TWO

TWO

OR
The Book of
TWINS AND DOUBLES
An Autobiographical
Anthology

WRITTEN AND EDITED BY
PENELOPE FARMER

A *Virago* Book

First published in Great Britain
by Virago Press 1996

This collection and introduction copyright © Penelope Farmer 1996

Acknowledgements on p.471ff constitute an extension
of this copyright page

A CIP catalogue record for this book
is available from the British Library.

ISBN 1 85381 705 8

Designed by Geoff Green
Typeset by Palimpsest Book Production Limited,
Polmont, Stirlingshire
Printed and bound in Great Britain by
Clays Ltd, St Ives plc

Virago
A Division of
Little, Brown and Company (UK)
Brettenham House
Lancaster Place
London WC2E 7EN

CONTENTS

ACKNOWLEDGEMENTS

All anthologists find themselves shamelessly picking the brains of most people they meet. It would be impossible to acknowledge every friend or acquaintance who offered suggestions for material. But to each and every one of them I express my gratitude. More specific thanks are due, however, to those whose comments, arising from their particular discipline or experience, and in several cases quoted here, helped me understand and take further my own thoughts and experience in relation to twinship and twoness. I list in no particular order: Nicholas Tucker, Marjorie Wallace, Colin Tudge, Maggie Mills and her sons, Max and Theo Hildebrand, Amos Oz, Colin Shorvon and Alison MacDonald. Jill Paton Walsh and John Rowe Townsend gave me the story of the Australian twins, referred to in the introduction on twin identity, which has haunted me throughout; Boris Wiseman alerted me to the work of Alessandra Piontelli, looking at twins in the womb, and thereafter corrected my translation from Lévi-Strauss; Lucy Bailey both translated the Gautier piece and checked my translations from René Zazzo; Joanna Carey put me on to the Detmold Twins and Lesley Gould allowed me to use the passage from Neil Gibson's film treatment; Jan Mark led me to Pierre Berton on the Dionne Quins; my gratitude to all of them. In Berkeley, California, I thank Catherine Robson who put me onto de Quincy and Jacques Lacan, and Martin Schwarz for his insights on the number two – in particular the distinction between dichotomy and polarity – and his suggestions for relevant material.

I owe special thanks to Victoria Nelson for not only translating the excerpt from the Cursor Mundi, but also suggesting and setting up my two months stay in Berkeley where, given such space and time, I was able to arrive at last at a shape for the book. I thank Tina Gillis, with whom I stayed, who endlessly allowed me to discuss my work with her in the course of our growing friendship, and who also, along with her colleague, Tom Laqueur, made this non-academic so generously welcome at the discussions and seminars in the Doreen Townsend Center – and the social events arising! – which in one way and another, too, helped form the book. I thank Robert Roper for letting me see his novel in progress on identical twins and use material from it.

Back in London, I thank both the editors I have worked with, Ruth Petrie and Lennie Goodings – herself the daughter of an identical twin! – for their invaluable encouragement and help, and my agent, Deborah Owen, who has understood better than most my need to undertake this anthology.

And finally I must acknowledge my long-suffering family, which has had to endure the sometimes painful consequences of twins and twin psyches not only in the flesh, but, over the past few years, so thoroughly in the head. In the light of which I'd like to dedicate the book, first to those progeny of twins in particular, my children, Clare and Thomas Mockridge, and my sister's children, William and Charlotte Rayner; second to all lone twins, like myself; and last but not least to the memory of my twin, Judith. With love.

DUALITY

N. *duality*, dualism; double-sidedness; double life, dual personality, split p., Jekyll and Hyde; positive and negative, yin and yang; dyad, two, deuce, duo, twain, couple, Darby and Joan, Jack and Jill, Romeo and Juliet; brace, pair, couple; doublets, twins, Castor and Pollux, Gemini, Siamese twins, identical t., Tweedledum and Tweedledee.

Adj. *dual*, dualistic; dyadic, binary, binomial; bilateral, bicameral; twin, biparous; bisexual, double-barrelled, duplex; paired, coupled etc. vb.; conjugate, binate; two abreast, two by two; in twos, both; in pairs, tête-à-tête, à deux; double-sided, double-edged, bipartisan; amphibious; ambidextrous; bifocal; biform, two-dimensional, two-faced; dihedral; di-, bi-.

Duplication
N. *duplication*, doubleness; doubling; gemination, reduplication, encore, repeat; iteration, echo; copy, carbon c., photocopy; double exposure; living image, look-alike.

Adj. *double*, doubled, twice; duplex, bifarious; biform; twofold, two-sided, two-headed, two-edged; bifacial, double-faced, two-faced; amphibious, ambidextrous; dual-purpose, two-way; of double meaning, ambiguous; ambivalent.

ROGET'S THESAURUS

Nigerian Twin Hymn

It is great God Almighty, the king
It is Lord God Almighty who blessed you with your twins
That's why you had two at once.

God grants twins to a person
Whose heart is pure.

Let she who dreams of having twins
Adopt a gentle character
Let him remain transparently honest.

I gather the firewood of splendour.

A twin wakes up to the beat of royal drums, like those
Of the Alaafin in heaven
Wakes up to fight for the art of beauty.

Twin sees the rich, passes them by
Twin loves persons in rags
Twin will transform a person in rags into a paragon of
Royal dress and richness.

Quoted in: R. FARIS THOMPSON, *The Face of the Gods*

———————

All life is replication . . . Of twinning we are born. This is both a
scientific verity and one of the oldest theological propositions on
the planet . . . In the beginning the Word was with God.

JOHN LASH, *Twins and the Double*

———————

The experience of duality can be described as the foundation
stone of human consciousness.

JOHN HERDMAN, *The Double*

———————

All things go in pairs, one the counterpart of the other;
he has made nothing incomplete.
One thing supplements the virtues of another.
Of his glory who can ever see too much?

ECCLESIASTICUS 42:24–5

———————

There is a cosmonogy in modern physics . . . in which they start with the idea that the whole cosmos originated from twin particles – from two electrons which were twin particles.

MARIE-LOUISE VON FRANZ, *Creation Myths*

DNA, the double helix, is perhaps the ultimate twin of our modern mythology. Twinhood is the generative cipher of all desire and division . . . Where our forbears resorted to sympathetic magic . . . totemic replication, masks, mimes, dances . . . for supernatural attunement to twins and twinning, we turn to genetics.

JOHN LASH, *Twins and the Double*

Etymologically, 'twin' denotes both union and separation, joining and parting. In the Middle English, 'twin' was frequently used as a transitive verb: to twin something meant to split or divide it . . . But 'twin' was also used to describe joining, juxtaposing or combining into one.

JOHN LASH, *Twins and the Double*

To parody a slogan of 1968: 'We are all twins . . .'

RENÉ ZAZZO, *Le Paradoxe des Jumeaux*

INTRODUCTION

ℬ&

L
ET ME declare an interest right away. My pursuit of twins far
from being dispassionate is deeply autobiographical. The idea
for this anthology arose from a piece I wrote for another collection
which insisted on centring itself round the death of my own twin sister,
five years ago.

It's not that the theme of twinship hadn't interested me before then
– how could it *not* interest me? Indeed twins, doubles, confusions
of identity have insinuated themselves into my writing from the
beginning, though in forms rarely recognised by me, since I found
writing about twinship directly very difficult. Partly I suppose I was
inhibited by the existence of my twin – at the best of times, our
relationship was not easy, and to have been open about my image
of our twinship might have seemed like betrayal. Much more, when
you are still living in such a relationship, it's as hard to define or
understand as the air you breathe – it *is* the air you breathe. Even
if you could define it you don't really need to; merely living it is
enough.

When your twin dies, though, when having always been two,
you are suddenly one, or at least appear so, that is quite another
matter. Then you need, you must – perhaps you always did need
to, had you but known – you need to separate; to confirm what it

5

means to be an individual, single, by beginning at last to decipher the doubleness. And even though I fell into it by mere accident, pursuing other people's thoughts on the subject has proved for me the best, most interesting way of doing so. The results are much richer, wider, more varied than anything I could write myself; appropriately so in pursuit of a theme which is, by virtue of its doubleness, profoundly ambiguous, thus more demonstrable when filtered through many minds.

At the same time, the way the theme builds up, layer on layer, juxtaposition by juxtaposition, the way narratives build up, within sections, throughout the book, it has become, after all, very much my book; my thesis; a thesis built out of quotations you could say. Wasn't it Walter Benjamin who suggested writing a novel out of quotations? Well, as a novelist I will say that this is my novel on twins. And so feel justified, somewhat, as an anthologist; if anthologising has to be justified – which I think in the present glut of anthologies it must be.

Any such search, of course, creates its own dynamic. What you end up with is not necessarily where you started out. In this case, what began as a book on twins, pure and simple, turned itself increasingly into a book on doubles, alter egos, generally, and so by degrees into one on the number two generally, on duality, dichotomy, division. And finally, to my own surprise, though I should not be surprised, I suppose, in the circumstances, that autobiography too here should be double, into a theme of writers; writers it would seem being a particularly duplicitous lot, in ways I will explain further in the part in which I arrive at writers as doubles.

I do not, I will not apologise for this. The themes of duality – doubleness – is where the particularity of twins moves into the area of the universal subconscious and general experience. Not least it explains the endless fascination with twins. This fascination is compounded of fear, I think; what comes up again and again is the feeling that identical twinship in particular confounds the sense that each person must be, is, unique. I discern longing, too, for that myth of perfect companionship and understanding which reveals itself particularly in the myth of twin souls; a condition for which twins are the paradigm and so deeply envied – erroneously in my experience, as I will demonstrate in the appropriate part. At the same time I suspect unwilling identification with a much less comfortable paradigm, given the many seemingly singular individuals who claim to sense that 'two souls are warring in my breast'. Finally, in light of the sheer oddity of twins – for my researches as well as my experience have led me to think more and more that we twins really are in some respects wholly peculiar, other, beasts – I am reminded of the zoologist, Ernst Mayr's, edict that most animal species can only be defined by what they aren't. In which case, could it not be, among other things, that some of the fascination with twins arises because our very differences help define the untwinned to themselves? In the same way that trying to work out singleness since the death of my twin, has helped me identify what it means to belong to that other human subspecies, twin?

Presumably it is this which also explains the wealth of material: on twins themselves, on doubleness, duality in general, literary, mythical, scientific, historical, biographical. In the first week I ever started to think, as a writer, about twins and twinship, the television schedules alone offered the film, *Dead Ringers* – Jeremy Irons as twin gynaecologists; an animated film about a pair of Siamese twins; Mengele's twin experiments at Auschwitz; and, in a news item about pensioners defrauded by Robert Maxwell, a pair of identical, identically clad, pensioner sisters. In the same week there also surfaced in London a French opera – *Jumelles* – based on the silent twins. Once you start looking we're everywhere, it seems.

But as for written material; I started with the keyword index in the British Library; pursuing the words 'twin', 'twins', 'Gemini', through its pre- and post-1970 catalogues yielded approximately 1,408 entries, despite including only works that had those words in the title, and despite excluding all articles, short stories, poems (excluding, too, most material not published in Britain).

Leaving aside such irrelevancies as twin-type motor bicycles and town twinning, much of the stuff listed both in the British Library and the other catalogues I investigated, in the United States and Australia mostly, concerns twin as gimmick, alas. Children's books are the worst offenders as you might expect; inflating the indices with countless jolly twin series, from Enid Blyton, via Chinese twins, French twins, and so on, through to the sagas of Sweet Valley High. But elsewhere, outside mythology, which has always been more subtle and ambiguous in such matters, what mainly interests writers up to the nineteenth century is the likeness between identical twins. Some, particularly those of eighteenth- and nineteenth-century ones, proceed to moral dichotomies – good twin/bad twin, and so on. Some, in biographical or autobiographical pieces mostly, report of telepathic communication between twins; identical twins falling ill or dying at the same moment, for instance. Otherwise, until the nineteenth century, literature mostly concerns itself with the narrative possibilities of the confusions between identical siblings; of which the Plautus play, the *Menaechmi*, was and is the prototype and in many cases the source; from The *Comedy of Errors* to Goldoni's *The Venetian Twins* – and countless poor imitations.

In the best of these, more aspects of twinship do emerge of course – Shakespeare registers the precise depths of longing felt by his separated pair ('I to the world am like a drop of water / that in the ocean seeks another drop') – and, wittingly or not, statements and events elsewhere can have a poignancy beyond their extrovert purpose, as in *The Venetian Twins*, when one twin dies and another character points out that death is the only way of resolving the confusions between twins; something which resonates uncomfortably in the feeling of this surviving twin. None the less, it is not until the nineteenth century and then not commonly, that twinship as such, the experience, feelings and psychic problems of twins are described – most notably and earliest by Georges Sand in her *La Petite Fadette*, which not only portrays the anguish of twin separation, but also advises parents how to rear twins so as to avoid such psychological problems. Nineteenth-century French literature in general seems to have been fond of using twins and look-alikes – though more often, as in much of Dumas, as devices of plot. If the nineteenth-century writer most obsessed with twinship and dualities in all aspects was the American with a schizoid pseudonym, Mark Twain, his twentieth-century successor, able, post-Freud, to pursue the subject to much greater depth, is Michel Tournier, author of *Gemini* and *The Erl King*. Another Frenchman. Maybe that follows.

A greater interest in the minds of twins went along – though not often directly connected – with the appearance of the double or *doppelgänger* – a concept not only coined by a German, Jean-Paul Richter, but in the beginning altogether more prevalent in German literature than elsewhere; notably in the work of E.T.A Hoffman. A word of warning: to quote the critic, Ralph Tymms, 'superficially, doubles are among the most facile and less reputable devices of fiction. A fairly frequent feature of magazine . . . plots is the character who clears himself of guilt . . . by producing a fortuitous double' and so on. After three years of immersing myself in twin and doubles literature I can vouch for this.

Yet there is no doubt of the power of the subject; the double/twin/ divided self appeared everywhere in nineteenth-century fiction, from Hoffman to Henry James, while two-faced works like *Frankenstein*,

Dr Jekyll and Mr Hyde and *The Picture of Dorian Gray* remain rooted in the public imagination. None the less, the fact that these, with the odd exception (James Hogg's *Confessions of a Justified Sinner*, perhaps, which is odd in all senses and wonderful besides) do not quite count as great literature is significant I think; as is the fact that now as then, in literary fiction, by writers particularly interested in matters of human duality, and who in some books use twins or doubles as illustration, such pairs are very often the least interesting – least subtle – aspect of the dualities they address. Nor is it surprising that twins and doubles were, and are, especially ubiquitous in genre fiction at the less reputable end of the literary spectrum; thrillers, horror stories, science fiction, and so on.

Here, of course, I cannot altogether avoid such stuff, given its significance to the subject. But nor can I claim to have covered everything; my own taste and inclination limited – was bound to limit – pursuit, even despite much offered – gratefully received – advice. (Shameless brain-picking, I discovered early, is the essence of this business.) I'm very conscious of the shortage of science fiction for instance. Such limitations apart, I have, as an anthologist, the advantage of not needing to concern myself with second-rateness, or with overused narrative device. A twin Little Jack Horner, I sit in my corner and pull out the plums to set alongside other plums which may illuminate – and in return be illuminated by – them. In such plum-picking and such juxtapositions, it is not always the hack writer who comes out worst, satisfactorily enough. Little gems of insight, of precise feeling, spring from the most surprising – and otherwise, and with good reason long forgotten, not to say disreputable sources. (Another justification for anthologising; of course.)

So much for content; as to the structure of the book in which it's set, I have arranged it, too, in twinned form, a pair of interconnected circles, beginning and ending in autobiography, and connected by a part which belongs in some respects to both.

The first circle is twins as existential; or twins in actuality – both in fiction and real life. The beginning of which is – or was – my own twinship, the starting point for this whole book. The part on birth and parenthood of twins is followed by one on twinship: like or identical twins – confusions of identity etc. – and unlike twins – twins as dichotomy – boy/girl twins and so on. This part concludes with material looking at the nature and psychology of twinship, that is, precisely what it means to be a twin.

Thereafter comes a part on love and hate; twins as lovers (the

9

usual confusions, twins falling in love with one person, lover unable to choose between twins; incest, heterosexual and homosexual (fictionally a much-written-about theme); twins as rivals (the prototype, Jacob and Esau, is only the first of many examples where inheritance is an issue between twins). Finally a part on separation of twins, leading to that ultimate separation, death – of my twin among others – completes the autobiographical circle.

The second circle turns round the myth of the twin; where the actuality of twinships interfaces with universal archetype and general experience. The part, in connecting this with the first circle (the life and times of twins), investigates freaks – extreme freakdom: Siamese twins, for instance – and the simple freakdom of mere doubleness; an aspect of twinship with which all twins, including myself, are well acquainted, since figuratively or actually it represents our official calling card. Not least, the freakdom leads to our usefulness, so this part goes on to look at the uses made of twins by scientists and psychologists: the infamous Dr Mengele; Francis Galton, who first saw comparisons between identical and fraternal twins as a way of disentangling the effects of nature from those of nurture; and so on. Also the uses made of twinship by those who invent themselves twins for financial, romantic, psychological reasons.

Thereafter we turn to actual myth: twins seen as sacred, as in some African tribes; twins as unholy, as taboo, in others. Discussions of the significance of the number two, mythologically speaking, also finds a place here, because of its likely connection with the way twins are seen and imagined; and this part concludes with a look at the equally mythical dream of twin souls.

The subject of the next part is symbolic twinship – shadows, reflections, alter egos, doubles – leading full circle finally, thematically and autobiographically, to the final part on writers; who not only write about twins, doubles, but frequently claim themselves – or their writing selves – as doubles: Borges and I; Henry James, Goethe, Maupassant, *ad infinitum*.

As with all anthologies – but the more so in this one, where practically every extract is, by definition, Janus-faced – almost any piece in any part could be used in another part, if not in three or four other parts. In particular, actuality and myth shade into one another at many points – actuality fed by myth, myth by actuality; some of the pieces illustrating myth could arguably be moved to actuality and vice versa. The ambiguities are inevitable, even intentional, reflecting the ambiguities – the duplicity, literally – of twins and twinship itself.

1

BIRTH AND
PARENTHOOD

ϑ&

T HERE WAS no such thing as ultrasound when our mother was
carrying us; no means therefore of monitoring closely the
occupant of her womb. But a second heartbeat – not to say a
second head – would have been noted more often than not, so I'd
guess she was not medically well served, even then. Apart from the
shock to her body and our father's nervous system, the main effect
was that where most – almost all – babies are awaited, eagerly or not,
my existence wasn't even suspected until 25 minutes or so after my
sister's birth. My urgent signs of wanting to follow her into the world
was heralded by a cry from the doctor 'My God there's another one.'
And out I came, leaving my mother doubly exhausted, and my father
also depleted in his own way. The maternity nurse, who went in search
of brandy to revive her, came up with the remains of a bottle of, if not
quite Napoleon brandy, something pretty aged and expensive, which
he'd been keeping for a special occasion; all of it she poured into the
glass that she put to my mother's lips. In the circumstances, I doubt if
our father would have objected to that expensive sip. But the nurse's
emptying the remainder of the glassful – most of it – down the sink
was another matter.

Presumably our father forgave us this alcoholic sacrilege. But the
way I've always felt obliged to proclaim myself, I sometimes wonder

if I've managed to forgive the world for denying my intra-uterine existence. I did not actually emerge from the womb shouting; though I was the heavier of the two, a mere 3 pounds is weakly, the more so then. But I made up for it later; starting you might say, along with my sister, by defying the doctor whose second reported comment was: 'I won't see those two alive when I come back.' Not only were we not having any of that, we suborned the maternity nurse into not having any of it either. She improvised a crude incubator out of a hot-water bottle, the success of which I demonstrate by being here and writing this, and by the burn scars still visible on my thumb and knee. Honourable battle scars I think in such a struggle; I've always felt proud of them. But for the rest, my life since has been one long yell for attention, not always let rip unblushingly, given the injunctions to reticence and modesty inflicted on me by my upbringing and education: I can still feel my shame, aged 8, confronted with one school report that claimed I was 'disturbing in class'. But nothing inhibited me for long, to the dismay, then, of my much more reticent, more easily embarrassed sister – and of my equally more modest husbands, friends and lovers thereafter. What else do you write for after all? Except to tell the world you're there and that what you think is to be counted. It's no profession for someone determined to hide their head; mine being hidden once was enough for me, I guess. (The precise identity, of course, of the person whose existence I so furiously proclaim is something else – with twins it always is. That little puzzle, though, I will leave till later.)

So much for birth. Of twin parenthood obviously, I can speak with even less authority. All I can say is that, if being a good parent generally is one of those skills, like driving, slightly beyond the average human capacity, the raising of twins is next to impossible. To begin with, the average parent has to come to terms with the disconcerting fact that whereas a single child relates at the start only to its mother, twins right from birth, and even before, have a relationship to which neither parent has any access. Faced with such challenges how can they begin to get it right? Our parents didn't get it right, certainly. They sent us for instance to schools so small that we always had to be in the same class, which was a disaster for my sister, since the inevitable comparisons between us, made by us if by no one else, were always to the disadvantage of a potential scientist like her in an arts-oriented school that suited me. But that was us. In other cases, other parents make the mistake of separating twins who might have done better kept together.

I do know from all the stories, though, how difficult it was for them, from the start. We were a trial; we were bound to be; one questing baby is hard work enough. To this day I sense the utter bemusement of my father in all things to do with us; as if he never quite got over his astonishment on hearing the unlooked for news of my arrival.

As to the birth and parenthood of other twins shown in the extracts here, many of them tell the same story: bemusement often; also pride, on the one hand, ambivalence, even downright shame on the other; sometimes both at once. Apart from alarm at the prospect of trying to rear two or more children at once, as in the extract from Patricia Ledward's *Twin Blessings*, a common theme is that there's something magical in it – something uncanny – hence the ambivalence; or else something animal. A frequent comparison is with animal litters – the distinction of humans being that they are born singly (along with calves, foals, elephants, and so on, but no one points that out the way they compare the birth of twins or multiples to litters of puppies or kittens). This animal resemblance is part, of course, of the still greater and sadder fascination with the birth of quins, such as the Dionne quins. It was the only reason given to Mary Kingsley for the banishment of twin mothers and the killing of the twins themselves in the part of West Africa through which she travelled, though suspicion of supernatural event, witchcraft, and so on, was almost certainly significant also.

At the opposite extreme is the perceived superiority of the mother who gives birth to the twins – as celebrated in some other African tribes; and as more prosaically, if succinctly, expressed in the extract from Marion Halligan's *Lovers' Knots*; and in the description of Violet Kray. One twin researcher compared the attitudes of middle-class mothers of twins, doing their best these days to maintain the individuality of even the most look-alike siblings, with those of the working-class ones who still, like Mrs Kray, stress the likeness of their twins – indeed glory in it. For many of these latter women it was the first thing in their lives that had made them feel different or important: of course they were going to make the most of it, the researcher said. Similarly, for some men, especially otherwise inadequate ones, fathering twins can seem a demonstration of extra potency, as demonstrated in Manuel Gonzales's 'The 'Clipse' – ironically here, and in similar tales I found: the poor little man who took such pride in his twin daughters, had in fact, the story makes clear, been cuckolded.

from Notes of an Anatomist

INDIVIDUAL human life begins this way: The fertilized egg cell, even before it is implanted in the womb, transforms itself into a spherical mass of tightly packed cells, each of enormous potential but hardly different from its neighbors. There is nothing to suggest the human form, yet the germ of a human being is locked up inside. In our earliest beginnings, nature makes us perfect, for the sphere is the ideal receptacle of perfection. The perfect being, independent of externals and utterly self-sustaining, said Plato, ought to be like the sphere of the cosmos.

[. . .] It seems preordained, however, that we should soon stray away from perfection. Soon there appears a streaklike ridge, or chine, over the surface of the embryonic cell mass, and henceforth we pass into the realm of symmetry: there shall be a central axis, and around this axis right- or left-sidedness. By virtue of a central divide, all organs can organize with reference to a plane, and it is fitting that the technical name for this dividing ridge should be that of 'organizer,' for it seems to inspire, inform, and direct future embryonic tissues rather than stand as a passive landmark. But the mysterious influences that direct these transformations, though miraculously precise, are not infallible. Thus a spherical embryo may be cleft into halves by one divider and then again, as if by accident, in two more halves by another divider whose very powers of organization, awesome in their complexity, continue to be exercised as if impelled by a blind design that took no notice of the original mishap and continued on, unswervingly, of its own inertia. The result is that in the end, where the birth of a human infant was expected, as is proper and right for the human species, the emergence of the first child is followed by another one that looks like its exact replica; and, sometimes, this is followed by another one, and, in some cases, by still more, so that human procreation, apparently designed for the nourishment and containment of one individual per cycle, comes to resemble the animal litters, wherein multiplicity is the rule.

Every gestation is fundamentally portentous, but one that so abruptly does away with predictable events and issues in two, or more, products leaves us dumbfounded.

[. . .] To explain multiple births, biologists multiply hypotheses. Identical twins may arise when the fertilized egg cell fortuitously splits into two spheres because of desultory changes in the environment. By recognizing this random disruption of a delicate ecology, biology does no more than acknowledge the existence of the fickle demon, without surprising his hand in the act of trickery. Or perhaps the splitting of the

15

primordial sphere is not the effect of chance but the result of a duplicating factor inherent in the father's sperm, carried into the egg cell,
much like a distraught burglar would leave behind a personal object in
the house he intended to loot. Alternatively, the duplicating impetus
may not be extraneous to the egg cell but may reside there waiting only
for the signal to make its presence felt. Or, yet, no extraneous factor
is required, nor is a signal needed, but human duplication could arise
from a deficiency of the conditions that preside over the formation of
singletons, as an absence of restraining influences instead of a surplus
of formative ones; in which case multiple conception would be thought
of as an excess resulting from a want, but neither of the two would be
explained. And from this baroque coiling of biological theories, we
infer that the biologist, like the maker of myths, is dumbfounded.
The swindling god keeps substituting the peas under his thimbles too
swiftly for anyone to detect the cheat; and the biologist, like all others,
wishing to expose the trickery, can only admire the contrivance.

Externally, the pathologist's approach seems somewhat different. As
usual, he adjusts his focus on the exceptional, the pathologic. Through
deviancy, he hopes for glimpses of the underlying order. Hence his interest
in monstrosities, which he so carefully classifies. And if he is not at the
same time an experimentalist, he will be wont to pronounce, *ut quum
facta sunt* (after the fact has occurred), 'the interpretation that verifies
his conjectures,' as Cicero scornfully said of seers and fortune-tellers.
To him, twinning per se is not 'pathologic enough'. Double conception,
after all, may be conducted in a normal atmosphere of shared harmony;
but any form of intrauterine discord is sure to polarize the pathologist's
attention. Such, for instance, the 'twin-to-twin transfusion syndrome,'
a form of imbalance in which one twin's circulation empties into placen-
tal vessels that divert the blood to his cotwin. As a result, the 'recipient'
twin is born large, ruddy, and plethoric, while his brother, the 'donor'
if he manages to survive, emerges pale, anemic, and wasted.

F. GONZALES-CRUSSI

And the first came out red, all over like an hairy garment; and
they called his name Esau.

And after that came his brother out and his hand took hold on
Esau's heel; and his name was called Jacob.

THE BOOK OF GENESIS

16

from Larousse Science of Life

ALL children who are born simultaneously to one mother are called twins; but there are two categories of twins. Twins of the first category resemble each other so strikingly that they are known as true or identical twins. The others resemble each other as do brothers and sisters born at different times: these are non-identical twins, and are called false or fraternal twins. The two categories of twins have a different origin. Identical twins arise from a single zygote, the result of one ovum fertilized by one spermatozoon. At the beginning of development the embryo is unique; then it doubles and separates into two independent embryos. Generally the two embryos share a part of the foetal membranes, the chorion and the placenta. Hence identical twins are also called 'uni-ovular' or 'mono-zygotic' or 'monochorionic' – synonyms which recall that they derive from a single ovum, a single zygote, and share a single chorion. They are always of the same sex. They are of the same genotype and are, indeed, two copies of the same individual. It is a case of human polyembryony.

Fraternal or false twins arise from different eggs which develop simultaneously like those of multiparous mammals which give birth to several offspring in one litter. For example, if two ova are detached from the ovary at about the same time and each is fertilized by different sperm the two resulting zygotes will develop side by side. Their foetal membranes will be distinct; they will have two amnions, two chorions, and two placentas. Fraternal twins are therefore known as 'bi-ovular', 'dizygotic' or 'dichorionic' to indicate that they arise from two ova, two zygotes, and have a chorion each. They can be of the same sex or brothers and sisters. Their resemblance to each other is neither more nor less than that of ordinary brothers and sisters. They are of different genotypes. It is a case of polyovulation.

[. . .] By a statistical method, known as Weinberg's method, it is possible to calculate the relative frequency of the two types of twins. In the white population of the United States 34.2 per cent of all twin births are of identical or monozygotic twins. In the coloured population the percentage is 28.9 per cent. The statistics for Germany give roughly the same results, although the frequency of identical twins is higher in towns than in the remainder of the country.

There would seem to be a correlation between the age of the

mother and the relative frequency of monozygotic and dizygotic births. From the age of fifteen to thirty-nine the frequency of twin births rises slightly for identical twins and appreciably more so for fraternal twins. After the age of forty the frequency of identical twins continues slowly to rise while the frequency of fraternal twins falls.

A woman less than twenty years of age has about the same chance of bearing identical twins as she has of bearing fraternal twins; while a woman between thirty-five and forty has three times as many chances of having fraternal twins.

Twins seem to run in families. Many cases are reported of women who not infrequently have two or even more children at a time. One, who brought thirty-two children into the world, gave birth eleven times, producing three pairs of twins, six sets of triplets and two of quadruplets. Another produced thirty children in twenty-two years by her first marriage, and by her second a further fourteen in the space of three years. Still another had forty-four children in thirty-three years – thirteen pairs of twins and six sets of triplets. Such cases – and there are many others – strongly suggest an individual predisposition to multiple births.

———————

In England, when a woman bore twins, she said she'd had Martin's hammer knocking at her wicket.

———————

In America, eating twin fruit is believed to induce the birth of twins, and planting under the sign of Gemini is believed to double the yield.

———————

The Galalareese are . . . of the opinion that if a woman were to consume two bananas growing from a single head she would give birth to twins. The Guarani Indians of South America thought that a woman would become a mother of twins if she ate a double grain of millet.

FRAZER, *The Golden Bough*

A ship is safer when two cables hold it, and an anxious mother, if she rears twins, has less to dread.

PROPERTIUS, *Elegies*

---

from The Profession of Violence

FOR Violet the arrival of the twins was the greatest event in her life. The last few years had been a struggle.

[. . .] She made the best of things. She was a good wife. According to her sister May, 'She always kept herself nice, Violet did. Never let herself go, like most women once they're married. She was a quiet one.' With the quietness went great strength of purpose; with twins she finally had something to be purposeful about. 'I never seen no babies like the twins,' she said proudly. 'They was so lovely when they was born, the two of them, so small and dark, just like two little black-haired dolls.'

Their brother, nearly four, was a placid, easy child, with his mother's personality and looks. The twins were different: they were demanding and brought out all their mother's deep protectiveness. They did something more: for the first time they gave Violet's life a touch of the glamour she had dreamt of when she eloped. Nobody else had twins; they were something special, and when she pushed them out in the big double pram they conferred on her the final accolade of cockney motherhood. It was a pretty sight; blonde young mother, gleaming pram and these two beautifully dressed little dolls, making their way past the pubs and stalls of the Bethnal Green Road. People would stop and look, neighbours inquired about them; her two sisters begged for a chance to take them out on their own.

'In those days everybody loved the twins and wanted a go with them,' says Violet.

JOHN PEARSON, *The Profession of Violence*

---

from Lovers' Knots

ELIZABETH Sullivan surprised everybody by getting married long after the rest of the family had taken it for granted that she never would. Her siblings and cousins were long past the first bloom of that state. Several of her own nieces and nephews had beaten her to it. Some of them had stopped pitying her singleness and started envying it; they wouldn't have minded the opportunity to be their own person again. She'd taken up tennis and met a carpenter who had a good business remodelling kitchens, a widower with three children already grown up. Andrew considered that this was enough family for any man, but said to Elizabeth that every woman had a right to a child and she could have one. Just one; at their time of life that would be enough. Perhaps he thought that at thirty-nine she might be past it and this need be no more than a generous gesture from an experienced husband to his new wife. But Elizabeth's body having dutifully produced eggs for two and a half decades all to no avail seemed to jump at the chance to make something of them at last; a month after the wedding she was pregnant. Thin Elizabeth became all round and willowy; she'd always been as gawky as an adolescent and now she lost that gawkiness but kept the youthfulness. She sat with those beautiful hands of hers resting on her belly with a smooth Madonna air that made people think, Elizabeth's not bad looking, after all. Clever Andrew just happened to notice it.

Then she produced twins. A girl and a boy. Daniel and Sarah. After that her husband regarded her with a certain distrust, as well as a lot of respect. Here was a woman who could bend life to her will. He told the story to his mates: Talk about giving her an inch and she takes a mile. One kid I said. So off she goes and produces twins. There was a certain upper-handedness about it that was good for Elizabeth in the early days of marriage; it set her up as a woman not to be trifled with.

MARION HALLIGAN

---

from Twin Blessings

NO one had ever heard of twins in either of our families: we were all much too timid and well-behaved to go in for anything so rash. Such a twist to our plans was ludicrous to contemplate.

I was sent to have an X-ray, but was so certain that a fuss was being made over nothing that when I paid my next visit to the doctor and she said triumphantly, 'Here's the X-ray, come and look at the two little spines,' I fainted with shock.

The first thing I heard when I revived were the doctor's words of encouragement, 'It'll be great fun!'

'*Fun?*' I shouted furiously.

'Wait and see,' came the cool, scientific advice.

I certainly hoped I wouldn't have much longer to wait. But as for the seeing – I was already in a state of rebellion. *I didn't want twins.*

We were to hear the doctor's words repeated many, many times. Our future was now perfectly clear. Life was going to be FUN – Charlie Chaplin and René Clair and the Marx Brothers all rolled into one were always to be there for our entertainment.

'Twins are such fun!' We heard it on the top of buses, we heard it in hospital waiting-rooms, we heard it in elegant drawing-rooms and on our steep, dark staircase. Such fun for all of us, for the parents and the grandparents to have two darling little babies to look after.

'My twin nephews were scamps,' chuckled Aunt Hannah, one of those aunts who wasn't really an aunt and in whose family children were reared by nannies and kept within the bounds of nurseries. 'They nearly pulled the house down.' She laid her painted cheek against the snarling silver fox on her shoulders and she smiled.

The loved one and I looked at our shabby, very much war-damage-repaired house that we were required to return to its free-holders in good condition when the lease expired. We looked at each other and we did not smile.

[. . .] What was going to be fun? Twice the number of nappies to wash? Twice the number of sleepless nights? The charm of trying to feed two hungry, screaming babies at the same time? Or just the challenge of the situation?

The only person we ourselves knew who had had a couple had been so overcome by fatigue that her life had moved on to a different plane altogether. She used to go shopping in her pyjamas, and so on, and had one day been found trying to wrap the infants up in brown paper in order to send them to a friend who repeatedly wrote in the most jolly style that she was dying to have them to stay.

We met only one person who showed us the dark side of the picture and she was a woman who seemed to pride herself not only on being worse off than anyone else but also on having friends everywhere who were doomed to misfortune. She came to visit us one morning and, sitting on the very edge of the chair and looking at us unhappily out of her worried little eyes, she told us about some people who had twin girls when their first child was about Alice's age: 'They had a terrible time with him – he screamed for a bottle, had to go back into napkins, crawled everywhere —'

At this point the thunder of Alice's tiny feet interrupted her mournful recital. 'I'm ready to go out now, Mummy,' she said. Her cheeks were daubed with lipstick and she must have emptied a whole box of powder over herself. She looked enchantingly buoyant and self-confident. I dreaded to think what might now lie ahead.

'– and once,' continued our merry friend, 'he hit them both on the head with a toy hammer – hard!'

PATRICIA LEDWARD

---

from The Faerie Queene

Her mother was the faire *Chrysogonee*,
   The daughter of *Amphisa*, who by race
   A Faerie was, yborne of high degree,
   She bore *Belphœbe*, she bore in like case
   Faire *Amoretta* in the second place:
   These two were twinnes, and twixt them two did share
   The heritage of all celestiall grace.
   That all the rest it seem'd they robbed bare
Of bountie, and of beautie, and all vertues rare.

It were a goodly storie, to declare,
   By what straunge accident faire *Chrysogone*
   Conceiu'd these infants, and how them she bare,
   In this wild forrest wandring all alone,

After she had nine moneths fulfild and gone:
For not as other wemens commune brood,
They were enwombed in the sacred throne
Of her chaste bodie, nor with commune food,
As other wemens babes, they sucked vitall blood.

But wondrously they were begot, and bred
Through influence of th'heauens fruitfull ray,
As it in antique bookes is mentioned.
It was vpon a Sommers shynie day,
When *Titan* faire his beames did display,
In a fresh fountaine, farre from all mens vew,
She bath'd her brest, the boyling heat t' allay;
She bath'd with roses red, and violets blew,
And all the sweetest flowres, that in the forrest grew.

Till faint through irkesome wearinesse, adowne
Vpon the grassie ground her selfe she layd
To sleepe, the whiles a gentle slombring swowne
Vpon her fell all naked bare displayd;
The sunne-beames bright vpon her body playd,
Being through former bathing mollifide,
And pierst into her wombe, where they embayd
With so sweet sence and secret power vnspide,
That in her pregnant flesh they shortly fructifide.

[. . .] Great father he of generation
Is rightly cald, th'author of life and light;
And his faire sister for creation
Ministreth matter fit, which tempred right
With heate and humour, breedes the living wight.
So sprong these twinnes in wombe of *Chrysogone*,
Yet wist she nought thereof, but sore affright,
Wondred to see her belly so vpblone,
Which still increast, till she her terme had full outgone.

Whereof conceiuing shame and foule disgrace,
Albe her guiltlesse conscience her cleard,
She fled into the wildernesse a space,
Till that vnweeldy burden she had reard,
And shund dishonor, which as death she feard:
Where wearie of long trauell, downe to rest
Her selfe she set, and comfortably cheard;

There a sad cloud of sleepe her ouerkest.
And seized euery sense with sorrow sore opprest.
. . . [Venus goes looking for the errant Cupid]

To search the God of love, her Nymphes she sent
   Throughout the wandry forrest eury where:
   And after them her selfe eke with her went
   To seeke the fugitiue, both farre and nere,
   So long they sought till they arriued were
   In that same shady couert wheras lay
   Faire *Chrysogone* in slombry traunce whilere:
   Who in her sleepe (a wondrous thing to say)
Vnawares had borne two babes, as faire as springing day.

Vnawares she them conceiued, vnaware she bore:
   She bore withouten pain, that she conceiued
   Withouten pleasure . . .

                       EDMUND SPENSER

---

from The Dionne Years

ELZIRE Dionne's travail began at 1:00 a.m. She lay on a big wooden bed in a bare room just off the kitchen, dimly lit by the mustard glow of a coal oil lamp. Though her body was bloated and her feet so badly swollen that her toes had vanished, she did not complain. She truly believed that she was dying, but she would not ask for help. Her husband, thoroughly alarmed, ran across the field to the two-room log house of her uncle Alexandre, fittingly surnamed Legros – a huge man, amiable in spite of an appearance rendered piratical by a pair of gold earrings and a red bandanna. It was Mme Legros whose aid Dionne was seeking. She was used to helping her neighbours in labour, a service for which she asked no fee. In eighteen years she had lost only one baby, but now it seemed she would lose a mother.

'Auntie,' her niece whispered as she walked into the room, 'I don't think I'll be able to pull through this time.' She asked for a rosary and the two women, in tears, began to pray. Mrs Dionne repeated aloud the Ave Maria and kissed the feet of the crucifix while her aunt continued to whisper 'O God, inspire me in my work,' and sensibly put some water on the wood stove to boil.

An hour passed. The pains increased. Dionne set off again, this time to seek out Mme Labelle, the midwife who had assisted at three of Mrs Dionne's previous confinements. This remarkable woman had borne eighteen children of her own, thirteen without a doctor's help. Married at sixteen and widowed at fifty-seven, she had followed her calling for ten years and had assisted at three hundred births, two hundred without a doctor present. When she was paid at all, she usually received a dollar; but she never refused a case, even though many of the calls came in the deep of the night with the thermometer at forty below.

Her first act on reaching the farmhouse was to fall on her knees with Mme Legros and pray. Dionne, meanwhile, hustled his older children off to neighbours and relatives and brought the eleven-month-old baby, Pauline, down to the kitchen. His wife was worse, her body ice cold. She continued to clutch her rosary, to move her lips in prayer, and to insist that she did not need a doctor. Mme Labelle thought otherwise; she sent Dionne off to Callander to find Dafoe. But as soon as he had gone, Elzire Dionne urged her to try to deliver the baby before the doctor arrived.

She was born just before four o'clock, the tiniest infant the two midwives had ever seen: a grotesque creature with the legs of an insect and a disproportionately large head, bright blue in colour and scarcely human except, oddly, for the large eyes with the long lashes and an appreciable shock of hair.

The baby was so small that Mme Labelle could easily hold her in her palm. She was not breathing. The midwife opened the oven door, held her in front of the heat, massaged her back, and blew air into the collapsed lungs. The baby struggled for breath like a drowning kitten; then from those blue lips there emerged a feline mew, a cry so thin and fragile that it seemed unreal. But there was no time for further ministrations – a moment only to wrap the infant in a scrap of woollen blanket and place her at the foot of the bed – for another birth was taking place. Mme Labelle breathed life into the second child while Mme Legros baptized them both. Neither woman believed the babies would survive for more than a few minutes.

Dafoe had already delivered one baby that night. Now, as he entered the farmhouse, he was faced with an astonishing sight: two babies lay wrapped in tattered woollen remnants on the bed and a third was emerging from the mother. 'Good God, woman,' said the doctor, 'put on some more hot water.' He quickly went to work, tying the third child's umbilical cord while Mme Legros scurried about searching for more pieces of cloth in which to wrap her. Now a fourth baby appeared. Dafoe's eyes bulged. 'Gosh!' he said and then 'Gosh!' again as a fifth followed almost immediately. These last two were still imprisoned in their amniotic sacs – tiny, spider-like creatures, moving feebly in a kind of slow motion behind the translucent walls.

Dafoe ruptured the sacs, gave the babies conditional baptism, and immediately turned to the mother. Elzire Dionne was close to death, her lips white, the tips of her finger's black. The doctor gave her an injection of pituitary to raise her blood pressure and another of ergot to prevent post-natal haemorrhage. At last she was told that she had given birth to five babies. 'Holy Mary!' she gasped.

The various narratives of the birth are vague about the whereabouts of Oliva Dionne at this moment. Most agree on two points: he had fled from the room, and he was in a state of nervous collapse that was heightened by the information that in the space of two hours his family had increased from seven to twelve. 'My God!' he was reported as saying, 'what am I going to do with five babies? It was bad enough to look after one; but how are we going to manage to look after five?' In the days that followed, Dionne continued to worry, publicly, about the heavy financial responsibility.

PIERRE BERTON

---

from Walt and Vult

WHEN Veronica began to feel the pains of their birth, he kept in her presence, as though she had been a Sicilian or an English queen, witnesses of the birth, who might afterwards be directed into witnesses at the baptism. The bed had been shoved into the territory of the nobleman, because she might bear a son, and through this artifice he would be withdrawn from the subjects of the prince, who would make him a soldier, instead, as already decided by his father, binding his brow with the laurel of Themis. In fact, as a citizen of the territory of the nobleman, Peter Gottwalt, the hero of this work, saw the light.

But the pains went on increasing; the father felt it both duty and prudence to replace the bed of the suffering mother in the territory of the prince, that each might receive his rights. 'It cannot be worse than a girl,' or he said, devoutly, '*Quod Deus vult*; What God wills!' It was the last, and no girl; therefore the boy received, from Shomaker's translation, the name of the Bishop of Carthage, namely, Quod Deus Vult, or Vult, as he was familiarly called. There were now established in the apartments sharp dividing lines and boundary treaties between the territories. Cradles, and all else were separated. Gottwalt slept and woke, and drank from his mother's breast as the Left; Vult did the same as the Right. Later, when both began to creep a little, Gottwalt was divided from his brother on the noble side by a little wicker-work fence, brought from the hen-house and manager, and placed before the doors of his apartment. But the wild Vult sprang so agilely behind these barriers, that with every effort he had the appearance of a leopard springing backwards and forwards behind his cage.

JEAN-PAUL RICHTER

---

from East of Eden

THE fire went out of Samuel's eyes and he said quietly, 'Your sons have no names.'

Adam replied, 'Their mother left them motherless.'

'And you have left them fatherless. Can't you feel the cold at night of a lone child? What warm is there, what bird song, what possible morning can be good? Don't you remember, Adam, how it was, even a little?'

'I didn't do it,' Adam said.

'Have you undone it? Your boys have no names.' He stooped down and put his arms around Adam's shoulders and helped him to his feet. 'We'll give them names,' he said. 'We'll think long and find good names to clothe them.' He whipped the dust from Adam's shirt with his hands.

[. . .] Lee brought out a table and two chairs and set the chairs facing each other. He made another trip for a pint of whisky and two glasses and set a glass on the table in front of each chair. Then he carried out the twins, one under each arm, and put them on the ground beside the table and gave each boy a stick for his hand to shake and make shadows with.

The boys sat solemnly and looked about, stared at Samuel's beard and searched for Lee. The strange thing about them was their clothing, for the boys were dressed in the straight trousers and the frogged and braided jackets of the Chinese. One was in turquoise blue and the other in a faded rose pink, and the frogs and braid were black. On their heads sat round black silken hats, each with a bright red button on its flat top.

Samuel asked, 'Where in the world did you get those clothes, Lee?'

'I didn't get them,' Lee said testily. 'I had them. The only other clothes they have I made myself, out of sail-cloth. A boy should be well dressed on his naming day.'

'You've dropped the pidgin, Lee.'

'I hope for good. Of course, I use it in King City.' He addressed a few short sung syllables to the boys on the ground, and they both smiled up at him and waved their sticks in the air. Lee said, 'I'll pour you a drink. It's some that was here.'

'It's some you bought yesterday in King City,' said Samuel.

Now that Samuel and Adam were seated together and the barriers were down, a curtain of shyness fell on Samuel. What he had beaten in with his fists he could not supplement easily. He thought of the virtues of courage and forbearance, which become flabby when there is nothing to use them on. His mind grinned inward at itself.

The two sat looking at the twin boys in their strange, bright-coloured clothes. Samuel thought, 'Sometimes your opponent can help you more than your friend.' He lifted his eyes to Adam.

'It's hard to start,' he said. 'And it's like a put-off letter that gathers difficulties to itself out of the minutes. Could you give me a hand?'

[. . .] 'Will you have another drink?' asked Adam.

'That I will, thank you. Names are a great mystery. I've never known whether the name is moulded by the child or the child changed to fit the name. But you can be sure of this – whenever a human has a nickname it is a proof that the name given him was wrong. How do you favour the standard names – John or James or Charles?'

Adam was looking at the twins and suddenly with the mention of the name he saw his brother peering out of the eyes of one of the boys. He leaned forward.

'What is it?' Samuel asked.

'Why,' Adam cried, 'these boys are not alike! They don't look alike.'

'Of course they don't. They're not identical twins.'

'That one – that one looks like my brother. I just saw it. I wonder if the other looks like me.'

'Both of them do. A face has everything in it right back to the beginning.'

'It's not so much now,' said Adam. 'But for a moment I thought I was seeing a ghost.'

'Maybe that's what ghosts are,' Samuel observed.

Lee brought dishes out and put them on the table.

'Do you have Chinese ghosts?' Samuel asked.

'Millions,' said Lee. 'We have more ghosts than anything else. I guess nothing in China ever dies. It's very crowded. Anyway, that's the feeling I got when I was there.'

Samuel said, 'Sit down, Lee. We're trying to think of names.'

'I've got chicken frying. It will be ready pretty soon.'

Adam looked up from the twins and his eyes were warmed and softened. 'Will you have a drink, Lee?'

'I'm nipping at the ng-ka-py in the kitchen,' said Lee and went back to the house.

Samuel leaned down and gathered up one of the boys and held him on his lap. 'Take that one up,' he said to Adam. 'We ought to see whether there's something that draws names to them.'

Adam held the other child awkwardly on his knee. 'They look some alike,' he said, 'but not when you look close. This one has rounder eyes than that one.'

'Yes, and a rounder head and bigger ears,' Samuel added. 'But this one is more like – like a bullet. This one might go farther but not so high. And this one is going to be darker in the hair and skin. This one will be shrewd, I think, and shrewdness is a limitation on the mind. Shrewdness tells you what you must not do because it would not be shrewd. See how this one supports himself! He's farther along than that one – better developed. Isn't it strange how different they are when you look close?'

Adam's face was changing as though he had opened and come out on his surface. He held up his finger, and the child made a lunge for it and missed and nearly fell off his lap. 'Whoa!' said Adam. 'Take it easy. Do you want to fall?'

'It would be a mistake to name them for qualities we think they have,' Samuel said. 'We might be wrong – so wrong. Maybe it would be good to give them a high mark to shoot at – a name to live up to. The man I'm named after had his name called clear by the Lord God, and I've been listening all my life. And once

29

or twice I've thought I heard my name called – but not clear, not clear.'

[. . .] Adam said desperately, 'Name me some names.'

'From the Bible?'

'From anyplace.'

'Well, let's see. Of all the people who started out of Egypt only two came to the Promised Land. Would you like them for a symbol?'

'Who?'

'Caleb and Joshua.'

'Joshua was a soldier – a general. I don't like soldiering.'

'Well, Caleb was a captain.'

'But not a general. I kind of like Caleb – Caleb Trask.'

One of the twins woke up and without interval began to wail.

'You called his name,' said Samuel. 'You don't like Joshua, and Caleb's named. He's the smart one – the dark one. See, the other one is awake too. Well, Aaron I've always liked, but he didn't make it to the Promised Land.'

The second boy almost joyfully began to cry.

'That's good enough,' said Adam.

Suddenly Samuel laughed. 'In two minutes,' he said, 'and after a waterfall of words. Caleb and Aaron – now you are people and you have joined the fraternity and you have the right to be damned.'

Lee took the boys up under his arms. 'Have you got them straight?' he asked.

'Of course,' said Adam. 'That one is Caleb and you are Aaron.' Lee lugged the yelling twins towards the house in the dusk.

'Yesterday I couldn't tell them apart,' said Adam. 'Aaron and Caleb.'

'Thank the good Lord we had produce from our patient thought,' Samuel said. 'Liza would have preferred Joshua. She loves the crashing walls of Jericho. But she likes Aaron too, so I guess it's all right. I'll go and hitch my rig.'

Adam walked to the shed with him. 'I'm glad you came,' he said. 'There's a weight off me.'

JOHN STEINBECK

———————

from Little Fadette

HE had already three children, when mother Barbeau, doubtless, taking into consideration that they had sufficient means for five, and no time to lose, thought fit to give him at a birth two fine boys, so much alike that it was almost impossible to distinguish one from the other.

Dame Sagette, who received them in her apron as they came into the world, did not omit to make a little cross with her needle upon the arm of the first born; 'for,' said she, 'a ribbon or a necklace may easily get changed, and then the right of primogeniture will be lost to the eldest; and as soon as the child is strong enough,' she added, 'you must make a mark which can never be effaced.' A piece of good advice which was not forgotten.

The eldest was christened Sylvain, which name was however quickly converted into Sylvinet, to distinguish him from his eldest brother, who had stood as godfather to him; while the younger was called Landry, a name which he preserved as he had received it at his baptism, since his uncle, who was his godfather, had from his youth upward been called Landriche.

Farmer Barbeau was somewhat astonished when he returned from market, to see two little heads in the cradle.

'Oh! oh!' said he, 'this cradle is too small. Tomorrow morning I must see if I cannot enlarge it.'

He knew something of joining, though he had never learnt it as a trade, and had made more than half of his own furniture. The worthy man gave no further evidence of surprise, but went to see his wife, who drank a large glass of warm wine, and declared that she never was better in her life.

'You labour so well, wife,' he said to her, 'that I must take fresh courage. Here are two more children to provide for, whom we did not absolutely need, and this is a hint to me that I must not flag in the culture of my lands and cattle. But, be easy, they too will work by and by; and take care you do not give me three next time, for that would be rather too much;' at this mother Barbeau began to shed tears, which greatly distressed her good man.

'Come, come,' said he, 'you must not grieve, wife. It was not to reproach you I spoke thus, but on the contrary to thank you. These two children are fine, well-made little fellows, sound in body and limb, and I am grateful.'

'Alas!' said the wife, 'I know well you did not mean to reproach me;

but I am sadly troubled, for they tell me there is nothing more difficult to rear than twins; that they wrong each other, and that frequently one of the two must perish that its twin may thrive.'

'Indeed,' said the farmer, 'is that true? As for me, these are the first twins I have seen. It is not a common event. But here is dame Sagette, who knows something about these things, and who will tell us all about it.'

Dame Sagette being thus called upon, replied: 'You may rely upon what I tell you: your twins will both thrive, and will not prove more sickly than other children. I have exercised my profession for half a century, and during that time I have seen all the children of the district born; these, therefore, are not the first twins I have brought into the world. Now, the resemblance does not affect their health at all; there are twins who are no more like each other than you and I; but it often happens that one is strong and the other weak, and this is why one lives and the other dies. But look at yours; they are both as strong and healthy as though they were only sons. They did each other no injury in the womb of their mother; they both came into the world without causing her to suffer, and without suffering themselves. They are beautiful children, and there is no fear of their dying. Console yourself therefore, mother Barbeau; it will be a pleasure to you to watch them grow; and, if they continue as they have begun, it will be only you, and those who see them every day, who will be able to distinguish between them, for I never saw twins so much alike. They resemble newly-hatched partridges; none but the mother-bird can tell one from the other.'

'This is all very well,' said farmer Barbeau, scratching his head; 'but I have heard it said that twins take such an affection for one another, that when they are separated, they refuse to live, and that one, at least, is often so consumed with grief as to perish.'

'And that is true,' returned dame Sagette. 'But listen to what a woman of experience is about to tell you, and be sure you do not forget; for when your children are old enough to be separated, I shall, perhaps, be no longer in the world to counsel and advise you. Take care, as soon as your twins begin to know each other, that you do not allow them to be always together. Set one to work, while the other remains in the house. When one goes fishing, send the other hunting; when one looks after the sheep, let the other attend to the oxen; when you give one wine to drink, let the other have water. Do not scold or correct them at the same time; do not dress them alike; when one has a hat, let the other have a cap; and, above all, do not let their blouses be of the same colour. In short, by all means you can devise, prevent them from being accustomed to be taken for each other. I fear greatly that what I am now telling you will go in at one ear and out of the other; but if you do not attend to it, you will some day bitterly repent.'

Dame Sagette spoke golden words. They promised to do as she directed, and dismissed her with a handsome present.

GEORGES SANDS

---

from The Robber Bride

ROZ puts on the bathrobe, over her hand-embroidered white-on-white batiste nightgown, bought to go with the bed, so who did she think was going to notice? She finds her purse, and transfers her half-empty pack of smokes to her pocket. *Not* before breakfast! Then she makes her way down the stairs, the back ones, the ones that used to be for maids, for toilet cleaners like her, clutching the banister so she won't trip. The stairs go straight into the kitchen, the sparkling austere all-white kitchen (time for a change!), where the twins sit on high stools at the tile-topped counter, wearing long T-shirts and striped tights and gym socks. These are the outfits they find it chic to sleep in, these days. It used to be such fun to dress them up, when they were little; such ruffles, tiny hats you could die for! Gone are the downy sleepers with plastic soles to their feet, gone too the expensive English cotton flannel nighties with rows of Mother Geese in bonnets and aprons printed on them. Gone are the books Roz used to read to the two of them when they wore those nighties, snuggling up to her, one under each arm – *Alice in Wonderland, Peter Pan, The Arabian Nights*, the reissues of lavish turn-of-the-century fairy tales with Arthur Rackham illustrations. Or not completely gone: stored in the cellar. Gone are the pink jogging suits, the raccoon bedroom slippers, the velvet party dresses, each frill and extravaganza. Now they won't let her buy them a thing. If she brings home even a black top, even a pair of underpants, they roll their eyes.

The two of them are drinking the yogourt-and-skim-milk-and-blueberry smoothies they've just made in the blender. She can see the melting package of frozen blueberries, and the puddle of blue milk lying like pale ink on the counter.

'So, you'll do me a favour, for once you'll put it in the dishwasher,' she can't help saying to them.

They turn their identical eyes towards her, lambent eyes like those of forest cats, and smile their identical heartless heart-crushing smiles, showing their slightly feral faun's teeth, blue at the moment, and shaking their moussey, fluffed-out manes; and she catches her breath, as she does almost every time she sees them, because they are so huge and so gorgeous and she still can't quite understand how she managed to give birth to them. One such creature would have been unlikely enough, but two!

They laugh. 'It's the Big Mom!' one of them shouts, the one on the right. 'The Big Mommy! Let's give her a hug!'

They leap down from their stools and grab hold of her and squeeze. Her feet lift from the ground, and she rises perilously into the air.

'Put me down!' she shrieks. They know she doesn't like this, they know she's afraid they'll drop her. They'll drop her and she'll break. Sometimes they have no sense of that; they think she's unbreakable. Roz the Rock. Then they remember.

'Let's put her on a stool,' they say. They carry her over and deposit her, and climb back onto their own stools, like circus animals who have done their trick.

'Mom, you look like a pumpkin in that,' says one. It's Erin. Roz has always been able to tell them apart, or so she claims. Two guesses and she's right every time. Mitch used to have trouble. But then, he only ever saw them for about fifteen minutes a day.

'Pumpkin, that's me,' says Roz, with heavy jocularity. 'Fat, orange, big friendly grin, hollow in the centre and glows in the dark.' She needs her coffee, right now! She pulls open the freezer door, sticks the frozen blueberry package back in there, finds the bag of magic beans, and fumbles around in one of the roll-out drawers for the electric grinder. Having everything stowed away in drawers wasn't such a hot idea, she can never find anything any more. Especially not the pot lids. *The uncluttered look*, said that fool of a designer. They always intimidate her.

'Aww,' says the other one. Paula. Errie and Pollie, they call each other, or Er and La, or, when they're speaking collectively, Erla. It's creepy when they do that. *Erla's going out tonight.* That means both of them. 'Aww. You rotten twin! You hurt the Mommy's feelings! You are just rotten, rotten to the core!' This last is an imitation of Roz imitating her own mother, who used to say that. Roz feels a sudden need for her, for her harsh, embattled, once-scorned, long-dead

34

mother. She's tired of being a mother, she wants to be a child for a change. She missed out on that. It looks like way more fun.

The twins laugh delightedly. 'Selfish rotten cesspool,' one says to the other.

'Unshaved armpit!'

'Festering tampon!'

'Used panty liner!' They can go on this way for hours, thinking up worse and worse insults for each other, laughing so hard they roll on the floor and kick their feet in the air with delight at their own outrageous humour. What puzzles her is how so many of their insults can be so – well, so sexist. *Bitch* and *slut* are among their mildest; she wonders if they'd let boys call them that. When they think she's not listening, they can get much more obscene, or what she thinks of as obscene. *Cunt gum.* Such a thing could never even have been thought of, when she was growing up. And they're only fifteen!

But people carry their vocabularies with them through their lives, like turtle shells, thinks Roz. She has a sudden flash of the twins at eighty, their beautiful faces raddled, their by-then-withered legs still encased in coloured tights, gym socks on their bunioned feet, still saying *cunt gum.* She shudders.

Touch wood, she corrects herself. They should live so long.

MARGARET ATWOOD

Livia, who was married to Drusus gave birth to twin sons. This as a rare event, causing joy even in humble homes, so delighted the Emperor that he did not refrain from boasting before the senators that to no Roman of the same rank had twin offspring ever before been born. In fact he would turn to his own story every incident however casual . . .

TACITUS, *Annales II*, 84

---

from The 'Clipse

CORNELIO came to see me and brought with him a couple of two-and-a-half-year-old girls, born in the same 'litter,' as he put it, called María de los Dolores and María del Pilar – both as blond

35

as a stalk of wheat, white and rosy like a ripe peach, and pretty as 'pictures' – that's one of Cornelio's expressions. There was a marked contrast between the childlike beauty of the twins and the truly irregular features of Cornelio – ugly as can be with dark brown skin and coarse, down to his dirty fingernails and the cracks in his heels. Naturally it occurred to me right away to ask him who was the happy father of that fair pair. The old man cackled with pride, twisted his prune face, wiped away the saliva with the back of his hairy hand, and answered:

'Well, I'm their daddy, believe it or not! They don't look much like me, but their mama really ain't so bad lookin', and fer the pow'r of ar great God, nothin's impossible.'

'But tell me, Cornelio. Is your wife a blonde or do they look like their grandparents?'

'Nope. In the whole family there's not a one that's been like them Siamese cats or fair-haired pups. We've all been half-breeds.'

'Well, then, how do you explain that the girls were born with that hair and coloring?'

The old man let loose with a loud guffaw, set his arms akimbo, and gave me a look of supreme disdain.

'What are you laughing about, Cornelio?'

'Well, didn't I hafta laugh, Mr Magón, when I see a poor, ignorant feller like me, a hick farmhand, knows more 'n a man like you, one that everyone says is so edgeecated and well read, so's ta even write laws fer the Presydent and his ministers?'

'O.K. then, explain it to me.'

'Now you'll see how it was.'

Cornelio took a good-sized lump of molasses out of his saddle-bags, gave a piece to each little girl, and drew up a stool, on which he eased himself down, gloating over his impending triumph; he blew his nose noisily, covering each opening with the respective forefinger while blowing violently through the other; he rubbed with the sole of his right paw, cleaning the floor; he wiped off his hands on the inside of his jacket, and began his explanation with these words:

'Ya know that 'bout this time in March, three years ago, there was a 'clipse, where the whole middle of the sun turned black; O.K., well 'bout twenty days before, Lina, my wife, turned up pregnant with those little girls. From then on, there was this real uneasiness got hold of her; it was amazin'. There was no stoppin' 'er. She'd leave the house day 'n night, always lookin' up at the sky; she'd go ta the empty lot, the brook, the thicket fence, 'n always accordin' to her fancy 'n that illness, so there weren't nothin' ta do but let 'er have 'er way. She'd always been full of cravin's, every time she's pregnant. Ya see, when the oldest was born, it was just the same; like one night she woke me up late at night 'n made me go look fer male plumtree shoots for her. Guess it was better ta go than have the poor little thing born with its mouth open. I brung her the shoots. After that there were other cravin's, but I'd never seen her so full of 'em as with these little girls. Well, now ya see, like I's sayin', spyin' at the sky, day 'n night, it got a hold of her, 'n the day of the 'clipse I'd been out in the brambles by the fence since the crack of dawn.

'So's not ta wear ya out with the story, things went on like that till these little girls was born. I don't deny that seein' 'em so blond and fair wasn't an uphill struggle fer me, but ever since it seems like they've brung God's blessing. The schoolmarm likes 'em 'n sews all their clothes for 'em; the politician gives 'em the loose change in his pockets; the priest asks me for 'em so's ta put 'em by the altar with pure linen petticoats 'n sequins fer Corpus Christi 'n the days of Holy Week; they take 'em out in the procession, puttin' 'em next ta the Nazarene 'n the Holy Sepulcher; fer Christmas Eve, they change 'em inta real purty dresses 'n put 'em by the manger, next ta the Holy Family. 'n all the expenses come outta the organizers' pockets, 'n they always give 'em a big coin, or even paper money, or some other good present. Blessed be ar God, who brought 'em ta serve Him from out of an ugly daddy like me! . . . Lina's even so stuck up 'bout 'er little girls that she just can't stand it when people don't praise 'em. She's already had some good fights with the old bags of the neighborhood over these orn'ry little kittens.'

I interrupted Cornelio, afraid that his panegyric would never end and I put him back on the track.

'O.K., but what about it?'

'What about it? Well, don'cha see that it's 'cause their mama saw the 'clipse that they're blondies? Din'cha know that?'

'No, I didn't, and I'm surprised you figured it out without having any education.'

'Why try 'n fool ya, Mr Magón; I wasn't the one as figured out the riddle. Ya know that Italian builder that made the church steeple in town? A big guy, with reddish hair 'n real white skin, who's been eatin' at ar house fer four years?'

'No, Cornelio.'

37

'Well, he's the one as explained the 'clipse thing ta me.'
MANUEL GONZALEZ ZELEDÓN (MAGÓN)
(*Translated by Roberta H. Kimble*)

---

from Travels in West Africa

TWINS are killed among all the Niger Delta tribes, and in districts out of English control the mother is killed too, except in Omon, where the sanctuary is.

There twin mothers and their children are exiled to an island in the Cross River. They have to remain on the island and if any man goes across and marries one of them he has to remain on the island too. This twin-killing is a widely diffused custom among the Negro tribes.

I doubt whether the Bantus do it so much, but I distrust those Bantus in the matter of twins. They lulled my mind into an unsuspicious, restful state regarding twins, and then played it low, so I won't go bail for them. It was this way. When I first came out to the Coast, my friends told me everything they could lay tongue on until I frequently smelt their souls scorching, and a brief experience of my friends' conversation warned me that the phrase, 'We've some very peculiar customs down here' was the *Leit Motif* of the entrance of twins into the conversation. Regarding this subject as unfit for general discussion, I therefore used to smother those twins by leading the conversation off by the ear immediately I heard the warning note, and exceedingly skilful in this I became.

When, however, I was past the Negro ports Bonny, Calabar, &c., and across the Bantu border line, below Cameroon, I found the subject did not arise, and I became lulled into a sense of false security. All went well for some time, until one day I was walking with an Englishman across a stretch of country where there were several villages. At one of these a high festival was evidently being held, a dance of women was taking place in the main street, the usual wriggle and stamp affair, to the thump, thump, thump of the native drums. Before one house, on either side of the doorway, stood a man and a woman. The remarkable point about the affair was that their legs were painted white, and as the view of them was not interrupted by clothes, the effect was somewhat startling. 'Dear me, Mr—,' I said, 'that's rather quaint.' 'We've some very peculiar customs down here regarding twins,' said he, before I, being unprepared, had time to turn the conversation.

These customs (Akele) amounted to the mother of twins being kept in her hut for a year after the birth. Then there was a great dance and certain ceremonies, during which the lady and the doctor, not the husband, had their legs painted white. When the ceremonials were over the woman returned to her ordinary avocations.

[. . .] The terror with which twins are regarded in the Niger Delta is exceedingly strange and real. When I had the honour of being with Miss Slessor at Okÿon, the first twins in that district were saved with their mother from immolation owing entirely to Miss Slessor's great influence with the natives and her own unbounded courage and energy. The mother in this case was a slave woman – an Eboe, the most expensive and valuable of slaves. She was the property of a big woman who had always treated her – as indeed most slaves are treated in Calabar – with great kindness and consideration, but when these two children arrived all was changed; immediately she was subjected to torrents of virulent abuse, her things were torn from her, her English china basins, possessions she valued most highly, were smashed, her clothes were torn, and she was driven out as an unclean thing. Had it not been for the fear of incurring Miss Slessor's anger, she would, at this point, have been killed with her children, and the bodies thrown into the bush.

As it was, she was hounded out of the village. The rest of her possessions were jammed into an empty gin-case and cast to her. No one would touch her, as they might not touch to kill. Miss Slessor had heard of the twins' arrival and had started off, barefooted and bareheaded, at that pace she can go down a bush path. By the time she had gone four miles she met the procession, the woman coming to her and all the rest of the village yelling and howling behind her. On the top of her head was the gin-case, into which the children had been stuffed, on the top of them the woman's big brass skillet, and on the top of that her two market calabashes. Needless to say, on arriving Miss Slessor took charge of affairs, relieving the unfortunate, weak, staggering woman from her load and carrying it herself, for no one else would touch it, or anything belonging to those awful twin things, and they started back together to Miss Slessor's house in the forest-clearing, saved by that tact which, coupled with her courage, has given Miss Slessor an influence and a power among the negroes unmatched in its way by that of any other white.

She did not take the twins and their mother down the village path to her own house, for though had she done so the people of Okyon would not have prevented her, yet so polluted would the path have been, and so dangerous to pass down, that they would have been compelled to cut another, no light task in that bit of forest, I assure you. So Miss Slessor stood waiting in the broiling sun, in the hot season's height, while a path was being cut to enable her just to get through to her own grounds. The natives worked away hard, knowing that it saved the polluting of a long stretch of market road, and when it was finished Miss Slessor went to her own house by it and attended with all kindness, promptness, and skill, to the woman and children. I arrived in the middle of this affair for my first meeting with Miss Slessor, and things at Okyon were rather crowded, one way and another, that afternoon. All the attention one of the children wanted – the boy, for there was a boy and a girl – was burying, for the people who had crammed them into the box had utterly smashed the child's head. The other child was alive, and is still a member of that household of rescued children all of whom owe their lives to Miss Slessor.

MARY KINGSLEY

The Japanese word for a twin pregnancy is '*chikusho-bara*' and means 'animal belly' . . . in earlier centuries this expression was one of the most obscene insults.

ALISON MACDONALD, *The Psychology and Inter-Relationship of Twins*

I know that in Northern Luzon among the Ingorots it was always the custom to kill a twin. I tried to find a reason for this and was told by the women that they did not wish to be like a dog and have a litter. Incidentally, there is one corporal in the constabulary who, when he was little, was put in a jar and left to die. His twin brother, however, beat him to it, whereupon they hastily retrieved him from the jar and he is alive today.

COLONEL THEODORE ROOSEVELT (governor of the Philippines), private communication to H.H. Newman, 1934

----

from At Hiruharama

THE doctor drove up bringing with him his wife's widowed sister, who lived with them and was a nurse, or had been a nurse. Tanner came out of the bedroom covered with blood, something like a butcher. He told the doctor he'd managed to deliver the child, a girl, in fact he'd wrapped it in a towel and tucked it up in the washbasket. The doctor took him back into the bedroom and made him sit down. The nurse put down the things she'd brought with her and looked round for the tea-tin. Brinkman sat there, as solid as his chair. 'You may be wondering who I am,' he said. 'I'm a neighbour, come over for dinner. I think of myself as one of the perpetually welcome.' 'Suit yourself,' said the sister-in-law. The doctor emerged, moving rather faster than he usually did. 'Please to go in there and wash the patient. I'm going to take a look at the afterbirth. The father put it out with the waste.'

There Tanner had made his one oversight. It wasn't the afterbirth, it was a second daughter, smaller, but a twin. – But how come, if both of them were girls, that Mr Tanner himself still had the name of Tanner? Well, the Tanners went on to have nine more children, some of them boys, and one of those boys was Mr Tanner's father. That evening, when the doctor came in from the yard with the messy scrap, he squeezed it as though he was wringing it out to dry, and it opened its mouth and the colder air of the kitchen rushed in and she'd got her start in life. After that the Tanners always had one of those tinplate mottoes hung up on the wall – Throw Nothing Away. You could get them then at the hardware store. – And this was the point that Mr Tanner had been wanting to make all along – whereas the first daughter never got to be anything in particular, this second little girl grew up to be a lawyer with a firm in Wellington, and she did very well.

PENELOPE FITZGERALD

2

LIKE AND UNLIKE TWINS: THE NATURE OF TWINSHIP

இ&

E VEN BEFORE the simplicities of DNA analysis, zygosity – that is whether twins are or are not identical – could usually be determined easily enough. In our case much of the evidence was ambiguous, and, we were told by the researchers in a twin study we took part in in the 1970s, more typical of identical twins, according to the thinking then. We had similar ear lobes, for instance, our hair grew in similar ways; we mirrored each other, moreover – right-handed, left-handed; right hair whorls, left hair whorls; her left-hemispheric intelligence practical, logical, scientific, my right one, more intuitive, imaginative, arts oriented. Of the same blood group, we were a short, brown-eyed, brown-haired, academic pair, amid tallish, blue-eyed, unacademic siblings. The same size and shape, we were sufficiently a pair to be exploited as bridesmaids, nativity-play pages, and so on, throughout our childhood, and could and did play some of the classic twin tricks on those who didn't know us well, like visiting dancing teachers, to whom we presented ourselves as each other on alternate weeks. None the less, we could always be told apart by those who knew us; and our own assumption that we weren't identical was finally borne out in a test for rhesus factors in our blood. The difference was small enough, however, to make me wonder sometimes if we were of that third, as yet unproven type of twinship – where the egg splits before conception, thus ensuring the pair gets identical genes from the mother and different ones from the father. More likely, our relative likeness lay within the statistical possibilities of likeness between any siblings. After all, theoretically it's possible that an untwinned pair could be given the same genes by both parents and so end up genetically identical.

In French, fraternal twins are called false twins (*faux jumeaux*), as against true twins (*vrai jumeaux*). Some identical twins also assert, arrogantly in my view, that us fraternals are mere siblings who happen to be born together, and therefore don't count. It is true that likeness is what non-twins find intriguing about twins above all – and creepy, too, as a visit to Twins restaurant in New York, where everyone from receptionists to bar staff to waiters – and often the customers – comes double may confirm, given the prevailing view that to be truly human is to be unique. Nevertheless, more subtly, in my opinion – and experience – if the popular glamour of twinship relates to perfect likeness, to all those endless tales of confusion, twinness as such relates to a good deal more than that. It's likely I would say that, of course. Being a twin is part of the self-myth and so not lightly to be relinquished. Fortunately for me, though, I am backed up by less biased observers of twins and relationships. Notably the French psychologist, René Zazzo, quoted at the end of this part, in whose view twinness stems not from genetic likeness and unlikeness, but from their being the ultimate couple.

The consequences of this resonates, not only within the couple so formed but on the twins as individuals – for they are individuals still, genetically identical or not, as Zazzo insists. And here again he makes complete sense to me as a twin. The problem is to find out in what that individuality – that identity – consists. The identity of a twin you could say is not having a sense of identity. A twin is one who from birth is compared with someone else. A problem all the more acute perhaps for fraternal twins, made to compare themselves with a person in some cases quite unlike them. The resultant confusion of identity, internal in this case, like the external confusion between the look-alike brothers in Goldoni's *Venetian Twins*, referred to earlier, can only be resolved by the death of one.

'From one half to the other', wrote my sister in her twenty-first-birthday present to me. Quite. It's no accident, I suspect, that review after review of my novels asserted that I was yet again in search of my identity. Or that my best-known book, *Charlotte Sometimes*, has two girls changing places without anyone noticing the difference, leading Charlotte herself to look in a mirror and ask if 'you were only a particular person because people recognised you as that?' For the fact is – something overlooked by those who assert that only genetic identity counts – that, before birth as after, a twin is never alone. And that whereas the primary relationship for the single child, the norm, is between mother and child, that is a hierarchical, or vertical relationship, the primary relationship for a twin is a horizontal one, with a peer. This may explain why we twins are in some sense so profoundly different from the rest of you. The more so if, as a psychologist friend asserts, the primary social norm, starting from that vertical relationship with the parent, is hierarchy, making horizontal relationships, between equals, experienced later, secondary by definition.

Not so with twins. Given the different role that each twin takes on within the couple relationship – Zazzo suggests, for instance, that one twin will always be effectively 'Minister for the Interior' and the other 'Minister for the Exterior' – a hierarchy can of course develop in any pair. Usually it does; one twin may be or at least appear dominant. But the hierarchies fluctuate, have to be created, defined, and subsequently, often, redefined; top twin in one respect is bottom twin in another. There is no inherent vertical structure between twins, as between parent and child. Evidence from ultrasound scanning of twins *in utero*, moreover, suggests that their relationship is not only paramount from the very womb, the nature of the intra-uterine relationship, whether amicable or inimical, is maintained thereafter. The affectionate continue to show affection. The fighters continue to fight.

As for us: who knows if our battles started in the womb. But I do know that in all images of our childhood, photographic or remembered, my twin was always there, alongside me; in our mother's arms, in our crib, dangling from our father's hands, in our playpen, in our school uniforms; twins; a couple. As I know, though this I remember less well, for our mother always managed to make each of us feel we were special to her, that it was not looking into her eyes that told me who I was, as in the case of the single-born. My sister, side by side with me, told me who I was; and who I wasn't. So that even now she's dead, what she was shadows what I am, defining me still relative to her, competitively more often than not. These days this comes down to 'Yah boo, I'm alive, and you're dead.' A feeling so primitive, I'm downright ashamed of it, at my age, and in such a condition, but it's so engrained I can't help it. Just so earlier, each of us reacted to my being the academically successful one, and her not; to her being the pretty, thin, sexually successful one and me fat, spectacled throughout adolescence, the wallflower. Despite my getting married earlier, it was not till much later when I lost the weight and the spectacles, both, that I aspired to her success in that area – coincidentally around the time she was discovering that, given the right subject, sociology, she was as academically able as I was, attending the London School of Economics as a mature student. Her reaction, then, was to stop bothering to make herself look good; mine – for we always went different ways in this – to consider doing another degree.

When they're not struggling to find identity, of course, the point of twins is precisely their twoness; what the psychologist, Dorothy Burlingham called the 'gang of two' – meaning the advantages of confronting the world always as a pair. Until late adolescence, I never had to confront any new situation without a twin at my side. From our earliest days, being independent and solitary, I'd sometimes chosen to, much to the discomfort of my twin, but leaving home and facing university alone was a different matter. Though it's hard for anyone, of course, I suspect that for me it was more painful than for most. Yet I don't think, weeping in my room, I fully understood then what made it so particularly painful. I hardly dared go to parties unless I could find someone to go with me; this did not do much for my social life.

Another stereotype has twins as a merry and enviable pair getting up to all sorts of fun and games by virtue of their twinship. Between us I don't remember much of that; maybe we weren't good enough friends to play two against the rest. Apart from our odd adventures tricking one teacher and another, we equipped ourselves with separate friends. It was not that we didn't have our own kind of symbiotic relationship, our own 'gangness'. But our way of facing the world as one was in my twin taking on the role of carer, while I took on the role of cared-for. Seeing Penelope as 'helpless' not to say 'hopeless' presumably helped compensate her for my greater academic success. Certainly till after we left school, she was the one who picked up after me; who found my lost pens, hats, gloves; got me up on time – something I was more than happy to go along with. At school in due course she was made prefect, head girl, because she was so competent and responsible – I was only appointed to any such role to encourage me to become more like her. Later still, I expected my partners to look after me the way she had, while an aspect of her deciding to marry pathologically needy men, addicts both, and follow a career in one caring profession or another, first voluntarily, then professionally, might have been her long practice in tending – her need to tend – me. It was an ongoing symbiosis therefore, though acted out with others in later life. But it was not of the kind whereby twin pairs, taking their cues from each other rather than being inhibited by parental – hierarchical – prohibitions, play at gangs in the more conventional sense, and egg each other on to ever more outrageous acts of villainy; the Kray twins the extreme outcome.

In the material here, I bow to conventional views of twinship (western views that are *à la* Lévi-Strauss) by starting with identical twins – including identical opposite-gender twins, actually something genetically impossible, though authors from Shakespeare on have ignored this inconvenient fact. Then, more willingly, I turn to fraternals, and general unlikeness, that is, twins as polarities and dichotomies – good twin/bad twin, upper class/lower class, and so forth, where twins otherwise identical are sometimes used as examples. The part looking at the nature of twinship, however, reflects Zazzo's assertion that twinness is about coupledom, mainly, so makes no such division.

In the light of which, let me end this introduction with one of the most poignant stories – for me – that I came across in my researches on twins, precisely because it raises so unambiguously the question whether it is genetics or the experience of being coupled that forms the twin. It concerns a pair of fraternal twins in Australia. One of this pair was at a football game, when the stares of those around him made him aware suddenly of a young man almost identical to him a few seats along. They began to talk, and in due course discovered that they'd been born the same day in the same hospital. It transpired they were indeed twins; the hospital had mixed up a double with a single birth, and sent the single child home as the second twin. So the real twins were reunited. A happy end you'd think – except in the case of the third, or rather non-twin, brought up to think he was one. Of the three it is he who continues to haunt me. Who did he now feel he was?

LIKE TWINS

Identical twins are, so to speak, the 'same individual of whom two copies have been printed . . .'

LAROUSSE *Science of Life*

———————

It might be said that the human being who possesses an identical twin is unusually fortunate, for in case of accident or sickness, he has a handy reserve of spare organs – always assuming that his twin is generous enough to make the necessary sacrifice.

Source unknown

———————

ADRIANA. I see two husbands or my eyes deceive me!
DUKE. One of these two men is genius to the other;
And so of these: which is the natural man,
And which the spirit? Who deciphers them?

WILLIAM SHAKESPEARE, *The Comedy of Errors*

———————

from History of Twins

ENOUGH has been said to prove that an extremely close personal resemblance frequently exists between twins of the same sex; and that, although the resemblance usually diminishes as they grow into manhood and womanhood, some cases occur in which the diminution of resemblance is hardly perceptible. It must be borne in mind that it is not necessary to ascribe the divergence of development, when it occurs, to the effect of different nurtures, but it is quite possible that

49

it may be due to the late appearance of qualities inherited at birth, though dormant in early life, like gout. To this I shall recur.

There is a curious feature in the character of the resemblance between twins, which has been alluded to by a few correspondents; it is well illustrated by the following quotations. A mother of twins says: –

> There seemed to be a sort of interchangeable likeness in expression, that often gave to each the effect of being more like his brother than himself.

Again, two twin brothers, writing to me, after analysing their points of resemblance, which are close and numerous, and pointing out certain shades of difference, add –

> These seem to have marked us through life, though for a while, when we were first separated, the one to go to business, and the other to college, our respective characters were inverted; we both think that at that time we each ran into the character of the other. The proof of this consists in our own recollections, in our correspondence by letter, and in the views which we then took of matters in which we were interested.

[. . .] Among my thirty-five detailed cases of close similarity, there are no less than seven in which both twins suffered from some special ailment or had some exceptional peculiarity. One twin writes that she and her sister 'have both the defect of not being able to come downstairs quickly, which, however, was not born with them, but came on at the age of twenty.' Three pairs of twins have peculiarities in their fingers; in one case it consists in a slight congenital flexure of one of the joints of the little finger; it was inherited from a grandmother, but neither parents, nor brothers, nor sisters show the least trace of it. In another case the twins have a peculiar way of bending the fingers, and there was a faint tendency to the same peculiarity in the mother, but in her alone of all the family. In a third case, about which I made a few inquiries, which is given by Mr Darwin, but is not included in my returns, there was no known family tendency to the peculiarity which was observed in the twins of having a crooked little finger. In another pair of twins, one was born ruptured, and the other became so at six months old. Two twins at the age of twenty-three were attacked by toothache, and the same tooth had to be extracted in each case. There are curious and close correspondences mentioned in the falling off of the hair. Two cases are mentioned of death from the same disease; one of which is very affecting. The outline of the story was that the twins were closely alike and singularly attached, and had identical tastes; they both obtained Government clerkships, and kept house together, when one sickened and died of Bright's disease, and the other also sickened of the same disease and died seven months later.

Both twins were apt to sicken at the same time in no less than nine out of the thirty-five cases. Either their illnesses, to which I refer, were non-contagious, or, if contagious, the twins caught them simultaneously; they did not catch them the one from the other. This implies so intimate a constitutional resemblance, that it is proper to give some quotations in evidence. Thus, the father of two twins says: –

> Their general health is closely alike; whenever one of them has an illness, the other invariably has the same within a day or two, and they usually recover in the same order. Such has been the case with whooping-cough, chicken-pox, and measles; also with slight bilious attacks, which they have successively. Latterly, they had a feverish attack at the same time.

Another parent of twins says: –

> If anything ails one of them, identical symptoms *nearly always* appear in the other; this has been singularly visible in two instances during the last two months. Thus, when in London, one fell ill with a violent attack of dysentery, and within twenty-four hours the other had precisely the same symptoms.

A medical man writes of twins with whom he is well acquainted—

> Whilst I knew them, for a period of two years, there was not the slightest tendency towards a difference in body or mind; external influences seemed powerless to produce any dissimilarity.

The mother of two other twins, after describing how they were ill simultaneously up to the age of fifteen, adds, that they shed their first milk-teeth within a few hours of each other.

[. . .] The last point to which I shall allude regards the tastes and dispositions of the thirty-five pairs of twins. In sixteen cases – that is, in nearly one-half of them – these were described as closely similar; in the remaining nineteen they were much alike, but subject to certain named differences. These differences belonged almost wholly to such groups of qualities as these: the one was more vigorous, fearless, energetic; the other was gentle, clinging and timid; or the one was more ardent, the other more calm and placid; or again, the one was the more independent, original and self-contained; the other the more generous, hasty, and vivacious. In short, the difference was that of intensity or energy in one or the other of its protean forms; it did not extend more deeply into the structure of the characters. The more vivacious might be subdued by ill health, until he assumed the character of the other; or the latter might be raised by excellent health to that of the former.

It has been remarked that a growing diversity between twins may be ascribed to the tardy development of naturally diverse qualities; but we have a right, upon the evidence I have received, to go farther than this. We have seen that a few twins retain their close resemblance through life; in other words, instances do exist of an apparently thorough similarity of nature, in which such difference of external circumstances as may be consistent with the ordinary conditions of the same social rank and country do not create dissimilarity. Positive evidence, such as this, cannot be outweighed by any amount of negative evidence. Therefore, in those cases where there is a growing diversity, and where no external cause can be assigned either by the twins themselves or by their family for it, we may feel sure that it must be chiefly or altogether due to a want of thorough similarity in their nature. Nay, further, in some cases it is distinctly affirmed that the growing dissimilarity can be accounted for in no other way. We may, therefore, broadly conclude that the only circumstance, within the range of those by which persons of similar conditions of life are affected, that is capable of producing a marked effect on the character of adults, is illness or some accident which causes physical infirmity. The twins who closely resembled each other in childhood and early youth, and were reared under not very dissimilar conditions, either grow unlike through the development of natural characteristics which had lain dormant at first, or else they continue their lives, keeping time like two watches, hardly to be thrown out of accord except by some physical jar. Nature is far stronger than Nurture within the limited range that I have been careful to assign to the latter.

[. . .] The steady and pitiless march of the hidden weaknesses in our constitutions, through illness to death, is painfully revealed by these histories of twins. We are too apt to look upon illness and death as capricious events, and there are some who ascribe them to the direct effect of supernatural interference, whereas the fact of the maladies of two twins being continually alike shows that illness and death are necessary incidents in a regular sequence of constitutional changes beginning at birth, and upon which external circumstances have, on the whole, very small effect. In cases where the maladies of the twins are continually alike, the clocks of their two lives move regularly on at the same rate, governed by their internal mechanism. When the hands approach the hour, there are sudden clicks, followed by a whirring of wheels; the moment that they touch it, the strokes fall. Necessitarians may derive new arguments from the life-histories of twins.

FRANCIS GALTON

———————

'like as two peas in a pod'
'made on similar blocks.'
'Like to a double cherry.'
'Two lovely berries moulded on one stem.'

———————

One river flowing in two beds.

ANATOLY PRISTAVKIN, *The Inseparable Twins*

———————

'You're so alike! Two boots of a pair! . . . No!' she exclaimed and bent down to look at them more closely. 'No, you're like two boots for the same foot! . . .

IBID.

———————

'You're a difficult problem,' said K, comparing them as he had already done several times. How am I to know one of you from the other . . . you're as like as two snakes.'

KAFKA, *The Castle*

———————

Rhea and Rhoda were the same girl; they'd wanted it that way. Only looking from one to the other could you see they were two.

JOYCE CAROL OATES, *Heat*

———————

A single person in two individuals.

ANATOLY PRISTAVKIN, *The Inseparable Twins*

———————

Two firm impressions made upon the wax
By the same seal are not more like each other
Than you two are . . .

WILLIAM RIDER, *The Twins*, 1655

———————

Her thoughts had been identical with those of her sister in every way, save only in one respect, and this cleavage can best be appreciated by the simple process of substituting Cora's name for her own whenever it appears in the reveries of the former.

MERVYN PEAKE, *Titus Groan*

———————

On Henry Vaughan the silurist and his alchemist twin brother, Thomas

What planet ruled your birth? What brittle star?
That you so like in souls as bodies are!
So like in both that you seem born to free
The slaine art from vulgar calumnie.
My doubts are solv'd, from hence my faith begins,
Not only your faces but your wits are Twins.

ANON.

———————

54

Sisters Crash. Twin sisters, Lorraine and Lavinia Christmas were recovering after a road crash on an icy road when they ran into each other's cars. The 31-year-old sisters, who live in different villages, ran into each other on a country road in Norfolk at Flitcham, Norfolk, on the morning of Christmas Eve.

The Independent, 26 December 1994

———————

The nightmare of swarming indistinguishable sameness.

ALDOUS HUXLEY, *Brave New World*

———————

A sudden noise of shrill voices made him open his eyes and ... look around. What seemed an interminable stream of identical eight-year-old twin males were pouring into the room. Twin after twin, twin after twin, they came – a nightmare. Their faces, their repeated face – for there was only one between the lot of them – puggishly stared, all nostrils and pale goggling eyes. Their uniform was khaki. All their mouths hung open. Squealing and chattering they entered. In a moment, it seemed, the ward was maggoty with them. They swarmed between the beds, clambered over, crawled under, peeped into the television boxes, made faces at the patients.

IBID.

———————

from Gemini

I could not sort out those pictures between Paul and myself except at random. What had happened was that I was being faced for the first time, unexpectedly, with a problem everyone else around us came up against several times a day: how to tell Paul and Jean apart. Everyone, that is, except us. Of course, we did not have everything in common.

55

We each had our own books and toys and above all our clothes. But while we could tell them by signs imperceptible to the rest – a special shine, a worn patch and, more than anything, by their smell, which for clothes was decisive – these criteria did not hold good for photos which looked at the pair of us from an outsider's point of view. I felt my throat swelling with tears but I was too old to burst out crying and so I did my best to carry it off. Confidently selecting six pictures, I drew them toward me, pushing the others across to Paul. My confidence deceived no one and Edouard smiled, stroking the tip of his small moustache with his forefinger. Paul said merely, 'We were both wearing shirts. Next time I'll put on a sweater. Then there can't be any mistake.'

MICHEL TOURNIER

---

from The Suicide and his Brother

BENITO Gandol and Amadeo Gandol were twins. They lived in San Feliu de Guixols, in the upper part of the town. Their similarity was so great, it was established without a doubt from the very first moment: they proceeded from the same ovum. A kind of sign hung on their chests: 'Gandol Brothers, Uniovular Twins.' For many years, they, as well as a hunchback and a once-beautiful woman who at that time went about constantly rubbing her wrists with alcohol, constituted a human diversion for the neighbors. 'Look at them, there they are! It's amazing.' 'Have you noticed? They walk in step!' 'What I don't understand is that they don't try to differentiate themselves, at least in their dress. On the contrary, the same suit, the same tie, the same shoes . . .' 'Yesterday they were at the beach and I observed a detail: they came out of the water together rubbing their eyes in the same way.'

The Gandol brothers, so identical – as children they always took each other's hand and the popular version was that, asleep in their bed, they made the same grimaces and turned over at the same instant – excited the mind and posed questions about free will and individual liberty. Here was a much more complex mystery than that of the hunchbacked man or of the woman who rubbed her wrists with alcohol. The fishermen of the town, especially versed in matters of monotony, asserted that they were more alike than two similar fish. The mushroom pickers couldn't remember ever seeing two mushrooms so conforming. The manufacturers of corks, basic industry in San Feliu

56

de Guixols, denied that the mass-produced corks that poured from the machinery attained such perfect parity. 'The stria in cork, their veins, always present some differences; the Gandol brothers, none.' Even the priest, with tongue in cheek, once said, 'I'd have enough with the confession of one of them.' Seemingly, only the doctor admitted the possibility that the fingerprints of Benito and Amadeo Gandol were different.

Red-haired, tall as castles, they were a duplicate force. Seeing them pass on the streets, people felt strangely protected, since it was obvious that in a moment of danger – of fire, of a ship off-course, of an epidemic – the Gandol brothers, uniting their vigor, could perform miracles. On their part, they both gave incessant proof of their love for the town and its inhabitants. Not only did they answer any call, but their presence was also inevitable at any public gathering that took place in San Feliu de Guixols. They were seen at the football games, in the cafes, at the movies; sometimes, at the fish auctions. When the great Fiesta came, the Gandol brothers were on the Organizing Committee and in the official program, year after year, they ordered a whole page of advertising: 'GANDOL BROTHERS, MANUFACTURERS OF CORKS.' There was something of lightning rods about them or of Psalms from the Bible. And, of course, no one imagined that they could die separately.

JOSÉ MARIA GIRONDELLA, from *Phantoms and Fantasies*

Dr David Lykken, a director of the Minnesota University study of twins reared apart, has reported several examples of cases where genes seem to be controlling not just broad tendencies, such as being intelligent or outgoing, but surprisingly detailed aspects of personal behaviour . . . For some time now the . . . study has been finding that twins separated at birth and reunited only in middle age shared such curiously specific things as: being brilliant storytellers, refusing to express controversial opinions, being habitual gigglers, and always wearing seven rings. There was even a pair who always entered the sea backwards and then only to their knees.

JEROME BURNE, *The Times*, January 1993

---

from Twins: A Study of Heredity and Environment

The Story of Ed and Fred

THE most interesting feature of this story is the remarkable parallelism in the lives of these twins in spite of the fact that they lived without knowledge of each other's existence for twenty-five years. They were both reared as only children by childless foster-parents, both being led to understand that they were own children. Though they lived a thousand miles apart, they had about the same educational experience, and both found employment as repair men in branches of the same great telephone company. They were married in the same year and each had a baby son. Each owned a fox terrier dog named Trixie. According to their statements, both of them from early boyhood were obsessed with the idea that they had a brother who died and often stated this to their playmates.

The story of their discovery of each other's existence is almost stranger than fiction. When Ed was twenty-two he was accosted by a jovial fellow who had just come from a distant city to work in Ed's department. 'Hello Fred! How's tricks?' he inquired. Ed explained that he was not Fred and denied that he knew the newcomer, but the latter was hard to convince, declaring that Ed was trying to cover up his identity. Soon afterwards another man accosted him as 'Fred' and stated that if he was not Fred Blank he was exactly like a fellow of that name with whom he had recently worked in a distant city. Ed was by this time rather disturbed about the matter and told his parents about it. Reluctantly, the parents were forced to admit that Ed was an adopted son and that he was one of a pair of twins, the other of whom had been adopted by a couple who lived in their home town but with whom they were not acquainted. They also revealed the fact that when the twins were small boys they had attended school together for a short time and that the other children had often noticed their close resemblance. It occurs to us that this early association of the twins may have led to the above-mentioned mutual feeling about a brother who had died.

Needless to say, Ed lost no time in getting in touch with Fred. The latter was out of work at the time and came to visit Ed. It was during this time that we succeeded in inducing them to come to Chicago to see the Fair and, incidentally, to be examined. Their visit with us was made even more interesting to them and to us by reason of a confusion of dates which resulted in their coming to us at the same time as a pair of

58

young women twins, Ethel and Esther. The two pairs of twins became great friends . . . The visits to the Fair were made together, each young man taking one of the young women. When they walked about, people were startled to see one couple walking ahead and a duplicate couple following behind. Everywhere they went they attracted attention and enjoyed the sensation they created. On one occasion they attended a side show featuring a pair of Siamese twins and, according to their statement, stole the show, attracting more attention than the exhibits.

H.H. NEWMAN

---

from The Old Capital

CHIEKO discovered the violets flowering on the trunk of the old maple tree. 'Ah. They've bloomed again this year,' she said as she encountered the gentleness of spring.

The maple was rather large for such a small garden in the city; the trunk was larger around than Chieko's waist. But this old tree with its coarse moss-covered bark was not the sort of thing one should compare with a girl's innocent body.

The trunk of the tree bent slightly to the right at about the height of Chieko's waist, and at a height just over her head it twisted even farther. Above the bend the limbs extended outward, dominating the garden, the ends of the longer branches drooping with their own weight.

Just below the large bend were two hollow places with violets growing in each. Every spring they would put forth flowers. Ever since Chieko could remember, the two violets had been there on the tree.

The upper violet and the lower violet were separated by about a foot. 'Do the upper and lower violets ever meet? Do they know each other?' Chieko wondered. What could it mean to say that the violets 'meet' or 'know' one another?

Every spring there were at least three, and sometimes as many as five, buds on the violets in the tiny hollows. Chieko stared at them from the inner corridor that opened onto the garden, lifting her gaze from the base of the trunk of the maple tree. Sometimes she was moved by the 'life' of the violets on the tree. Other times their 'loneliness' touched her heart . . .

'Go on upstairs in the back. The two of you make yourselves

59

at home and talk.' Shige was the one finally able to express herself.

Chieko took Naeko's hand as they crossed the narrow veranda, went upstairs, and lit the heater.

'Naeko, come here a moment,' Chieko called her to the dressing mirror. Chieko stared at their two faces.

'We certainly do look alike.' Chieko felt a hot rush enter her body. They changed sides. 'We're really the very images of each other.'

'That's what twins are,' Naeko said.

'What would happen if everyone had twins?'

'People would always be mistaking one another. It would certainly cause problems.' When Naeko stepped back, her eyes were moist. 'One can never know fate.'

Chieko stepped toward Naeko and grasped her shoulders firmly. 'Naeko, couldn't you stay here always? Father and Mother have said they want you to. I'm very lonely here by myself. Maybe the cedar mountains are a pleasant place, but . . .'

Naeko seemed unable to remain standing. Kneeling down as if otherwise she might stagger, she shook her head. Teardrops fell on her knees.

'Miss, our lives and our upbringing have been different. I couldn't live in a place like Muromachi. Once, just this once, I've come to your home. I wanted to show you the kimono you gave me. . . . And you were kind enough to come visit me twice in the cedar mountains.'

Chieko was silent, so Naeko continued, 'Miss, you are the one that our parents abandoned. I don't know why.'

'But I've forgotten that,' Chieko said without pausing. 'I don't even think of it. It's as though I never had any such parents.'

'I think . . . maybe both of them have received their punishment. I was just a baby, but please forgive me.'

'What kind of sin, what kind of responsibility could you have?'

'It's not that. I told you before I don't want to be even the slightest obstacle to your happiness.' Naeko lowered her voice. 'I'd rather disappear completely.'

'No, don't say that.' Chieko spoke firmly. 'It seems so unfair. Naeko, are you unhappy?'

'No, I'm lonely.'

'"Good fortune is short, while loneliness is long." Isn't that true?' Chieko asked. 'Let's lie down. I want to talk some more.' Chieko took the bedding from the closet. Naeko helped her.

'Happiness. This is happiness.' Naeko was listening to a sound coming from the roof.

Seeing Naeko straining to hear, Chieko stood motionless and asked, 'Is it winter rain? Or sleet? Or both?'

'Maybe. Or is it snow?'

'Snow?'

'It's quiet. Hardly enough to call snow . . . just a fine powder. In the mountain village sometimes a snow like this comes while we're working and before we know it, the surfaces of the leaves turn white like flowers . . . and even the tips of the fine twigs of the dead winter trees.'

Chieko listened.

'Sometimes it stops, or turns to sleet or a winter rain.'

'Shall we open the shutter and see? We'll know right away.' Chieko got up, but Naeko held her back.

'Don't! It's cold, and besides it would destroy the illusion.'

'Illusion? Did you say "illusion"? You talk about illusions quite a bit.'

Naeko smiled. There was a faint sorrow about her beautiful face.

Naeko hurriedly spoke as Chieko was about to spread out the futon. 'Chieko, just this once let me prepare your bedding for you.'

Chieko got into her futon. The two lay side by side.

'Oh, Naeko, it's so warm.'

'Our labor is different . . . just like the places we live.'

Naeko embraced Chieko. 'It will be cold on a night like this,' Naeko said, as if she were not the least bit chilled. 'Tonight the powder snow will drift down . . . stop . . . then flutter down again.'

Takichiro and Shige came upstairs to the next room. Being older, they used an electric blanket to warm the bed.

Naeko whispered in Chieko's ear, 'Your bed is warm now so I'll get into mine.'

Later, Chieko's mother opened the sliding door a crack to peep into the girls' room.

The next morning, Naeko got up very early. She shook Chieko to awaken her. 'Miss, this has been the happiest time of my life. I'm going to leave now before anyone sees me.'

Just as Naeko had said, a light powder snow had been falling off and on during the night. Now the cold morning glistened.

Chieko got up. 'You don't have a raincoat do you? Here, take this.' She got out her best velvet coat, a collapsible umbrella, and high clogs for Naeko.

'These are for you. Come again . . . please.'

Naeko shook her head. Chieko stood against the Bengara lattice door, watching as Naeko walked away. Naeko did not look back. A few delicate snowflakes fell on Chieko's hair and quickly vanished. The town was as it should be, still silent in sleep.

YASAHARI KAWABALA

---

from Castor and Pollux

APOLLO Can't you tell me how to distinguish Castor and Pollux, for they are so alike that I'm constantly out.

HERMES He that was with us yesterday is Castor.

APOLLO How can you possibly distinguish between two persons so like one another?

HERMES Pollux's face is all black and blue with the blows he received in wrestling, and particularly from Bebryx, in the expedition of the Argonauts.

APOLLO I am very much obliged to you for letting me know this distinguishing mark, for I always confounded them, each having alike his egg-shell, helmet, his white horse, his javelin and his star. But I say, why do we never see Castor and Pollux at the same time?

HERMES Well, they are so fond of each other that when fate decreed one of them must die and only one be immortal, they decided to share immortality between them.

LUCIAN AD 120–80

A former Army officer carried out a 'carefully planned and brutally executed double murder' of his parents, a court in Gibraltar was told . . . Roderick Newell, 27, was not arrested for the murder till five years later . . . In July 1992, Mr Newell met his uncle and aunt, Stephen and Gaye Newell for tea at a hotel in Perthshire, Scotland. There Mr Newell . . . confessed he would be blamed for the crime. During the . . . conversation, the accused gazed in the face of his father's identical twin and there spurted from his lips the pent-up guilt he held for so long.

The Independent, October 1993

---

from Double Exposure

I had to wait in Paris three days before my ship was to sail. On the day before the last I lunched with a friend at the Ritz. As the coffee was poured, I looked up from the table. To my horror, I spied Junior staggering in. I had no idea what I should do. If he came over to me, I was sure he would make a scene. Even if he didn't, it would be extremely hard for me to get away from him. I hoped he hadn't heard I was sailing the next day and decided, on his own, to sail with me. I turned my face away, hoping somehow that if I didn't see him, he, by some force of sympathetic magic, would not be able to see me. But my stratagem was useless; when next I looked up he was standing beside me, trying to put his arm around me, and babbling with a thick tongue, 'Thelma, darling, oh, Thelma, darling!'

Suddenly I had one of my reliable inspirations. I looked up with a stony glare. 'Really, Junior,' I said, 'you must be drunker than you look. Surely you should be able to tell the difference between your own wife and her sister. I'm Gloria.'

For a moment he seemed stunned. Then, relying on that pseudo-dignity drunkards try to assume when they are caught in embarrassing situations, he drew himself up stiffly and said, with the greatest formality, 'I'm sorry, Gloria. For a moment I thought you were my wife.' He then carefully and slowly navigated his way out of the room.

GLORIA VANDERBILT AND THELMA, LADY FURNESS

---

from Plum Pie

'THAT'S no good, either. No,' said George, 'this is the end. I'm a rat in a trap. I'm for it. Well-meaning, not to be blamed, the victim of the sort of accident that might have happened to anyone when lit up as I was lit, but nevertheless for it. That's Life. You come to Monte Carlo to collect a large fortune, all pepped up with the thought that at last you're going to be able to say No to old Schnellenhamer, and what do you get? No fortune, a headache, and to top it all off the guillotine or whatever they have in these parts. That's Life, I repeat. Just a bowl of cherries. You can't win.'

Twin! I uttered a cry, electrified.

'I have it, George!'

'Well?'

'You want to get on the yacht.'

'Well?'

'To secure your passport.'

'Well?'

'Then go there.'

He gave me a reproachful look.

'If,' he said, 'you think this is the sort of stuff to spring on a man with a morning head who is extremely worried because the bloodhounds of the law are sniffing on his trail and he's liable to be guillotined at any moment, I am afraid I cannot agree with you. On your own showing that yacht is congested with sergeants of police, polishing the handcuffs and waiting eagerly for my return. I'd look pretty silly sauntering in and saying "Well, boys, here I am" Or don't you think so?'

'I omitted to mention that you would say you were Alfred.'

He blinked.

'Alfred?'

'Yes.'

'My brother Alfred?'

'Your twin brother Alfred,' I said, emphasizing the second word in the sentence, and I saw the light of intelligence creep slowly into his haggard face. 'I will go there ahead of you and sow the good seed by telling them that you have a twin brother who is your exact double. Then you make your appearance. Have no fear that your story will not be believed. Alfred is at this moment in Monte Carlo, performing nightly in the revue at the Casino and is, I imagine, a familiar figure in local circles. He is probably known to the police – not, I need scarcely say, in any derogatory sense but because they have caught his act and may even have been asked by him to take a card – *any* card – and memorize it before returning it to the pack, his aim being to produce it later from the inside of a lemon. There will be no question of the innocent deception failing to succeed. Once on board it will be a simple matter to make some excuse to go below. An urgent need for bicarbonate of soda suggests itself. And once below you can find your passport, say a few graceful words of farewell and leave.'

'But suppose Schnellenhamer asks me to do conjuring tricks?'

'Most unlikely. He is not one of those men who are avid for entertainment. It is his aim in life to avoid it.

[. . .] 'But what would be Alfred's reason for coming aboard?'

'Simple. He has heard that Mr Schnellenhamer has arrived. It would be in the Society Jottings column. He knows that I am with Mr Schnellenhamer——'

'How?'

'I told him so when I met him yesterday. So he has come to see me.'

The light of intelligence had now spread over George's face from ear to ear. He chuckled hoarsely.

'Do you know, I really believe it would work.'

'Of course it will work. It can't fail. I'll go now and start paving the way. And as your raiment is somewhat disordered, you had better get a change of clothes, and a shave and a wash and brush-up would not hurt. Here is some money,' I said, and with an encouraging pat on the back I left him.

Brichoux was still at his post when I reached the yacht, inflexible determination written on every line of his unattractive face. Mr Schnellenhamer sat beside him looking as if he were feeling that what the world needed to make it a sweeter and better place was a complete absence of police sergeants. He had never been fond of policemen since one of them, while giving him a parking ticket, had recited Hamlet's To be or not to be speech to give him some idea of what he could do in a dramatic role. I proceeded to my mission without delay.

'Any sign of my nephew?' I asked.

'None,' said the sergeant.

'He has not been back?'

'He has not.'

'Very odd.'

'Very suspicious.'

An idea struck me.

'I wonder if by any chance he has gone to see his brother.'

'Has he a brother?'

'Yes. They are twins. His name is Alfred. You have probably seen him, sergeant. He is playing in the revue at the Casino. Does a conjuring act.'

'The Great Alfredo?'

'That is his stage name. You have witnessed his performance?'

'I have.'

'Amazing the resemblance between him and George. Even I can hardly tell them apart. Same face, same figure, same way of walking, same coloured hair and eyes. When you meet George, you will be astounded at the resemblance.'

'I am looking forward to meeting Mr George Mulliner.'

'Well, Alfred will probably be here this morning to have a chat with me, for he is bound to have read in the paper that I am Mr Schnellenhamer's guest. Ah, here he comes now,' I said, as George appeared on the gangway. 'Ah, Alfred.'

'Hullo, uncle.'

'So you found your way here?'

'That's right.'

'My host, Mr Schnellenhamer.'

'How do you do?'

'And Sergeant Brichoux of the Monaco police.'

'How do *you* do? Good morning, Mr Schnellenhamer, I have been wanting very much to meet you. This is a great pleasure.'

I was proud of George. I had been expecting a show of at least some nervousness on his part, for the task he had undertaken was a stern one, but I could see no trace of it. He seemed completely at his ease, and he continued to address himself to Mr Schnellenhamer without so much as a tremor in his voice.

'I have a proposition I would like to put up to you in connection with your forthcoming Bible epic Solomon And The Queen Of Sheba. You have probably realized for yourself that the trouble with all these ancient history super-pictures is that they lack comedy. Colossal scenery, battle sequences of ten thousand a side, more semi-nude dancing girls than you could shake a stick at, but where are the belly laughs? Take *Cleopatra*. Was there anything funny in that? Not a thing. And what occurred to me the moment I read your advance publicity was that what Solomon And The Queen Of Sheba needs, if it is really to gross grosses, is a comedy conjuror, and I decided to offer my services.

[. . .] I was aghast. Long before the half-way mark of this speech the awful truth had flashed upon me. It was not George whom I saw before me – through a flickering mist – but Alfred, and I blamed myself bitterly for having been so mad as to mention Mr Schnellenhamer to him, for I might have known that he would be inflamed by the news that the motion-picture magnate was within his reach and that here was his chance of getting signed up for a lucrative engagement. And George due to appear at any moment! No wonder that I reeled and had to support myself on what I believe is called a bollard.

P. G. WODEHOUSE

from The Three Crump Twins of Damascus

[*IBAD, Syahouk and Babekan, three hump-backed twin brothers, 'crooked behind and before, blind of the left eye, lame of the right foot and so perfectly like one another in face, shape and clothes, that even their father and mother sometimes mistook one for the other' are exiled from Damascus because Babekan had wounded a child who'd been teasing them, and none of the three would admit which of them it was. Babekan, the actual criminal, goes to Baghdad, apprentices himself to a cutler and makes good, ending up married to the cutler's wife. Ibad and Syahouk meanwhile are destitute. Hearing of their brother's good fortune they come to Baghdad to seek his help. But Babekan flies into a rage, and offers them only a small amount of gold to settle in another city. When his wife, Nohoud remonstrates with him, he says he will kill her too, if she gives them help. The brothers leave but are forced back to Baghdad by illness; only to find that this time their brother is away from home.*]

Nohoud could not help knowing these were his brothers, they resembled her husband so exactly. So touched was she by their poverty and tears, that despite his warnings she set some victuals before them. It was now dark night, and Ibad and Syahouk had scarce satisfied their first hunger, when somebody rattled at the door and the voice of Babekan was heard, though he was not to have returned until three days longer. The brothers and Nohoud turned pale as death, and Nohoud hastily hid the two in the cellar behind five or six tubs of brandy.

Babekan knocked ever louder. When the door was opened to him at last, he suspected his wife of having some gallant hid in a corner and beat her soundly. Afterwards he visited every hole

67

with the greatest care but never thought of looking behind the brandy tubs.

He did not go out again until the next evening. Then Nohoud ran immediately to the cellar; but she was in the utmost surprise at finding Ibad and Syahouk without the least signs of life. Taking her resolution, she shut up the shop and ran to look for a porter from Sivrihifar, a town famous for the foolishness of its inhabitants. Having told him that a little hump-backed man had died at her house, she proffered him four sequins of gold if he would put him in a sack and throw him into the Tigris.

The porter took one Crump upon his shoulders and did as he was asked. But when he returned to Nohoud for his money, she went behind the counter on pretence of fetching it and fell back with a loud cry. The porter, following her, was struck mute as a fish when he saw the same body lying there which he thought he had thrown into the Tigris. I am sure, said he, I did throw that plaguey crooked rascal over the bridge; how then could he come hither? However, continued he, let's try if he will get out again; then having put the second Crump into the same sack, he carried him to the bridge, and choosing the deepest part of the Tigris, threw in poor Syahouk. He was again returning merrily to Nohoud, when he saw coming towards him a man with a lanthorn in his hand. He was ready to drop down dead with fear at the sight of Babekan. Finding, moreover, that Babekan took the ready way to the house from which he had fetched the two Crumps, he seized him furiously by the collar. Ah, rogue, cried he, you think to make a fool of me all night, do you? Then being a lusty fellow he threw his sack over his shoulder and forced Babekan into it, tied the mouth with a strong rope, and running to the bridge flung the poor man into the river, sack and all. Then he returned to the cutler's to demand the money which had been offered him. Do not fear him coming any more, said he. The wag only pretended to be dead, but I have done his business for him now so thoroughly that he will never come to your house any more.

Nohoud, surprised, demanded to know what he meant – upon hearing about the porter's meeting with the third Crump, she cried, Ah, Sirrah, you have now drowned my husband, and do you think I will reward you for this murder? No, no, I will avenge his death, and go this moment to make my complaint to the Cady.

The porter gave very little heed to all the threats. I swear by my head, he cried, in a violent rage, if you do not give me my sequins this moment, I will send you to keep company with that crooked monster I have thrown three times into the river. Taking her by the hair he pulled Nohoud into the street. But when a neighbour came to her assistance, he took to his heels, and was on his way home when he met three men, each with a load upon his shoulder. He that went first took the porter by the arm and said, Take this bundle off my head and walk before me.

The porter would have refused, but the stranger shook a sabre four foot broad and threatened to cut off his head, so that he was forced to take up the load and go in company through the streets until they came to a little door which was presently opened by an old woman: they passed through a long passage very dark and arrived in a magnificent hall: but what was the porter's amazement and terror when by the light of many tapers he saw the crooked brothers he had thrown into the Tigris; two upon the shoulders of a slave and a fisherman; and the third upon his own head. The Devil take this cursed, Crump-backed, one-eyed son of a whore, cried he, I believe I shall do nothing all night but throw him into the river and not get rid of him at last.

He addressed these words to no less than the Caliph, Watik-Billah, himself. For it was the Caliph walking the streets privately that night accompanied only by a slave had met the unfortunate fisherman who in place of the fish had caught the Crump brothers in his nets; upon which he had ordered the three to be taken to his palace. Made still more curious by the porter's complaint, the Caliph now desired him to explain so whimsical an adventure.

[. . .] The Caliph took abundant pleasure in this story. Then viewing the three brothers more narrowly he thought he perceived in them some signs of life. He sent for a physician who finding that Ibad and Syahouk threw up with the water they had swallowed a great deal of brandy, did not doubt that their drunkenness was the occasion of their being thought dead. As for Babekan nothing but want of air had suffocated him; as soon as his head was out of the sack he recovered by degrees, whereupon the Caliph had all three brothers taken to bed in different chambers and locked up.

[*The wife sent for next morning cannot tell which brother is her husband, the three having been dressed by the Caliph in identical suits. In their turn each of the brothers claims her as his wife, until the Caliph says he only wants to know which is Babekan in order to punish him with the bastinado for treating his siblings so cruelly. Babekan then repents of his meanness, and promises to divide his fortune with his brothers . . . So all live happily ever after . . .*]

ANON., 1795

One face, one voice, one habit and two persons. . . .
An apple cleft in twain is not more twin
Than these two creatures. . . .

WILLIAM SHAKESPEARE, *Twelfth Night*

---

from Twelfth Night

[*Enter Antonio*]
ANTONIO Put up your sword. If this young gentleman
   Have done offence, I take the fault on me:
   If you offend him, I for him defy you.
SIR TOBY You, sir! why, what are you?
ANTONIO One, sir, that for his love dares yet do more
   Than you have heard him brag to you he will.
SIR TOBY Nay, if you be an undertaker, I am for you.
FABIAN O, good sir Toby, hold! here come the officers.
SIR TOBY I'll be with you anon.
VIOLA [*To Sir Andrew*] Pray, sir, put your sword up, if you please.
SIR ANDREW Marry, will I, sir; and, for that I promised you, I'll be
   as good as my word. He will bear you easily and reins well.

[*Enter two Officers*]
FIRST OFFICER This is the man; do thy office.
SECOND OFFICER Antonio, I arrest thee at the suit
   Of Count Orsino.
ANTONIO You do mistake me, sir.

FIRST OFFICER No, sir, no jot: I know your favour well,
    Though now you have no sea-cap on your head.
    Take him away: he knows I know him well.
ANTONIO I must obey. – [*To Viola*] This comes with seeking you:
    But there's no remedy: I shall answer it.
    What will you do, now my necessity
    Makes me to ask you for my purse? It grieves me
    Much more for what I cannot do for you
    Than what befalls myself. You stand amaz'd:
    But be of comfort.
SECOND OFFICER Come, sir, away.
ANTONIO I must entreat of you some of that money.
VIOLA What money, sir?
    For the fair kindness you have show'd me here,
    And part, being prompted by your present trouble,
    Out of my lean and low ability
    I'll lend you something: my having is not much:
    I'll make division of my present with you.
    Hold, there is half my coffer.
ANTONIO   Will you deny me now?
    Is't possible that my deserts to you
    Can lack persuasion? Do not tempt my misery,
    Lest that it make me so unsound a man
    As to upbraid you with those kindnesses
    That I have done for you.
VIOLA   I know of none;
    Nor know I you by voice or any feature.
    I hate ingratitude more in a man
    Than lying, vainness, babbling drunkenness,
    Or any taint of vice whose strong corruption
    Inhabits our frail blood.
ANTONIO   O heavens themselves!
SECOND OFFICER Come, sir: I pray you, go.
ANTONIO Let me speak a little. This youth that you see here
    I snatch'd one-half out of the jaws of death,
    Reliev'd him with such sanctity of love,
    And to his image, which methought did promise
    Most venerable worth, did I devotion.
FIRST OFFICER What's that to us? The time goes by: away!
ANTONIO But O! how vile an idol proves this god.
    Thou hast, Sebastian, done good feature shame.

71

In nature there's no blemish but the mind;
None can be call'd deform'd but the unkind:
Virtue is beauty, but the beauteous evil
Are empty trunks o'erflourish'd by the devil.
FIRST OFFICER The man grows mad: away with him!
Come, come, sir.
ANTONIO Lead me on. [*Exeunt Officers with Antonio*]
VIOLA Methinks his words do from such passion fly,
That he believes himself; so do not I.
Prove true, imagination, O, prove true,
That I, dear brother, be now ta'en for you!

WILLIAM SHAKESPEARE

---

from The Heavenly Twins

LADY Adeline, having seen the children safely and beautifully dressed for the ceremony, Angelica as a bridesmaid, Diavolo as page, left them sitting, with a picture book between them, like model twins.

'Really,' she said to Mr Hamilton-Wells, 'I think the occasion is too interesting for them to have anything else in their heads.'

But the moment she left them alone, those same heads went up, and set themselves in a listening attitude.

'*Now*, Diavolo; *quick!*' said Angelica, as soon as the sound of her mother's departing footsteps had died away.

Diavolo dashed the picture book to the opposite side of the room sprang up, and followed Angelica swiftly but stealthily, to the very top of the house.

When the wedding party assembled in the drawing-room the twins were nowhere to be found. Mr Hamilton-Wells went peering through his eye-glass into every corner, removed the glass and looked without it, then dusted it, and looked once more to make sure, while Lady Adeline grew rigid with nervous anxiety.

The search had to be abandoned, however; but when the party went down to the carriages, it was discovered, to everybody's great relief, that the children had already modestly taken their seats in one of them with their backs to the horses. Each was carefully covered with an elegant wrap, and sitting bolt upright, the picture of primness. The wraps were superfluous, and Mr Hamilton-Wells was about to remonstrate, but Lady Adeline exclaimed: 'For heaven's sake, *don't* interfere! It is such a *trifle*. If you irritate them, goodness knows *what* will happen.'

But, man-like, he could not let things be.

'Where have you been, you naughty children?' he demanded, in his precisest way. 'You have really given a great deal of trouble.'

'Well, papa,' Angelica retorted, hotly, at the top of her voice through the carriage window for the edification of the crowd; 'you said we were to be good children, and not get into everybody's way, and here we have been sitting an hour as good as possible, and quite out of the way, and you aren't satisfied! It's quite unreasonable, isn't it, Diavolo? Papa can't get on, I believe, *without* finding fault with us. It's just a bad habit he's got, and when we give him no excuse, he invents one.'

Mr Hamilton-Wells beat a hasty retreat, and the party arrived at the church without mishap, but when the procession was formed, there was a momentary delay. They were waiting for the bride's page who descended with the youngest bridesmaid from the last carriage, and the two came into the church demurely hand in hand. 'What darlings.' 'Aren't they pretty?' 'What a sweet little boy, with his lovely dark curls!' was heard from all sides; but there was also an audible titter. Lady Adeline turned pale, Mrs Frayling's fan dropped. Evadne lost her countenance. The twins had changed clothes.

SARAH GRAND

---

from The Yellow Dress

[*TWIN brother and sister on a southern plantation are separated when the brother Lum is sent to work elsewhere. The sister, Lessie, pining for him agrees reluctantly to marry, and is given distinctive yellow material to make a wedding dress by her employer, the narrator of the story. One day he goes to see Lessie, but she will not admit him; through the crack in the door, however, he see a pair of checked trousers lying on a chair, and assumes her lover is visiting. Later he sees the distinctive yellow material of the wedding dress crossing a field. Lessie, as he thinks, makes no answer when he shouts after her, and soon disappears. That night he finds an angry mob upon his doorstep.*]

I had done forgot about the dress and Lessie and her man, too, after I got back from the river that night, when they come. I was settin' reading the paper with my shoes off and thinking about going to bed when they tromped up on the front porch. They pounded on the door a couple of times before I could get a lamp lit in the front room, and I wouldn't have opened up if I hadn't thought I knew the voice that spoke.

He come inside by hisself, but some stood in the doorway. He was a big stout fellow and had on a double-bill hunting cap. 'I want you to show us where a nigger named Lum McRae lives,' he said. He looked from a little book in his hand up at me his eyes squinting together like a pair of scissors shuttin'.

I started off to tell him that Lum had left the Bite, but he stopped me. He said he knew all about that, but he had reason to believe Lum had come back home that day. It was plain that Lum was in trouble. I asked the man (I couldn't place him but I knowed I'd seen him before in Dublin) what it was, and he said Lum had raped a white girl there.

It sort of shook me up, his saying that, and I couldn't come to the idea right off that Lum or any other Big Bite nigger 'ud do such a thing. I asked him how he knowed it was Lum. There wasn't no doubt, he said. Lum was the only nigger on the place when it happened and the white girl had said it was a nigger in a checked suit. Lum was last seen in Dublin after it happened though the switchman didn't know about the raping in the railroad yard, still wearing a checked suit.

I was about to tell him I didn't think Lum would come back home if he did a thing like that, when I recollected those checked pants I seen through the door crack.

There looked to be twenty to twenty-five men in the bunch, when I stepped outside – I couldn't tell so good in the dark. The big fellow in the hunting cap put me in the front car with him. And he told me going over to Tink's that the girl's uncle was settin' on the back seat.

Tink's shanty was plumb cold when we got there. It looked like nobody was home and I would have left this crowd at the gate, but the big fellow wouldn't let me. He took six other men – they all had guns and pistols, but I didn't bring any – and made me come along with them to the house. They surrounded it and then he rapped on the door with his pistol butt and yelled, 'Hey, ole nigger!' I didn't go in, but all they found was Matt sick in the bed. They turned the place upside down, but it didn't do any good.

The big fellow, when he come out of the house, yelled, 'Hey you men, don't let anything get by you – that nigger's somewhere around here – he's been here tonight.' They had been standing quiet under the trees; now they got noisy. They broke up in bunches and searched the outhouses, the cowshed, the barn, the scuppernong arbors. They even threw down the rail fences and climbed up the trees. A couple of 'em broke down the smoke-house door.

It looked like they weren't goin' to find anything when a high-pitch voice hollered from the barn, 'Here he is!' A squat fellow and a tall one come through the barnlot gate dragging him between them. There was a moon, but all I could see was somebody being drug. The crowd gathered around and a couple of them said it was Lum, they knew him. I held back, thinking maybe they'd let me go now, but the fellow in the hunting cap made me get in the car with him.

We only went about a mile and turned off the road into an oak grove, where the old Nall house used to stand. Our car pulled over beyond a big low-limbed oak and stopped in what had been the yard once. When we got back to the tree, the two men who found the nigger were standing under it with him, and one of them was holding a railroad lantern. The rest of the crowd was getting out of their cars and coming up.

Just as we got there a man in our bunch – tall thin man with mustaches – stepped out of a sudden and slapped the nigger in the face. The two men holding him had turned him loose and he went down. The big fellow with me grabbed this mustached man by the arm and said, 'Hold on Ed, we ain't ready for that yet.'

The crowd gathered into a circle around the nigger on the ground and the two men who'd been holding him. I could see now he had on the checked suit. The big man in the hunting cap was sort of running things. He kicked the nigger's foot and told him to get up. The nigger come up slow, the man with the railroad lantern holding his arm.

Somebody played a flashlight on him when he was on his feet. He looked like a man I saw once who took hold of a live wire and couldn't turn it loose, but his eyes were closed. I know I thought, 'Poor Lum, your buckeye won't do you no good now' though I could laugh about that afterward.

Then the big man stepped in the ring and said in a sharp way, 'Nigger, you going to meet your Maker in a minute – you better clean your conscience while you can.' He waited a while and then he said, 'We're giving you this last chance to get right with God.'

The nigger stood there like something cut out of clabber. His eyes were still closed and you could only tell he wasn't asleep by his breathing and a sort of fluttering in his throat. There were flashlights playing on him from all around the ring now, and the men who held his arms shook him, but he didn't open his mouth once.

75

The big man stepped toward him of a sudden and said, 'You raped that girl! Didn't you?'

His eyes come open, like when you shove a stick of fire at a fellow's face. They kept staring at the big man, staring at 'im, but that was all.

About that time the man with the mustaches hit the nigger in the face with his pistol butt and kicked him in the privates after he was on the ground. Then the ring broke up and everybody started kicking him. It turned me sick at my stomach and I stepped away and bent over a bush for a minute. The crowd was spreading out from the tree when I come back and the nigger was already swinging from the rope. As I made my way into the circle, I saw he was barefooted. I stood there staring and it come to me about that afternoon Cap'n Day took him off to Dublin. Me and Cap'n had come back from fishing on the river and picked up Lessie at the forks of the swamp road. It wasn't until we got over to Tink's that Cap'n found out – and me too for that matter – we had Lessie and not Lum in the car. Cap'n hollered at our mistake. While this thing was running through my mind the rope slipped on the limb or something and the nigger's body turned. The flashlights were playing on his stretching neck and rumpled checked suit. My eye fixed on the back of his heel. I realized of a sudden that I was looking at a white crooked scar on the nigger's heel: that day trying to get out'n the back of the car and away from us, Lessie had busted open the door and fell out on the ground, splittin' her heel on a piece of glass. I knew that scar – I knew damn well I knew it.

I was so taken, I just lifted my arms and started running toward the nigger without saying a word. I couldn't make words come for a minute. By the time I had got there, several of the crowd had grabbed me. I thought I wasn't never going to make 'em understand. I had to tear off the coat and shirt, too, and show 'em. It was Lessie all right, but it was already too late when we cut her down. And I'd thought all the time she was wearing that yellow wedding dress.

BRAINARD CHENEY

'He's swimming to me.'
'Why to you? It might as well be to me.'
'Why?'
'Because we're just the same.'

'That's our glory.'
'*And* our pride. Don't forget that.'

MERVYN PEAKE, Titus Groan

One twin is always the theme and the other the variation.

JANE SMILEY, from Ordinary Love

The difference was in the key-note not in the melody.

FRANCIS GALTON

I am always in awe when I watch identical twins. You are on occasion struck with the similarity and then on other occasions you are struck with the difference. It's . . . like this glass: is it half empty or half full? And each of these perspectives is, I think, a valid one.

From transcript of 'Freedom in the Genes' in the series,
Cracking the Code, BBC2

UNLIKE TWINS

The stars of Castor and Pollux appear identical at first glance, but upon closer examination differences appear. With the aid of telescopes, astronomers have discovered that Castor is actually two white stars revolving round each other forty-five light years away. While Pollux is a giant orange star only thirty-five years from Earth.

KAT DUFF, *Gemini and the Path of Paradox*

---

from Gemini

I HAVE said that Jean showed no interest in the glasses I loved so much. This may be the moment to mention the way his tastes and preferences differed slightly from mine even from our childhood. Many games and toys which instantly found their way to my heart were rejected by him, much to my distress. Of course, we coincided most of the time in a happy and harmonious unison. But there were times – and more and more frequently as we grew to adolescence – when he would dig his heels in and say no to something, even though it was in the direct line of twinship. It was in this way that he refused stubbornly to use a little battery-operated telephone with which we could have talked to one another from different rooms in the house. With no one to talk to, I did not know what to do with the toy, which I was delighted with and of which I had had such high hopes. But there was real anger in his rejection of one of those tandem bicycles that husbands and wives are to be seen pedaling out together on Sundays, got up in identical plus fours, roll-necked sweaters, and flat caps. It was true that he was willing to admit into our cell things which undoubtedly had a subtle bearing on our condition, but he could not bear too blatant references to our twinship.

He liked things whose function was clearly contradicted by being duplicated but which we were given two of, against all apparent common sense, in accordance with our demands. For instance, the two little pendulum clocks to hang on the wall, imitations of Swiss cuckoo clocks, each with a little wooden bird that shot out twittering to mark the hours and half hours. Outsiders never failed to express surprise at those two identical clocks hanging on the same wall within a few inches of each other. 'To do with being twins!' Edouard once told one of them. To do with being twins, in other words, one of the mysteries of twinship. But what no one realized, apart from Jean-Paul, was that Jean's clock persisted in chiming a few seconds *before* mine, even when the hands of both were in exactly the same position – seconds enough so that never, not even at midday or midnight, did the two chimes overlap. From a *singular*, which is to say a trivial point of view, a difference in the making is enough to explain the slight time lag. To Jean, it was something far different, what he called the 'something or other,' although he always refused to explain what he meant by it.

But even more than the clocks, he liked the barometer, of which we were likewise given two, as going further in the direction of twinship. It was a dear little wooden house with two doors and a figure to come out of each: a little man with an umbrella on one side and a little woman with a sunshade on the other, one forecasting rain, the other shine. But these, too, were slightly out of phase, so that Jean's little people were always ahead of mine, by twenty-four hours sometimes, so that occasionally they met, by which I mean that Jean's man would come out while my little lady was doing the same.

We had at least one passion in common, for things that brought us into direct contact with cosmic facts – clocks and barometers – but it seemed as if these only began to interest Jean the moment they revealed a fault, some defect through which his famous 'something or other' could creep in. Presumably that is why the binoculars – visually instruments of astronomically long range but faultless accuracy – filled him only with indifference.

MICHEL TOURNIER

from My Sister

WE´RE not identical, my sister and I. Not alike at all. That's what I tell people when they learn I have a twin. They are fascinated till I tell them 'But we're not identical'. For some reason they seem less interested then, as if the novelty isn't valid any more. I don't know why. I think it makes us more unusual. But not everyone seems to agree, so when I see their interest waning I add: 'We're not very close, really' and they nod, feeling sorry for me. I think sometimes they're thinking 'If only you were identical, you'd be closer then'.

That's what I used to think. It was my way of explaining things. Identical twins are generally closer, I remember espousing with great authority when our older sister compared us with her identical twin friends.

'Well that's for sure,' our older sister laughed. 'You two aren't real buddy-buddies are you?'

Buddies?

There is a photo of us on our first day of school. We're standing together in the backyard, holding hands. We have big straw hats on our heads, with elastic catching us under the chin, and belts on our uniforms that seem to wrap us at chest level. My sister's head is tilted slightly. She is grinning at the camera. I look a little unsure, a little wary. But I am holding my sister's hand. We look, for all the world, like buddies . . .

I do not remember ever being buddies with my sister. But the photo suggests something different. I look at it sometimes and imagine my mother on the other side of the camera, holding it a little unsteadily so that we are framed at an angle. And I imagine her thinking, as she watches another two of her children step out into a wider world away from her, that 'at least they have each other'.

We were a pair then, my sister and I. We must have done everything together. We must have been inseparable, referred to always as 'the twins'. I do remember that and growing, later, to dislike people for doing it to us, for lumping us together. But it had its advantages then – the correlation, the assumption of some equation between us.

My sister could draw. I couldn't. We sat next to one another at school. In all our primary classes we sat next to one another. That surprises me now but I think I liked it then. I must have.

In second grade we had to draw a picture for a school inspector who was coming the next week.

'Anything you like', said the teacher, an old nun who in memory appears two foot tall, but must have been taller than me. I think. She had soft hands, that nun. Unbelievably soft. She had found a kitten in the playground once and brought it into the class. We were allowed to crowd around while she nursed it, gently stroking the kitten. We could touch it too – if we were gentle – and I did, brushing the nun's fingers as she held the kitten in her lap. So soft.

So when she said 'Anything you like', I drew a cat because I knew she would like it.

But my cat ended up fat and ugly, spreading out all over the page in one big smudge. On their way round the room the soft hands hesitated by my side of the desk. Then they moved on behind me.

My sister had drawn a tree – light and clear and beautifully unsmudged. The soft hands fell upon it and from behind our desk a voice crooned, 'Lovely, lovely . . .' Then those same hands fell upon us both – one each, caressing the nape of our necks.

'Such talented twins.'

I could feel the whole class smiling.

I remember tapping my sister's thigh under the desk, then finding her hand.

My sister and I don't say much to one another. Ours is a fairly quiet household when both of us are home. We do not argue. I am trying to think if we have ever argued – this sister of mine who is not my buddy . . .

I can't recall ever having had a conversation with my sister that lasted beyond a couple of sentences, let alone an argument. My mother would say that is a cruel thing to say. But it is true. I mean no harm. When we travel together in the car, I reach for the radio automatically. My sister used to joke about it – my reflex action – and I could see the joke. But that is our way.

We have not always been so keen to see the joke together, though I think we have understood much more together than people would assume. At opposing ends at times, yes, but understanding all the more.

When I was fourteen I got a five-year diary for my birthday. It had a lock and key. I kept the key hidden under the carpet beside my bed. I remember one day writing on the inside back cover of that diary. I wrote with my fountain pen because I thought it was more lasting. If I had had one of those indelible pens I would probably have used that. 'I DO NOT BELIEVE – AND WILL NEVER BELIEVE – THAT THE PERSON THEY CALL MY TWIN SISTER IS REALLY MY

TWIN. SHE IS NOT MY SISTER AT ALL. SHE IS NOT EVEN RELATED.' And I signed and dated it and even noted the time.

Every day after that when I made an entry in my diary, I would turn to the inside back cover and read my pledge.

I think I had been influenced by a book I'd read – about a baby mix-up in a hospital – in which two boys discover they had grown up in the wrong families. It is the stuff of movies and cheap tabloids. I remember that the idea became something of a family joke. Even now our family refers, laughingly, to 'the fire at the hospital' on the day my sister and I were born.

I never knew if she actually did read it – and I will never ask her – but after a few months, I suspected my sister had seen the pledge at the back of my diary. I think I burnt the diary a year or so later – I remember a ceremonial burning of some of my things in the backyard incinerator. But I'm not sure. Maybe the diary just disappeared like so many other things.

TRISH MCNAMARA

I must trust the substance not the shadow: you are most like me but are not the same.

WILLIAM RIDER, *The Twins* 1655

They were one in name as they were in devotion, for each of them was called Henwald, with this distinction, taken from the colour of their hair, that one was called Henwald the Black, the other Henwald the White.

BEDE, *Ecclesiastical History* c. 800 AD

At school the twins . . . had been known respectively as Tune and Cartoon. For nature, in her most prankish mood, having fashioned those two in like mold, yet had so slightly, so deftly, so fiendishly overemphasized in Hannah what was perfection in Hilda that perfection became grotesquerie – or almost that . . . It was as though . . . having wrought this perfect thing, [she] had said pettishly, 'What! You expect me to achieve this miracle a second time! No! Here, I'll make a rough copy of it. But a masterpiece is a masterpiece. One doesn't repeat.'

EDNA FERBER, 'One Basket', *Our Very Best People*

———————

Valentine thus growing up in the love of the court, and all the while his brother, Orson, lives in the forest all rough and covered with hair like a bear, leading the life of a beast. . . .

———————

My brother, Esau, is the Hairy man, and I, Jacob, am the smooth man.

Beyond the Fringe

———————

Only their brother could tell them apart. And he said he saw no likeness.

MARY GRANT BRUCE, *Twins of Emu Plains*

———————

When . . . but a very short time has intervened between two conceptions the embryos, both of them, proceed to maturity; as was seen with Hercules and his brother Iphicles [sons of Jupiter and Amphytrion respectively]. This was the case also with the woman who brought forth two children at one birth, one of whom bore a resemblance to her husband, the other to her paramour.

PLINY, *Natural History*, Book 6

———————

from Histoire de Lynx

IN response to the conundrum of twinship, the Old World favoured one of two extremes; its twins were identical or they were opposites, antithetical. The New World prefers intermediate forms. The Old World did not, of course, entirely ignore these. Plato's myth of Prometheus and Epithemeus could almost be Brazilian! It appears, however, that in the mythology of the Old World, that formula rarely surfaced, whereas it constitutes a kind of seminal cell in the mythology of the New.

Dumezil has always insisted on the equality, even the indistinguishability of twins in the Indo-European tradition; the Vedic hymns portray the Asvins as a single entity; in the Mahabharata their twin sons . . . play a subordinate role. The authors of the hymns were not interested in a theology of difference; they demonstrate the enduring tendency of Indo-European thought to erase the differences between twins, though there are indications that in the earliest versions disparities between the Asvins were more marked. The story of Romulus and Remus, too, attests to the persistence of still more ancient tradition, surviving in a much attenuated form both in the diverse talents of Castor and Pollux (one a horseman, the other a warrior) and in the equally diverse attributes of the Castor and Pollux – wisdom and beauty respectively.

In the case of Castor and Pollux, one twin is mortal and given burial, and the other, immortal, is raised to the sky as a celestial body. Greek myth, however, rejects this disparity and and makes the two equal, whereas American myth incorporates disparity and does not seek to amend it. In Europe, popular conceptions of twinship always turn on themes of absolute likeness between twins; they are physically indistinguishable, to the extent of dressing alike and using the same make-up. They have similar tastes, thoughts, characters; stories have them falling in love with the same woman, or else make them so hard to tell apart, that the wife of one brother mistakes the other for her husband. They fall ill at the same time, cannot survive without each other. And so on. Georges Sands's *La Petite Fadette* epitomises these beliefs.

For its part, native American thought challenges the conception of twins as identical beings . . . Lynx and Coyote started off as like twins according to one myth. But then Lynx, having some grievance against Coyote proceeds to elongate the the jaws, ears and paws of his enemy. In reprisal Coyote shortens Lynx's mouth, ears and tail – that is why the canine and feline kinds are unlike to this very day. Such a hypothesis suggests that by its nature likeness can only be temporary or provisional. It cannot endure.

Indeed, in native American thought, symmetry is seen as negative, even malign . . . As it is also worth noting that in America one twin invariably takes on the role of trickster; the principle of imbalance . . . lies at the heart of any twin relationship. Whereas in ancient Greece, once all differences between the Dioscuri are eliminated, the principal disequilibrium has to be sought elsewhere; thus the role of trickster falls to a third being, Eurymas – whom one author designates the devil – a term which translates as trickster well enough; of him, frustratingly little is known, apart from his having been killed by Pollux with one blow, as punishment for mixing him up with his brother, Castor.

Thus such traces which lingered in the Indo-European tradition of a more archaic concept of twinship were progressively eroded. Unlike the Indians, Indo-Europeans did not explain the world in terms of difference. For them the ideal of perfect twinship survived in conditions seemingly inimical to any such thing. Amerindian thought, on the other hand, finds a kind of philosophical disparity indispensible; whether cosmically or socially, matters never stay the same; at the heart of any unstable duality at whatever level it is perceived lies always the possibility of yet another unstable duality.

CLAUDE LÉVI-STRAUSS (translated by Penelope Farmer)

---

from The City of God

CICERO says that Hippocrates, that excellent physician, wrote that two children that were brethren, falling sick, and the sickness waxing and waning in both alike, were hereupon suspected to be twins. And Posidonius, a Stoic, and one much addicted to astrology, labours to prove them to have been born both under one constellation and conceived both under one. So that which the physician ascribes to the similitude of their temperatures of body, the astrologer attributes to the power and position of the stars in their nativities. But truly in this question, the physician's conjecture stands upon more probability, because their parents' constitution might be easily transfused into them both alike at their conception: and their first growth might participate equally of their mother's disposition of body, and then being nourished both in one house, with one nourishment, in one air, country, and other things corresponding, this now might have much power in the proportioning of both their natures alike, as physic will testify. Besides, use of one exercise equally in both might form their bodies into a similitude, which might very well admit all alterations of health alike, and equally in both. But to draw the figure of heaven and the stars into this parity of passions (it being likely that a great company of the greatest diversity of effects that could be might have originated in diverse parts of the world at one and the same time) were a presumption unpardonable. For we have known two twins that have had both diverse fortunes and different sicknesses both in time and nature: whereof (methinks) Hippocrates gives a very good reason, namely the diversity of nourishment and exercise, which might be the cause of different health in them; yet that diversity was effected by their will and inclination, and not by their bodily constitution. But neither Posidonius, nor any patron of this fate in the stars, can tell what to say in this case, if he will not delude the simple and ignorant with a discourse of that they know not. As for their talk of the space of time between the twins' nativities, due to a particular spot in the heavens where the hour of birth is signified, which they call the horoscope – it is either not so significant as the diversity of will, act, manners, and fortune of the twins born doth require; or else it is more significant than their difference of honours, state, nobility, or meanness will permit: both which diversities they place only in the hour of the nativity. But if they should be both born before the horoscope were fully varied, then would I require a unity in each particular of their fortunes which cannot be found in any two twins that ever yet were born. But if the horoscope be changed before both be born, then for this diversity I will require a difference of parents, which twins cannot possibly have.

ST AUGUSTINE

---

from Twin Brothers or Vice and Virtue Contrasted

IT happened one day when Bob was not well, some sugar was put into his milk, upon which Jack who was quite hearty began to cry out for sugar too, but Hannah would not give him any and went out of the room, under pretext of telling his father that he was obstinate and would not take his milk without sugar. Whilst she was out of the room, Bob says, 'Brother Jacky had Bobby's milk,' putting the basin towards him and taking Jack's in exchange. The latter, though he knew his poor brother was unwell, took the sugared milk and was eating it when Hannah returned, who knew not but that it was his own.

[*As adults: Jack who'd run away to sea now returns.*]

'Aye,' said Jack with an horrid oath, turning towards his brother and twisting an enormous quid of tobacco in his mouth. 'Let's know how the land lays, Bob; no sailing on an unknown coast without chart or compass; am I to bear down to the old woman in the country, or can the business be settled here without her?'

'If you mean to speak of our worthy mother,' replied Robert, while a glow of indignation flushed his face, 'Do it with more respect, or all further intercourse ceases between us.' 'With all my heart,' cried his brutal brother; 'Only tip me the wink, and steer off on what tack you like.'

[. . .] Surely, my young readers, I need make no comment on the twin brothers. You will see that virtue is its own reward; and that vice seldom fails to meets its appropriate punishment, I flatter myself, that the readers of this story . . . warned by the example of Jack Tomkinson, the baneful paths of vice and idleness as they must see it will lead to certain misery and destruction; on the other hand who would not wish to practise the virtues of Robert.

ANON., 1802

from Voices from the River

THEY were an odd pair, so entirely different from each other that you would never have taken them for twins. Davy was the big one, a huge giant of a man, with almost unnatural reserves of strength. I've seen him lift up the rear end of a Land Rover without visibly straining; and one night at the local hotel, he ripped the counter right off the bar, a great length of solid mahogany two and a half inches thick, and hurled it into the back mirror. That was after the manager had tried to stop them going in there. Later, Davy claimed in court (probably with justification) that they'd been discriminated against.

It was a particularly sore point with him. Understandably, because although he was as black as any African, his hair was smooth and wavy and he had the features of a European – the nose and mouth so finely formed that they could almost have been copied from one of those Renaissance paintings of Italian noblemen. Jonno was the same peculiar mixture, only in reverse. From a distance, you'd have sworn he was white, his hair and skin very nearly fair; but up close he had the face and hair texture of a negro. It was as if fate, in a spirit of mockery, had deliberately chosen to divide their ancestry unequally between them, confusing rather than blending the races.

VICTOR KELLEHER

from The Compendio Historial – El Cid

NOTE also inasmuch as some say that the Cid was a bastard they are mistaken about it. And the way in which those who have not read his history and chronicle say this is as follows: that is, that Don Diego Lainez, father of the Cid, before marrying Doña Teresa Nuñez, mother of the Cid, on Saint James Day in Vivar forced a peasant woman, a miller's beautiful wife, at her house and she conceived a son at that time. And the peasant, her husband, when he came home from the mill, seized her that same day and she conceived another son at that time. And when they were to be born, the knight's son was born first. And he looked like his father, very lively and full of grace; and the peasant's [son looked] like his [father], very coarse. And when both brothers were five or six years old, the knight's son made hobby-horses out of wood and lances and swords and other things pertaining to arms. And he called the young boys 'knights' and ran about from one place to another and all his activities had to do with weapons and knighthood. And the peasant's son made little oxen out of clay and plows of wood. And with these things and other sticks, which he had in his hand, he would plow along the floor, saying 'Gee up here!' and 'Gee up there!' And those who saw them marvelled at it. Don Diego Laínez then took his son, who was called Fernán Díaz. And when he was of age to bear arms he was a good knight and very brave.

Quoted in: DONALD WARD, *The Indo-European Divine Twins*

from One Old Maid

SHE was at home – a plain but spacious house, with what had been in its day a handsome flight of stone steps leading to the front door. It was a dingy quarter, from which fashion had long since fled, although it remained perfectly respectable. Miss Boyle let herself in with a latch-key and went along a dimly lighted entry to a back room, whence issued an odd sound, like the plaining of a cross child, uttered in a coarse masculine voice. Shriller tones made response as Aunt Co's hand touched the lock.

'Hush up that noise! You'd ought to be well shaken, you had ought! It ain't my fault she isn't here to give you your supper. If I'd my way you would go to bed without it. Be quiet, or she shan't ever come home!'

Amid the burst of lamentations aroused by this threat Miss Boyle entered. Something sat on the floor in the middle of the room, whimpering and rubbing one eye with a big fist – a woman as tall as Miss Boyle herself, and obese to unsightliness: with a thick hanging jaw and small eyes set very far apart, low forehead, beetling brows, long upper lip and a mane of coarse gray hair hanging over her shoulders – a creature from which sane humanity turned, sick at the caricature of itself. The face was wet with tears and smeared with dirt from her soiled hands, but she stopped crying at sight of her sister. Springing up, clumsy and eager, she ran to her, caught hold of her dress and babbled in furious gibberish illustrating her meaning by angry gestures toward the other occupant of the apartment. This was a shrewish little woman in cap and spectacles, who without noticing the pantomime stooped to lift a tea-pot from the hearth to a round table set on one side of the fire.

'Yes, my baby; sister knows,' responded the guardian, patting the fat cheek, and smiling fondly. 'Sister didn't mean to leave her so long. Now Lulu will be good and she shall have something nice for her supper. Has she been very troublesome, Mattie?' to the sharp little maid.

''Bout's usual. She's always ugly as sin. She throwed a new handkerchief of yours into the fire, and would 'a sent your work-box after it if I hadn't ketched it as 'twas goin'. You was out later'n common, and she worried awful 'bout that. She knows when time's up well as you do.'

'It is wonderful how smart she is!' commented Miss Boyle, in plaintive admiration. 'I didn't mean to be away so long – I just ran in for a minute to see Juliana.'

She was washing the idiot's face with a wet cloth, and panted out the broken bits of sentences in a frightened way that seemed to be habitual to her.

'Hold still, my precious child! You see I hadn't seen her for an age – and they were just at dinner – such an elegant affair it was, too – I wish you had seen it, Mattie – and Emma's betrothed was there, a very handsome, agreeable young man he is – and they would make me sit down, although I told them I hadn't time – and I ran away the minute I was through eating. That is,' with conscientious accuracy, 'the instant Juliana had this basket ready. Yes, there is something in it for Lulu,' the idiot was tugging at the cover; 'but she must eat her bread and milk first, like a nice girl, and not slop it over the table or pull the cloth off as she did at dinner-time.'

Lulu began to cry again; then stopping suddenly laughed yet more disagreeably, and pointed to a large grease-spot on the carpet.

'The carpet will have to come up before that can be cleaned,' snapped Mattie. 'I've been at work scouring it, off and on, the whole afternoon. If she'd been mine I'd a boxed her ears for that job. She knowed better.'

Lulu spit at her spitefully, and Miss Boyle stepped between them.

[. . .] They were twins – these two – and the fond mother, who had just finished Madame de Staël's popular romance, had them christened respectively Corinne and Lucile. Corinne grew up shapely in body and intellect; Lucile had never spoken an articulate word, never passed in mind the first year of babyhood. It was a sore affliction to the father . . . But to the mother and Corinne, Lulu was the most interesting member of the household. When the father spoke of hiding what he was disposed to regard as a family disgrace in the safe seclusion of an asylum, Mrs Boyle's terror and indignation were like the rage of a bereaved lioness. The subject was never broached again while she lived. She survived her husband but a year; and dying bequeathed the unfortunate girl – a sacred legacy – to her twin-sister's keeping, exacting from her a promise that she would never be overpersuaded to abandon her to the care of hirelings; that while Corinne lived her household should be Lucile's also.

MARION HARLAND

from I Like to Look

'I SPENT twenty-nine days alone in the Gobi desert; I've got a pilot's licence; I've tickled the soles of the feet of the Dalai Llama for nearly an hour and, believe me, he didn't move a muscle. I've been in three movies, but you won't have seen them – it was in Turkey. I lost half a million dollars at cards – wasn't mine, but it would have been if I hadn't lost it. Easy come, easy go. Look at my arm, see? It was done in Hong Kong by a bearded lady. Took over forty hours. And look at the muscle too. I took cyanide in a hijack death-pact and came to just as they were about to bury me. I've got three passports. I didn't do much in the antipodes – too burnt out. Lived in a cave, had a baby, got it adopted, joined a theatre group. Then I met the Sheik –'

Bill refilled our glasses. The ice had melted into small shivers; it was old and made the drink taste faintly of metal. Dee paused to swallow.

'What about you, er –' Bill said, 'do you share your sister's passion for adventure?'

'Yes,' I replied, 'but –'

'She was always the quiet one,' Dee cut in. 'It was the Sheik, you see, who gave me the half a million. He wanted to marry me, but I slipped out one morning and left for Canada. Now this might have got back: I killed someone in a bar in Montreal. Self-defence. I was tried, but I got off, of course. You didn't hear? After that, I went to the Soviet Union, in the summer, mind you. Left, my jacket padded with manuscripts, just before they kicked me out –'

Yes, I thought, I like to look. In trains, buses, gardens, at films, even those in languages I don't understand, on pavements and curbstones, in mirrors and water there's much to see and I look. I look at faces, the folds round eyes, the sculpture of flesh that grows with time to reflect habits of thought and feeling, the many textures and colours of skin. I look at litter, wet paper, September leaves. I look at the sea: sometimes the sky is darker than the water, a negative. Sometimes the beach is smooth and damp, and as the sun sets the sand blazes brazen-gold. On the rocks, mussels build themselves into tight black bouquets. I like to look at the fossils, exposed in shale that softens, blurring in a matter of hours the sharp record of past millennia, dissolving them within a day. I like to look at the shadows of twigs mingled with clots of leaves, just stirring in the wind. At sand blown round grasses and debris, at frost on windows, at gulls landing like a scattering of crumbs on the sea. I like to look at the wind seen through glass, at

the flow of traffic, its motorway lights tailing into the distance, red
retreat, oncoming white.

'Miles away,' Dee said to Bill, meaning me. 'We're twins, you
know.'

'You're not at all alike!' Bill said to Dee conspiratorially.

KATHY PAGE

Portrait of a Younger Twin

'ON aime mieux dire du mal de soi-même que de n'en point parler.'
LA ROCHEFOUCAULD

When were you last at my house – or I at yours?
Tumbling a cruster of brandy, here, by the fire,
I realise it is not only that I want to show
what I have done to remodel this old house, newly bought,
(we have never courted each other's approval)
it is more that I acknowledge a chafe somewhere
between us. Why don't you call round sometime?
I'll get some beer in, we'll make it a party.

Looking at us, no one would ever have thought we were twins:
the hour that pushed us out allotted us separate stars,
two days of birth. Yet our differences were distinct enough
to hold us together: your black hair made mine more fair,
olive skinned and active, you emphasised my left-handedness.

We split into the sides of a pattern, then,
light and shadow, or hard and soft, given and gift.
Growing up separately, boys in the one classroom,
we still needed each other, we were both slow
to make friends.
In our shared bedroom I used to read in books
of twins playing tricks of identity on others. I dreamed
epiphanies. If I put my arms round your shoulders
you were embarrassed.

But one night you woke,
choking and dumb, and your shout of fear and panic
came from my throat, summoning the others,
bringing them heavily and urgently in to be witnesses.
Do you remember that night? Just once it happened.
     I am asking,
do you remember?

THOMAS SHAPCOTT

---

from Le Paradoxe des Jumeaux

GESELL was undoubtedly the first to note the differences [between twins] at a time when most scientists were blinded by their likenesses, by an obsession with questions of heredity . . .

The perception of, the taking of differences into consideration, fits a more individualist conception of human identity. To be human, Gesell says, is to be unique, and twins are not, cannot be, an exception to that rule. Within each child, and that includes each and every twin, are the marks of its uniqueness. In short, for him, the chief value of twins lies in their demonstrating, despite their identical heredity and shared environment the principle of singularity . . .

[With twins] I used to be under the impression that they played at imitating one another simply to confuse me, to make a monkey of me. I vacillated between amusement, wonder, and a bewildering sense of unease.

Until the day that is when I realised that psychologically speaking *they were not alike*, or at least only superficially so. At once the spell was broken. And I was struck by the paradox; was it naivety made me assume them so alike? For though identical in the eyes of science the twins were not actually the same. I need to say more and at greater length about this sudden understanding, this new light on the nature of twinship. I want to set it down not just for the benefit of psychologists, but for non-psychologists, not just for twins and their parents but for non-twins, not just for identical twins but for non-identical twins also.

And in that way I want to unite two separate modes of thought, two different intellectual worlds; that of scientific explanation, on the one hand, and of intuitive understanding signified by myth and dream, on

93

the other. To limit, decode the exuberant excess of myths of twinship and at the same time to tear off the blinkers of science, would be to give each kind of truth its due weight.

. . . In brief, it was my resistance to certain . . . received ideas that made me brutally aware one day of what had been staring me in the face all along . . . I saw the two twins sitting in front of me as a couple; no longer simply as a pair of individuals, the equivalent of two indistinguishable drops of water, of interchangeable jars, or even of two gloves, different only in the way of mirror images, one for the right hand, one for the left.

. . . This intuition both demonstrates and helps resolve the major paradox at the heart of my book; that twins, though genetically identical, are not psychologically identical. Paradoxical because one would assume that the psychic development of a pair nurtured within the same physical and cultural environment would be no less determined by biology. Same genes, same environment; thus even the same personality, except in the case of an accident or illness affecting only one of a pair. The formula – *identical twins are two copies of one individual* – is so well known that it blinds us from the start to the fundamental non-identity of any pair. Once struck by the differences, I proceeded to eliminate any chance of errors of observation in each new pair that I investigated, thereafter invoking, firstly, the well-established philosophical principle; that two living creatures, be they identical twins or two leaves on the same tree, cannot be literally identical. A respectable enough belief, but only a belief. I followed this up, therefore, by noting the small differences in the physical make-up of twins, discernable from birth, prophetic distinctions of distinct personalities. For instance, one twin might weigh a hundred grammes more than his brother. As we will see, however, that this type of explanation for subsequent differences, though not insignificant, cannot be more than secondary. Thus gradually, as I set my own observations alongside those of other researchers, the idea of the couple began to take root. The couple, that is, as a more or less equal distribution of tasks, of daily activities, a distribution which organises itself very early, an organisation in which each has a defined place, duties, roles. By which the personality of each, with the connivance of the other, is affirmed.

. . . The concept of the couple, of course, is as old as society itself. It has been known almost as long that there is no such thing as a couple that does not take on different roles, making it likely that each partner influences the personality of the other. The mother forms the infant and the infant transforms the mother; lovers and friends alike adjust and modify the selves they were before they met. Up to what point, how deeply, and for what traits may not be clear. But whether a couple by birth (mother–child) or a couple by choice, the differences exist from the start.

In the case of twins, the calculation starts at zero. Any differences observed cannot be ascribed to pre-existing differences. The effects of coupledom that are hard to describe, let alone distinguish in an ordinary couple can be isolated in twins unexpectedly different in appearance despite identical genes.

As if in an experiment devised by nature herself, these perfectly matched pairs demonstrate for all of us the power of the couple, of all kinds of couples, in the formation, eventually the deformation, of personality.

RENÉ ZAZZO (translated by Penelope Farmer)

THE NATURE OF
TWINSHIP

In this book, Miss Farmer is looking for her identity again.
from a review of a book by Penelope Farmer

---

from Untitled novel in progress

MY brother understood me, though. Say what you will about twinhood
– in our case, semi-mirror identical twinhood, very rare – it guarantees
that at least one person understands you, knows you down to the
bottom of your worthless soul. You may hate him, you may wish he
was dead, but he knows even this about you, and that's something.
As we grew older, my brother tended to stake out the temperamental
high ground between us, but part of him was always with me down
in the lowlands, on the scruffy outskirts. At age twenty we were even
more physically similar than we'd been as infants, if that's possible:
without our clothes on we were interchangeable, fully fungible, and
even our father had a hard time telling us apart. (Our mother had
always been easy to fool. I think she didn't really care and she
liked to joke that we'd been switched at birth, whatever that could
mean.) With our clothes on, though, and impersonating the people
we wanted to be, we became distinguishable. Mark was the lanky,
lank-haired blond with the strange eyes, attractive to all, shamefully
good at everything he tried, agreeably self-possessed; since at least
the second grade he'd been the most popular boy around, the best
student, destiny's undoubted favorite. I'd had trouble learning to read,

96

by way of contrast, and I wet my bed till I was nearly twelve. Our Uncle Allan, thinking he saw signs of unusual musical talent, arranged for us to have lessons with some of the best teachers in the East, causing my brother to take off like a prodigy at first. I, on the other hand, had to learn everything through pure skullwork and sweat, and I never achieved anything like his startling facility. (I did, however, stick with the instrument longer, becoming a grimly correct first violin in our high school orchestra.)

If you think the 'secret' of what I'm telling you is that I nursed a murderous resentment of my brother, yet somehow failed to recognize this in myself, you must think again. Twinness and twin relations are more complex, a double helix double doubled, which all the developmental psychologists, all the Human Genome Projects in the world can never spell out. I truly loved my brother, I hated him, he was myself and I hated that, he was different from me and I loved that, and I *was* that. This puzzling, eternally perturbing condition is neither so rare nor so remarkable as one might think, according to the dominant voices in contemporary anthropological neonatology: by statistical manipulations too arcane for me to reproduce here, these authorities demonstrate that the mystique of twinhood encoded in such stories as those of Jacob and Esau, Romulus and Remus, Pharez and Zarah, Castor and Pollux, etc., expresses nothing but a stubborn affinity for graphical duplication – symmetry, in a word – and that the cultures with 'isomerous' representational styles feature more myths about twinning, and tell them more often. Q.E.D.

Sometimes, though, twin statistics do have a repellent interest, even for me, and in this regard I'd like to mention that while only a third of all twins are identical, and only a fourth of identicals are true mirror twins, ten per cent of all living births are of the twin type. Furthermore, some eighty per cent of twin pregnancies are lost in utero, the shadow-fetus being fully or partly resorbed, which by my calculations means that over half of all the people in the world began their existence in a twinful state. We who actually see the light of day, therefore, in the company of another are not so strange, so 'anomalous' as some experts would make us out to be: we walk the earth with our living shadows, and are shadows ourselves, while the rest of humanity must wander eternally unpartnered, doomed to sense but not find its other half.

ROBERT ROPER

from The American Dream

MRS Dyson inhales and then coughs. She stares intently at him. 'Tell me what it's like to be a twin,' she says. 'Tell me the good and bad, all of it. How does it feel to have someone around who looks like you and talks like you, and maybe even thinks like you? I haven't met Josephine, of course, but Roberta tells me you're very alike. I imagine you must get compared all the time. Are you able to have any kind of separate life and identity?'

No one has asked these questions before. The questions he and Josephine do get asked are usually no more than social and incurious and jokey enquiries: 'Are you the Heavenly Twins?' or 'Which twin has the Toni?' – requiring no more than a frown in reply. Mrs Dyson's questions, he senses, are real ones, but he hasn't any answers. Being a twin is just a fact of his life. He's known nothing else, so how can he say?

GEORGINA HAMMICK

And the Frog brown as cork, what did he want from me? Didn't he know that I was just a twin, and twin girls are never princesses?

HART WEGNER, *The Houses of Ivory*

A twin baby did not have an easy life, right from the beginning he had to learn the hard way and discover very young how to work out his own lonely little salvation. Where a single baby would be petted and dandled when things went wrong, a twin very often cried for the comfort of warm arms.

PATRICIA LEDWARD, *Twin Blessings*

The fact of his existence was like that of an important text, an explanation or commentary without which the text of my life would be unreadable; he himself was like a copy of the book, no more, no less.

JOHN HOLLANDER, *The Twin's Story*

He hardly liked to look the real facts in the face as he now realised that one half of his business and all he owned belonged to Jack. But even this disturbed him less than the thought that his personality would be halved. Instead of being John Holdaway, he would be one of the Holdaway brothers. No longer a power and a name, but a unit.

F.J. RANDALL, *The Bermondsey Twin*

from Identity and Intimacy in Twins

ACCORDING to psychoanalytic theory, single children identify with the mother or primary caretaker and through this process become aware of their separateness. In the case of twins, each infant must go through identification and separation with the mother and with the twin . . . The relationship between infant twins is elusive and nonverbal, and there is a lack of differentiation that precedes awareness of body boundaries. Further, the need for the twin is different than the need for the mother, as the twin is experienced as part of the self in infancy. Maturation of sensory perception is necessary before one twin can begin to perceive himself/herself as separate from the other. Perhaps twin differentiation begins through touching and poking each other. Separation occurs more naturally from the mother, who already has attained her own sense of separateness from the child.

Gradually, a twin baby perceives that his/her twin is really another individual, not an extension of himself/herself or a mirror image. In early childhood there appears to be a continuum, never a sharp delineation, between a sense of oneness and the realization of separation. At this stage the primary intertwin identification resembles the primary identification with the mother in that it is based on play and ego gratification. The influence of the primary intertwin identification is evident in later stages of development and in some instances throughout the life of the twins.

BARBARA SCHAVE AND JANET CIRIELLO

---

from Notes of An Anatomist

THE identical twin, like the identical triplet, or any identical multiple, gazes into the shattered mirror of his own individuality with a perplexity that is directly proportional to the number of his brethren.

Locke defined self as consciousness and said that the little finger, while comprehended under that consciousness, is as much part of the self as what is most so; and that if the little finger were to be cut off and carry with it this consciousness, 'it is evident that the little finger would be the person, and self would have nothing to do with the rest of the body.' But a twin sees an entire being, an autonomous thinking and feeling homologue, whose compound nature more strongly than a severed little finger represents to the mind that it, too, has consciousness. And since this being, outwardly the same person as he, shared his beginnings in time and space, thus fulfilling the requisites that logic demands of identity, he must experience the odd sensation that his consciousness is shared and his self cleft twice, thrice, or more. In a sense, one might say that the twin is 'beside himself,' and the connotation of being dazzled or confounded that is embodied in the expression is more telling of the problems of identity besetting twins than many a learned treatise.

F. GONZALES-CRUSSI

---

the feeling I get when I look at her, or when I look very self-consciously into a mirror, a feeling of being pulled apart and put together . . .

DOROTHY BAKER, *Cassandra at the Wedding*

The me I'm telling you about got here ahead of me, so that means I got here, oh dear, before myself . . .

VON KLEIST, *Amphytrion*, trans. M. Greenberg

Mark Twain: 'My twin and I got mixed up in the bathtub when we were only two weeks old and one of us drowned, but we didn't know which. Some think it was Bill and some think it was me. One of us had a peculiar mark – a large hole on the back of his left hand; but that was me. That child was the one that was drowned!'

quoted HAL HOLBROOK, *Mark Twain Tonight*

Someone once looked at us and said: 'If you two could be put together in one person, you'd have everything; you'd be perfect.'

PENELOPE FARMER

---

from Year King

AND now he waited again; in a much less agitated state than he had waited before. The sense of flickering was now gone altogether. He thought about the whole thing with a cool rather frightening clarity which somehow dissected his mind and feelings as effectively as his mind and his body had been separated before. It is like a duel, he thought; a duel to some kind of death. We both declared it; we could both choose weapons, and I chose first and I tried mine and it didn't win. Now I have to wait for him to choose his. He saw it all; yet he was not frightened.

He thought once: I was trying to kill his mind and my body. Now he will try to kill my mind and his body. It is not murder; murder does not encompass crimes like that, and anyway we are not two people, we are one person.

But we are not one person; my mind does not fit his body; his mind will not fit mine. That night he awoke screaming. But in the morning he rose calm and easy and went about his work very cheerfully . . .

[. . .] He had no physical sensations at all initially. He was not a body at all, he was simply a mind that hovered between bodies and could not insert itself into either. He saw himself twice over; had to remind himself that the second body wasn't actually his; only his on a loan he had not asked for and did not actually want, even if he had been expecting it.

He saw himself on the sofa first, in the cottage with his cup of coffee, head bowed, feet apart; having just turned from moonlight – he had gone out in a moment of impulse and walked up to the churchyard to view the drowned silver countryside and listen to the owls, then felt scared and creepy suddenly and come in again, with relief. It would have been much more appropriate if it had happened then, while he was out, than now, surrounded as he was by empty cups of coffee and crumpled newspapers and debris from his supper. Christ, he had been thinking, it's about time I cleaned up in here.

He saw this other figure now besides; exposed; clinging to a wall as if with sticky feet like a fly's – you would think – till you noticed the rope, and the careful jamming in crevices of hands and feet. There were lights on either side of the arched gateway of another building ten yards or so away, which picked out the near sides of pinnacles on the same building but left the far ones dark, by comparison. They were very eccentric pinnacles, having more character than obvious function, set with vertical rows of blunt spikes, like some kind of armoured yet fabulous animal. Though symmetrically arranged they did not look man-made at all; it was more as if small rock pinnacles from the Arizona desert had transported themselves here and multiplied. As far as Lan could judge in this light the stone was even desert-coloured too. His mind hovered above them, eyeing mean-while the other quite different building, not angular at all, actually round and set regularly with pairs of smooth round pillars. The figure which had not changed its position since he saw it first was jammed between two of these, halfway up, feet and backside taking the strain, chimneying, or semi-chimneying, the pillars being set into the wall and not wholly three-dimensional, so that a fair amount of the body jutted out sideways. He watched it begin to creep upwards. He did not yet seem responsible for its progress; he was not aware of his mind ordering it on. But when it reached a point just below the capitals of the pillars it stopped, being able to get no further by that particular method. His mind was quite coolly assessing now how it should navigate this next obstacle, and as if in answer to that he saw a shoulder turn and an arm reach up to grasp a capital – and then a foot in turn alter its position, refit itself, push. This first overhang was not too bad, foot and handholds being provided by decorative stone garlands; above that though was a fifteen-foot stretch of naked wall, bearing one thin line of moulding only – and above that again was a much deeper overhang, beneath an ornamental stone balustrade.

There was a rope round Lew's waist, attached to an efficient-looking harness. Lan was beginning to be able to feel the harness. The figure in the cottage had altogether gone from his sense by now, leaving only this other one. He was and yet was not inside it, though definitely directing it at last. Twice he told himself, hold still – and found the other body waited. He paused hopefully in case it would move again without him, but it did not. Now it had no other mind but his.

He was it. Yet wasn't it. He found himself remembering tests he'd done once in a psychology lab to help a psychologist friend of his mother's – he'd had to guide a brass pointer round an elaborate circuit, allowed to see neither circuit nor hand directly, having to watch them in a mirror instead, the effect of this to make him very clumsy and uncertain, moving his fingers one way when he'd intended to move them in another. Every time he had made a mistake and touched the circuit walls he'd set off an electric bell.

The effect of such clumsiness now would be infinitely more dangerous.

But as his mind could not take in bodily sensation except in the vaguest and fuzziest way, so the sense of fear would not translate itself to the body. This perhaps was the greatest danger of all. Neither mind nor body felt in any way real at all.

How beautiful this place was; the moonlight; its reflections on the spires and pinnacles beyond; the texture it laid on pale stone.

Cautiously Lan used feet as levers now – heaved up – then the body stood straight again; such ornamental stone-work was much more helpful than protuberances on rock – this close to he could not define the shapes they made, only be thankful for such regular, substantial feet and handholds. He used the rope too, hanging outwards at one point like a steeplejack – it occurred to him no proper climber would operate like that, but he was not a proper climber, he told himself, walking the feet up the wall while the hands clutched at the rope, praying that whatever anchored it would hold fast. The body had almost reached the next overhang now – this, however, being by no means as accommodating as the last, its ornamentation geometric, providing square, edged downward-facing hunks, too large for hands to grasp, and quite useless to feet. His mind did not know what the body should do next; into it came brief flashes from Lew's climbing books – diagrams of pegs and slings to be used when natural hand and footholds were not available. But there was nothing like that to help him now. There was nothing to help him now except the rope. The companionship it suggested he had somewhere here, far from encouraging him made him feel still more disjointed and alien. He had visions of remaining like that – mind, body, ill-fitting, each one on a different man-made precipice, for all the rest of time. Was that what Lew wanted? Should he throw the body off and so solve the problem instantly – was that what Lew wanted? How cold it was now; he did not know whether he felt the cold or not; then a clock struck and another and another, low chimes echoing, pulling sense and sensation together, dinning through them. What ears heard them, his ears? – *whose* ears? – he could not see how this overhang was to be negotiated. Lew's body could not instruct Lan's captive mind. Lan's ill-fitting mind knew nothing at all.

PENELOPE FARMER

To be like us isn't easy, it requires constant attention to detail. I've thought it out; we've thought it out together. I've tried to explain to my doctor that it's a question of working ceaselessly at being as different as possible because there must be a gap before it can be bridged. And the bridge is the real project.

DOROTHY BAKER, *Cassandra at the Wedding*

---

from The Twin Pupils

NURSE began early to teach Annette that she was not to live for herself alone, but to make it her constant endeavour to promote Lisa's happiness; and the little thing understood easily the different position in which her sister's affliction placed them, and saw intuitively the kind of protection of which she stood in need. Unfortunately, she was not contented with understanding it herself, but was excessively desirous that her sister should do the same; not being aware that many years would necessarily elapse before the mind could be sufficiently advanced to form any correct notion of the first of wonders – sight. In spite, therefore, of Nurse's remonstrances, she was continually assuring Lisa how happy she was to do anything for her, *because* she could not see to do it herself; upon which her sister invariably replied, (much to her discomfiture) 'But I can see if you can, why can't I?' And one day, on her giving this her accustomed answer, Annette (much to the amusement of her adult auditors) adopted the words she had so frequently heard used in reference to her sister, and replied, 'No dear, you tan't see, you are blind; mamma, and papa, and we are all very sorry, but nothing can be done for you.'

'But I am not blind, more blind than you,' was the immediate reply; 'for a lady said yesterday we were just alike, as much alike as two pins.'

'That means to look at,' reasoned Annette, 'but the difference is, dear, I can see that table and you tan't.'

'Yes, but I tell you I tan,' was the positive rejoinder; 'for I knocked my head this morning and Nurse said it was the table.'

'Well,' resumed Annette, feeling somewhat shaken by her sister's pertinacity, 'I will tell Nurse what you think, dear; but I very afear *you* make the mistake, not her. Nurse,' she immediately exclaimed, while running up to the other end of the room, 'Lisa says she tan see, she won't believe us.'

'I am not at all surprised at that,' rejoined the Nurse; 'you had better not talk about it, and I have told you so before, Annette, because she thinks it unkind to be told she cannot do anything you can; and while she is so young, it is impossible for her to form any idea of what seeing means.'

'Poor little ting,' said Annette, compassionately.

ANON., 1855

Twins, as a group of two, use each other to accomplish what one cannot do alone, that is, they have the strength of two and are invincible. They fight each other's battles and ally themselves against the rest of the world when they feel themselves threatened or find that they are in danger. They can withdraw from the rest of the world when it is too disagreeable and still have a world of their own.

DOROTHY BURLINGHAM, *Twins*

from Twins, Triplets and More

DISCIPLINING twins can be unexpectedly problematic even for experienced parents. Many have been disconcerted to find how ineffective are the forms of control they had successfully used with their older children. Why is this? It is probably due to the support provided by the twin-partner. A child responds to discipline largely because he wants the love and respect of the person on whom he most depends. For most children that is a parent. But in the case of a twin the person whose respect and cooperation he most wants is by his side egging him on to worse and worse misdemeanours or demonstrating quite new ones. It is not therefore surprising that a parent needs to exert much more disciplinary pressure to have any effect. It has been found that parents have to use more overt verbal control and more reprimands to twins than to single children.

The pranks of twins can, moreover, be much more hair-raising than those of single children. With children of different ages one of them will be either sensible enough to foresee danger or physically incapable of performing the reckless act. Twins tend to push each other way beyond the limits that a single child of the same age would risk. Triplets show a further magnification of the problem, and it would be amazing if any house could be made quad-proof.

A further complication is that, because of their companionship, twins tend to have far greater perseverance. Twins will happily play for hours with the contents of their mother's make-up bag and I've lost count of the number of refrigerators that have been raided before dawn and the contents used with masterful ingenuity, usually on the least stain-proof furniture. One mother resorted to setting her alarm for 3.30 a.m. so that she could protect her kitchen from the inevitable invasion at 4.00.

Disconcerting habits may also be acquired which no child on its own could keep up. Rachel and Rebecca, a bright pair of identical twins, became known as the 'whispering twins'. It had all started when they were about 2½ years old. When strangers appeared they would only talk in a whisper. This drew attention from both their parents and their friends as they tried to persuade them to break their silence. Initially the children would give in after a few minutes. Later they became increasingly skilful and determined, obviously regarding it as a challenge. By the time I met them at 4½ years they could hold out all day and against all incentives including treat outings and much-wanted presents. Even their beloved grandmother, with whom they spent whole days, could not induce them to speak above a whisper. Indeed, they would sometimes actually announce to their mother their intention of not speaking all day. I cannot imagine a single child having the confidence and determination to perform such a feat.

ELIZABETH BRYAN

---

from The Birthday Gift

AFTER a bit the seesaw became just part of the backyard. Birds from the loquat tree dirtied the seat. Benno liked his trike best. When Ben wanted a seesaw he had to ask. Ben liked the regular up and down motion and could do it for hours (if Benno would). Just at dusk was one time the two boys ended up most using it. Smell of dinner cooking upstairs, and knowing you had to wait. Up and down till there was hardly enough light. Six o'clock, the moon sometimes beginning to colour, flying foxes swooping up the gully to the loquats, their noise not really spooky, only a playground squabble, a before-tea restlessness.

The boys would sometimes end up balancing halfway up, halfway down. They could have reached toes to the ground, but they discovered just that right balance and let the thing pause – the slightest movement of one would topple it. It was a delicate skill, sensitive as a compass. After, Ben might make a move suddenly, uptilting his end, so Benno bumped down on the tyre. Ben tried to catch him out, if only sometimes. Benno was more likely to break the balance first, ramming feet down quick. They would compete then to see who could bounce hardest. It was more exciting just because of the stillness before.

They developed a pattern. By the end of April this had become regulated, instinctive, so they got impatient with the other kids if they did not follow the rules. Ben started counting aloud. That made it easier for the others, and soon counting was part of the proper game: One – two – three – four – five – six – seven – stop. One – two – three – four – five – six – seven – eight – nine – ten – *push*. Then they would go as fast as they could, pushing against the strength of each other, until one gave in, shouting, 'One!' And it would return to the steady up-down, seven turns. Then the hold-on-to-ten. Then *push*.

Only Benno and Ben really managed the middle up to ten. The

other kids were too heavy or too light or too wriggly or just *had* to reach down their feet. Afraid to balance.

THOMAS SHAPCOTT

---

from My Twin Joe

ONE day in high school we were taking an examination in Latin. Our class had been reading and translating Virgil's Æneid. And the test consisted in translating certain passages which had been selected from that noble classic. Along with the other members of our class, we did the work in silence, placing our translations in writing on sheets of paper and handing them to our teacher at the close of the examination period for inspection and report. Our Latin teacher that year, a Mrs Livingood, was a large, heavy woman, loud in her manner, positive in her convictions, quick in her decisions. When she handed the papers back to the class she said:

'I am handing all of the papers back but those of the twins. I have discovered that the twins cheated in their examinations. Their translations were identical, word for word; and I have not yet decided what the punishment will be.'

'Cheated!' said Joe, who was always a ready advocate for his twin. 'My twin would not cheat under any circumstances. You ought to know that.'

'You cannot talk me out of it with that ready smile, Charles,' calling Joe the wrong name. 'Here are the papers. They are the same, word for word. You cannot disprove the physical facts. Besides, Joe shows his guilt on his face,' pointing to me.

'Guilt! That is not guilt.'

Joe might have made a more eloquent reply. He might at least have said something about our past record with respect to the trait of character involved; but he was merely a sixteen-year-old boy unexpectedly confronted with this accusation by a person of superior authority. I admit we were dumb, dumb like a sheep before its shearer. Nevertheless, Joe continued his smiling all the while. It has always been that way. You cannot get him provoked no matter what the provocation.

'You were sitting close together, and you copied each other's papers. You do not have to knock a person in the head with a brick in order to get an idea across. You cheated.' There was a lot of fight in her voice and countenance. You could see that she expected support from the other scholars in the room. But many of them had come up through the grades with the twins.

'We are twins,' we both put in.

'Don't I know you are twins? That is no excuse for doing wrong.'

'What we mean,' said Joe, translating, 'is this: Because we are twins we do the same things and think the same thoughts, and the papers might be the same for that reason.'

'This is not an age of spiritualism. If you had not been sitting so close together the papers would not have been alike,' and she looked around with a smile of satisfaction.

'We believe they would.'

'Then prove it,' she said, with an air of victory. 'One of you sit on this side of the room and one on the other. I shall give you another examination right now. Joe, you come over here,' looking at me and waving me over with her arm and hand.

I went. That was the diplomatic thing to do. We loved to have our identities confused, and anyway, we had long since learned by experience that a time like this was no time in which to take up with a teacher such a trifling and irrelevant matter as a mistake in identity.

Well, she gave us another test in a room that was filled with excited and curious faces, a stern and high-tempered teacher presiding, the clock ticking slowly on the north wall of that silent room.

When she examined our papers she found them again to be identical. Would she give up? No, she still had contention in her.

'There has been some trick. You have got a communication across in spite of my care. I shall require another examination. But not today. It is too late. Tomorrow I shall have Principal Williamson help me look after you.'

We went home sensing the idea that somehow we were the victims of a serious mishap in which we were not to blame.

Before we went to bed that night we sat together, working together, until we had again reviewed the Æneid as far as we had taken it.

The next morning Principal Williamson was on hand. He took part in the proceedings. More mystery, much concealed excitement, the scholars looking out of the corners of their eyes.

'Joe will come into my office for the examination,' Professor Williamson said, and he led Joe away, leaving me alone and desolate. Mrs Livingood handed me the memoranda for the test and told me to go to work. I looked them over, and I could easily see that we were facing a longer and more difficult examination than we had taken before. I sat there chewing the end of my pen.

'Why don't you get to work?' after the lapse of fifteen minutes.

'I am not ready.'

And so I sat there. I was confused, embarrassed, and I looked to neither right nor left.

'Why don't you get to work?' after another long period of silence.

'I am not ready.' And I was not. It seemed to me that there was some wheel in my brain which was not ticking with its accustomed rhythm.

'Your brother will be through before you get started,' she said after another long pause. 'Why don't you get to work?' There was a note of triumph in her voice.

'I am not ready.' It was a dumb thing to repeat, but I could not go forward with the work. The lines of Latin looked far away and vague.

Just then Professor Williamson came hurrying into the room.

'I want my copy of the memoranda for the test. I have been delayed by my other work, and Joe has been waiting in my office.'

So we took that examination at the same time even though we were not in the same room. We took it under a stress and strain which tried our hearts, but the identical wheels in our brains seemed to be working rhythmically. After the work was over and the papers had been handed in, after Joe had come back to his accustomed seat and I had him near again, there was a suspense which seemed to last interminably. The years go by so quickly, but sometimes the minutes seem so long.

At the noon recess Professor Williamson called the teacher and the twins into his office. He was all goodwill.

'Boys, your Latin papers are identical. The same words, the same syntax, the same grammar, but, strangest of all, the same mistakes. But of one thing I am sure, you did not cheat. It must be because you are twins.'

CHARLES CRAILL

––––––––––

Language is for relating to others: C'est pour les autres.

JOHN BARTH

––––––––––

from The Bridge of San Luis Rey

BECAUSE they had no family, because they were twins, and because they were brought up by women, they were silent. There was in them a curious shame in regard to their resemblance. They had to live in a world where it was the subject of continual comment and joking. It was never funny to them, and they suffered the eternal pleasantries with stolid patience. From the years when they first learned to speak they invented a secret language for themselves, one that was scarcely dependent on the Spanish for its vocabulary, or even for its syntax. They resorted to it only when they were alone, or at great intervals in moments of stress whispered it in the presence of others. The Archbishop of Lima was something of a philologist; he dabbled in dialects; he had even evolved quite a brilliant table for the vowel and consonant changes from Latin into Spanish and from Spanish into Indian-Spanish. He was storing up notebooks of quaint lore against an amusing old age he planned to offer himself back on his estates outside Segovia. So when he heard one day about the secret language of the twin brothers, he trimmed some quills and sent for them. The boys stood humiliated upon the rich carpets of his study while he tried to extract from them their *bread* and *flower* and their *I see* and *I saw*. They did not know why the experience was so horrible to them. They bled. Long shocked silences followed each of the Archbishop's questions, until finally one or the other mumbled an answer. The priest thought for a while that they were merely in awe before his rank and before the luxury of his apartment, but at last, much perplexed, he divined the presence of some deeper reluctance and sadly let them go.

This language was the symbol of their profound identity with one another, for just as *resignation* was a word insufficient to describe the spiritual change that came over the Marquesa de Montemayor on that night in the inn at Cluxambuqua, so *love* is inadequate to describe the tacit, almost ashamed oneness of these brothers. What relationship is it in which few words are exchanged, and those only about the details of food, clothing, and occupation; in which the two persons have a curious reluctance even to glance at one another; and in which there is a tacit arrangement not to appear together in the city and to go on the same errand by different streets? And yet side by side with this there existed a need of one another so terrible that it produced miracles as naturally as the charged air of a sultry day produces lightning. The brothers were scarcely conscious of it themselves, but telepathy was a common occurrence in their lives, and when one returned home the other was always aware of it while his brother was still several streets away.

Suddenly they discovered that they were tired of writing. They went down to the sea and found an occupation in loading and unloading vessels, not ashamed of working side by side with Indians. They drove teams across the provinces. They picked fruit. They were ferrymen. And always they were silent. Their sombre faces took on from these labours a male and gipsy cast. Their hair was seldom cut, and under the dark mat their eyes looked up suddenly surprised and a little sullen. All the world was remote and strange and hostile except one's brother.

THORNTON WILDER

———————

from Gemini

ONE of the nicest effects of our 'monstrousness' was undoubtedly this cryptophasia, the unfathomable jargon we called Aeolian, which enabled us to talk together for hours on end without others present being able to understand a word we said. The cryptophasia which most real twins create between themselves constitutes for them a definite strength and source of pride in relation to other individuals. But in the majority of cases they pay a heavy price for this advantage since the geminate jargon can be seen clearly to develop at the expense of normal speech and so of social intelligence. Statistics have established that a rich, abundant and complex cryptophasia goes with an ordinary language that is poor, meager, and rudimentary. This imbalance is all the more serious because of the constant relationship that exists between sociability and intelligence on the one hand and the level of language development on the other. Here we put our finger on the drawback of exceptions, anomalies, and teratological forms which frequently possess some dazzling, superhuman gift, for this superiority has been purchased at the cost of some serious flaw on the most ordinary, basic level. I regarded myself for a long time as a superman. I still believe I am destined for something out of the common run. But I no longer conceal from myself – as how could I after my twofold amputation? – the terrible price I have had to pay for it.

The mistake made by all the psychologists who have dealt with the enigma of cryptophasia is to have considered it as an ordinary language. They have treated it as they would have done some African or Slavonic dialect, trying to amass a vocabulary and extract a syntax from it. This is the fundamental contradiction of translating a geminate phenomenon into individual terms. Geminate speech – wholly dictated and structured by twinship – cannot be equated with an individual language. To do so is to overlook the essence and retain only the incidental. For in Aeolian, *the words are incidental, silence is the essence*. That is what makes a geminate language a phenomenon absolutely incomparable to any other linguistic form.

MICHEL TOURNIER

---

from The Silent Twins

JUNE and Jennifer were at school now but still did not speak much. At the end of their first year the teacher wrote in her Service Children's Report about June: 'At first rather unsettled and inseparable from her twin sister. Has settled better since. Is a little more independent. If upset will cry for a long time. Will not talk to me. Talks to other children.' A year later the report was a little better. 'June is beginning to write but still lacks confidence to speak or read.' The teacher added an observation which was to follow the twins' progress throughout their schooling: they 'tend to be too content to do very little. They show very little initiative or imagination.' The school decided to send the girls for weekly speech therapy, but it does not seem to have helped. They brought home exercise books filled with sounds and words they were meant to practise, but never did. Gloria clung to her belief that they were just a little backward and would catch up in their own way. In any case, with five children to care for, there was little time for practising grunts and whistles. So by the time they were eight, although their school reports refer to them as reading fluently and writing, the twins were still not speaking. 'Jennifer,' says her report, 'has no oral response, but writes diligently.' June is 'still silent and won't converse. Both of them are very shy.'

This charitable explanation became the acceptable excuse for the twins' odd behaviour. It followed them to their next school at Braunton, Devon, where they went when Aubrey was posted to RAF, Chivenor, in 1971. The twins, then eight and a half years old, found themselves in a new environment with no familiar faces, and little sympathy among their peers for children who did not speak properly and had black skin. They were laughed at in class and bullied and baited in the playground, thus forced to cling even more tightly to the safe world of each other, to strengthen the walls of their twinship and to withdraw behind them. They stopped trying to communicate with outsiders and, even within the family, became more isolated. Gloria and Aubrey would hear them chatter endlessly to one another and to their dolls, but could only make out an occasional word. It was as though they had deliberately distorted their speech into a secret code to prevent others from understanding it.

Private languages used by twins are not unknown. A French film director made a film about the secret language of a pair of twins in San Diego, California, in 1977. From early childhood, these twins had invented a 'code' which sounded so foreign that at first people thought they had developed a new language. Like the Gibbons twins, these two girls, who called themselves Poto and Cabengo, spoke rapidly in staccato bursts. By slowing down the tapes and analysing them word by word, their secret 'language' turned out to be ordinary English mixed with German (their family was bilingual), but spoken fast and with many repetitions and such altered stress on individual syllables that the words took on the opposite emphasis to normal. In the case of Poto and Cabengo, once their game was discovered and they were separated and placed in different schools, they abandoned their own language and spoke normally.

With June and Jennifer, there was no such easy outcome. Their lack of speech to outsiders and their high-speed 'patois' between themselves were only symptoms of the more serious conflict which soon dominated their lives. No-one knows when it began, whether it started in infancy, or in their first school, or at Braunton, but by the time they were eleven the battle lines had been firmly drawn both against the outside world and internally, between twin and twin.

MARJORIE WALLACE

---

from Voo and Doo

I trotted to the dugout for my glove. 'Andy' Anderson had his back turned to me. I never did care for him. He has got shifty eyes. In left field I heard the song change to 'Why didn't you go home Bill Bailey, why didn't you go home.' Over the rest of the play I will 'draw a merciful curtain,' until the end of the fifth with the score still 'knotted' at nothing all, and the singing dying down in the stands. In the fifth I escaped – that is the word – for a little while in the clubroom beneath the stands. To get there you walk up a long dark tunnel, on boards cut and frayed by cleats, and turn left and there it is. I walked in and found two players there ahead of me. 'In a trice' I identified them. The twins. I was about to speak but then realized that they both had off their jackets. The pitcher's number was 7 and the catcher's number was 11 – I could see the numbers on the backs of their jackets and watched, 'in shocked silence,' while they passed in the swap from one player to the other. They put them on, fast, and started buttoning up. They were tucking in the tails when they saw me. They stopped 'in mid gesture,' and just stared, with their mouths and eyes wide open. Then those mouths and eyes thinned and chilled, and my throat and mouth got dry and my stomach restless. They walked to me, and stood one at each side, and slightly in front of me.

'Fellows,' I said, trying to be calm and pleasant, 'but fellows, this is not right.'

They seemed to draw closer to me, without moving. They were a sort of presence there, and I remembered the fire beneath the pot, and the two witches, and how the twins had looked in the light, their faces long and thin, like twin devils.

'Mr Anderson knows,' said the new pitcher, and the new catcher said, 'And if it is all right with him, it is all right with everybody.'

'But tell me,' I said, swallowing, curious though frightened, 'have you two been swapping, changing the battery, in every game?'

They nodded, together, grinning a little thin grin, watching me with those eyes of ice.

'But why?' I said.

'We are really both pitchers,' said the new pitcher, and the new catcher said, 'We could not decide which one of us would be the pitcher.'

'Why not both of you?'

'We would have a better chance if only one of us was the pitcher.'

'And you could win more games, one of you coming in in the middle of the game.'

'It did not start that way. It started because we could not agree and we had a fight. It just worked out that way. Now you are going to keep quiet about it.'

I did not want to keep quiet about it. This was wrong – it was against all the rules of fair play and baseball. But I could remember all the years in the bushes, and all the years on the bench, and the catchers who did not take off their gear, and the song they had just sung in the stands and caused me to get picked off third base. I did not want the bench again, I did not want the bushes again. I wanted what I had.

I decided – I suppose that Marv Engles would say that I sold my soul to the devil. 'Let us go and talk to Mr Anderson,' I said.

We went out together, a twin on each side of me, like a convoy. Mr Anderson was shouting at his third base coach who turned his back now and returned to his post. Mr Anderson sat down, his face red and his breath coming hard. He saw us together in the door and got up and walked slowly to us. He looked into our faces, licked his lips and went from red to white.

'Mr Anderson,' said the new pitcher, 'he knows.'

'Mr Anderson,' said the new catcher, 'he knows, and has promised to behave if you will not trade him or send him down again.'

'Mr Anderson,' I said, 'I have promised to behave if you will play me every day.'

Mr Anderson went through the expected sputters and oaths, and nodded and went back to his seat and held his head in his hands. He seemed to have suddenly lost weight. I went back to left field, and the new pitcher won the game. I am still in left field, and a little overweight, and batting .199, but will come on strong later, and feel better now that I have got it all down, out of my system and on to paper.

HOKE NORRIS

---

from Those Extraordinary Twins

NEXT morning all the town was a-buzz with great news; Pudd'nhead Wilson had a law case! The public astonishment was so great and the public curiosity so intense, that when the justice of the peace opened his court, the place was packed with people, and even the windows were full. Everybody was flushed and perspiring; the summer heat was almost unendurable.

Tom Driscoll had brought a charge of assault and battery against the twins. Robert Allen was retained by Driscoll, David Wilson by the defense. Tom, his native cheerfulness unannihilated by his back-breaking and bone-bruising passage across the massed heads of the Sons of Liberty the previous night, laughed his little customary laugh, and said to Wilson:

'I've kept my promise, you see; I'm throwing my business your way. Sooner than I was expecting, too.'

'It's very good of you – particularly if you mean to keep it up.'

'Well, I can't tell about that yet. But we'll see. If I find you deserve it I'll take you under my protection and make your fame and fortune for you.'

'I'll try to deserve it, Tom.'

A jury was sworn in; then Mr Allen said:

'We will detain your honor but a moment with this case. It is not one where any doubt of the fact of the assault can enter in. These gentlemen – the accused – kicked my client at the Market Hall last night; they kicked him with violence; with extraordinary violence; with even unprecedented violence, I may say; insomuch that he was lifted entirely off his feet and discharged into the midst of the audience. We can prove this by four hundred witnesses – we shall call but three. Mr Harkness will take the stand.'

Mr Harkness, being sworn, testified that he was chairman upon the occasion mentioned; that he was close at hand and saw the defendants in this action kick the plaintiff into the air and saw him descend among the audience.

'Take the witness,' said Allen.

'Mr Harkness,' said Wilson, 'you say you saw these gentlemen, my clients, kick the plaintiff. Are you sure – and please remember that you are on oath – are you perfectly sure that you saw *both* of them kick him, or only one? Now be careful.'

A bewildered look began to spread itself over the witness's face. He hesitated, stammered, but got out nothing. His eyes wandered to the twins and fixed themselves there with a vacant gaze.

'Please answer, Mr Harkness, you are keeping the court waiting. It is a very simple question.'

Counsel for the prosecution broke in with impatience:

'Your honor, the question is an irrelevant triviality. Necessarily, they both kicked him, for they have but the one pair of legs, and both are responsible for them.'

Wilson said, sarcastically:

'Will your honor permit this new witness to be sworn? He seems to possess knowledge which can be of the utmost value just at this moment – knowledge which would at once dispose of what every one must see is a very difficult question in this case. Brother Allen, will you take the stand?'

'Go on with your case!' said Allen, petulantly. The audience laughed, and got a warning from the court.

'Now, Mr Harkness,' said Wilson, insinuatingly, 'we shall have to insist upon an answer to that question.'

'I – er – well, of course, I do not absolutely *know*, but in my opinion –'

'Never mind your opinion, sir – answer the question.'

'I – why, I *can't* answer it.'

'That will do, Mr Harkness. Stand down.'

[. . .] The third witness too had seen the twins kick the plaintiff. Mr Wilson took the witness.

'Mr Rogers, you say you saw these accused gentlemen kick the plaintiff?'

'Yes, sir.'

'Both of them?'

'Yes, sir.'

'Which of them kicked him first?'

'Why – they – they both kicked him at the same time.'

'Are you perfectly sure of that?'

'Yes, sir.'

'What makes you sure of it?'

'Why, I stood right behind them, and *saw* them do it.'

'How many kicks were delivered?'

'Only one.'

'If two men kick, the result should be two kicks, shouldn't it?'

'Why – why – yes, as a rule.'

'Then what do you think went with the other kick?'

'I – well – the fact is, I wasn't thinking of two being necessary, this time.'

'What do you think now?'

'Well, I – I'm sure I don't quite know what to think, but I reckon that one of them did half of the kick and the other one did the other half.'

Somebody in the crowd sung out: 'It's the first sane thing that any of them has said.'

The audience applauded. The judge said: 'Silence! or I will clear the court.'

Mr Allen looked pleased, but Wilson did not seem disturbed. He said:

'Mr Rogers, you have favored us with what you think and what you reckon, but as thinking and reckoning are not evidence, I will now give you a chance to come out with something positive, one way or the other, and shall require you to produce it. I will ask the accused to stand up and repeat the phenomenal kick of last night.' The twins stood up. 'Now, Mr Rogers, please stand behind them.'

A Voice: 'No, stand in front!' (Laughter. Silenced by the court.) Another Voice: 'No, give Tommy another highst!' (Laughter. Sharply rebuked by the court.)

'Now, then, Mr Rogers, two kicks shall be delivered, one after the other, and I give you my word that at least one of the two shall be delivered by one of the twins alone, without the slightest assistance from his brother. Watch sharply, for you have got to render a decision without any if's and and's in it.' Rogers bent himself behind the twins with his palms just above his knees, in the modern attitude of the catcher at a base-ball match, and riveted his eyes on the pair of legs in front of him. 'Are you ready, Mr Rogers?'

'Ready, sir.'

'Kick!'

The kick was launched.

'Have you got that one classified, Mr Rogers?'

'Let me study a minute, sir.'

'Take as much time as you please. Let me know when you are ready.'

For as much as a minute Rogers pondered, with all eyes and a breathless interest fastened upon him. Then he gave the word: 'Ready, sir.'

'Kick!'

The kick that followed was an exact duplicate of the first one.

'Now, then, Mr Rogers, one of those kicks was an individual kick, not a mutual one. You will now state positively which was the mutual one.'

The witness said, with a crestfallen look:

'I've got to give it up. There ain't any man in the world that could tell t'other from which, sir.'

'Do you still assert that last night's kick was a mutual kick?'

'Indeed, I don't, sir.'

'That will do, Mr Rogers. If my brother Allen desires to address the court, your honor, very well; but as far as I am concerned I am ready to let the case be at once delivered into the hands of this intelligent jury without comment.'

MARK TWAIN

———

from 'The Case for the Defence'

IT was all over, you would have said, but the hanging.

After the formal evidence had been given by the policeman who had found the body and the surgeon who examined it, Mrs Salmon was called. She was the ideal witness, with her slight Scotch accent and her expression of honesty, care and kindness.

The counsel for the Crown brought the story gently out. She spoke very firmly. There was no malice in her, and no sense of importance at standing there in the Central Criminal Court with a judge in scarlet hanging on her words and the reporters writing them down. Yes, she said, and then she had gone downstairs and rung up the police station.

'And do you see the man here in court?'

She looked straight at the big man in the dock, who stared hard at her with his pekingese eyes without emotion.

'Yes,' she said, 'there he is.'

'You are quite certain?'

She said simply, 'I couldn't be mistaken, sir.'

It was all as easy as that.

'Thank you, Mrs Salmon.'

Counsel for the defence rose to cross-examine. If you had reported as many murder trials as I have, you would have known beforehand what line he would take. And I was right, up to a point.

'Now, Mrs Salmon, you must remember that a man's life may depend on your evidence.'

'I do remember it, sir.'

'Is your eyesight good?'

'I have never had to wear spectacles, sir.'

'You are a woman of fifty-five?'

'Fifty-six, sir.'

'And the man you saw was on the other side of the road?'

'Yes, sir.'

'And it was two o'clock in the morning. You must have remarkable eyes, Mrs Salmon?'

'No, sir. There was moonlight, and when the man looked up, he had the lamplight on his face.'

'And you have no doubt whatever that the man you saw is the prisoner?'

I couldn't make out what he was at. He couldn't have expected any other answer than the one he got.

'None whatever, sir. It isn't a face one forgets.'

Counsel took a look round the court for a moment. Then he said, 'Do you mind, Mrs Salmon, examining again the people in court? No, not the prisoner. Stand up, please, Mr Adams,' and there at the back of the court with thick stout body and muscular legs and a pair of bulging eyes, was the exact image of the man in the dock. He was even dressed the same – tight blue suit and striped tie.

'Now think very carefully, Mrs Salmon. Can you still swear that the man you saw drop the hammer in Mrs Parker's garden was the prisoner – and not this man, who is his twin brother?'

Of course she couldn't. She looked from one to the other and didn't say a word.

There the big brute sat in the dock with his legs crossed, and there he stood too at the back of the court and they both stared at Mrs Salmon. She shook her head.

What we saw then was the end of the case. There wasn't a witness prepared to swear that it was the prisoner he'd seen. And the brother? He had his alibi, too; he was with his wife.

And so the man was acquitted for lack of evidence. But whether – if he did the murder and not his brother – he was punished or not, I don't know. That extraordinary day had an extraordinary end. I followed Mrs Salmon out of court and we got wedged in the crowd who were waiting, of course, for the twins. The police tried to drive the crowd away, but all they could do was keep the road-way clear for traffic. I learned later that they tried to get the twins to leave by a back way, but they wouldn't. One of them – no one knew which – said, 'I've been acquitted, haven't I?' and they walked bang out of the front entrance. Then it happened. I don't know how, though I was only six feet away. The crowd moved and somehow one of the twins got pushed on to the road right in front of a bus.

He gave a squeal like a rabbit and that was all; he was dead, his skull smashed just as Mrs Parker's had been. Divine vengeance? I wish I knew. There was the other Adams getting on his feet from beside the body and looking straight over at Mrs Salmon. He was crying, but whether he was the murderer or the innocent man nobody will ever be able to tell. But if you were Mrs Salmon, could you sleep at night?

GRAHAM GREENE

from Crime as Destiny

IN the first part of these investigations we applied the Twin method with regard to criminals in a purely statistical manner. With the help of the records we ascertained in the case of all available twins whether they themselves and their fellow-twins had come into conflict with the law or not. In every single case we also endeavoured to find out conclusively whether we were dealing with monozygotic twins, i.e. those with the same heredity, or dizygotic pairs, i.e. those with different heredity. In addition we confined ourselves exclusively to those of the same sex and such pairs of whom at least one partner had been sentenced.

[. . .] The concordant monozygotic pairs should reveal to us the similar effect of similar innate tendencies, whilst the differences in their cases should enable us to estimate the importance of environmental factors. Nevertheless, if we consider their histories from this point of view, we are struck by finding complete agreement, far beyond what we might have reasonably expected, in the behaviour of a whole number of pairs. I only wish to remind the reader of the brothers Heufelder, Meister, Lauterbach, and Ostertag, as well as the Dieners and Maats, and the sisters Messer. In all these cases the type of crime is absolutely similar, the criminal careers begin at about the same age, and the behaviour of both in court and in prison corresponds absolutely. The Heufelders are old burglars, both of whom have been behind iron bars for nearly two decades and both of whom show paranoiac symptoms in prison. Both brothers Meister commit puerile offences against the laws of property, and both in prison suffer deeply owing to their terrified imaginations. The Lauterbachs are quite unusual swindlers, crooks almost of genius, who keep the upper hand even in court, and whose 'respectability' in prison is almost as great as their unblushing impudence. Both brothers Ostertag have just too little sense and will-power, at least in view of the ambitions induced in them by their happy, prosperous youth. The two Dieners, guttersnipes, but good fellows at heart, cannot stand alcohol; it makes them rabid and draws the knives from their pockets. The Maat brothers have not a scrap of affection for anyone in the whole wide world except their own unpleasant selves. Their abnormal sexuality leads them into intimate relationships, but even these only seem to be of value to them if they can exploit those with whom they are involved. Finally, the sisters Messer suffer from a degree of nymphomania which must be rare. In all these cases we see the results of the common law which binds these pairs of twins to one another.

JOHANNES LANGE (translated by Charlotte Haldane)

---

from The Krays

THE second of March 1952 was a grey day at the end of another London winter, and the Tower of London gave a grim welcome to the two quiet young men in identical blue suits who arrived among that morning's sparse crop of tourists at the main gate by the Shrewsbury Tower. They showed the Yeoman Warder the official form they had received three weeks earlier, and he directed them past Traitor's Gate to the Waterloo Building opposite the White Tower, the headquarters of the Royal Fusiliers.

Few regiments excel at the welcome of newcomers, and the Waterloo Building – a Victorian block of old-fashioned military ferocity – was enough to make any recruit wonder what he was in for. But the twins seemed unconcerned. They smiled at no one and said nothing. A sergeant put them in line and led them off to the other-ranks' mess for a meal. When they had eaten and were ordered outside to collect their uniforms and equipment, they went along with thirty or so other new recruits. Their squad corporal took over. He showed them their barrack room, allocated beds, and prepared to start the hard sharp lesson that turns mere boys into grown soldiers. He began by showing them how to lay their kit out – small pack above large pack, greatcoat above the bed with brasses gleaming, back and front. He told them the toe-caps of both pairs of boots must be shiny enough to see their faces in by the weekend. And he paused to explain how pride in appearance was the mark of all good soldiers, but that if you were lucky enough to be a Fusilier . . .

Before the corporal could explain what was so special about the Royal Fusiliers the two recruits in the identical blue suits started walking towards the door.

The corporal stopped. He was not the man to take nonsense from recruits but had never faced a situation quite like this before.

'And where might you be going?'

The twins paused, faces expressionless except for a faint but identical raising of the eyebrows.

'I said, where d'you think you're off to, you lovely pair?'

One of the twins spoke then, as quietly as if telling somebody the time.

'We don't care for it here. We're off home to see our mum.' They continued to walk towards the door.

The corporal felt the two boys were trying to make a fool of him, and grabbed one by the arm.

There was something strange about what happened then. Violence is usually accompanied by some sign of emotion but the faces of the twins remained expressionless. There was a thud. The corporal staggered back against the wall, holding his jaw – and still unspeaking, still unhurrying, the twins, in their dark blue suits, walked down the stairs and out across the square where the ravens perched and the last of the afternoon sightseers was being shown the spot where Queen Anne Boleyn lost her head four hundred years or so before.

Ronald and Reginald Kray of the Royal Fusiliers were back at Vallance Road in time for tea.

The ending of National Service is often seen as a factor in the rise of lawlessness among the young. Perhaps. But for the Kray twins it is undeniable that without the two years they were now to spend in contact with the army, they would never have been able to take over the East End with the speed and ruthlessness they showed when finally released in the spring of 1954.

Next morning, just before daybreak, the police called at Vallance Road. The twins, who had spent their first night of service to Queen and Country at a dance-hall in Tottenham, were asleep. But they had been expecting the police. They yawned, dressed, made no attempt to resist, and telling their mother not to worry as they'd soon be back, went downstairs and into the police car which carried them to Bethnal Green police station where a military escort returned them to the Tower. They were placed in a cell, presented with a fresh uniform apiece, told to get shaved, given a slice of bread and mug of army tea, and informed they would be appearing in the Commanding Officer's orderly room next morning charged with being absent without leave.

From the day the Fusiliers tried teaching them the rudiments of discipline and military training, the twins found something they could never really do without – an enemy.

They also discovered certain skills they needed from the army – lessons in organization and morale, of leadership and weaponry and propaganda which were to prove invaluable when the time came to organize a private army of their own. They learned about themselves as well – how much they could take and just how tough they really were; together with the advantages of being twins. They learned how vulnerable a large organization can be, and taught themselves new ways of making officials ridiculous. They tested out their powers of resistance – and found them more than adequate.

Next morning the twins were lined up among the other petty offenders to face the charge of absence without leave and striking an NCO in the lawful exercise of his duty. By army standards these were serious charges. The corporal gave his evidence and normally this would have led to a court-martial. But there would have been something faintly ridiculous about court-martialling a pair of boys for knocking out an NCO on their first afternoon in the army. There was also a practical difficulty which no one had thought of until that moment. Which of these identical young tearaways landed the actual blow?

The corporal wasn't sure, but thought it was the one on the far left.

'Were you the one who attacked the corporal?' the CO asked Private Ronald Kray.

'No, sir.'

'Then it must have been you.'

'Oh no, sir.'

'Well, one of you did it.'

This was a situation the twins had faced since childhood and they knew exactly how to act.

'Did what, sir?'

'Struck this NCO.'

'But which one of us are you accusing, sir?'

'Whichever of you made this cowardly assault. Who did?'

The twins shrugged their shoulders – an impertinent gesture and a slightly uncanny one, for they did it together.

[. . .] In the early fifties a large hotel off Piccadilly Circus was leading one of the strangest double lives of any eating place in London.

During the day the tea-rooms and the downstairs restaurants with their Odeon-style décor and absolute respectability were a great place for children's teas and maiden-ladies' outings with the most reliable poached egg in Central London.

But around midnight with the aunts and school children safely in their beds, their places in the Lloyd-Loom chairs would be taken by a very different clientele. And by one o'clock the downstairs tea-room, which stayed open through the night, was transformed into an informal club – part sanctuary, part labour exchange – for half the petty thieves and criminals in London.

'A regular den of thieves,' is how one of the regulars remembers it. It was certainly convenient, and cheap – and close to all the places where criminals could work.

It was not the place for the upper echelons of crime. They had more exclusive social territory. But in the old days, after midnight in the big downstairs lounge of the hotel, one saw the social side of West End crime – the small-time fences and ponces, the informers and thieves and pickpockets, the villains and the bouncers who required work or a chat and the society of their own kind. This was where the twins were brought by Dickie Morgan, and they soon began to make their mark on this nocturnal criminal society.

Almost everyone who met them now agrees there was a strange air of innocence about them which marked them out from other villains round about them. Some thought them shy. They were extraordinarily polite to anyone older who took the trouble to talk to them. They never bragged, were never loud-mouthed, never seemed to swear. Among a race of almost universal gamblers they never gambled. Among womanizers and ponces they showed no interest in women. Among hard-drinkers they were never drunk.

Most of the time they would just sit – slightly apart from everybody else – usually silent and impassive, watching and listening to what went on. Several who knew them now remark upon their eyes. 'There was something about them that bored right through you, especially if you were lying to them. You always felt they knew.'

They also had an air of weirdness and danger, which everybody noticed from the start. Some say they cultivated this quite consciously. Certainly they did so later. Natural actors that they were, they picked up all the tricks of instilling fear with an economy of effort and projecting their presence to maximum effect. But what distinguished them even now from all the other violent characters around them, is that they had an extraordinary presence to project.

It remains something of a mystery. Part of it was due to their behaviour as identical twins. With their telepathy and uncanny similarity their effect was literally double that of a normal individual, and this certainly explains much of their effectiveness. So does their imperviousness to pain and danger. They were so fit and vicious that they had already perfected a technique of synchronized and ruthless combat which rendered them invulnerable as long as they stayed together.

But there was something else. 'They were,' says one old villain who came up against them shortly afterwards, 'a thoroughly evil pair of bastards.' And from now on in their story, the idea continually recurs that they were uniquely and positively 'evil'.

Largely because of this the twins were accepted as true villains from the start. Without knowing exactly why, older and more experienced thugs were wary of them. One or two who weren't were dealt with efficiently and unemotionally, but these were 'unimportant nobodies' – 'liberty-takers' who hadn't the good sense to understand the twins for what they were. There was an old wrestler, working as a doorman at a club in Berwick Street who had the stupidity to refer to the twins as 'boys' and whose jaw was nearly broken by a punch that sent all sixteen stone of him down the stairs to the men's room.

People who befriended them were shrewder. 'You never knew who you'd be needing next time. You weren't getting any tougher or any younger and it was common sense to keep on the right side of a pair of up-and-coming youngsters like the twins.'

[. . .] The Kray trial might have been not just the longest, but the most fascinating murder trial in history. That it was not was really the twins' own decision. They wanted privacy and got it; they were the ones who stopped the one defence that could conceivably have shaken the prosecution's case, a defence based upon the nature and responsibility of twins.

The fact that there had never been a case like this argued in law before need not have mattered. There had never been a pair of criminal twins like the Krays before, and only in recent years has the relationship between identical twins been understood. It seems indisputable that Reggie Kray could have built a powerful defence along the lines of diminished responsibility, had he chosen to. But this would have meant betraying Ronnie and denouncing him as his evil genius. It would also have meant the end of Ronnie's world, the destruction of the twins and of the violent dream that had sustained them both since childhood.

Gratefully the court was spared the task of settling responsibility for crimes committed when one disordered mind can dominate two separate bodies. Whatever may have been the truth, the twins were judged as separate and responsible individuals. This was what everybody wanted, themselves included. And it was as separate and responsible murderers that they were sentenced to life imprisonment, 'which I would recommend should not be less than thirty years', by Mr Justice Melford Stevenson on 8 March 1969.

The twins were thirty-four. Their active life was over.

JOHN PEARSON, *The Profession of Violence*

3

LOVE AND HATE

ঙ&

D ID MY sister and I love each other? I'm afraid so. We might have found life much easier if we hadn't; for I don't think we liked each other very much, and even the love was profoundly suspicious – on my sister's side anyway. I was partly to blame for that, of course. I was the high-profile, 'successful' twin, the university entrant, the one who'd published a book and been given all the attention that being published so young tends to entail. Yet how could I not glory in this – when, still worse from her point of view, I was not taking it for granted? At that stage one does take such success as one's due, rather, not realising the precariousness of things. The problem for her, it seemed, was that it wasn't her due; which must have felt quite unfair. We were twins after all, and she could not duck the inevitable questions, from tactless outsiders, as well maybe from her own psyche; if your twin's going to Oxford/getting published, why aren't you? A situation made worse by a subsequent decision of our parents. Having agreed, reluctantly – my father did not believe in further academic education for females – to let me go to university, they made her stay at home and take a secretarial course in the nearby town rather than in London as she'd been promised. They couldn't afford Oxford for me and London for her, they said. Such is the material which weaves itself into twin relationships, transforming love into hate, setting guilt to crush some of the joy in achievement – and resentment to fester on both sides.

But we did love each other, also. Love between twins can be a very powerful and touching thing – as between twins already quoted in this book; the sister who gave her life to looking after her deformed and mentally defective twin; the girl who swapped clothes with her twin brother when he was being pursued by a lynch mob. Just so, I woke from the emergency Caesarian which launched my first child, to find my sister by my bedside, to my huge surprise. We had agreed, both of us, I did not need her. She had been in Scotland; but something kept telling her that I was in trouble, as I was. And so she had come. That was, I think, the first time in our lives we actually embraced.

Till then our physical contact had always been fighting, no holds barred: between siblings at least, our family never had gone in for physical affection. In the piece here René Zazzo suggests that sexual games between twins are more common than is usually suspected; and that repressed desire may be a factor where the incest taboo operates with particular fury, and physical contact is shunned. I never fancied my twin in the slightest. Quite the reverse – the thought of her sexuality did – still does – appal me. So, who knows.

Certainly, to judge from the large amount of fiction about incestuous – or would-be incestuous – twins, the possibility of physical activity between such close siblings lies deep within universal consciousness: much traditional prejudice against twins, particularly boy/girl twins, arises from the assumption that they will have had such relations in the womb. The Balinese, for instance, as we see here, insist on twins being brought up apart – if they are commoners that is. For some reason, in Bali, incest is all right if the pair are aristocratic.

What may be less common than supposed – though there are endless fictions to the contrary – is twins being attracted to the same person – or one person being attracted to both twins, even seemingly look-alike ones. Recent American research has suggested that in reality the sexual partner of one twin rarely fancies the other, nor is it common for both twins to fall for the same person – clearly sexual chemistry at least is not a matter of genetics. Human nature being what it is, of course the desire to collect operates in the sexual sphere as any other, meaning that, for some, making love to both of a pair of twins would seem a prize worth pursuing. To judge from the piece here about the twins bought for $40,000, we were not the only female twins to see a particular gleam in the eye of some of our suitors. Not that it ever came to anything in our case – I never fancied any of her sexual partners in the slightest; whether she fancied mine I don't know. It was one of the many subjects we never discussed.

In some stories, competition over lovers leads to acts of generosity between twins – as with Angela Carter's pair, one of whom gave the other a night with her lover as a twenty-first birthday present, unbeknown to the boy himself. Alternatively, it leads to hate and even murder between previously amicable twins, or brings the warring of inimical twins to a climax. For some twins are inimical from the start – if Esau and Jacob are the paradigm, from the womb itself. But twins are not necessarily twin souls; far from it. We weren't. Whether or not we fought in the womb there is no knowing, but certainly we fought thereafter. As toddlers, we could be issued with nothing but soft toys, since anything might be used as a weapon to beat over our heads. Aged 12, at boarding school, we survived one term of being allowed to sleep in the same bedroom, because our other roommates could not bear the sight of us fighting to the death all over the floor. But as girls we were spared at least that particular cause of rivalry among male twins – Esau and Jacob again the paradigm – where inheritance of the first-born is at stake; another rich source of fiction, though which twin is supposed to inherit varies. (In France, for instance, logically, if almost certainly inaccurately, the second-born is imagined to be the first conceived and so the eldest. Among the Yoruba, the first twin born is sent to test or taste the world on behalf of the other, making the second-born twin again ascendant.) One interesting variant of the theme, the story by Algernon Blackwood, has the twins' father objecting to his heirs coming double, not the twins themselves quarrelling.

Perfect love between twins can be found, probably, and perfect hate. But if intense rivalry may be more of an issue between fraternal twins who have all these differences to counter, identical twins, too, may have their problems; some of the writings of the Gibbons – the Silent Twins – make that clear, leading me to guess that twins of most kinds usually swing between the two extremes of feeling. We certainly did; bound willingly and unwillingly by each other; to the extent that relations with others, friends and lovers alike, were, are, contaminated by the extremes of feeling generated by our twin; feelings that, like many twins, no doubt, we sought (in my case still seek?) vainly and sometimes fatally to find in other partnerships. Or, on the contrary, tried avoiding there. Yet since no amount of willpower could stop us attempting to make new twins of these partners, all too often we did end up re-enacting aspects of our difficult twinship with them; something not uncommon between twins and their intimates, I suspect.

TWINS AS LOVED
AND LOVERS

She turned as she drew the bolt on the tall gate . . . to let me out and asked suddenly with a benign look, 'You love your sister?' Love! *Love*, Roz? A searching question indeed, one I could only stammer over.

'Yes . . . No! I don't know . . . I could not say, 'She is my twin, twins do not love one another!' which was what came to my lips.

IANTHE JERROLD, *My Twin and I*

Everything is still asleep, except that in one of the St Brigitte's dormitories a faint light is burning. Our glory hole. Our clothes peel off. We curl up together head to tail, laughing to find ourselves so salty. Will we complete our seminal communion or will sleep overcome our ritual?

MICHEL TOURNIER, *Gemini*

Love indeed. Here maybe we have the most absolute, the most indisputable form of union between two human souls.

RENÉ ZAZZO

from The Faerie Queene

FOR at that berth another Babe she bore,
   To weet the mighty *Ollyphant,* that wrought
   Great wreake to many errant knights of yore,
   And many hath to foule confusion brought.
   These twinnes, men say, (a thing far passing thought)
   Whiles in their mothers wombe enclosed they were,
   Ere they into the lightsome world were brought,
   In fleshly lust were mingled both yfere,
And in that monstrous wise did to the world appere.

So liu'd they euer after in like sin,
   Gainst natures law, and good behauioure:
   But greatest shame was to that maiden twin,
   Who not content so fowly to deuoure
   Her natiue flesh, and staine her brothers bowre,
   Did wallow in all other fleshly myre,
   And suffred beasts her body to deflowre:
   So whot she burned in that lustfull fyre,
Yet all that might not slake her sensuall desyre.

EDMUND SPENSER

---

from Twins in Bali

Description of the Ritual at Sukawană, District of Kintamani, Bali

ON the night of September 18, 1933, twins were born to woman of Sukawană. When the family saw that the twins were a boy and a girl, they knew that this was a great wrong, that disaster had come upon their house and upon their village.

[. . .] On the morning following the birth of the twins the men of the village tore down the house where they were born. It did not take long, for the houses of Sukawană are but a single chamber fitted with a raised sleeping-platform on either side of a low hearth – three stones on a mud floor. The walls are of solid two-inch boards, the roof a shingle of split bamboo, turned inner side upward to make gutters for the rain. When the house was in pieces, the men loaded it on their shoulders and carried it off down the steep trail to the edge of the graveyard. Behind them came the women bearing mats, baskets, clay pots, a coconut spoon, all the furnishings and contents of the house. When they had finished, the place where the house had stood lay bare and empty, a break in the trim line of the compound, like the gap of a fallen tooth.

If the new house which was to be built up out of the materials of the old had been to accommodate only the family of the twins, the building would have been easy, for the wood is joined, the pillars fit into the beams, and the roof bamboos hang on their supports by slits cut in the lower side of each shingle. But the new *kubu* was to accommodate some fifty men. These were the watchmen, the *gĕbagan*, relatives and villagers who would take turns sleeping there beside the graveyard. Why must they watch – what must they watch for? Are they the keepers of the unlucky parents? No, the people say they come out of compassion, to help the banished ones, for it is lonely beside the grave-yard and evil creatures (*léyak*) roam there at night, and one would not dare to be there alone, no, not even ten strong men would dare to sleep there, but if there are fifty it is noisy and no one is afraid.

So the villagers brought bamboo poles and rough mats of woven coconut fronds and sheaves of the long grass which grows upon the hillsides. With the posts of the old house and a few green trees as supports, they patched together a shelter some forty feet long by twelve feet wide. (The original house measured perhaps fifteen feet by nine.) At the northwest end (*tĕbènan*) of the building a private room was walled off for the parents with the twins, provided with a hearth for their use. The watchmen have two long rows of boards laid on stones for their sleeping place, and a kitchen outside to the southeast. The mother and the father of the twins may not cook their food in the same kitchen with the watchmen, for they are too unclean.

By evening the *kubu* was ready, a draughty and uncomfortable place, for the reception of the unlucky family. The mother of the twins, still weak from a difficult birth, was carried down the hillside and installed in this prison which she might not leave for a month and seven days.

[. . .] I have heard in Bali that twins such as these are 'wrong' because the boy and the girl are as if married in the womb. I have heard also that if a boy child brings his wife with him out of the womb, it is a birth such as only gods and kings may have. For the common *sudră* it is an affront to the *rajă* (*mamadă rajă dalĕm*) to have children in this way.

JANE BELO

Luca . . . seemed aware of the presence of his sister inside the womb and frequently reached out for her with gentle touching and stroking motions . . . When one year old Alice and Luca could often be seen engaged in their favourite game of using the curtain of their living room as a kind of dividing membrance, gently stroking their heads through it as they had in their pre-natal past.

ALESSANDRA PIONTELLI, From Fetus to Child

---

from Absolute Hush

THERE came a sudden muffled cry from the top of the house.

'I said they'd got some animal,' groaned Mrs Lovage.

Sissy and George, in the servants' bedroom, chair up against the door, window shutters closed, were struggling strenuously to emulate the illustrated postures of the fucking satyrs and the big-bottomed nymphs on the bedspread. The small room got hot, their awakened bodies gave off unfamiliar smells, and the quilt began to smell sharply of antique lanoline fermented in the body odours of the Plague House guests.

Excited, they thrashed about wildly and let out little screams.

George felt such a thrill at the sight of Sissy's fat red mouth that he pressed his own against it. It felt warm and wet and tasty. He ran his tongue across her teeth and felt stirred when he encountered their sharp smoothness.

They rubbed their fat soft cheeks together, sucked and nibbled each other, and every now and again would study the quilt. After a while, they felt confident enough to try out experiments of their own with toes and tongues.

They discovered that George's tits stood up as well as Sissy's. Sissy did not want to appear jealous but it seemed unfair that George, with his own large talent, should compete so favourably with her small ones.

Then George found, nestled among Sissy's scarlet petals, a tiny willy that stiffened when he caressed it with his tongue.

He sprang up excited, as though he had unburied a treasure. 'Look! Look!' he cried.

Sissy tried to see too, curling her body round like a Chelsea bun, but there were too many bits of her and George in the way.

'I'll tiptoe down and get Mummy's mirror,' said George.

But Sissy clung to him crying, 'No! No! Keep doing it! I don't mind not seeing!'

Down in the kitchen Mrs Lovage said, 'I could go and look, dear, if you're worried.' She spoke without conviction and was disappointed when Elizabeth agreed enthusiastically, 'Oh, do, Mrs Lovage. What an angel you are.'

'Well, are you really sure, dear? I mean there's not much harm they can get up to in the attics, is there?' There were an awful lot of stairs to the top of the house, and Mrs Lovage's knees were aching from having just finished the kitchen floor.

But ever since Elizabeth had seen the children furtively slinking, she had been troubled by a sense of unease.

'Oh, be a love and have a look all the same,' she cried fervently. If Mrs Lovage went, then Elizabeth would not have to be confronted with her children doing something really ghastly and Mrs Lovage would be able to break it to her gently.

Mrs Lovage gave just the right sort of sigh as she put down her cup, balanced her fag on the edge of the ashtray, then rose stiffly. She did these things very slowly in case Elizabeth had second thoughts and said, 'Don't worry, Mrs L. It doesn't matter,' but Elizabeth just kept leaning forward and smiling at her hopefully.

'Off I go, then,' said Mrs Lovage, making herself sound weary but willing, so that Elizabeth, instead of sensing reluctance, said, 'You are kindness itself, Mrs L.'

Mrs Lovage gave her one last brave smile as she went towards the door.

Elizabeth sighed, leant back in her chair, and began luxuriously to plan the party for which Mrs Lovage's Myrtle's Yank's PX – what a vulgar word, only Americans would buy their provisions from somewhere known only by initials – would provide.

Dealing with the children always aggravated Mrs Lovage and she considered, as she puffed her way through the hall, that you would never have imagined that someone as gracious as Elizabeth could have such coarse children. She was determined to catch the children unawares, for there was no point in puffing and grunting to the top if, when she arrived, they had hidden the evidence. Tiptoeing, she came on to the first landing and from overhead she heard another of those strange shrill cries.

'You haven't got a hole,' George said.

'You must be trying in the wrong place,' said Sissy, offended and frustrated. 'Try again. Ouch!'

'You can't expect me to be like those satyrs if you're going to scream all the time,' complained George.

'It hurts!' cried Sissy. 'The nymphs are all smiling as though they're having fun. None of them is in agony!'

The pair examined the figures on the quilt yet again.

'True,' sighed George. 'But there seems to be quite a lot of difference between them and you. You are fatter in the middle and they are fatter higher up and lower down.'

'It's no use pointing out my faults,' snapped Sissy. 'The nymphs – all except for that one who's doing something funny that I wouldn't exactly like to do myself – are looking blissful. I think I should be able to lie looking blissful while you do things to me, George. I mean, I didn't have to do anything when it was the Italian prisoner. He did it all.'

After a sad pause, George said in a low voice, 'There seems to be a big difference between me and the satyrs too.'

'Yes. Well. You haven't got hooves. So what?' said Sissy crisply. 'The Italian prisoner didn't have hooves and he would have got his huge big thing in me without any trouble at all if you hadn't gone screaming for Mummy.'

They heard Mrs Lovage calling from the bottom of the stairs.

'Don't make a sound,' breathed Sissy, pressing her fingers against her brother's mouth.

'Kiddies, are you up there?' called Mrs Lovage in a high and quavery voice.

George and Sissy held their breath.

Mrs Lovage sighed, felt tired, and could not face another flight, nor bear the thought of hunting the dirty children through the little attic bedrooms. Suppose they were hiding from her. It had happened before. She had gone from room to room, looking for them and feeling sure they watched her, unseen, silently sniggering, filthy little things. Then she would have climbed up all those stairs for nothing.

She called, 'George! Sissy! If you are there, answer me at once!' in her strict voice and when this received no answer either, gave up and returned to the kitchen, saying, 'Behaving perfectly.'

'Good,' said Elizabeth. Softly drawing on her cigarette, she gazed out of the window and felt that even her children must have been purified by such a day.

*   *   *

Mrs Lovage had often hinted at something dirty that George and Sissy, sharing a bed, might be doing.

'What sort of thing?' they would ask, longing to know, loving dirtiness, and not able to guess how to proceed with what Mrs Lovage suspected them of. Until today, when they realized that the instructions for dirtiness were all embroidered on the Nymph bedspread.

'It's what Teddy must have been doing to Mummy,' giggled George,

'They weren't laughing,' said Sissy. 'They were struggling and grunting and serious.'

George, thoughtful for a moment, said, 'Well, Mummy never could see a joke.'

'Mr and Mrs Lovage must do it,' gasped Sissy after a moment.

'Perhaps everybody you see walking about does,' said George.

SARA BANERJI

from The Valkerie

SIEGLINDE   (*beside herself*)
    Was Wälse your father,
    and are you a Wälsung?
    Then it is yours,
    that sword in the tree!
    So now let me name you
    as I have loved you:
    Siegmund—
    that is your name!

SIEGMUND
        [*He leaps up, hurries to the trunk, and grasps the sword hilt*]
    Siegmund call me,
    and Siegmund am I!
    The proof is the sword,
    my hand soon shall hold it!
    Promised by Wälse
    in hour of need,
    now it is found;
    I grasp it now!

Holiest love
in highest need,
yearning desire
in longing and need,
burning bright in my breast,
drives to deeds and death.
  Notung! Notung!
  So name I the sword!
  Notung! Notung!
  Bright, shining steel!
  Show me your sharpness,
  glorious blade!
  Come forth from the scabbard to me!

[*With a powerful effort, Siegmund draws the sword from the tree, and
shows it to the astonished and enraptured Sieglinde*]

Siegmund, the Wälsung,
here you see!
As bride-gift
he brings you this sword:
he claims with it
his loveliest bride;
and from this house
he leads her away.
Far from here,
follow me now,
forth to the laughing
land of bright Spring.
Your guard is Notung, the sword,
should Siegmund die, conquered by love!

[*He has embraced her, to draw her away with him*]

SIEGLINDE
  [*In highest excitement she tears herself away and stands before him*]

Is this Siegmund,
standing before me?
Sieglinde am I;
I longed for you.
  Your own dear sister
and bride you have won with the sword!

SIEGMUND
  Bride and sister
  be to your brother;
the blood of the Wälsungs is blessed!

[*He draws her to him with passionate fervour; with a cry, she falls on
his breast. The curtain falls quickly*]

RICHARD WAGNER: trs. Andrew Porter

---

from The Blood of the Walsungs

'MAY I come in, Gigi?' asked Sieglinde.

'Yes, come in,' he answered.

She was already dressed, in a frock of shimmering sea-green silk,
with a square neck outlined by a wide band of beige embroidery.
Two embroidered peacocks facing each other above the girdle held
a garland in their beaks. Her dark brown hair was unadorned; but a
large egg-shaped precious stone hung on a thin pearl chain against
her bare skin, the colour of smoked meerschaum. Over her arm she
carried a scarf heavily worked with silver.

'I am unable to conceal from you,' she said, 'that the carriage is
waiting.' He parried at once:

'And I have no hesitation in replying that it will have to wait patiently
two minutes more.' It was at least ten. She sat down on the white velvet
chaise-longue and watched him at his labours.

Out of a rich chaos of ties he selected a white piqué band and began
to tie it before the glass.

'Beckerath,' said she, 'wears coloured cravats, crossed over the way
they wore them last year.'

'Beckerath,' said he, 'is the most trivial existence I have ever had
under my personal observation.' Turning to her quickly he added:
'Moreover, you will do me the favour of not mentioning that German's
name to me again this evening.'

She gave a short laugh and replied: 'You may be sure it will not be
a hardship.'

He put on the low-cut piqué waistcoat and drew his dress coat over
it, the white silk lining caressing his hands as they passed through the
sleeves.

'Let me see which buttons you chose,' said Sieglinde. They were the amethyst ones; shirt-studs, cuff-links, and waistcoat buttons, a complete set.

She looked at him admiringly, proudly, adoringly, with a world of tenderness in her dark, shining eyes. He kissed the lips lying so softly on each other. They spent another minute on the chaise-longue in mutual caresses.

'Quite, quite soft you are again,' said she, stroking his shaven cheeks.

'Your little arm feels like satin,' said he, running his hand down her tender forearm. He breathed in the violet odour of her hair.

She kissed him on his closed eyelids; he kissed her on the throat where the pendant hung. They kissed one another's hands. They loved one another sweetly, sensually, for sheer mutual delight in their own well-groomed, pampered, expensive smell. They played together like puppies, biting each other with their lips. Then he got up.

'We mustn't be too late today,' said he. He turned the top of the perfume bottle upside down on his handkerchief one last time, rubbed a drop into his narrow red hands, took his gloves, and declared himself ready to go.

He put out the light and they went along the red-carpeted corridor hung with dark old oil paintings and down the steps past the little organ. In the vestibule on the ground floor Wendelin was waiting with their coats, very tall in his yellow paletot. They yielded their shoulders to his ministrations; Sieglinde's dark head was half lost in her collar of silver fox. Followed by the servant they passed through the stone-paved vestibule into the outer air. It was mild, and there were great ragged flakes of snow in the pearly air. The coupé awaited them. The coachman bent down with his hand to his cockaded hat while Wendelin ushered the brother and sister to their seats; then the door banged shut, he swung himself up to the box, and the carriage was at once in swift motion. It crackled over the gravel, glided through the high, wide gate, curved smoothly to the right, and rolled away.

The luxurious little space in which they sat was pervaded by a gentle warmth. 'Shall I shut us in?' Siegmund asked. She nodded and he drew the brown silk curtains across the polished panes.

They were in the city's heart. Lights flew past behind the curtains. Their horses' hoofs rhythmically beat the ground, the carriage swayed noiselessly over the pavement, and round them roared and shrieked and thundered the machinery of urban life. Quite safe and shut away they sat among the wadded brown silk cushions, hand in hand. The carriage drew up and stopped. Wendelin was at the door to help them out. A little group of grey-faced shivering folk stood in the brilliance of the arc-lights and followed them with hostile glances as they passed through the lobby. It was already late, they were the last. They mounted the staircase, threw their cloaks over Wendelin's arms, paused a second before a high mirror, then went through the little door into their box. They were greeted by the last sounds before the hush – voices and the slamming of seats. The lackey pushed their plush-upholstered chairs beneath them; at that moment the lights went down and below their box the orchestra broke into the wild pulsating notes of the prelude.

Night, and tempest . . . And they, who had been wafted hither on the wings of ease, with no petty annoyances on the way, were in exactly the right mood and could give all their attention at once. Storm, a raging tempest, without in the wood. The angry god's command resounded, once, twice repeated in its wrath, obediently the thunder crashed. The curtain flew up as though blown by the storm. There was the rude hall, dark save for a glow on the pagan hearth. In the centre towered up the trunk of the ash tree. Siegmund appeared in the doorway and leaned against the wooden post beaten and harried by the storm. Draggingly he moved forwards on his sturdy legs wrapped round with hide and thongs. He was rosy-skinned, with a straw-coloured beard; beneath his blond brows and the blond forelock of his wig his blue eyes were directed upon the conductor, with an imploring gaze. At last the orchestra gave way to his voice, which rang clear and metallic, though he tried to make it sound like a gasp. He sang a few bars, to the effect that no matter to whom the hearth belonged he must rest upon it; and at the last word he let himself drop heavily on the bearskin rug and lay there with his head cushioned on his plump arms. His breast heaved in slumber. A minute passed, filled with the singing, speaking flow of the music, rolling its waves at the feet of the events on the stage . . . Sieglinde entered from the left. She had an alabaster bosom which rose and fell marvellously beneath her muslin robe and deerskin mantle. She displayed surprise at sight of the strange man; pressed her chin upon her breast until it was double, put her lips in position and expressed it, this surprise, in tones which swelled soft and warm from her white throat and were given shape by her tongue and her mobile lips. She tended the stranger; bending over him so that he could see the white flower of her bosom rising from the rough skins, she gave him with both hands the drinking horn. He drank. The music spoke movingly to him of cool refreshment and cherishing care. They looked at each other with the beginning of enchantment, a first dim recognition, standing rapt while the orchestra interpreted in a melody of profound enchantment.

[. . .] The storm whistled, a gust of wind burst open the door, a flood of white electric light poured into the hall. Divested of darkness they stood and sang their song of spring and spring's sister, love!

Crouching on the bearskin they looked at each other in the white light, as they sang their duet of love. Their bare arms touched each other's as they held each other by the temples and gazed into each other's eyes, and as they sang their mouths were very near. They compared their eyes, their foreheads, their voices – they were the same. The growing, urging recognition wrung from his breast his father's name; she called him by his: Siegmund! Siegmund! He freed the sword, he swung it above his head, and submerged in bliss she told him in song who she was: his twin sister, Sieglinde. In ravishment he stretched out his arms to her, his bride, she sank upon his breast – the curtain fell as the music swelled into a roaring, rushing, foaming whirlpool of passion – swirled and swirled and with one mighty throb stood still.

Rapturous applause. The lights went on. A thousand people got up, stretched unobtrusively as they clapped, then made ready to leave the hall, with heads still turned towards the stage, where the singers appeared before the curtain, like masks hung out in a row at a fair . . .

Siegmund pushed back his chair and stood up. He was hot; little red patches showed on his cheek-bones, above the lean, sallow, shaven cheeks.

'For my part,' said he, 'what I want now is a breath of fresh air. Siegmund was pretty feeble, wasn't he?'

'Yes,' answered Sieglinde, 'and the orchestra saw fit to drag abominably in the Spring Song.'

'Frightfully sentimental,' said Siegmund, shrugging his narrow shoulders in his dress coat. 'Are you coming out?' She lingered a moment, with her elbows on the ledge, still gazing at the stage. He looked at her as she rose and took up her silver scarf. Her soft, full lips were quivering.

They went into the foyer and mingled with the slow-moving throng, downstairs and up again, sometimes holding each other by the hand.

'I should enjoy an ice,' said she, 'if they were not in all probability uneatable.'

'Don't think of it,' said he. So they ate bonbons out of their box – maraschino cherries and chocolate beans filled with cognac.

THOMAS MANN

_____

from Le Paradoxe des Jumeaux

CONTEMPORARY fiction abounds in stories of twin love, of incest between twin brothers and sisters. The scientific literature, on the other hand is almost silent on these issues. Are we then about to open a wholly new chapter in twin studies . . .? I'm not sure. Are such loves the exception or simply the extreme? Even writing the word 'love' I'm not sure what exactly it evokes.

Best to begin, maybe, by letting twins speak for themselves, using extracts from much longer interviews already published elsewhere. I interviewed each twin separately, with the proviso that the twin seen first had to promise not to communicate to his fellow twin either my questions or his answers. I'd known all of my subjects for several years, and I don't think that any of them concealed the truth from me, intentionally at least. Indeed, the fact that their statements almost always tallied validates all the more those instances where the pair disagreed as to the significance of the acts reported.

. . . All the couples in my study were monozygotic, thus by definition of the same sex. Heterosexual incest, therefore, escaped my net. As, too, what might have been an interesting comparison between monozygotic and dizogotic twins of the same sex . . .

Irene and Lucienne. 14 years, 3 months.

Irene. We often 'play' with each other. Each night. It's not just a matter of pleasure, there's feeling in it. I'm in love with my sister. She's in love with me . . . I'm jealous of her physically.

Lucienne. I've played with my twin since we were about two years old. Once or twice a week . . . it's a need for physical pleasure linked to a need for affection. But I don't think it's real love.

Jacques and Michel. 28 years.

Michel. We always shared a bed – and then at night, involuntarily . . . it always left a feeling of shame the next day. But these physical contacts, these sex games did not put me off girls. I had my first girlfriend at the age of 15, my first affair at 17.

. . . (3 years earlier – trying to prevent his brother's marriage. Michel had defined the different kinds of love, of pairings, thus.

> Yes, I love women, that's not the issue. To make love – fine; but to tie yourself to a woman for life, that's crazy. You wouldn't understand – you're not a twin. A man like you must be looking in love for another self. But we twins, we've had this alter ego, this double, right from day one. When you've experienced the intimacy of twinship, all other kinds seem like pale imitations – altogether illusionary. Sexual union with a woman is great, of course. But she remains an unknown – how can you pair for life with an unknown? With only pots and pans and bed linen in common . . .

> We can't allow our twin real friends, either. I remember breaking up one friendship my twin had – to me it seemed out of the question. I always had such great feeling for him. When – very rarely – he allowed me a tender smile, it roused in me the deepest sense of love . . .)

Jeanne and Marie. Aged 30. Had shared a bed till the age of seventeen. At the time of the interview, Marie had been married for nine years.

Jeanne. With my sister? Never! As a child I played that way with a cousin. But with my sister it would have seemed utterly repugnant. When we had to sleep in the same bed we put a bolster between us. I've never kissed her in my life.
Marie. No, absolutely not. We tried to avoid sharing a bed. We've never even kissed.

(On the other hand, Jeanne, like Michel with Jacques, never accepted her sister's marriage. She said she'd get her own back some day. When she'd returned to France after an absence of several years, she'd thrust her own lover into her sister's arms. Both twins told me of these goings-on. Marie, however, . . . claimed her twin suspected nothing. Was she lying, or had she been unknowingly manipulated by Jeanne? I never got that point clear . . . But then one day they arrived in tandem at my laboratory and said their lover was deceiving them with a third woman . . . They wanted me to persuade him to get rid of this rival, and to tell him that the twins would not let him go.

When I roundly refused this commission, they chanted, simultaneously; 'You have known us for fifteen years. As a psychologist, you must have discerned our secret. Left to ourselves we're in danger of falling into the worst kind of perversion . . . If you're our friend, help us. We want to stay normal. Our lover is a carnal link between us, the kind we don't want to have directly.'

Marie's husband had been a rival. The lover was an accomplice. He played the role of intermediary, and also that of the bolster, which had been put between them during their childhood.

I never saw them again. But they wrote to me that they had 'won'. The other woman had been routed. They'd taken off with the man on a pleasure cruise . . .)

RENÉ ZAZZO, trs. Penelope Farmer

---

from Twin Sisters of Marigny

'BUT now, Luigi,' said I. 'Suppose again that there had been two Eves just alike in the garden; and that Adam had found and loved one, and that their love had become sacramental love together, and by and by when she has gone out of his sight he meets the other, but does not know it is another, and loves her; this love becomes sacramental love between them – would this *his* love then be holy love? I don't speak now of her?'

'Only, I should think,' said he, 'Before he knew there were two.'

J.F. BINGHAM

They were as much alike as two bales of cotton . . . Just what the twins would do should Scarlett accept either of them, the twins did not ask. They would cross that bridge when they came to it. For the present they were quite satisfied to be in accord again about one girl, for they had no jealousies between them.

MARGARET MITCHELL, *Gone With the Wind*

---

from Esau and Jacob

I HAVE spoken of Flora's hallucinations before. Truly, they were extraordinary.

On the road, after they left the dock, though the twins were traveling separately and alone, each in his own coupé, she thought she heard them speak – this was the first part of the hallucination. Second part: the two voices fused, so alike were they, and became one. In short, her imagination made of two young men a single person.

I do not believe that this phenomenon is very common. On the contrary, there will no doubt be someone who will not believe me at all and will put down as pure invention what is actually the purest truth. Well, you will be interested to learn that, during her father's mission, Flora heard the two voices fuse into the same voice and the same person, and more than once. And now, in the house in Botafogo, the phenomenon was repeated. When she heard the two brothers without seeing them, her imagination completed the fusion of sound with that of sight, and there appeared to her one single man saying extraordinary words.

All this is no less extraordinary, I admit. If I consulted my own feelings in the matter the two young men would not thus became *one* lad, nor would the young lady remain one damsel. I would rectify nature by doubling Flora. Since this cannot be, I accept the unification of Pedro and Paulo. Because, this effect of vision would be repeated in their presence, as well as in their absence, when she allowed herself to forget the time and the place, and let herself go. At the piano, during a conversation, while out walking in the chácara, at the dinner table, she would have these sudden, brief visions, at which she herself smiled, in the beginning.

[. . .] It was a vague, dark, mysterious spectacle, in which the visible figures became intangible, double became single, single double, a fusion, confusion, diffusion.

[. . .] Now that the nature of the phenomenon has been stated, it is necessary also to state that Flora thought it droll and charming in the beginning. No, I am wrong: in the very beginning, as she was far away, she did not think much about it. Later, it gave her a kind of start or dizzy feeling, but when she got used to passing two into one and one into two, the alternation came to hold a certain charm for her, and she would evoke it just to have a change of scenery. Finally, not even this was necessary, the alternation took place of itself.

Sometimes it was slower than others, on occasion it was instantaneous. The alternations were not so frequent as to border on delirium. In short, she was becoming used to them and taking pleasure in them.

Once in a while, as she lay in bed, before dropping off to sleep, the phenomenon occurred, after much resistance on her part since she did not want to lose her sleep. But sleep would come, and dream complete the waking vision. In the dream, Flora walked, on the arm of the same loved youth, Paulo, if it was not Pedro, and they went along gazing at stars and mountains, or perhaps the sea, as it murmured lovers' sighs, or raged, and at the flowers and the ruins. Not infrequently they were alone, against a piece of sky bright with moonlight, or all studded with stars like a strip of dark blue cloth. It was at the window, for example, from outside came the song of soft winds, a great mirror hanging from the wall reproduced her outline and his, in confirmation of her imagination. As it was a dream, her imagination conjured unheard of sights, so great and so many that one would scarcely believe they could all fit into the space of a single night. But they did, and with room to spare. It sometimes happened that Flora suddenly awoke, lost the picture and the shape, persuaded herself that it was all illusion, and then she rarely went back to step. If it was early, she got up, walked about till she was tired, fell asleep again, and dreamed of something else.

Other times, the vision remained after the dream had gone – a single handsome figure, with the same caressing voice, the same beseeching gesture. One night, as she was about to place her arms on its shoulders with the unconscious aim of locking her fingers behind its neck, reality, though absent, demanded its rights, and the single youthful figure became two – the two persons that so resembled each other.

This change gave the two waking visions such a stamp of phantas-magoria that Flora was afraid and thought of the devil.

MACHADO DE ASSIS

---

from Laquelle des Deux

LAST winter, I found myself rather often in the company of two sisters – two young English girls. Whenever you saw one sister, you could be sure that the other was not far away, and so they became known as the inseparable beauties.

One had brown hair and the other blonde, and although they were twins, they had only one thing in common: you could not know them without loving them, for they were two of the most charming and yet most utterly different creatures ever seen together. They seemed, however, to be the best of friends.

I do not know if it was purely by instinct that they had realised the value of contrast or if there was a genuinely strong bond between them; whatever the case, they showed each other off to great advantage and this, I think, was the reason for their apparent unity, for it strikes me as very unlikely that two sisters of the same age, each equally, yet distinctively beautiful, would not hate each other cordially. It was not so, however, and the adorable pair were always to be found side by side in the same corner of the salon, leaning against each other with the most graceful ease or reclining together on the same love-seat. Each was the other's shadow, forever at the other's side.

I thought all this most strange, and it certainly drove all the young men of their acquaintance to distraction: it was impossible to say a word to Musidora without Clary hearing; impossible to slip a note into Clary's pretty little hand without Musidora noticing. It really was most provoking. The two girls thought all these fruitless attempts hugely amusing, and took a mischievous delight in encouraging and then ruining them at a stroke by some childish banter or unexpected joke. It was most amusing to see the look of discomfiture on the faces of the poor dandies, forced to take back their compliments and love letters. My friend, Ferdinand, was quite stunned with disappointment and for a week his tie was as unkempt as that of a married man.

I was just as bad as the rest of them: I hovered around the two girls, launching myself first at Clary, then at Musidora, always without success. So vexed was I one night that I seriously entertained the idea of blowing out what was left of my brains. All that prevented me from carrying out this plan was the thought that I would leave the way clear for Ferdinand and the realization that I would not be able to try on the suit that my tailor was to bring round the next day. So I set my suicidal notions aside for another time, although I still cannot decide whether I acted wisely or unwisely in so doing.

When I searched the depths of my soul, I made a dreadful discovery: I was in love with both sisters at the same time. Yes, Madame, it is absolutely true, though utterly disgraceful – and perhaps even because it is so disgraceful: both of them! I can hear you cry, 'The monster!' as you sit pulling that pretty face of yours. But I can assure you that I am the most harmless chap in the world; it is just that the heart of a man, whilst far from being as peculiar as that of a woman, is nonetheless quite peculiar enough, and no-one – not even you, Madame – can answer for it. Had I known you earlier I would probably have loved no-one but you: but, alas, I did not.

Clary was a veritable Diana, tall and slender, with the most beautiful eyes in the world, eyebrows which looked as though they had been drawn with a paintbrush, and a fine and beautifully-shaped nose. Her skin was lit by a transparent glow, her hands delicate and elegant, her arms delightful, if a little thin and her shoulders as perfect as those of a young girl can be (for truly beautiful shoulders do not appear until thirty). In short, she was a real stunner.

Was I wrong?

Musidora had translucent skin, a head all blonde and white and angelically limpid eyes. Her hair was so fine and silky that a single breath of air set it fluttering, seemed to double its volume, and she had the daintiest feet and the tiniest waist: she was like a little fairy.

Was I not right?

After searching my soul a second time, I made a discovery even more dreadful than the first: I loved neither Clary nor Musidora. Clary, alone, was no more than half-lovable; Musidora, when separated from her sister, lost almost all her charm. When they were together, my ardour was once more awakened and I found both of them equally adorable. It was not the brunette or the blonde who inflamed me – it was the synthesis of the two types of beauty which the two sisters so perfectly represented. What I loved was a sort of abstract being which was neither Musidora nor Clary but which was made up of both of them; a graceful phantom born of the communion of these two beauties, flitting from one to the other, borrowing here a gentle smile and there a passionate glance, compensating for the melancholy of the little blonde one with the vivacity of the brunette, taking the choicest features from each and thus making the other whole. Something utterly charming and yet intangible surrounded the two girls, which somehow dissipated as soon as they were apart. My love had merged the two together; they had truly become for me one and the same person.

THEOPHILE GAUTIER, translated by Lucy Bailey

[*Article on Hollywood hookers – story told by police vice officers*

in charge of monitoring.] 'Once a man, a middle-Eastern magnate, saw a pair of twins on TV and asked Alex, the high-class
madam to approach them. She got them for her client at a price
of $40,000.'

Cosmopolitan, February 1993

When twins were asked to evaluate their twin's spouse, in more
than half the cases they expressed merely neutral feelings. The
spouses, for their part, returned the favor – although one might
have expected them to be at least somewhat attracted to the
identical twin. 'We are left with a curious and disconcerting
conclusion,' Lykken and Tellegen wrote, 'Although most human
choice behavior . . . reflects the characteristics of the chooser, the
most important choice of all – that of the mate – seems to be an
exception . . . another person like ourselves (our identical twin)
is not likely to be drawn to the same choice we make.'
LAWRENCE WRIGHT, 'Double Mystery', *New Yorker*, August 1995

from Twin Sombreros

'SHORE. I'm – a liar . . . an' a miserable hombre.'
'*Brazos!*' Janis darted to him and knelt, one hand on his shoulder.
'What did she mean? What do you mean?'
'Aw, Jan, it's no use. June saw through me . . . I fell in love with
yu both. I cain't tell you apart . . . I've been honest with June – an'
with yu, too. I did ask her to marry me. An' when – those times I've
been alone with yu – I thought *yu* was June! . . . But now I know yu,
it doesn't make no difference. I love yu just the same – just as turrible
. . . An' after last night – when yu let yoreself go – Aw! I'm a gone
goslin'.'
'You loved me – thinking I was June?' she asked, her voice
breaking.
'I reckon I did.'
'But you love me, too?'
'Yes, I love yu, Jan.'

'Just as much as you do June?'

'I cain't tell my love apart any more than I can yu girls.'

'But Brazos,' cried Janis, frantically. 'We can't be absolutely the same to you.'

'Yes, yu air. Only June makes me happy, quiet, shore of myself – an' yu drive me wild with yore kisses . . . Jan, I'd go to hell for one of those kisses.'

Janis slipped her other arm around Brazos and embraced him passionately, as if she could never let him go. Then she looked up at her sister in anguish. 'June, I forgive him. We – *I* am most to blame. But I can't hate him now . . . I can't bear to let him go . . . Oh, merciful heaven, what *can* I do?'

'Jan, you need not give Brazos up,' said June, her voice strong and sweet. 'You shall marry him.'

Brazos heard aright and he sprang up, almost lifting Janis with him.

'What's thet?' he demanded, roughly.

'Jan shall have you, Brazos.'

He stared at her, only conscious through sight of her drawn face and wonderful eyes that for the first time he was realizing the true June Neece.

'I cain't consent to thet.'

'Nor I, June,' added Janis. 'It wouldn't be fair. To cheat you of everything? No, no! All my life I have let you put me first. I won't do it here . . . But I'm not big enough to give him to you . . . We must be brokenhearted together.'

'Janis, neither of us needs be brokenhearted. He shall marry you and we'll all be happy.'

'But – but – ' faltered Janis.

'What yu got in yore haid, girl?' interposed Brazos, sternly, and letting go of Janis he squared toward June, studying her pale face with narrow piercing eyes. She was proof against his scrutiny. She was the strongest of the three.

'Brazos, I'd give my very life to make Jan happy.'

'Shore. But it cain't be done.'

'Jan shall be your wife, Brazos . . . and you can have me, too.'

Janis leaped to her. 'June! . . . I – he – Oh, if it could only be!'

'It can, sister.'

Brazos seized her shoulders in rough grasp. He felt the blood rush back to his heart leaving his skin tight and cold.

'What air – yu sayin'?' he demanded, huskily.

'I said Jan shall be yore wife . . . and you can have me too. We're twins, you know, almost the same as *one* girl . . . I'd never marry. I'd always be true to you, Brazos. No one would ever know.'

'My Gawd!' gasped Brazos and he fell back overcome.

ZANE GRAY

from The Decameron

SUPPER now was served up in the most delicate order, with the best and richest wine, greatly to the king's liking; and whilst he was eating, with great admiration of the beauty of the place, two young damsels, of about fifteen years of age, entered the garden, with their hair like golden wire, most curiously curled, and garlands of flowers upon their heads, whilst their mein and deportment bespoke them rather angels than mortal creatures: their garments were of fine linen cloth, as white as snow, which were girt round their waists, and hung in large folds from thence to their feet. She that came first had two fishing-nets, which she carried in her left hand upon her shoulder, and in her right was a long stick: the other that followed had a frying-pan upon her left shoulder, and under the same arm a faggot of wood, with a trevet in her hand, and in the other hand a bottle of oil and a lighted torch; at which the king was greatly surprised, and waited attentively to see what it meant.

The damsels being come before him, made their obeisance in the humblest and modestest manner; and at the entrance of the pond, she that had the pan with the other things, laid them down upon the ground; and taking up the stick which the other carried, they both stepped into the canal, the water of which came up to their breasts. A servant immediately kindled a fire, and laying the pan upon the trevet, and putting oil therein, he began to wait till the damsels should throw him some fish. So one of them beating the places where the fish lay, and the other holding the net, they soon caught fish enough, to the great diversion of the king; and throwing them to the servant, who put them alive as it were into the pan, they took out some of the finest, as they had been before instructed, and cast them upon the table before the king, Count Guido, and their father. The king was highly delighted with seeing them jump about, and he took and tossed them about in like manner, and so they diverted themselves, till the servant had fried that which he had in his pan, which was set before the king by Signor Neri's order, more as a curiosity than anything nice and dainty. The damsels, thinking they had now done enough, came out of the water, with their garments hanging about them in such a manner as scarcely to conceal any part of their bodies, and modestly saluting the king as before, they returned into the house. The king, with the count and gentlemen that attended, were much taken with their extraordinary beauty and modest behaviour: the king especially, who was perfectly lost in admiration, and finding a secret passion stealing upon him, without knowing which to prefer, they were so exactly alike, he turned to Signor Neri, and asked who those two damsels were? When he replied, 'My lord, they are my daughters, born at a birth, one of whom is called Gineura, the pretty, and the other Isotta, the fair.' The king commended them very much, and advised him to marry them; but he excused himself, alleging that he was not in circumstances to do it. Nothing now remained to be served up but the dessert, when the two ladies came attired in rich satin, with two silver dishes in their hands, full of all manner of fruit, which they set before the king; and retiring afterwards to some distance, they sang a song, beginning in the following manner:

Thy power, O love! who can resist? &c.,

with such exquisite sweetness, that it seemed to the king as if choirs of angels were descended from heaven for his entertainment. No sooner was the song ended, but they fell upon their knees before him, to take their leave, which the king, though he was secretly grieved at it, seemed graciously to comply with. When supper was concluded, the king, with his attendants, mounted their horses, and returned to the palace, where, being unable to forego the love that he had conceived for Gineura, for whose sake he also loved her sister, as resembling each other, he grew so uneasy that he could think of nothing else; upon which account he cultivated, under other pretences, a strict friendship with the father, and used frequently to visit him at his garden, in order to see Gineura; till, unable to contain any longer, seeing he could think of no better way, he resolved to take not one only, but both from him by force, and he signified his intention to Count Guido, who, being a nobleman of strict honour, said to this effect: 'My liege, I am greatly surprised at what you now say, and more perhaps than any other person would be, since I have known you more, even from your infancy, and as I never remember any such thing of you in your youth, when love has the greatest power over us, it seems so odd and out of the way, that I can scarcely give credit to it. Did it become me to reprove you, I know very well what I might say, considering that you are yet in arms in a kingdom newly conquered, amongst a people not known to you, abounding with treachery and deceit, and have many great and weighty affairs upon your hands; yet you can sit down at ease in such circumstances, and give way to such an idle passion as love. This is not like a great king, so much as an inglorious stripling. And what is worse, you say you are resolved to take the two daughters away from a poor gentleman, whom he had to wait upon you out of his abundant respect, as well as to shew his great confidence in you, believing you to be a generous prince, and not a rapacious wolf. Have you so soon forgotten that it was Manfredi's taking the same liberties which opened your way to this kingdom? Can there be a baser crime than to take away from one that honours you, his honour, his hope, and entire comfort? What will people say in such a case? Do you think it any excuse, his being of a different party? Is this kingly justice, to treat people in that manner, be they of what party they will, that throw themselves under your protection? It was great glory to conquer Manfredi, but, let me tell you, it will be much greater to conquer yourself. You, therefore, who are ordained to correct vice in others, learn to subdue your own; curb that unruly appetite, nor stain with so foul a blot the character you have so gloriously acquired.' These words touched the king to the quick, and so much the more as he knew them to be true: therefore he sighed, and said, 'Count, I hold it an easy conquest over any enemy, however formidable, compared to one's own passion; but, be the difficulty ever so great, such is the force of your words, that, before many days are past, I will convince you, if I know how to conquer others, that I am able also to withstand myself.' So he went to Naples soon after, when, to put it out of his power to do a base thing, as well as to reward the knight for the favours shewn him, he resolved, however grating it seemed, to give another the possession of that which he himself coveted, to marry both the ladies, not as Signor Neri's daughters, but his own. Bestowing, then, large fortunes upon them, Gineura, the pretty, he gave to Signor Maffeo da Palizzi; and Isotta, the fair, to Signor Gulielmo della Magna, both worthy knights, retiring himself afterwards to Puglia; where, with great pains and trouble, he got the better at last of his passion, and lived with ease and quiet ever after. Now some people, perhaps, may say, that it is a small thing for a king to have bestowed two ladies in marriage. I allow it: but for a king to give away the very lady that he himself was in love with, and without plucking the least bud, flower, or fruit of his love, that I will maintain to be great indeed – Such, then, were the virtues of this most generous king; rewarding the courtesy of a noble knight, shewing a great and proper regard to his beloved fair one, and subduing his own desires with strict resolution and honour.

BOCCACCIO 1313–1375

from Tales of Home

DURING the separation no letters passed between them. When the neighbors asked Jonathan for news of his brother, he always replied, 'He is well,' and avoided further speech with such evidence of pain that they spared him. An hour before the month drew to an end, he walked forth alone, taking the road to the nearest railway station. A stranger who passed him at the entrance of a thick wood, three miles from home, was thunderstruck on meeting the same person shortly after, entering the wood from the other side; but the farmers in the near fields saw two figures issuing from the shade, hand in hand.

Each knew the other's month, before they slept, and the last thing Jonathan said, with his head on David's shoulder, was, 'You must know our neighbors, the Bradleys, and especially Ruth.' In the morning, as they dressed, taking each other's garments at random, as of old, Jonathan again said, 'I have never seen a girl that I like so well as Ruth Bradley. Do you remember what father said about loving and marrying? It comes into my mind whenever I see Ruth; but she has no sister.'

'But we need not both marry,' David replied, 'that might part us, and this will not. It is for always now.'

'For always, David.'

Two or three days later Jonathan said, as he started on an errand to the village: 'I shall stop at the Bradleys this evening, so you must walk across and meet me there.'

When David approached the house, a slender, girlish figure, with her back towards him, was stooping over a bush of great crimson roses, cautiously clipping a blossom here and there. At the click of the gate-latch she started and turned towards him. Her light gingham bonnet, falling back, disclosed a long oval face, fair and delicate, sweet brown eyes, and brown hair laid smoothly over the temples. A soft flush rose suddenly to her cheeks, and he felt that his own were burning.

'Oh Jonathan!' she exclaimed, transferring the roses to her left hand, and extending her right, as she came forward.

He was too accustomed to the name to recognize her mistake at once, and the word 'Ruth!' came naturally to his lips.

'I should know your brother David has come,' she then said; 'even if I had not heard so. You look so bright. How glad I am!'

'Is he not here?' David asked.

'No; but there he is now, surely!' She turned towards the lane, where Jonathan was dismounting. 'Why, it is yourself over again, Jonathan!'

As they approached, a glance passed between the twins, and a secret transfer of the riding-whip to David set their identity right with Ruth, whose manner toward the latter innocently became shy with all its friendliness, while her frank, familiar speech was given to Jonathan, as was fitting. But David also took the latter to himself, and when they left, Ruth had apparently forgotten that there was any difference in the length of their acquaintance.

On their way homewards David said: 'Father was right. We must marry, like others, and Ruth is the wife for us, – I mean for you, Jonathan. Yes, we must learn to say *mine* and *yours*, after all, when we speak of her.'

'Even she cannot separate us, it seems,' Jonathan answered. 'We must give her some sign, and that will also be a sign for others. It will seem strange to divide ourselves; we can never learn it properly; rather let us not think of marriage.'

'We cannot help thinking of it; she stands in mother's place now, as we in father's.'

Then both became silent and thoughtful. They felt that something threatened to disturb what seemed to be the only possible life for them, yet were unable to distinguish its features, and therefore powerless to resist it. The same instinct which had been born of their wonderful spiritual likeness told them that Ruth Bradley already loved Jonathan: the duty was established, and they must conform their lives to it. There was, however, this slight difference between their natures – that David was generally the first to utter the thought which came to the minds of both. So when he said, 'We shall learn what to do when the need comes,' it was a postponement of all foreboding. They drifted contentedly towards the coming change.

The days went by, and their visits to Ruth Bradley were continued. Sometimes Jonathan went alone, but they were usually together, and the tie which united the three became dearer and sweeter as it was more closely drawn. Ruth learned to distinguish between the two when they were before her: at least she said so, and they were willing to believe it. But she was hardly aware how nearly alike was the happy warmth in her bosom produced by either pair of dark gray eyes and the soft half-smile which played around either mouth. To them she seemed to be drawn within the mystic circle which separated them from others – she, alone; and they no longer imagined a life in which she should not share.

Then the inevitable step was taken. Jonathan declared his love, and was answered. Alas! he almost forgot David that late summer evening, as they sat in the moonlight, and over and over again assured each other how dear they had grown. He felt the trouble in David's heart when they met.

'Ruth is ours, and I bring her kiss to you,' he said, pressing his lips to David's; but the arms flung around him trembled, and David whispered, 'Now the change begins.'

'Oh, this cannot be our burden!' Jonathan cried, with all the rapture still warm in his heart.

'If it is, it will be light, or heavy, or none at all, as we shall bear it,' David answered, with a smile of infinite tenderness.

For several days he allowed Jonathan to visit the Bradley farm alone, saying that it must be so on Ruth's account. Her love, he declared, must give her the fine instinct which only their mother had ever possessed, and he must allow it time to be confirmed. Jonathan, however, insisted that Ruth already possessed it; that she was beginning to wonder at his absence, and to fear that she would not be entirely welcome to the home which must always be equally his.

David yielded at once.

'You must go alone,' said Jonathan, 'to satisfy yourself that she knows us at last.'

Ruth came forth from the house as he drew near. Her face beamed;

she laid her hands upon his shoulders and kissed him. 'Now you cannot doubt me, Ruth!' he said, gently.

'Doubt you, Jonathan!' she exclaimed with a fond reproach in her eyes. 'But you look troubled; is any thing the matter?'

'I was thinking of my brother,' said David, in a low tone.

'Tell me what it is,' she said, drawing him into the little arbor of woodbine near the gate. They took seats side by side on the rustic bench. 'He thinks I may come between you: is it not that?' she asked. Only one thing was clear to David's mind – that she would surely speak more frankly and freely of him to the supposed Jonathan than to his real self. This once he would permit the illusion.

'Not more than must be,' he answered. 'He knew all from the very beginning. But we have been like one person in two bodies, and any change seems to divide us.'

'I feel as you do,' said Ruth. 'I would never consent to be your wife, if I could really divide you. I love you both too well for that.'

'Do you love me?' he asked, entirely forgetting his representative part.

Again the reproachful look, which faded away as she met his eyes. She fell upon his breast, and gave him kisses which were answered with equal tenderness. Suddenly he covered his face with his hands, and burst into a passion of tears.

'Jonathan! Oh Jonathan!' she cried, weeping with alarm and sympathetic pain.

It was long before he could speak; but at last, turning away his head, he faltered, 'I am David!'

There was a long silence.

When he looked up she was sitting with her hands rigidly clasped in her lap: her face was very pale.

'There it is, Ruth' he said; 'we are one heart and one soul. Could he love, and not I? You cannot decide between us, for one is the other. If I had known you first, Jonathan would be now in my place. What follows, then?'

'No marriage,' she whispered.

'No!' he answered; 'we brothers must learn to be two men instead of one. You will partly take my place with Jonathan; I must live with half my life, unless I can find, somewhere in the world, your other half.'

'I cannot part you, David!'

'Something stronger than you or me parts us, Ruth. If it were death, we should bow to God's will: well, it can no more be got away from than death or judgment. Say no more.

ANON., 1885

———————

I've met countless examples of twins using their likeness to pass themselves off as one another with the same woman. The most touching case was that that of a professional soldier, confined to barracks for several months, who got his brother, also a soldier, to take over his mistress, during his absence without her knowledge. Using his double as proxy was a means of keeping her faithful to him meanwhile.

RENÉ ZAZZO Le Paradoxe des Jumeaux

———————

from The Twin Brothers

THE stranger rode on, without further speech, to the king's palace, where the king and the princess both took him for his twin brother, and called out: 'Why have you tarried so long away? We thought something evil had befallen you.'

When night came and he slept with the princess, who still believed him to be her husband, he laid his sword between them, and when morning came he rose early and went out to hunt. Fate led him by the same way which his brother had taken, and from a distance he saw him and knew that he was turned to stone. Then he entered the hut and ordered the old woman to disenchant his brother. But she answered: 'Let me first touch your dog with my wand, and then I will free your brother.'

He ordered the dog, however, to take hold of her, and bite her up to the knee, till she cried out: 'Tell your dog to let me go and I will set your brother free!'

But he only answered: 'Tell me the magic words that I may disenchant him myself;' and as she would not he ordered his dog to bite her up to the hip.

161

Then the old woman cried out: 'I have two wands, with the green one I turn to stone, and with the red one I bring to life again.'

So the hunter took the red wand and disenchanted his brother, also his brother's horse, and his dog, and ordered his own dog to eat the old woman up altogether.

While the brothers went on their way back to the castle of the king, the one brother related to the other how the cypress tree had all at once dried up and withered, how he had immediately set out in search of his twin, and how he had come to the castle of his father-in-law, and had claimed the princess as his wife. But the other brother became furious on hearing this, and smote him over the forehead till he died, and returned alone to the house of his father-in-law.

When night came and he was in bed the princess asked him: 'What was the matter with you last night, that you never spoke a word to me?'

Then he cried out: 'That was not me, but my brother, and I have slain him, because he told me by the way that he had claimed you for his wife!'

'Do you know the place where you slew him?' asked the princess, 'and can you find the body?'

'I know the place exactly.'

'Then to-morrow we shall ride thither,' said the princess.

Next morning accordingly they set out together, and when they had come to the place, the princess drew forth a small bottle that she had brought with her, and sprinkled the body with some drops of the water so that immediately he became alive again.

When he stood up, his brother said to him: 'Forgive me, dear brother, that I slew you in my anger.' Then they embraced and went together to the Fairest in the Land, whom the unmarried brother took to wife.

Then the brothers brought their parents to live with them, and all dwelt together in joy and happiness.

THE BROTHERS GRIMM

---

from The Twins

[*Enter* Charmia *as in her chamber*]

CHAR. Here let me freely mourn for my offence, and if I thought that I might expiate my fault with tears, and that I should live ever, I'd ever weep. My too much injur'd Lord, how shall I look on him when he comes home? I would give millions for an honest face, but I'm all Strumpet; how now?

[*enter* Gratiano]

GRAT. What alwaies weeping? I am come to comfort you.

CHAR. If so y'ar welcome; you need not then have stoln this private way: this is an honest work, and not an Incest.

GRAT. Come, come, you harp too much upon that string, I'm come to claim you once again.

CHAR. Is this comfort? go to your chamber, brother, and repent what you have done, and do not sin afresh.

GRAT. Sister, I vow again I must enjoy you.

CHAR. By heaven you shan't while I'm alive: 'tis the least sinne o'th two.

[*Draws her knife*]

GRAT. Hold dearest *Charmia*; see I am *Gratiano*.

CHAR. You *Gratiano*?

GRAT. I am by heaven.

CHAR. A perjur'd man in swearing so; if you be he, He give you a good reason why you should never lye with me agen: I have abus'd thy bed with thy own brother: Nay, what may make you loath me ten times more, I was the tempter, I solicited, and vow'd my death in case he did deny: If you be *Gratiano* you will kill me, and will not let such an incestuous strumpet be partner in your state: Honour won't let you: I know by this you are not *Gratiano*: Where's all your rage? this calmness of your spirit fits not an injur'd husband: Were you he, you would not let me live to beg for death but with a wing'd revenge would cut me off.

GRAT. You are too quick, death is the end of torment; Ile have a torture of continuance to punish Incest; to which death compar'd shall seem a curtesie and not a torment; death shall but be an Epilogue to the Tragedy Ile act in you.

CHAR. O now me-thinks you are my much wrong'd Lord, you look and speak like him like on that had been wrong'd beyond sufferance: Deal with me as you please.

GRAT. My lustfull Brother durst boldly tell me, he would lye with you and do me a curtesie, but in conclusion, rage and revenge set a new point and edge upon my Rapier, and I kild the Monky.

CHAR. And for my sin my brother *Fulvio*'s slain, would I had perist when I thought of it, he had liv'd good, I dy'd less full of sin.

GRAT. Nay more, to aggravate your misery, my Brother never lay with you, 'twas I (when *I* had stript him, put on his clothes) that lay with you.

CHAR. Then *I* am free, my Lord, from wronging you, unless it were in intention: And say a man intend to kill another, and miss his aym, can the Law hang that man?

GRAT. Your argument is built upon the air; for say you should intend to kill this man, and missing of your aim murder another, yet think you have hit right, this merits death no less than t'oher would: This is your; you thought you had ly'n with my Brother *Fulvio*, but lay with me, contrary to your will; thus you'ar incestuous with your own husband.

CHAR. I see my sin more fully now than ever.

[*Enter* Julietta]

JULIET. Where are you mother? here's a Letter for you: Uncle, how doe you?

CHAR. Prithee girle be gone, leave me a little while – 'Tis my Lords hand; 'tis sent from my Lord *Fidelie*'s: Is this well Brother? When with the Lyons skin you can't prevail, you put the Foxes on to cosen me: and you are *Gratiano* in *Fulvio*'s clothes, I wish you were.

GRAT. Indeed *I* am the same; this Letter was forg'd by me, it was my plot; but he, alas is dead: yet after all, if now you'l be obedient and yeeld to me, Ile pardon you.

CHAR. He not beleeve a sillable: fine tricks! are you my husband for all this: How cunningly you'd satisfie your lust on me, for all this evident proof I have that you are *Fulvio*, and that my Lord is now at Lord *Fidelio*'s.

GRAT. Think you so still: be confident Ile not solicite you to lye with you again, unless you'l yeeld *I* am your husband: if you'l see the sports Ile go with you, and if you'l call me brother Ile answer to't.

CHAR. Ile never call you otherwise.

Exeunt.

WILLIAM RIDER, 1655

from Wise Children

I FELT as if I'd met him somewhere else before, although I never had. I didn't think of love or passion when I thought of him; I only thought about the down on his delicious cheek.

As if it were yesterday. The show was called *Over to You*. Nora was ready for a change. She ditched the aged drummer and took up with a wee scrap of a lad pale as a lily, blond as a chick. He didn't know what hit him. Nora used to give her all. Because we shared the dressing room, I used to have to sit on the stairs outside and listen to them through the wall going at it like hammer and tongs on the horsehair sofa where we were supposed to put our feet up between shows. He muttered broken phrases, sometimes sobbed. Something about him touched my heart. Nora said, he was young enough to be grateful but it wasn't that.

I sat on the stairs outside and listened to them and my mind began to change, until I came to a decision: by hook or by crook, I said to myself, come what may, the day that I am seventeen, I'll do it on that horsehair sofa.

Do *what* on the horsehair sofa?

What do you think?

It was late April but still chilly. Little cold winds whipped round the wings and the bare backstage corners. We turned up our gas fire and plucked our eyebrows. There was a bunch of flowers for our birthday and a cake with candles ready for the party after the show.

'Nora . . .'

'Yes?'

'Give me your fella for a birthday present.'

She put down her tweezers and gave me a look.

'Get your own fella,' she said.

They'd sent us early lilac. The scent of white lilac always brings it back. Seventeen hurts.

'He's the only one I want, Nora.'

I'll only do it once, I said. He's really stuck on you, Nora, he's crazy about you and he's never given me a second look. But won't he be able to tell the difference? I don't know, we won't know until we try; but why should he notice any difference? Same eyes, same mouth, same hair. If it was only the once and if I keep my mouth shut . . . he is as innocent as asparagus, his heart as pure as Epps' cocoa, poor lamb. Why should he guess?

'Nora, I want him so.'

'Oh, *Dora*,' she said, for then she knew that only he would do.

She put on my Mitsouko and I put on her Shalimar. She had a new dress, floral chiffon, peonies, rhodies, dusty pink and misty blue and mauve, long skirts were back, I looked romantic. We took big breaths and blew out the candles on the cake; our wish at seven had come true and ever since I was a true believer in birthday-candle magic so you can guess what it was I wished for at seventeen. I smelled the unfamiliar perfume on my skin and felt voluptuous. As soon as they started to call me Nora, I found that I could kiss the boys and hug the principals with gay abandon because all that came quite naturally to her. To me, no. I was ever the introspective one.

As for Nora/Dora, she kept herself to herself until she'd had a couple and then she forgot to behave herself and carried on in her usual fashion but by the time she started dancing on the table most of the party was plastered so nobody noticed she was behaving out of character and that's how Dora got off with the pianist, to my considerable embarrassment in subsequent months.

There was a scratchy gramophone going full tilt. I laid claim to my birthday present as soon as he came shyly through the door. His face was still shining with cold cream. I took his hand. 'Let's dance,' I said.

'Nothing for me but to love you, just the way you look tonight . . .' sang the voice on the gramophone.

I know I wanted him more than anything, that his sweet face and his silken floss of flaxen hair moved me like nothing else had done in the masculine line before, but, all the same, I scarcely knew what it was I wanted, when all is said and done, in spite of Grandma's comprehensive sex education and all I'd seen during my life in the chorus and, more than all that, I'd seen my sister cry for love, and nearly bleed to death for love, and I'd listened while the one she loved made her shout out loud, when I was full of envy and desire. I thought I knew the lot, didn't I?

And yet I didn't know a thing.

Lilac; and a wind blowing in through the window they'd opened to let the fug out; and the smoke of the candles that I'd just blown out, still lingering in the room, catching at the throat; and the first kiss. I nearly fainted when we kissed, I was scared witless, I thought he'd recognise the ruse at once and suddenly I didn't want to go through with it. I wanted to go home to Grandma, to go back to yesterday's things we'd lost already – back to Mrs Worthington's piano, to our shorn sausage curls, to pick up our discarded liberty bodices and encase ourselves again in them. But he was just my own age, just seventeen, a child, too; nothing to be afraid of. And for the purpose of the act, I wasn't Dora, any more, was I? Now I was Nora, who was afraid of nothing provided it was a man.

So I kissed him back and we slipped off.

He went to have a wash in the basin, first, while I stripped off and lay on the sofa watching him, the back of his neck bent humbly as he attended to himself. The water purled. Just the lights round the mirror were burning. A cab stopped outside and panted like a dog; there was a chink of coins: 'Ta, guv'nor.' These sounds might have come from another world.

He was too young for body hair. His tender flesh was all rosy in the light behind him. He smiled as he came towards me. It stuck out like a chapel hat peg. What did? What do you think? I couldn't keep my eyes off it. I'd never seen a naked man before although Grandma had drawn us pictures. There was a little clear drop of moisture trembling on the tip, it came to me to lick it off. He gave a gasp. His nipples were quite stiff, too. He was shivering a bit, not that it was cold, we'd left the gas fire on.

He never said: 'Nora, there's something different about you, something more enchanting, tonight.' I never wanted him to, either. I'd have been ashamed. I'll never know if he could tell the difference. If he did, he was too much of a gent to say. Skin like suede. Eyes the blue of the paper bags they used to sell you sugar in, years ago. I never bled or hurt; a decade and a half of *fouettés*, *jetés* and high kicks had done in the membrane without leaving a trace. He used a French letter, don't ever believe them if they tell you it takes away the romance. He sighed, his eyes rolled back so you could see the whites. Eyelashes a foot long.

Some things you can't describe.

ANGELA CARTER

---

from Sweet Adversity

BEVERLY stands in the door. 'Let's stay here awhile, it's nicer,' she says, locking the door. Twins sit up, pour her a glass, drop their shoes. She sits crosslegged on the bed, twins facing her, bottle midway. Leo pulls the lightstring and they talk in the shadows of the streetlamp.

'You were wonderful,' she says, her face milky darkness. 'I saw you limping. Are you sure you're all right?'

'Maybe we should look,' Leo says.

Strip off their pants, stand by the window. 'I can't tell anything in this light,' Teddy says. 'But it feels awful.'

'Put on the light,' Beverly says. 'Oh my lord, doesn't that hurt?'

Their joined thighs, bluerotten. 'That's the worst we've ever had,' Leo says. 'We'll feel this for a while.'

'Oh, it looks horrible,' Beverly says. 'You better go to bed.'

Teddy pulls the lightstring. Beverly against the wall by Leo. 'You're trembling,' she says. 'Boy, you guys were great. Are you in pain?'

'We'll live,' Teddy says.

'We been hurt before,' Leo rasps.

'I won't forget how you protected me. When he knocked you down, it hurt me worse than it did you, believe me.'

Leo takes her hand. 'We're here with you. That makes up for everything, doesn't it?'

'Sure does,' Teddy says.

Twins ambushed by nerves, the bed spidery with silence.

'How'd you like to go swimming in the morning?' Leo asks.

'Great,' Beverly says. 'Where? I brought my suit.'

'There are some private beaches past the fence,' Leo says. 'Sleep here.'

'This blouse stinks,' she says.

'Take it off,' Leo says.

Teddy takes Beverly's hand. 'Make love with us,' he says.

'Well' – she sighs – 'it may as well be you twins as anyone else.'

'You're a virgin?' Leo husks.

'Yep,' she says.

'So'm I,' Leo says.

'Me too,' Teddy says. 'Technically.' She throws her blouse on the chair. 'Oh, stand up on the bed,' he begs. 'We've never really seen a girl with nothing on.'

'You haven't even kissed me,' Beverly says.

'Oh come here!' Leo says.

Leo kisses her, then strokes her back and unhooks her bra as she slips fully into Teddy's arms. 'Stand up,' Teddy whispers, sighing.

She stands, strips her panties, hands on hips. Small-breasted, plump. 'Not so great, huh?' she asks. 'I never thought it would be like this! I mean. *Si*amese twins, holy Christmas.'

'You're beautiful,' Leo says.

'Oh, lovely,' Teddy says.

Twins rise, undress. Peel rubbers. 'I'll go first,' Teddy says, 'since I know a little bit about it.'

'I don't think it's gonna work,' Beverly says under Teddy.

'Put your leg over our band,' Teddy says.

Beverly gasps.

'Does it hurt?' Teddy asks.

'No. Forget about me.'

Teddy begs strength in the golden sluice. A cellar door opens on wheatfields. 'Oh,' he says. 'Oh. *Heaven!*'

She changes legs, Leo mounts. 'Help me,' he says.

Teddy rides the wall, eyes closed on sunmemories.

'Lovely,' Leo says.

'I never felt anything like this before!' she cries.

An angel dies, dropping through Leo's earth.

Twins wash their privates in the bathroom, check droopy rubbers for wholeness.

'Let's go swimming now and make love on the beach,' Leo asks Beverly.

'Rest one minute,' she begs. 'My heart just beat a million beats!'

DONALD NEWLOVE

---

from The Pillow Boy of the Lady Onogoro

'THERE was once in Ch'ang An Province in China a poet called Yü Hsüan-chi, who became the concubine of a minor official. Since the ways of China are harsher than ours, the official's wife, jealous of her husband's new mistress, tortured her and forced her from the house. The homeless Yü Hsüan-chi wandered far and wide through the province, and all she had to comfort her were these lines of Li Po, which she recited to herself over and over again:

> Journeying is hard
> Journeying is hard
> There are many turnings
> Which am I to follow?
> I will mount a long wind some day
> And break the heavy waves.

'Eventually the girl came to a monastery high on a red-ochre rock, where the monks, had she but known it, were renowned for their licentiousness. As she climbed the steep rock steps she saw them above her, leaning over the parapet and giggling at her progress. When Yü knocked at the carved gate a hatch was drawn back and two merry identical faces peered out at her. Brother Li and Brother Hu were twins, and it was to them that she was presently to owe her initiation, not only into the Taoist Scriptures, but also into less devout practices.

'The Brothers conducted Yü to a clean bare cell, and brought washing water, food, and a hempen robe to replace her soiled and tattered garments. Then they left her alone to fall into the blissful sleep of exhaustion.

'In the morning the resilience of her youth reasserted itself, and Yü sprang up, eager to explore this sanctuary in which, the Brothers had reassured her, she could remain as long as she pleased. That there was a price to be paid for her lodging Yü did not discover until later that day.

[. . .] 'During the evening meal in the refectory Yü was obliged to suffer many curious stares and whispers, but after it was over the Brothers knocked shyly on the door of her cell. There were a few formalities to be observed, they told her: initiation rites which must be carried out before a woman could be admitted as a novice. So saying, the congenial twins brought in a jug of water, a sharp blade, and a red-ochre inkstone and brushes.

'Yü sat calmly on her pallet and bent her neck, since she fully expected her head to be shaved and was perfectly willing to sacrifice her long lustrous hair should this be required.

'However, with a blush that enveloped his tonsured pate, Brother Li shook his head and nudged his more forthright twin Hu, who informed Yü that the nether hair only was to be shaved, and if she would be so good as to uncover the parts, his brother would carry out the purification without delay.

'Yü was surprised, but the request was put with such delicacy that she obediently opened her hempen robe and spread her thighs so that Brother Li could shave her *hisho*. This the young *bonze* did with great artistry, leaving not a single hair and tweaking not at all, and although he murmured simple words of appreciation as the small pink bud emerged, never once did he utter an immodest or irreligious one.

'When Li had completed his task his twin Hu, with many gentle encouragements, instructed Yü to kneel on the *tatami* mat and place her hands on the floor before her. Trustingly Yü complied, turning her head to watch Brother Hu as he mixed a red-ochre ink and wetted a brush fastidiously with the tip of his tongue, and if she had thought Brother Li an artist with the razor, she was to find that his twin surpassed him a hundredfold with the brush.

'Kneeling behind her, Hu parted her plump cheeks to reveal her whorled orifice, while Brother Li stroked her hair soothingly and murmured words of encouragement. If Yü found the ministrations to her nether regions somewhat shocking, the teasing sensations of the brush and the coolness of the red-ochre were far from unpleasant. Gravely Brother Hu licked his brush and carried on with his work, until he had painted a perfect circle of red-ochre around the now-expanding orifice. Then he bowed deeply to Yü and asked her if she was now ready for the final rites of initiation.

'So mischievously did he ask, and so meekly did his brother echo the question, that Yü would have thought herself mean indeed to refuse, so deep was her urge to follow the Way of her new friends. Indeed, if all the rites were as pleasurable as what had gone before, she could not imagine why anyone ever chose to leave the priesthood!

'By all means, she replied, and Brother Hu left the room to return a few moments later with two other monks as sweet-faced as himself, and several vials of the aromatic oils for which the monastery was famed throughout the province.

'Opening one of the vials Brother Hu poured a little oil of thyme first into Yü's palm, and then on to the outstretched hands of the other monks. Yü bent her head and sniffed devoutly, but this was not, Li explained, what orthodoxy dictated.

'At a sign from Brother Hu, Li and the other monks, Brother Chen and Brother Yung, knelt down and drew back their cassocks to reveal their erect members, and Brother Hu indicated that Yü should anoint each one with scented oil. As Yü stood before them, she was anointed in her turn, both the shaven anterior orifice and the perfect painted O of her nether opening, while the kneeling priests chanted an arcane *sutra* in reverent voices.

'Brother Hu, whose personality was suited to leadership, motioned his twin to lie down on the pallet, and guided the by now sweet-smelling Yü into a posture astride him. Despite the ineptitude of her one and only previous lover, Yü understood quite quickly what was required. Sliding her orifice on to Brother Li's blushing and well-slicked member, she began to move her hips with some enthusiasm, until halted by a command from Brother Hu.

'Putting his hands round Yü's slender waist, Hu lifted her up until the head of his twin's member barely touched the entrance of her budded cleft. Meanwhile he inserted an oil-anointed finger into the inviting red circle of her nether opening until it flowered out, and in its whole-hearted blooming easily admitted his questing member, which burrowed eagerly as a bee into the moist interior. Once snugly rooted between Yü's cheeks Brother Hu slowly withdrew, so that his fortunate twin below could once more reclaim the honeyed depths of Yü's anterior cleft, and so they thrust in perfect tandem, one twin withdrawing while the other dove deep, and vice versa, in a harmonious seesaw motion which all but ravished Yü's inexperienced senses.

'As if this were not enough, Brother Chen and Brother Yung approached with pious faces. Straddling the torso of the recumbent Li, Brother Chen offered his member to the panting Yü, who gobbled at this sweetmeat with a greedy abandon only intensified by the intervention of Brother Yung who, with eyes devoutly averted, laid his head on Li's belly and proceeded to ply his tongue with unerring flicks across Yü's pulsating bud, which burgeoned and thrust forward now as never before, until she felt herself draw near to Heaven.

'And God said to her in a sonorous voice, . . . "One who has a man's wings and a woman's also is in himself a womb of the world, and being a womb of the world, continually, endlessly gives birth . . ."

'Hearing this, Yü surrendered to the holiness of all things, and when, heavy with sweet delight, she returned at last to this earth, it was to hear the voice of Brother Hu offering thanks in the immortal words of Lao-Tzu himself:

> These are the four amphitheatres of the universe
> And a fit man is one of them:
> Man rounding the way of earth
> Earth rounding the way of heaven
> Heaven rounding the way of life
> Till the circle is full.

'And this is how the poet Yü Hsüan-chi took her first and faltering steps on the Way to enlightenment.'

ALISON FELL

172

from The Tiger in the Kitchen

THESE few words came as a shock to him. He had expected that his brother would also hold out his arms and say, 'Brother.' So he was forced to repeat foolishly:

'Yes, it's me.' Though his brother's words were not in themselves difficult to understand, they were so incomprehensible to him that he felt they struck him to the brain. He let his arms fall and looked about helplessly. So it happened he caught sight of Fanny.

'Oh, it's you,' he said reluctantly.

Fanny felt as if something very strange that she knew nothing about was going to happen and hastened to say:

'We've come to ask you to be godfather to our child.'

'Certainly, with pleasure,' he said in confusion. 'But where is the child?'

'This is my wife,' Otto said.

'Your wife? I must congratulate you.'

'Thank you,' said Fanny. 'Actually we're not married yet. We've come here to earn some money to pay for the priest, the verger and the wedding bells.'

'You're very welcome,' Otto said, several times over. 'Won't you sit down? You won't hurt the floor.'

Fanny smiled and sat down on the floor, but her smile was only visible from the outside. Otto again held out his hand to his brother, but the other ignored it.

'How lucky you turned up just today! I've been given notice from tomorrow unless I can manage to be in two places at once. We can both go along tomorrow and do the job between us, so there's no need for you to be hard up any more. You see, I move bicycle racks, in and out.'

Otto did not reply.

As a last resort his brother appealed to the memory of their happy, vanished childhood together.

'Otto, do you remember when we were born no one could tell which of us was which. I've often thought that perhaps I am you and you are me.'

'Won't you ever grow up?'

Otto recoiled as if he had been whipped and kicked over the cycle rack with a crash.

'I've come to give you back this picture,' Otto said, and taking his brother's photograph out of his pocket he put it on the table by the side of the similar picture that was already there.

'We'll be leaving here tomorrow. Can we sleep here for tonight? We haven't any money to go to an hotel, because my wife's purse was her heart.'

'Yes,' Fanny went on quickly, because she wanted to keep some sort of a conversation going. 'My fiancé gave me back my heart in a way you'll perhaps be interested to hear about. He . . .'

'I don't know anything about that,' Otto said and set the cycle rack up again.

Shortly afterwards they all lay down on the floor to sleep, as there was no bed. Only Fanny found it impossible to go to sleep. The moon shone in through the window and by its light she saw on either side of her the same sleeping man. Anxious not to take the wrong man for her fiancé she woke one of them and whispered:

'Is it you?'

'Yes,' he replied.

'Otto, don't be angry with me . . . I love you so much . . . every time I see you . . . and I've been with you all the time lately . . .'

'Not while I was in the Town Hall!'

'No . . . but apart from then . . . every time I see you I get wild with love, and now I've seen you and your brother together you're so alike that I am twice as much in love . . . I cannot bear it, nor will I keep my maidenhood a moment longer. Otto, I know we're not married yet, but . . .'

'Be quiet,' he said, infinitely gently, 'or he will hear us. It is a good thing, after all, that we are lying on the floor, a sofa always creaks so. Come here, into the moonlight, so I can see you . . . Just help me move him over a bit . . . Mind the cycle rack! . . . dearest!'

Next morning Otto awoke to find Fanny kissing his still sleeping brother. In one bound he was on his feet and gave Fanny a well-aimed box on the ears. The noise roused Otto, who sprang up, afraid that the cycle rack had been upset.

'What are you kissing him for?' thundered Otto.

'I thought it was you,' wept Fanny and threw her arms round his neck and kissed him too. But he was angry and pushed her away.

'What are you kissing him for?' the other Otto thundered before Fanny had even fallen to the floor. The two men faced each other, fire in their eyes.

'It's no good our fighting,' one of them roared at the other, 'we're both as strong as each other.'

'It's no good our fighting,' the other said, 'we're both as strong as each other.'

'We'll hire a pair of pistols and shoot it out to the death,' roared the first.

'Hire a pair of pistols . . .' the other stammered, but his brother was already out of the house and he had to follow. Last of all came Fanny, crying noisily. In all probability one of them would be shot and how would she know whether it was her fiancé or not? In the street the twins faced each other, equal distances apart, and raised their pistols. Perhaps one of them was a little more eager to raise his pistol than the other, but the result was the same: both pistols were lifted and fired at the same moment. And as was to be expected of two who had always been each other's equals, their aim was equally good, and they sank to the ground, equally dead.

A policeman had heard both the shots and now came up. He went from one to the other with a chicken's feather in his hand and by its help he established the fact that they were both dead.

'That was a piece of luck!' he growled. 'Now we don't have to condemn them to death for murder.'

Long did Fanny run, screaming, backwards and forwards from one to the other, but at last she had to give up trying to decide which was her fiancé. It was after all not so important, as he was dead anyway, but she sat herself down between the two and began tearing her garments to shreds.

'They both killed each other for my sake,' she said ecstatically to all who chanced to pass by.

VILLI SORENSEN

---

from The Black Prince

CANON de Mondez, concealing the panama behind his soutane, asked the solicitor: 'Can you explain that indecent corpse the Marquis kept in his drawing-room, Maître?'

'As far as I have been able to determine the facts, Monsieur le Chanoine, I believe the corpse was brought back from Louisiana, by the Marquis Théodore, nearly two centuries ago. She was a woman of those parts with whom he had fallen passionately in love. Even dead, she was able to arouse the most extraordinary emotions!' said the solicitor, leading the Canon a little apart. 'The last Marquis and his twin brother, when still children, found the corpse one day when playing in the Château attics, to which the glass coffin had been relegated long before and forgotten. They told no one. Then when they succeeded jointly, as you know, to their father, the Marquis was able to take advantage of the fact that the coffin appeared in no inventory to appropriate it to himself. This may well have been the underlying reason for the quarrel that divided the two Paluselles for over forty years. It is a fact that neither of them ever married; and my predecessor here told me that they had never even – how shall I put it? – well, you understand, Monsieur le Chanoine . . . But the fact was, that whenever they met a woman, they became obsessed by the memory of the corpse, and they were never able to find one that resembled it sufficiently.'

MAURICE DRUON

from Man Overboard!

I HAVEN'T been at many weddings in my life, and I don't suppose you have, but that one seemed to me to be all right until it was pretty near over; and then, I don't know whether it was part of the ceremony or not, but Jack put out his hand and took Mamie's and held it a minute, and looked at her, while the parson was still speaking.

Mamie turned as white as a sheet and screamed. It wasn't a loud scream, but just a sort of stifled little shriek, as if she were half frightened to death; and the parson stopped, and asked her what was the matter, and the family gathered round.

'Your hand's like ice,' said Mamie to Jack, 'and it's all wet!'

She kept looking at it, as she got hold of herself again.

'It don't feel cold to me,' said Jack, and he held the back of his hand against his cheek. 'Try it again.'

Mamie held out hers, and touched the back of his hand, timidly at first, and then took hold of it.

'Why, that's funny,' she said.

'She's been as nervous as a witch all day,' said Mrs Brewster severely.

'It is natural,' said the parson, 'that young Mrs Benton should experience a little agitation at such a moment.'

Most of the bride's relations lived at a distance, and were busy people, so it had been arranged that the dinner we'd had in the middle of the day was to take the place of a dinner afterwards, and that we should just have a bite after the wedding was over, and then that everybody should go home, and the young couple would walk down to the cottage by themselves. When I looked out I could see the light burning brightly in Jack's cottage, a quarter of a mile away. I said I didn't think I could get any train to take me back before half-past nine, but Mrs Brewster begged me to stay until it was time, as she said her daughter would want to take off her wedding dress before she went home; for she had put on something white with a wreath, that was very pretty, and she couldn't walk home like that, could she?

So when we had all had a little supper the party began to break up, and when they were all gone Mrs Brewster and Mamie went upstairs, and Jack and I went out on the piazza to have a smoke, as the old lady didn't like tobacco in the house.

The full moon had risen now, and it was behind me as I looked down toward Jack's cottage, so that everything was clear and white, and there was only the light burning in the window. The fog had rolled down to the water's edge, and a little beyond, for the tide was high, or nearly, and was lapping up over the last reach of sand, within fifty feet of the beach road.

Jack didn't say much as we sat smoking, but he thanked me for coming to his wedding, and I told him I hoped he would be happy; and so I did. I daresay both of us were thinking of those footsteps upstairs, just then, and that the house wouldn't seem so lonely with a woman in it. By and by we heard Mamie's voice talking to her mother on the stairs, and in a minute she was ready to go. She had put on again the dress she had worn in the morning.

Well, they were ready to go now. It was all very quiet after the day's excitement, and I knew they would like to walk down that path alone now that they were man and wife at last. I bade them good-night, although Jack made a show of pressing me to go with them by the path as far as the cottage, instead of going to the station by the beach road. It was all very quiet, and it seemed to me a sensible way of getting married; and when Mamie kissed her mother good-night I just looked the other way, and knocked my ashes over the rail of the piazza. So they started down the straight path to Jack's cottage, and I waited a minute with Mrs Brewster, looking after them, before taking my hat to go. They walked side by side, a little shyly at first, and then I saw Jack put his arm round her waist. As I looked he was on her left, and I saw the outline of the two figures very distinctly against the moonlight on the path; and the shadow on Mamie's right was broad and black as ink, and it moved along, lengthening and shortening with the unevenness of the ground beside the path.

I thanked Mrs Brewster, and bade her good-night; and though she was a hard New England woman her voice trembled a little as she answered, but being a sensible person she went in and shut the door behind her as I stepped out on the path. I looked after the couple in the distance a last time, meaning to go down to the road, so as not to overtake them; but when I had made a few steps I stopped and looked again, for I knew I had seen something queer, though I had only realised it afterwards. I looked again, and it was plain enough now; and I stood stock-still, staring at what I saw. Mamie was walking between two men. The second man was just the same height as Jack, both being about a half a head taller than she; Jack on her left in his black tail-coat and round hat, and the other man on her right – well, he was a sailor-man in wet oilskins. I could see the moonlight shining on the water that ran down him, and on the little puddle that had settled where the flap of his sou'wester was turned up behind: and one of his wet shiny arms was round Mamie's waist, just above Jack's. I was fast to the spot where I stood, and for a minute I thought I was crazy. We'd had nothing but some cider for dinner, and tea in the evening, otherwise I'd have thought something had got into my head, though I was never drunk in my life. It was more like a bad dream after that.

I was glad Mrs Brewster had gone in. As for me, I couldn't help following the three, in a sort of wonder to see what would happen, to see whether the sailor-man in his wet togs would just melt away into the moonshine. But he didn't.

I moved slowly, and I remembered afterwards that I walked on the grass, instead of on the path, as if I were afraid they might hear me coming. I suppose it all happened in less than five minutes after that, but it seemed as if it must have taken an hour. Neither Jack nor Mamie seemed to notice the sailor. She didn't seem to know that his wet arm was round her, and little by little they got near the cottage, and I wasn't a hundred yards from them when they reached the door. Something made me stand still then. Perhaps it was fright, for I saw everything that happened just as I see you now.

Mamie set her foot on the step to go up, and as she went forward I saw the sailor slowly lock his arm in Jack's, and Jack didn't move to go up. Then Mamie turned round on the step, and they all three stood that way for a second or two. She cried out then – I heard a man cry like that once, when his arm was taken off by a steam-crane – and she fell back in a heap on the little piazza.

I tried to jump forward, but I couldn't move, and I felt my hair rising under my hat. The sailor turned slowly where he stood, and swung Jack round by the arm steadily and easily, and began to walk him down the pathway from the house. He walked him straight down that path, as steadily as Fate; and all the time I saw the moonlight shining on his wet oilskins. He walked him through the gate, and across the beach road, and out upon the wet sand, where the tide was high. Then I got my breath with a gulp, and ran for them across the grass, and vaulted over the fence, and stumbled across the road. But when I felt the sand under my feet, the two were at the water's edge; and when I reached the water they were far out, and up to their waists; and I saw that Jack Benton's head had fallen forward on his breast, and his free arm hung limp beside him, while his dead brother steadily marched him to his death. The moonlight was on the dark water, but the fog-bank was white beyond, and I saw them against it; and they went slowly and steadily down. The water was up to their armpits, and then up to their shoulders, and then I saw it rise up to the black rim of Jack's hat. But they never wavered; and the two heads went straight on, straight on, till they were under, and there was just a ripple in the moonlight where Jack had been.

It has been on my mind to tell you that story, whenever I got a chance. You have known me, man and boy, a good many years; and I thought I would like to hear your opinion. Yes, that's what I always thought. It wasn't Jim that went overboard; it was Jack, and Jim just let him go when he might have saved him; and then Jim passed himself off for Jack with us, and with the girl. If that's what happened, he got what he deserved. People said the next day that Mamie found it out as they reached the house, and that her husband just walked out into the sea, and drowned himself; and they would have blamed me for not stopping him if they'd known that I was there. But I never told what I had seen, for they wouldn't have believed me. I just let them think I had come too late.

When I reached the cottage and lifted Mamie up, she was raving mad. She got better afterwards, but she was never right in her head again.

Oh, you want to know if they found Jack's body? I don't know whether it was his, but I read in a paper at a Southern port where I was with my new ship that two dead bodies had come ashore in a gale down East, in pretty bad shape. They were locked together, and one was a skeleton in oilskins.

FRANCIS MARION CRAWFORD

———————————

TWINS: HATING
AND HATED

from Creation Myths

IN our Iroquois myth when the woman arrived on earth she gave birth to a girl and that girl later was impregnated by the spirit of the tortoise; during her labour pains she heard the twins talking in her womb. The one said to the other, 'That is the place where we shall come out, it is the shorter way and the light is already shining through.' But the other said, 'Oh, no! We should kill our mother if we did that! We should go out by another way, the one which all human beings will take later. We will turn downwards.' The first speaker gave in and the other said that was how it should be from now on. Thus the first quarrel arose. The second then said the other should go first, but the latter said his brother should go first, and so they fought with each other till the second gave in, turned over, and came out head first. The grandmother received him and then turned her attention to the woman for the second child, but the second twin did not come out the normal way but from under his mother's armpit. The apex of his head was a firestone knife, and with that he pierced his mother and came out. This killed her. The grandmother was furious and said, 'You have killed your mother!' But the firestone twin accused the other and persisted so vehemently in this that the grandmother finally took the innocent human-shaped twin and threw him away into the bushes; the one with the firestone body became her beloved son whom she nursed and cared for. The grandmother then took her dead daughter and out of her corpse formed the Sun and the Moon and all the other lights. The twin who had been thrown away into the bushes recovered and grew up and became the positive creator called Maple Sprout and was in constant battle and difficulties with Tawiskaron, the son with the firestone body.

MARIE LOUISE VON FRANZ

The pathology of twinning is largely the history of sibling rivalry before birth. If the feud dates back to the stage when each twin was close to the sphere, its effect may be profound. In their clash for the womb's territory one may encroach upon the other.

F. GONZALEZ-CRUSSI, *Notes of an Anatomist*

Here we go again the other one struck again with its fist . . . now they have started fighting as before . . . one blow after the other . . . again . . . again . . ., again.

Ultrasonic observation of twins in the womb; ALESSANDRA PIONTELLI, *From Fetus to Child*

'Twins. Here! Lay the big one aside, nurse. It has all but killed the other in a struggle to be first . . .'

MRS E. F. BROOKE, *Twins of Skirlaugh Hall*

Born in a shotgun shack built by his father . . . Elvis Aron Presley entered the world wrapped in a shroud. A twin brother, Jesse Garon, was stillborn. His mother, Gladys . . . focussed all her considerable love on the surviving twin, telling Elvis that 'when one twin died, the one that lived got all the strength of both.' A suitable beginning for a mythic hero.

Review of biography of Elvis Presley, *New York Times Book Review*, October 1994

---

from Cursor Mundi

THERE was never, since the world began, a war like this,
such strife between twin children in their mother's womb.
Their struggle was stupendous, a spectacle to behold,
that blind battle between the unborn, locked in a bitter embrace!
The one who lay on the right – the other shoved him aside;
The one who lay on the left – the other stole his spot.
The lady, full of foreboding, was a woman sorely tried.
But our Lord had given her, through His truthful prophecy,
sure knowledge of the story of those children –
their fate, their lives, and what their battle betokened.

A FOURTEENTH-CENTURY NORTHUMBRIAN POEM
(translated by Victoria Nelson)

---

from The Silent Twins

THE pressures of the wait and successive postponements began to tell on the girls and both suffered nightmares, often the same nightmare, a particularly terrifying experience which they called the Beast. It was a sensation which would overcome them when they were dozing or just waking up or falling asleep. On 29th April they both record such an experience. It was just after dinner. Jennifer had eaten and enjoyed kidneys and cabbage and two sponges in custard. June had eaten her main course but donated her sponge to Jennifer. For once, there seemed to be harmony. Both girls lay on their beds and fell asleep.

June woke an hour later. She felt a great heavy breathing weight enveloping her as though a fat man had lain on top of her, smothering her in the folds of his flesh. She lay scared and rigid, unable to struggle against the hands which she felt were moving towards her throat. The Beast had in the past tickled her stomach as though in play. She felt like a tiny baby who was being suffocated, too weak to struggle against the presence. Both girls likened the sensation to what a baby must feel before a cot death. June heard Jennifer moaning in the bunk above her. She, too, was lying paralysed under the unknown weight, but June did not know. 'If I don't struggle to move, I know I will die,' wrote June. 'Will he ever leave me? Perhaps when I die I will die in my sleep, though you and I shall only know the truth; the monster has won.'

The twins could offer no explanation of their nightmare, which they had experienced for the first time only two years before. It may simply have been an extension of their waking quarrels, or perhaps it was some subconscious recollection of an infant trauma. Did someone, a jealous brother or sister, hold a pillow over the faces of the toddler twins? Or did June and Jennifer's rivalry start in Gloria's womb because there was not enough room for two of them to grow and flourish there? The position in which they were born – June head first; Jennifer breech – may have meant that June literally was sat upon by her sister. They had, even before birth, crowded each other out. The Beast was the other twin.

MARJORIE WALLACE

from Esau and Jacob

BARBARA questioned them. Natividade told why she had come, and handed her her sons' pictures and locks of their hair, since, she said, she had been told this would be all that was necessary.

'It is,' Barbara assured her. 'The babies are your sons?'

'Yes.'

'The face of one is the face of the other.'

'They are twins. They were born a little over a year ago.'

'You may sit down, ladies.'

Natividade said to her sister in a low voice that the cabocla was 'friendly.' Not in such a low voice, however, that the cabocla could not hear. Perhaps Natividade feared the prophecy, and wanted to make sure of a favorable destiny for her sons. The cabocla went and sat down at a round table in the center of the room, and facing the two women. She placed the locks of hair and the pictures before her. By turns she looked at these and at the mother, asked the latter several questions, then remained staring at the pictures and the locks of hair, her lips parted, her brows drawn together. It pains me to say that she lit a cigarette, but I must say it, because it is the truth, and the smoke accords with the rites. Outside, her father drew his fingers across the guitar, and softly sang a ballad of the tropic Northern wilderness:

> Naiad with skirts of white,
> Over the stream with leap . . .

While the smoke from the cigarette curled upward, the face of the fortuneteller changed expression, radiant, somber, now questioning, now full of answers. As she leaned over the pictures, she clasped the locks of hair in either hand, and held them to her face, staring at them, smelling them, listening to them. And none of this seemed strange or ridiculous, as it does in the telling. Natividade did not take her eyes off her, as if determined to read her thoughts. And it was not without amazement that she heard her ask if the boys had fought before they were born.

'Fought?'

'Yes, fought, Senhora.'

'Before they were born?'

'Yes, Senhora. I asked if they had not fought in their mother's womb. Don't you remember?'

Natividade, who had not had an easy pregnancy, answered that she had, to be sure, felt strange motions repeated, and pains, and sleeplessness . . . But then what did it mean? Why would they fight? The cabocla did not answer. A few minutes later she got up and walked around the table, slowly, like a person walking in her sleep, her eyes open and fixed. Then she returned to the mother and the pictures, looking at one and the other. She began to move restlessly, and breathe hard. All of her, face and arms, shoulders, legs, all of her was on the verge of wresting the *word* from Fate. At last, she grew quiet, sat down exhausted, then leaped up and came toward the two women, so radiant, her eyes so alive, so full of fire, that Natividade hung on them and could not keep from grasping her hands and asking her in an anxious tone, 'Well? Tell me, I can hear everything.'

Barbara, brimming with soul and with laughter, took a long breath. The first word seemed to fill her mouth, but withdrew again to her heart, without reaching the prophetess' lips or the ears of others. Natividade pressed for the response: she could tell her everything, without leaving out anything . . .

'Things fated to be!' the cabocla finally murmured.

'Bad things?'

'Oh! no! no! Fine things! things fated to be!'

'But that's not enough. Tell me the rest. This lady is my sister, and in my confidence, but if need be, she'll leave us, and I alone remain. Tell me in my ear . . . Will they be fortunate?'

'Yes.'

'Will they be great men?'

'They will be great, oh! very great! God will give them many blessings. They will go up, up, up . . . They fought in their mother's womb . . . well? They will fight outside in the world. Your sons will be glorious. That is all I can tell you. As for the kind of glory, it rests with the future: things fated to be!'

From the inner court, the voice of the old caboclo went on with the song of the wilderness:

> Climb up my coconut tree,
> Throw down the côcos to me.
> MACHADO DE ASSIS (translated by Helen Caldwell)

---

from Rivalry

OUR model of being male came to us across an immense space. My mother's bitterness towards men did little to reconcile us to our gender. She used to say, 'I've had to be father and mother to you as well.' It was a fierce, expiatory, over-protective love, saturated by her own guilt and unhappiness.

It seemed to me a pity to have had two fathers, and to have known neither of them, a bit of a waste really, since I had such a fragile sense of my own sexual identity. To make it worse, the separation of the men in her life was mirrored in her relationship with her twin boys. I think she feared above everything the possibility that we might combine against her. To forestall this, she kept us apart, as she had kept her husband and our father apart. We grew up as strangers to each other. Our personalities were constructed by her in such a way that we were mutually incomprehensible. I was clever, he was slow. He was handsome, I was ugly. He was well-behaved, I was troublesome. He was practical, I was supposed to be 'creative'. As it turned out, he had inherited his father's craftsmanship, and I his radicalism. But what could such beings possibly have in common? We grew up estranged from one another in the claustral intensity of our narrow family group; and so effective was it that it has persisted all our lives. She praised us endlessly to outsiders, but never to our faces. She also complained to each about the other. 'He'll never amount to anything.' 'He hasn't got a ha'porth of common sense.' 'He'll never get anywhere.' 'He'd better learn to hold a brush properly, because sweeping the roads is all he'll ever be fit for.' 'He isn't sharp enough to give handbills out.' 'He's a great dream of delight.' But she gave us to understand that each was the preferred one; and this was perhaps the best way of keeping us apart. We savoured, in secret, our superior status, not knowing that this was part of a competitive separation, which was destined to last a lifetime.

JEREMY SEABROOK, *The Independent on Sunday*, 1994

from Gemini

THERE were two of us, and we were born of one birth, but I swear to you that I was born the first, and Ram Dass is the younger by three full breaths. The astrologer said so, and it is written in my horoscope – the horoscope of Durga Dass.

But we were alike – I and my brother who is a beast without honour – so alike that none knew, together or apart, which was Durga Dass. I am a Mahajun of Pali in Marwar, and an honest man. This is true talk. When we were men, we left our father's house in Pali and went to the Punjab, where all the people are mud-heads and sons of asses. We took shop together in Isser Jang – I and my brother – near the big well where the Governor's camp draws water. But Ram Dass, who is without truth, made quarrel with me, and we were divided. He took his books, and his pots, and his Mark, and became a *bunnia* in the long street of Isser Jang, near the gateway of the road that goes to Montgomery.

[. . .] The people of Isser Jang were my portion, and the *jaghirdar* and the out-town was the portion of Ram Dass; for so we had arranged. I was the poor man, for the people of Isser Jang were without wealth. I did what I could, but Ram Dass had only to wait without the door of the *jaghirdar*'s garden-court, and to lend him the money; taking the bonds from the hand of the Steward.

In the autumn of the year after the lending, Ram Dass said to the *jaghirdar*: – 'Pay me my money,' but the *jaghirdar* gave him abuse. But Ram Dass went into the Courts with the papers and the bonds – all correct – and took out decrees against the *jaghirdar*; and the name of the Government was across the stamps of the decrees.

[. . .] This was in the month of *Phagun*. I took my horse and went out to speak to the man who makes lac-bangles upon the road that leads to Montgomery, because he owed me a debt. And I went forward till I came to the orange-bushes by the *jaghirdar*'s house. Here met me four men with their faces bound up, laying hold of my horse's bridle and crying out: – 'This is Ram Dass! Beat!' Me they beat with their staves – heavy staves bound about with wire at the end, such weapons as those swine of Punjabis use – till, having cried for mercy, I fell down senseless. I cried aloud that I was not Ram Dass but Durga Dass, his brother, yet they only beat me the more, and when I could make no more outcry they left me.

[. . .] When these four had gone away laughing, my brother Ram Dass came out of the crops and mourned over me as one dead. But I opened my eyes, and prayed him to get me water. When I had drunk, he carried me on his back, and by bye-ways brought me into the town of Isser Jang. My heart was turned to Ram Dass, my brother, in that hour because of his kindness, and I lost my enmity.

But a snake is a snake till it is dead; I was wrong in that I trusted my brother – the son of my mother.

When we had come to his house and I was a little restored, I told him my tale, and he said: – 'Without doubt, it is me whom they would have beaten. But the Law Courts are open, and there is the Justice of the Sirkar above all; and to the Law Courts do thou go when this sickness is overpast.'

[. . .] My heart was opened to my brother in my sickness, and I told him the names of those whom I would call as witnesses – all men in my debt, but of that the Magistrate Sahib could have no knowledge, nor the *jaghirdar*. The fever stayed with me, and after the fever, I was taken with colic, and gripings very terrible. In that day I thought that my end was at hand, but I know now that she who gave me the medicines, the sister of my father – a widow with a widow's heart – had brought about my second sickness. Ram Dass, my brother, said that my house was shut and locked, and brought me the big door-key and my books, together with all the monies that were in my house – even the money that was buried under the flour.

One night, when I had told Ram Dass all that was in my heart of the law-suit that I would bring against the *jaghirdar*, and Ram Dass had said that he had made the arrangements with the witnesses, giving me their names written, I was taken with a new great sickness, and they put me on the bed. When I was a little recovered – I cannot tell how many days afterwards – I made inquiry for Ram Dass, and the sister of my father said that he had gone to Montgomery upon a law-suit. I took medicine and slept very heavily without waking. When my eyes were opened, there was a great stillness in the house of Ram Dass, and none answered when I called – not even the sister of my father. This filled me with fear, for I knew not what had happened.

Taking a stick in my hand I went out slowly, till I came to the great square by the well, and my heart was hot in me against the *jaghirdar* because of the pain of every step I took.

I called for Jowar Singh, the carpenter, whose name was first upon the list of those who should bear evidence against the *jaghirdar*, say-ing:– 'Are all things ready, and do you know what should be said?'

Jowar Singh answered: – 'What is this, and whence do you come, Durga Dass?'

I said: – 'From my bed, where I have so long lain sick because of the *jaghirdar*. Where is Ram Dass, my brother, who was to have made the arrangement for the witnesses? Surely you and yours know these things!'

Then Jowar Singh said: – 'What has this to do with us, O Liar? I have borne witness and I have been paid, and the *jaghirdar* has, by the order of the Court, paid both the five hundred rupees that he robbed from Ram Dass and yet other five hundred because of the great injury he did to your brother.'

The well and the *ber*-tree above it and the square of Isser Jang became dark in my eyes, but I leaned on my stick and said: – 'Nay! This is child's talk and senseless. It was I who suffered at the hands of the *jaghirdar*, and I am come to make ready the case. Where is my brother Ram Dass?'

But Jowar Singh shook his head, and a woman cried: – 'What lie is here? What quarrel had the *jaghirdar* with you, *bunnia*!' . . .

I cried again, saying: – 'By the Cow – by the Oath of the Cow, by the Temple of the Blue-throated Mahadeo, I and I only was beaten – beaten to the death! . . . And I tottered where I stood, for the sickness and the pain of the beating were heavy upon me.

Then Ram Narain, . . . came up and said: – 'To-day is the one and fortieth day since the beating, and since these six days the case has been judged in the Court, and the Assistant Commissioner Sahib has given it for your brother Ram Dass, allowing the robbery, to which, too, I bore witness, and all things else as the witnesses said. There were many witnesses, and twice Ram Dass became senseless in the

Court because of his wounds, and the Stunt Sahib – the *baba* Stunt Sahib – gave him a chair before all the pleaders. Why do you howl, Durga Dass? These things fell as I have said: Was it not so?'

And Jowar Singh said: – 'That is truth. I was there, and there was a red cushion in the chair.'

[. . .] Then a new fear cam upon me and my bowels turned to water, and, running swiftly to the house of Ram Dass, I sought for my books and my money in the great wooden chest under my bedstead. There remained nothing: not even a cowrie's value. All had been taken by the devil who said he was my brother. I went to my own house also and opened the boards of the shutters; but there also was nothing save the rats among the grain-baskets. In that hour my senses left me, and, tearing my clothes, I ran to the well-place, crying out for the Justice of the English on my brother Ram Dass, and, in my madness, telling all that the books were lost. When men saw that I would have jumped down the well, they believed the truth of my talk; more especially because upon my back and bosom were still the marks of the staves of the *jaghirdar*.

Jowar Singh the carpenter withstood me, and turning me in his hands showed the scars upon my body and bowed down with laughter upon the well-curb. He cried aloud so that all heard him, from the well-square to the Caravanserai of the Pilgrims: – 'Oho! The jackals have quarrelled, and the grey one has been caught in the trap.'

RUDYARD KIPLING

from The Magic Ring

WHEN he was lost in these reflections, lo! there appeared, through the morning fogs, a tall figure of an armed knight on the opposite half of the cleft rock. With his visor thrown back, he gazed around him, just as Sir Otto had before done, till suddenly their eyes met together, and both trembled with affright, – for it was indeed Ottur and Otto who had thus encountered each other.

At length, 'This cannot and shall not longer be endured,' cried Ottur. 'At the sight of thee my senses are again confused, and I am driven to madness. In this world one champion only must live with that form and those features. Besides, thou hast, in this last night, beaten us from the battle-field; but, if I could make an end of thee, the faithful servants of Odin and Valhalla might hope ere long to redeem their lost honours, and inflict just vengeance on their foes. Therefore raise thy spear, and defend thyself, for the cleft of the rocks forbids us to use our swords; but ere the sun has fully risen in the heavens, our lances must determine who is to have the right of wearing such features, – thou or I.' – With these words he brandished his massive javelin high over his head.

'Yet halt a moment,' said Sir Otto; 'methinks by the combat which thou hast now proposed neither of us will arrive at peace of mind. How might that man live for the future who had put to death his own double? – were not that to say that he had killed himself?'

'Truly it would be so,' answered Ottur; 'but, remember, we shall fight with closed visors. One cannot mark then how his own features are stained with blood, or grinning in death's agony.' – Thereupon he closed his iron beaver with a great crash, and again poised his javelin.

'Yet, methinks, we might become friends and brethren in arms,' answered Sir Otto, 'and this on terms more intimate than those which bound any two heroes that the world has yet ever known.'

'Wilt thou then follow the banners of Gerda? – or would I forsake her?' said Ottur, in a hollow voice from his closed helmet; – 'since these are questions that may never be peaceably answered betwixt us, let us straightway to our bloody work! – If thou wilt not begin the attack, I shall at all hazards hurl my spear against thee; and surely, since thou wear'st the semblance of Ottur, thou canst not prove a runaway and a coward!'

'Heaven forbid!' answered the Knight of Trautwangen, who now drew down his visor, and prepared himself, like his antagonist, for the combat. For a little space thereafter, the two tall champions stood with their shields uplifted, and watching each other, when, lo! the Knight of Trautwangen beheld a new and strange assailant, who was rushing from the thickets against his adversary; – a wild bull, which had perchance been disturbed and enraged by the movements of the troops, came forth foaming, bellowing, and tossing his horns – directing all his wrath against Ottur, whom he would doubtless have hurled from the precipice; for the youth seemed never to observe his approach. In a moment the Knight of Trautwangen sent forth his javelin with irresistible strength, and so correct an aim, that it passed clear over the head of his pagan foe, and struck deep into the neck of the raging animal, which immediately fell, wrestling with death, among the deep snow.

'What meanest thou, Otto?' said the pagan youth, at the same time dropping his spear; 'it is impossible that thou couldst have been so bad a marksman, as to throw the weapon over my head! – or, peradventure, thou hast done this but in mockery?' – Sir Otto made a signal that he should look behind him; and, on turning round, Ottur saw the wild beast with the arrow in his neck, which was now stretching his convulsed limbs in the last agonies of death. At this sight he paused, and at length, turning to the Knight of Trautwangen, he threw back his visor, whereupon the latter followed his example; and the sun, which just then rose, shone brightly on the features of both the young heroes.

BARON FOUQUÉ

from Tweedledum and Tweedledee

ALICE was just going to say 'Good-night' and leave them, when Tweedledum sprang out from under the umbrella, and seized her by the wrist.

'Do you see *that*?' he said, in a voice choking with passion, and his eyes grew large and yellow all in a moment, as he pointed with a trembling finger at a small white thing lying under the tree.

'It's only a rattle,' Alice said, after a careful examination of the little white thing. 'Not a rattle-*snake*, you know,' she added hastily, thinking that he was frightened: 'only an old rattle – quite old and broken.'

'I knew it was!' cried Tweedledum, beginning to stamp about wildly and tear his hair. 'It's spoilt, of course!' Here he looked at Tweedledee, who immediately sat down on the ground, and tried to hide himself under the umbrella.

Alice laid her hand upon his arm, and said in a soothing tone, 'You needn't be so angry about an old rattle.'

'But it isn't old!' Tweedledum cried, in a greater fury than ever. 'It's new, I tell you – I bought it yesterday – my nice NEW RATTLE!' and his voice rose to a perfect scream.

All this time Tweedledee was trying his best to fold up the umbrella, with himself in it: which was such an extraordinary thing to do, that it quite took off Alice's attention from the angry brother. But he couldn't quite succeed, and it ended in his rolling over, bundled up in the umbrella, with only his head out: and there he lay, opening and shutting his mouth and his large eyes – 'looking more like a fish than anything else,' Alice thought.

'Of course you agree to have a battle?' Tweedledum said in a calmer tone.

'I suppose so,' the other sulkily replied, as he crawled out of the umbrella: 'only *she* must help us to dress up, you know.'

So the two brothers went off hand-in-hand into the wood, and returned in a minute with their arms full of things – such as bolsters, blankets, hearth-rugs, table-cloths, dish-covers, and coal-scuttles. 'I hope you're a good hand at pinning and tying strings?' Tweedledum remarked. 'Every one of these things has got to go on, somehow or other.'

Alice said afterwards she had never seen such a fuss made about anything in all her life – the way those two bustled about – and the quantity of things they put on – and the trouble they gave her in tying strings and fastening buttons – 'Really they'll be more like bundles of old clothes than anything else, by the time they're ready!' she said to herself, as she arranged a bolster round the neck of Tweedledee, 'to keep his head from being cut off,' as he said.

'You know,' he added very gravely, 'it's one of the most serious things that can possibly happen to one in a battle – to get one's head cut off.'

Alice laughed loud, but managed to turn it into a cough, for fear of hurting his feelings.

'Do I look very pale?' said Tweedledum, coming up to have his helmet tied on. (He *called* it a helmet, though it certainly looked much more like a saucepan.)

'Well – yes – a *little*,' Alice replied gently.

'I'm very brave generally,' he went on in a low voice: 'only to-day I happen to have a headache.'

'And *I've* got a toothache!' said Tweedledee, who had overheard the remark. 'I'm far worse than you!'

'Then you'd better not fight to-day,' said Alice, thinking it a good opportunity to make peace.

'We *must* have a bit of a fight, but I don't care about going on long,' said Tweedledum. 'What's the time now?'

Tweedledee looked at his watch, and said 'Half-past four.'

'Let's fight till six, and then have dinner,' said Tweedledum.

'Very well,' the other said, rather sadly: 'and *she* can watch us – only you'd better not come *very* close,' he added: 'I generally hit everything I can see – when I get really excited.'

'And *I* hit everything within reach,' cried Tweedledum, 'whether I can see it or not!'

Alice laughed. 'You must hit the *trees* pretty often, I should think,' she said.

Tweedledum looked round him with a satisfied smile. 'I don't suppose,' he said, 'there'll be a tree left standing, for ever so far round, by the time we've finished!'

'And all about a rattle!' said Alice, still hoping to make them a *little* ashamed of fighting for such a trifle.

'I shouldn't have minded it so much,' said Tweedledum, 'if it hadn't been a new one.'

'I wish the monstrous crow would come!' thought Alice.

'There's only one sword, you know,' Tweedledum said to his brother: 'but you can have the umbrella – it's quite as sharp. Only we must begin quick. It's getting as dark as it can.'

'And darker,' said Tweedledee.

It was getting dark so suddenly that Alice thought there must be a thunderstorm coming on. 'What a thick black cloud that is!' she said. 'And how fast it comes! Why, I do believe it's got wings!'

'It's the crow!' Tweedledum cried out in a shrill voice of alarm: and the two brothers took to their heels and were out of sight in a moment.

LEWIS CARROLL, from: *Through the Looking Glass*

---

from The Flemish Double Portrait

IN this painting which hangs in the Hermitage in St Petersburg
(the artist is unknown but the style is Flemish fifteenth century)
two aristocratic women wearing elegant silk & brocade dresses
are seated facing each other on elaborately carved fauteuils
we see them in profile, they are looking at each other as if engaged
   in conversation
their dresses are similar in cut but one is red and one is green

as we approach the painting we take the ladies to be sisters
on nearer inspection they appear to be twins
but when we look very closely they are indisputably one and the
    same person
the same coiffures, the same beaded slippers, the same gold-chain
    necklaces
a small mole (reversed of course) in the cheeks near the mouth
the ladies are staring at each other with unconcealed hatred
you might say that they are trying to set fire to each other with
    their eyes
their hands are clenched tight in their laps
if you linger before this painting for only a few moments
you may become hypnotized by the enmity it contains (such hatred,
    such hatred)
you may even feel hallucination stealing into your mind
you may imagine that you hear the women hissing at each other (in
    whatever is your language)
one asks, what are you doing inside me that I feel such excruciat-
    ing pain?
and the other replies, it is you who have no right to be in me, I demand
    that you go,
    I never wanted you, I never loved you, go now, you must
    go!

In describing the painting I neglected to say
that there are two small pet monkeys perched on the backs of the
    armchairs
they are different in color, one a slightly darker brown than the
    other
they show no animosity toward each other
in fact one is about to toss a little silver ball to the other.

                                                JAMES LAUGHLIN

——————

Nobody suffers the way I do. Not with a sister. With a
husband – yes. With a wife – yes. With a child – yes. But
this sister of mine, a dark shadow, robbing me of sunlight is
my one and only torment. June Gibbons. We have become
fatal enemies in each other's eyes ... We scheme, we plot

and who will win? A war which has gone on too long, when will it reach its climax? . . . A deadly day is getting closer each minute . . . I say to myself how can I get rid of my one shadow?

MARJORIE WALLACE, *The Silent Twins*

———————

There's another man within me that's angry with me.

SIR THOMAS BROWNE

———————

It does not arouse remorse in us when we slay a twin; it is too much like suppressing an aspect of ourselves.

JOHN UPDIKE, *Invention of the Horse Collar*

———————

from The Book of Genesis

AND it came to pass that when Isaac was old, and his eyes were dim, so that he could not see, he called Esau his eldest son, and said unto him, 'My son': and he said unto him, 'Behold, here am I.'

And he said, 'Behold now, I am old, I know not the day of my death. Now therefore take, I pray thee, thy weapons, thy quiver and thy bow, and go out to the field, and take me some venison; and make me savoury meat, such as I love, and bring it to me, that I may eat; that my soul may bless thee before I die.'

And Rebekah heard when Isaac spoke to Esau his son. And Esau went to the field to hunt for venison, and to bring it. And Rebekah spoke unto Jacob her son, saying,

'Behold, I heard thy father speak unto Esau thy brother, saying, "Bring me venison, and make me savoury meat, that I may eat, and bless thee before the Lord before my death." Now therefore, my son, obey my voice according to that which I command thee. Go now to the flock, and fetch me from thence two good kids of the goats; and I will make them savoury meat for thy father, such as he loveth: and thou shalt bring it to thy father, that he may eat, and that he may bless thee before his death.'

And Jacob said to Rebekah his mother, 'Behold, Esau my brother is a hairy man, and I am a smooth man. My father peradventure will feel me, and I shall seem to him as a deceiver; and I shall bring a curse upon me, and not a blessing.'

And his mother said unto him, 'Upon me be thy curse, my son: only obey my voice, and go fetch me them.'

And he went, and fetched, and brought them to his mother; and his mother made savoury meat, such as his father loved. And Rebekah took goodly raiment of her eldest son Esau, which were with her in the house, and put them upon Jacob her younger son; and she put the skins of the kids of the goats upon his hands, and upon the smooth of his neck; and she gave the savoury meat and the bread, which she had prepared, into the hand of her son Jacob.

And he came unto his father, and said, 'My father': and he said, 'Here am I; who art thou, my son?'

And Jacob said unto his father, 'I am Esau thy firstborn; I have done according as thou badest me: arise, I pray thee, sit and eat of my venison, that thy soul may bless me.'

And Isaac said unto his son, 'How is it that thou hast found it so quickly, my son?'

And he said, 'Because the Lord thy God brought it to me.'

And Isaac said unto Jacob, 'Come near, I pray thee, that I may feel thee, my son, whether thou be my very son Esau or not.'

And Jacob went near unto Isaac his father; and he felt him, and said, 'The voice is Jacob's voice, but the hands are the hands of Esau.'

And he discerned him not, because his hands were hairy, as his brother Esau's hands: so he blessed him. And he said, 'Art thou my very son Esau?'

And he said, 'I am.'

And he said, 'Bring it near to me, and I will eat of my son's venison, that my soul may bless thee.'

And he brought it near to him, and he did eat: and he brought him wine, and he drank. And his father Isaac said unto him, 'Come near now, and kiss me, my son.'

And he came near, and kissed him: and he smelled the smell of his raiment, and blessed him, and said,

> 'See, the smell of my son
> Is as the smell of a field which the Lord hath blessed:
> Therefore God give thee of the dew of heaven,
> And the fatness of the earth,
> And plenty of corn and wine:
> Let people serve thee,
> And nations bow down to thee:
> Be lord over thy brethren.
> And let thy mother's sons bow down to thee:
> Cursed be every one that curseth thee,
> And blessed be he that blesseth thee.'

And it came to pass, as soon as Isaac had made an end of blessing Jacob, and Jacob was yet scarce gone out from the presence of Isaac his father, that Esau his brother came in from his hunting. And he also had made savoury meat, and brought it unto his father, and said unto his father, 'Let my father arise, and eat of his son's venison, that thy soul may bless me.'

And Isaac his father said unto him, 'Who art thou?'

And he said, 'I am thy son, thy firstborn Esau.'

And Isaac trembled very exceedingly, and said, 'Who? where is he that hath taken venison, and brought it me, and I have eaten of all before thou camest, and have blessed him? yea, and he shall be blessed.'

And when Esau heard the words of his father, he cried with a great and exceeding bitter cry, and said unto his father, 'Bless me, even me also, O my father.'

And he said, 'Thy brother came with subtilty, and hath taken away thy blessing.'

And he said, 'Is not he rightly named Jacob? for he hath supplanted me these two times: he took away my birthright: and, behold, now he hath taken away my blessing.' And he said, 'Hast thou not reserved a blessing for me?'

And Isaac answered and said unto Esau,

'Behold, I have made him thy lord, and all his brethren have I given to him for servants; and with corn and wine have I sustained him: and what shall I do now unto thee, my son?'

And Esau said unto his father, 'Hast thou but one blessing, my
father? bless me, even me also, O my father.'
And Esau lifted up his voice, and wept.
And Isaac his father answered and said unto him,

> 'Behold, thy dwelling shall be the fatness of the earth,
> And of the dew of heaven from above;
> And by thy sword shalt thou live,
> And shalt serve thy brother;
> And it shall come to pass when thou shalt have the dominion.
> That thou shalt break his yoke from off thy neck.'

And Esau hated Jacob because of the blessing wherewith his father
blessed him: and Esau said in his heart, 'The days of mourning for
my father are at hand; then will I slay my brother Jacob.'

THE BOOK OF GENESIS

---

from The Twin-Rivals

[*Enter* Elder Wou'dbe *and* Subtleman]
My Brother! dearest Brother, welcome! [*Runs and embraces him*]
ELDER WOU´DBE I can't dissemble, Sir, else I wou'd return your false
Embrace.
YOUNG WOU´DBE False Embrace! still suspicious of me! I thought
that five Years Absence might have cool'd the unmanly Heats of
our childish days – that I am overjoy'd at your Return, let this
testify, this Moment I resign all Right and Title to your Honour,
and salute you Lord.
ELDER WOU´DBE I want not your Permission to enjoy my Right, here
I am Lord and Master without your Resignation; and the first Use
I make of my Authority, is, to discard that rude bull-fac'd Fellow
at the Door; where is my Steward,

[*Enter Steward*]
MR CLEARACCOUNT, let that pamper'd Sentinel below this Minute
her discharg'd – Brother, I wonder you cou'd feed such a swarm
of lazy idle Drones about you, and leave the poor industrious Bees
that fed you from their Hives, to starve for want – *Steward*, look to't,
if I have not Discharges for every Farthing of my Father's Debts

upon my Toylet to morrow morning, you shall follow the Tipstaff I can assure you.

YOUNG WOU´DBE Hold, hold, my Lord, you usurp too large a Power, methinks, o'er my Family.

ELDER WOU´DBE Your Family!

YOUNG WOU´DBE Yes, my Family, you have no Title to lord it here – Mr *Clearaccount*, you know your Master.

ELDER WOU´DBE How! a Combination against me! – Brother, take heed how you deal with one that, cautious of your Falshood, comes prepar'd to meet your Arts, and can retort your Cunning to your Infamy: Your black unnatural Designs against my Life before I went abroad, my Charity can pardon; but my Prudence must remember to guard me from your Malice for the future.

YOUNG WOU´DBE Our Father's weak and fond Surmise! which he upon his Death-bed own'd; and to recompence me for that injurious unnatural Suspicion, he left me sole Heir to his Estate – Now, my Lord, my House and Servants are – at your Service.

ELDER WOU´DBE Villany beyond Example! have I not Letters from my Father, of scarce a Fortnight's Date, where he repeats his Fears for my Return, least it should again expose me to your Hatred.

SUBTLEMAN Well, well, these are no Proofs, no Proofs, my Lord; they won't pass in Court against positive Evidence – here is your Father's Will, *signatum & sigillatum*, besides his last Words to confirm it, to which I can take my positive Oath in any Court of *Westminster*.

ELDER WOU´DBE What are you, Sir?

SUBTLEMAN Of *Clifford*'s-Inn, my Lord, I belong to the Law.

ELDER WOU´DBE Thou art the Worm and Maggot of the Law, bred in the bruis'd and rotten parts, and now art nourish'd on the same Corruption that produc'd thee – the *English* Law as planted first, was like the *English* Oak, shooting its spreading Arms around to shelter all that dwelt beneath its shade – but now whole Swarms of Caterpillars, like you, hang in such Clusters upon every Branch, that the once thriving Tree now sheds infectious Vermin on our Heads.

YOUNG WOU´DBE My Lord, I have some Company above, if your Lordship will drink a Glass of Wine, we shall be proud of the Honour, if not, I shall attend you at any Court of Judicature whenever you please to summon me. [*Going*]

ELDER WOU´DBE Hold sir, – perhaps my Father's dying Weakness was impos'd on, and he has left him Heir; if so, his Will shall freely be obey'd. [*Aside*] – Brother, you say you have a Will.

SUBTLEMAN Here it is. [*Shewing a Parchment*]

ELDER WOU´DBE Let me see it.

SUBTLEMAN There's no President for that, my Lord.

ELDER WOU´DBE Upon my Honour I'll restore it.

YOUNG WOU´DBE Upon my Honour but you shan't – [*Takes it from Subtleman and puts it in his Pocket*]

ELDER WOU´DBE This over-caution, Brother, is suspicious.

YOUNG WOU´DBE Seven thousand Pound a Year is worth looking after.

ELDER WOU´DBE Therefore you can't take it ill that I am a little inquisitive about it – Have you Witnesses to prove my Father's dying Words.

YOUNG WOU´DBE A Couple, in the House.

ELDER WOU´DBE Who are they?

SUBTLEMAN Witnesses my Lord – 'tis unwarrantable to enquire into the Merits of the Cause out of Court – my Client shall answer no more Questions.

ELDER WOU´DBE Perhaps, Sir, upon a satisfactory Account of his Title, I intend to leave your Client to the quiet Enjoyment of his Right, without troubling any Court with the Business; I therefore desire to know what kind of Persons are these Witnesses.

SUBTLEMAN Oho, he's a coming about [*Aside*] I told your Lordship already, that I am one, another is in the House, one of my Lord's Footmen.

ELDER WOU´DBE Where is this Footman?

YOUNG WOU´DBE Forthcoming.

ELDER WOU´DBE Produce him.

SUBTLEMAN, That I shall presently – The day's our own, Sir, [*To Young Wou'dbe*] but you shall engage first to ask him no cross Questions.

[*Exit Subtleman*]

ELDER WOU´DBE I am not skill'd in such: But pray Brother, did my Father quite forget me, left me nothing.

YOUNG WOU´DBE Truly, my Lord, nothing – he spake but little, left no Legacies.

ELDER WOU´DBE 'Tis strange! he was extreamly just, and lov'd me too – but, perhaps—

[*Enter Subtleman with Teague*]

SUBTLEMAN My Lord, here's another Evidence.

ELDER WOU´DBE *Teague*!

YOUNG WOU´DBE My Brother's Servant! [*They all four stare upon one another*]

SUBTLEMAN. His Servant!

TEAGUE Maishter! see here Maishter, I did get all dish [*Chinks Money*] for being an Evidensh dear Joy, an be me shoule I will give the half of it to you, if you will give me your Permission to maake swear against you.

ELDER WOU´DBE My Wonder is divided between the Villany of the Fact, and the Amazement of the Discovery. *Teague*! my very Servant! sure I dream.

TEAGUE Fet, dere is no dreaming in the cashe, I'm sure the Croon pieceish are awake, for I have been taaking with dem dish half hour.

YOUNG WOU´DBE Ignorant, unlucky Man, thou hast ruin'd me; why had not I a sight of him before.

SUBTLEMAN I thought the Fellow had been too ignorant to be a Knave.

TEAGUE Be me shoule, you lee, dear Joy – I can be a Knave as well as you, fen I think it conveniency.

ELDER WOU´DBE Now Brother! Speechless! Your Oracle too silenc'd! Is all your boasted Fortune sunk to the guilty blushing for a Crime? but I scorn to insult – let Disappointment be your Punishment: But for your Lawyer there – *Teague*, lay hold of him.

SUBTLEMAN Let none dare to attach me without a legal Warrant.

TEAGUE Attach! no dear Joy, I cannot attach you – but I can catch you by the Troat, after the fashion of *Ireland*. [*Takes* Subtleman *by the Throat*]

SUBTLEMAN An Assault! An Assault!

TEAGUE No, no, tish nothing but choaking, nothing but choaking.

ELDER WOU´DBE Hold him fast *Teague* – Now Sir [*To Young Wou'dbe*] because I was your Brother you wou'd have betray'd me; and because I am your Brother, I forgive it, – dispose your self as you think fit, – I'll order Mr *Clearaccount* to give you a thousand Pounds. Go take it, and pay me by your Absence.

YOUNG WOU´DBE I scorn your beggarly Benevolence: Had my Designs succeeded, I wou'd not have allow'd you the weight of a Wafer, and therefore will accept none. – As for that Lawyer, he deserves to be Pillory'd, not for his Cunning in deceiving you; but for his Ignorance in betraying me. – The villain has defrauded me of seven thousand Pounds a year. Farewel. – [*Going*]

[*Enter* Midnight *out of the Closet, runs to* Young Wou'dbe *and kneels*]

MIDNIGHT My Lord, my dear Lord *Wou'dbe*, I beg you ten thousand Pardons.

YOUNG WOU´DBE What Offence hast thou done to me?

MIDNIGHT An Offence the most injurious. – I have hitherto concal'd a Secret in my Breast to the Offence of Justice, and the defrauding your Lordship of your true Right and Title. You *Benjamin Wou'dbe* with the crooked Back, art the Eldest-born, and true Heir to the Estate and Dignity.

OMNES How!

TEAGUE Arah, how?

MIDNIGHT None, my Lord, can tell better than I, who brought you both into the world. – My deceas'd Lord, upon the sight of your Deformity, engag'd me by a considerable Reward, to say you were the last born, that the beautiful Twin, likely to be the greater Ornament to the Family, might succeed him in his Honour. – This Secret my Conscience has long struggled with, – upon the News that you were left Heir to the Estate: I thought Justice was satisfied, and I was resolv'd to keep it a Secret still: but by strange Chance overhearing what past just now, my poor Conscience was rack'd, and I was forc'd to declare the Truth.

YOUNG WOU´DBE By all my forward Hopes I cou'd have sworn it: I found the Spirit of Eldership in my Blood: my Pulses beat, and swell'd for Seniority. – Mr *Hermes Wou'dbe*, – I'm your most humble Servant. [*Foppishly*]

GEORGE FARQUHAR, 1702

---

from The Inheritors

IN short, Reb Shimshen left behind a seat in the old Kasrilevka Synagogue. But he forgot one small detail. He didn't indicate who was to inherit the seat – Maier or Schnaier.

Obviously Reb Shimshen – may he forgive me – did not expect to die. He had forgotten that the Angel of Death lurks always behind our backs and watches every step we take, else he would surely have made a will or otherwise indicated in the presence of witnesses to which of his two sons he wanted to leave his fortune.

Well, what do you suppose? The very first Saturday after they arose from mourning, the quarrel began. Maier argued that according to law the seat belonged to him; since he was the older (by a good half-hour). And Schnaier had two arguments in his favor: first, they were not sure which of the two was older because according to their mother's story they had been exchanged as infants and he was really Maier and Maier was really Schnaier. In the second place, Maier had a rich father-in-law who also owned a seat along the east wall of the synagogue, and since the father-in-law had no sons the seat would eventually be Maier's. And when that happened Maier would have two seats by the east wall and Schnaier would have none whatever. And if that was the case, where was justice? Where was humanity?

When he heard of these goings-on, Maier's father-in-law, a man of means, but one who had made his money only recently, entered the battle. 'You've got a lot of nerve!' he exclaimed. 'I am not forty yet and I have every intention of living a long time, and here you are, dividing up my inheritance already. And besides, how do you know that I won't have a son yet? I may have more than one, see!' he stormed. There is impudence for you!'

So their neighbors tried to make peace between them, suggested that they determine how much the seat was worth and then have one brother buy his share from the other. That sounds reasonable enough, doesn't it? The only trouble was that neither brother wanted to sell his share. They didn't care a thing about the money. What was money – compared to stubbornness and pride?

'How can one's own brother be so pigheaded as to keep a person away from his rightful seat?' 'Why should you have our father's place, and not I?' It became a matter not so much of having things his own way as it was of preventing the other from having his. As the saying is: If I don't, you don't either. And the rivalry between the Maiers and the Schnaiers increased in fury. Stubbornness gave way to cunning as each tried to outwit the other!

The first Sabbath Maier came early and sat down in his father's seat; and Schnaier remained standing throughout the services. The second Sabbath Schnaier came first and occupied his father's place, while Maier remained standing. The third Sabbath Maier got there still earlier, spread himself out in the seat, pulled his *tallis* over his head, and there he was . . .

The next time it was Schnaier who hurried to get there first, sat down in the coveted seat, pulled his *tallis* over his face – and just try to budge him! The following week Maier was the first to get there . . . This went on week after week till one fine Sabbath both of them arrived at the same time – it was still dark outside – took their posts at the door of the synagogue (it was still shut) and glared at each other like roosters ready to tear each other's eyes out. It was like this that long ago the first two brothers stood face to face in an empty field, under God's blue sky, full of anger, ready to annihilate one another, devour each other, spill innocent blood . . .

But let us not forget that the Maiers and Schnaiers were young men of good family, respectable and well behaved – not rowdies who were in the habit of assaulting each other in public. They waited for Ezriel, the *shammes*, to come and open the door of the synagogue. Then they would show the whole world who would get to their father's seat first – Maier or Schnaier . . .

The minutes passed like years till Ezriel arrived with the keys. And when Ezriel, with his tangled beard, arrived he was not able to reach the door because the brothers stood against it – one with the left foot, the other with the right foot, and would not budge an inch.

'Well, what's going to happen?' said Ezriel casually, taking a pinch of snuff. 'If the two of you insist on standing there like mean scarecrows I won't be able to open the door and the synagogue will have to remain closed all day. Go ahead and tell me: does that make sense?'

Apparently these words had some effect, because the Maiers and Schnaiers both moved back, one to the right, the other to the left, and made way for Ezriel and his key. And when the key turned in the lock and the door swung open, the Maiers and Schnaiers tumbled in headlong.

'Be careful, you're killing me!' yelled Ezriel the *shammes*, and before he could finish the words the poor man lay trampled under their feet, screaming in horror: 'Watch out! You're trampling all over me – the father of a family!'

But the Maiers and Schnaiers cared nothing for Ezriel and his family. Their only thought was for the seat, their father's seat, and jumping over benches and praying stands they made for the east wall. There they planted themselves firmly against the wall with their shoulders and the floor with their feet and tried to shove each other aside. In the scuffle they caught each other's beards, grimaced horribly, gritted their teeth and growled: 'May the plague take you before you get this seat!'

In the meantime Ezriel got up from the floor, felt to see if any of his bones were broken, and approached the brothers. He found them both on the floor clutching each other's beards. At first he tried to reason with them.

'Shame on you! Two brothers – children of the same father and mother – tearing each other's beards out! And in a Holy Place at that! Be ashamed of yourselves!'

But Ezriel gathered that at the moment his lecture was in vain. Actually, his words added fuel to the flame so that the two children of one father became so enraged that one of them clutched in his fist a tuft of black hair (from Maier's beard) and the other a tuft of red (Schnaier's beard); blue marks showed on both faces and from the nose of one streamed blood.

As long as it was merely a matter of pulling beards, slapping and pummeling each other, the *shammes* could content himself with reading a lecture. But when he saw blood streaming, Ezriel could stand it no longer, for blood, even though only from a punched nose, was an ugly thing fit for rowdies and not God-fearing men.

He wasted no time, but ran to the tap, grabbed a dipper of water, and poured it over the two brothers. Cold water has always – since the world was created – been the best means of reviving a person. A man may be in the greatest rage, but as soon as he gets a cold bath he is strangely refreshed and cool; he comes to his senses. This happened to the Maiers and the Schnaiers. At the unexpected shower of cold water to which Ezriel had treated them, they woke up, looked each other in the eyes, and grew ashamed – like Adam and Eve when they had tasted of the forbidden fruit of the Tree of Knowledge and saw their nakedness . . .

And that very Saturday night the Maiers and Schnaiers went together with their friends and neighbors to the home of Reb Yozifel, the Rabbi, to have the dispute settled.

SHOLOM ALEICHEM

---

from The Vivisector Vivisected

'DURING this extraordinary conversation the wind had risen still more, and the turret was plainly felt to rock to and fro. The evening, too, began to hasten in, aided by the black, scurrying rack that obscured the sky. We had been toiling for more than an hour, having to keep time like rowers. My arms were getting tired, and I was profusely perspiring. Maculligan was shouting and laughing like a maniac or drunkard, his face bloated with exertion and his long light hair hanging over his eyes. Suddenly I cast my eyes on the thermometer in the bath which maintained the heat of the blood at the necessary 100°. It stood at 97.4°. The fire in the stove was getting low.

'I said: "The fire is getting low; it must be replenished."

'"You pile it up then," said Maculligan; "we must both leave off together."

'At a signal from him we both ceased pumping and I, who was nearest, rushed to the stove, knocked the lid off and poured in, in my haste, the whole scuttle full of coals. When I returned the patient had fainted: we immediately resumed.

'I said: "He was nearly out then, Maculligan."

'"Wot's that?" muttered the patient, coming round. "Tarnation take you deevils, how did you gumption that my name was Maculligan?"

'"Is that so?" inquired Maculligan.

'"Is that so! I guess it is – Josephus Maculligan av Maculligan Castle, County Lietrim, son av old Maculligan av the same, and be damned to yer!"

'No sooner were these words uttered than my companion uttered the most horrible yell I ever heard.

'"You are my brother," he shrieked; "Ha! ha! look at this!" showing the long scar on his face. The patient's jaw dropped, and he struggled violently; but when my friend relaxed the speed of pumping he fell back, and began to groan.

'"Oh! oh! Is it me brother they have put to plague me, me twin brother, who I knocked about and gashed down the cheek because he was after bein' five munutes older than myself and had got all the proparty? Ye are not dead, Pathrick dear? Ye are no ghost, avic? Ye will not tormint me though your father and me druv you to Ameriky?"

'"No, no," shouted Maculligan. "I am alive! You are alive! We are all alive! I am surgeon of the Snogginsville Infirmary. I have made an invention for reviving the dead by means of injecting hot, fresh blood into his veins. I required a case for experiment, which had merely bled to death. You were the first that presented. If we leave off pumping for five minutes, or the stove goes out, letting the hot water cool, the blood will clot in the machine and you will die immediately."

'I cannot describe the face of Josephus Maculligan during this recital. He burst forth into oaths, upbraiding his brother for attempting such an experiment, and shrieking for help. But the wind out-shrieked him. He prayed and cried alternately. My arms were getting intensely tired, and my back was aching, owing to the necessary stoop of the body. Suddenly the setting sun, which was almost touching the horizon, gleamed out from the clouds, and poured a red glow on Patrick Maculligan's face. I shall never forget its expression: he seemed to have become more like an ape than a man. His face was turbid and red; his mouth drawn back at the corners, showing all his teeth and the very gums. His tongue hung out, the large veins of the throat and forehead stood prominent, the long scar on the cheek glistened white, and seemed to have contracted in length, drawing up the upper lip, and showing the canine tooth of that side. His necktie and collar had burst open, and he panted quickly like a dog; while his eyes, round and lidless, glared on his brother, not with anger or fear, but without any expression at all. The one beam of blood-red light, streaming in from the window seemed to rest upon him on purpose, and, as it were, moved and twined amongst his hair. He alone was visible: all the rest of the room was dark; for the ray, after touching him passed into the workshop beyond. I could see that his hands which were working the pump were swollen and veined.'

SIR RONALD ROSS

---

from The Terror of the Twins

THAT the man's hopes had built upon a son to inherit his name and estates – a single son, that is – was to be expected; but no one could have foreseen the depth and bitterness of his disappointment, the cold, implacable fury, when there arrived instead – twins. For, though the elder legally must inherit, that other ran him so deadly close. A daughter would have been a more reasonable defeat. But twins——! To miss his dream by so feeble a device——!

The complete frustration of a hope deeply cherished for years may easily result in strange fevers of the soul but the violence of the father's hatred, existing as it did side by side with a love he could not deny, was something to set psychologists thinking. More than unnatural, it was positively uncanny. Being a man of rigid self-control, however, it operated inwardly, and doubtless along some morbid line of weakness little suspected even by those nearest to him, preying upon his thought to such dreadful extent that finally the mind gave way. The suppressed rage and bitterness deprived him, so the family decided, of his reason, and he spent the last years of his life under restraint. He was possessed naturally of immense forces – of will, feeling, desire; his dynamic value truly tremendous, driving through life like a great engine: and the intensity of this concentrated and buried hatred was guessed by few. The twins themselves, however, knew it.

On the occasion of their final visit to the asylum, preceding his death by a few hours only, very calmly, but with an intensity that drove the words into their hearts like points of burning metal, he had spoken. In the presence of the attendant, at the door of the dreadful padded cell, he said it: 'You are not two, but *one*. I still regard you as one. And at the coming of age, by h—, you shall find it out!'

The lads perhaps had never fully divined that icy hatred which lay so well concealed against them, but that this final sentence was a curse, backed by all the man's terrific force, they quite well realised; and accordingly, almost unknown to each other, they had come to dread the day inexpressibly. On the morning of that twenty-first birthday they shared the same biting, inner terror, just as they shared all other emotions of their life – intimately, without speech. During the daytime they managed to keep it at a distance, but when the dusk fell about the old house they knew the stealthy approach of a kind of panic sense. Their self-respect weakened swiftly . . . and they persuaded their old friend, and once tutor, the vicar, to sit up with them till midnight.

[. . .] The library was the quietest room in the house. It had shuttered bow-windows, thick carpets, heavy doors. Books lined the walls, and there was a capacious open fireplace of brick in which the woodlogs blazed and roared, for the autumn night was chilly. Round this the three of them were grouped, the clergyman reading aloud from the Book of Job in low tones; Edward and Ernest, in dinner-jackets, occupying deep leather arm-chairs, listening. They looked exactly what they were – Cambridge 'undergrads', their faces pale against their dark hair, and alike as two peas. A shaded lamp behind the clergyman threw the rest of the room into shadow. The reading voice was steady, even monotonous, but something in it betrayed an underlying anxiety, and although the eyes rarely left the printed page, they took in every movement of the young men opposite, and noted every change upon their faces. It was his aim to produce an unexciting atmosphere, yet to miss nothing; if anything did occur to see it from the very beginning. Not to be taken by surprise was his main idea. . . . And thus, upon this falsely peaceful scene, the minutes passed the hour of eleven and slipped rapidly along towards midnight.

[. . .] The clergyman had been reading aloud for some considerable time, one or other of the twins – Ernest usually – making occasional remarks, which proved that his sense of dread was disappearing. As the time grew short and nothing happened they grew more at their ease. Edward, indeed, actually nodded, dozed, and finally fell asleep. It was a few minutes before midnight. Ernest, slightly yawning, was stretching himself in the big chair. 'Nothing's going to happen,' he said aloud, in a pause. 'Your good influence has prevented it.' He even laughed now. 'What superstitious asses we've been, sir; haven't we—?'

Curtice, then, dropping his Bible, looked hard at him under the lamp. For in that second, even while the words sounded, there had come about a most abrupt and dreadful change; and so swiftly that the clergyman, in spite of himself, was taken utterly by surprise and had no time to think. There had swooped down upon the quiet library – so he puts it – an immense hushing silence, so profound that the peace already reigning there seemed clamour by comparison; and out of this enveloping stillness there rose through the space about them a living and abominable Invasion – soft, motionless, terrific. It was as though vast engines, working at full speed and pressure, yet too swift and delicate to be appreciable to any definite sense, had suddenly dropped down upon them – from nowhere. 'It made me think,' the vicar used to say afterwards, 'of the *Mauretania* machinery compressed into a nutshell, yet losing none of its awful power.'

'. . . haven't we?' repeated Ernest, still laughing. And Curtice, making no audible reply, heard the true answer in his heart: 'Because everything has *already happened* – even as you feared.'

Yet, to the vicar's supreme astonishment, Ernest still noticed – nothing!

'Look,' the boy added, 'Eddy's sound asleep – sleeping like a pig. Doesn't say much for your reading, you know, sir!' And he laughed again – lightly, even foolishly. But that laughter jarred, for the clergyman understood now that the sleep of the elder twin was either feigned – or *unnatural*.

And while the easy words fell so lightly from his lips, the monstrous engines worked and pulsed against him and against his sleeping brother, all their huge energy concentrated down into points fine as

Suggestion, delicate as Thought. The Invasion affected everything. The very objects in the room altered incredibly, revealing suddenly behind their normal exteriors horrid little hearts of darkness. It was truly amazing, this vile metamorphosis. Books, chairs, pictures, all yielded up their pleasant aspect, and betrayed, as with silent mocking laughter, their inner soul of blackness – their *decay*. This is how Curtice tries to body forth in words what he actually witnessed. . . . And Ernest, yawning, talking lightly, half foolishly – still noticed nothing!

For all this, as described, came about in something like ten seconds; and with it swept into the clergyman's mind, like a blow, the memory of that sinister phrase used more than once by Edward: 'If father doesn't come, he will certainly – *send*.' And Curtice understood that he had done both – both sent and come himself. . . . That violent mind, released from its spell of madness in the body, yet still retaining the old implacable hatred, was now directing the terrible, unseen assault. This silent room, so hushed and still, was charged to the brim. The horror of it, as he said later, 'seemed to peel the very skin from my back.' . . . And, while Ernest noticed nothing, Edward slept . . . The soul of the clergyman, strong with the desire to help or save, yet realising that he was alone against a Legion, poured out in wordless prayer to his Deity. The clock just then, whirring before it struck, made itself audible.

'By Jove! It's all right, you see!' exclaimed Ernest, his voice oddly fainter and lower than before. 'There's midnight – and nothing's happened. Bally nonsense, all of it!' His voice had dwindled curiously in volume. 'I'll get the whisky and soda from the hall.' His relief was great and his manner showed it. But in him somewhere was a singular change. His voice, manner, gestures, his very tread as he moved over the thick carpet toward the door, all showed it. He seemed less *real*, less alive, reduced somehow to littleness, the voice without timbre or quality, the appearance of him diminished in some fashion quite ghastly. His presence, if not actually shrivelled, was at least impaired. Ernest had suffered a singular and horrible *decrease* . . .

The clock was still whirring before the strike. One heard the chain running up softly. Then the hammer fell upon the first stroke of midnight.

'I'm off,' he laughed faintly from the door; 'it's all been pure funk – on my part, at least . . .!' He passed out of sight into the hall. *The Power that throbbed so mightily about the room followed him out*. Almost at the same moment Edward woke up. But he woke with a tearing and indescribable cry of pain and anguish on his lips: 'Oh, oh, oh! But it hurts! It hurts! I can't hold you; leave me. It's breaking me asunder—'

The clergyman had sprung to his feet, but in the same instant everything had become normal once more – the room as it was, before, the horror gone. There was nothing he could do or say, for there was no longer anything to put right, to defend, or to attack. Edward was speaking; his voice, deep and full as it never had been before: 'By Jove, how that sleep has refreshed me! I feel twice the chap I was before – twice the chap. I feel quite splendid. Your voice, sir, must have hypnotised me to sleep. . . . He crossed the room with great vigour. 'Where's – er – where's – Ernie, by the bye?' he asked casually, hesitating – almost searching – for the name. And a shadow as of a vanished memory crossed his face and was gone. The tone conveyed the most complete indifference where once the least word or movement of his twin had wakened solicitude, love. 'Gone away, I suppose – gone to bed, I mean, of course.'

Curtice has never been able to describe the dreadful conviction that overwhelmed him as he stood there staring, his heart in his mouth – the conviction, the positive certainty, that Edward had changed interiorly, had suffered an incredible accession to his existing personality. But he *knew* it as he watched. His mind, spirit, soul had most wonderfully increased. Something that hitherto the lad had known from the outside only, or by the magic of loving sympathy, had now passed, to be incorporated with his own being. And, being himself, it required no expression. Yet this visible increase was somehow terrible. Curtice shrank back from him. The instinct – he has never grasped the profound psychology of *that*, nor why it turned his soul dizzy with a kind of nausea – the instinct to strike him where he stood, passed, and a plaintive sound from the hall, stealing softly into the room between them, sent all that was left to him of self-possession onto his feet. He turned and ran. Edward followed him – very leisurely.

They found Ernest, or what had been Ernest, crouching behind the table in the hall, weeping foolishly to himself. On his face lay blackness. The mouth was open, the jaw dropped; he dribbled hopelessly; and from the face had passed all signs of intelligence – of spirit.

ALGERNON BLACKWOOD

from The Twins of Warsaw

LINDOFF Whereof I joy, my lord, to tell you
　　Your brother Orloff is at liberty –
　　Young Edgar gained his pardon from the kind . . .

COUNT CARLOVITZ [*transported*] My brother! –
　　My dear brother! – Where is he?

LINDOFF Now in the house; – the tempest drove him hither,
　　As all of us – he has retired to rest
　　In yonder chamber.

CARLOVITZ Then I will fly and clasp him to my heart.
　　[*Rushes into the chamber in which he as Count Orloff, entered a
　　few minutes before, exclaiming, in the voice of Carlovitz*] Orloff!
　　My dear, dear brother! – he sleeps and hears me not! – Orloff!
　　'tis I, thy brother Carlowitz! – Oh speak me!
　　[*Then answers as the brother, Orloff, in a rough and angry voice*]
　　Hence detested viper! From my sight!
　　[*again as Carlovitz*] Oh, spurn me not, my brother! – my dear,
　　dear brother . . .
　　[*as Orloff*] Avaunt thee, serpent! An thou cling to me, I'll prove
　　a second Cain and strike thee dead!—
　　[*This alternation is introduced to gain time for the change of dress,
　　etc.*] Enters as Count Orloff . . .

[*Ending*]
ORLOFF To Orloff there's a word of deeper import than power –
　　freedom, gold or even *life*!
　　It is *revenge*! Orloff and Carlovitz,
　　As brother twins came into this vile world,
　　And to perdition shall they both be hurled hurled
　　Together! – Witness – Orloff is no liar!
　　Behold! he keeps his promise! Fire! Fire!

[*He fires the thatch of the building and laughs, maliciously*]

ANON., melodrama, c.19

from Japanese Tales of Mystery and Imagination

FIRST let me repeat that I was born as one of a pair of twins so strangely identical, so completely the same that it seemed as if we had been cast in the same mold. There was, however, a single distinguishing feature. This was a mole on my thigh, the one sign that made it possible for our parents to tell us apart. If our hairs had been counted, I would not have been surprised had the number been the same. This very singular similarity between us was, I now believe, the seed which gradually took root in my mind, tempting me to kill my other half.

When I finally decided to kill my brother I really had no special reason to be bitter towards him other than that of a burning jealousy on my part. The fact of the matter was that he inherited an immense fortune as first-born son and heir, while my share was incomparably smaller. At the same time, the woman whom I had loved became his wife; her parents had forced her to marry him because of his superiority over me in fortune and position. Naturally, this was our parents' fault rather than his. If I wanted to hate, I should have become bitter against my deceased parents rather than against my brother. Besides, he was innocent of the knowledge that his wife had once been my heart's desire. But hate him I did – with all my soul.

So, if I had been capable of thinking rationally, nothing would have happened. But, unfortunately, I was born wicked, and I didn't know how to get on in the world. And to make matters worse, I had no definite aim in life, being a confirmed wastrel. I had become the kind of rogue who is satisfied only with living a life of idleness, living from day to day without a thought for tomorrow. Therefore, after losing both my fortune and my love at one stroke, I suppose I became desperate. At any rate, I immediately squandered foolishly the money I received as my share.

Consequently, there was nothing for me to do but to appeal to him for financial help. And I used to give him a great deal of trouble. He gradually became annoyed at my repeated calls for help, and one day he told me flatly that he would put a halt to his generosity unless I mended my ways.

One afternoon, on my way home from his house after having been refused another loan, a terrible idea suddenly occurred to me.

[. . .] Please believe that my wicked resolution did not grow out of any feelings of animosity. As a born rogue, I only wanted to obtain pleasure at any cost. But in spite of my wicked nature, I was still a coward and would never have made such a resolution had I anticipated the slightest danger. But there was not the faintest chance of failure – or at least so I believed.

I quickly began to put my plans into operation. First, as a preliminary step, I visited his house more frequently and studied his and his wife's daily behavior closely. Painstakingly, I tried to observe and to remember every detail of their lives, overlooking nothing . . .

After about a month, when I had completed all my observations, I suddenly announced without any warning that I was all set to go to Korea to find work. At the time I was still a confirmed bachelor, so my sudden announcement did not arouse any suspicion . . .

One day soon after – it was a day which suited all my plans perfectly – I boarded a Shimonoseki-bound train at Tokyo Station and waved farewell to my brother and his wife. But after only an hour or so I stole off the train at Yamakita and, after waiting some time, took a train back to Tokyo. Traveling by third class and mingling with the crowd, I was soon back in Tokyo without anyone's knowing.

I should explain at this point that while I waited for the Tokyo train at Yamakita Station, I went into the rest room and cut out the mole on my thigh with a razor – the one and only mark which distinguished me from my brother. After this simple operation, my brother and I were carbon copies, so to speak.

When I arrived at Tokyo, dawn was just breaking. This too was part of my plan. Without losing any time, I quickly changed into a kimono I had had made for the purpose before starting out; it was of the same Oshima silk which my brother used for everyday wear. Furthermore, I also put on the same kind of underwear, wore the same sash, the same clogs, in fact, everything that he usually wore. Then I went to his house at the right time, carefully figured out to a split second. Taking extra care that nobody should see me, I climbed over the back fence and stole into his spacious garden.

It was still very early in the morning and dark, so no one noticed me as I crept up to the side of the well in one corner of the garden. This old abandoned well was one of the most important factors which prompted me to commit the crime. It had run dry long ago, and had not been used since. I remembered my brother's having said at one time that it was dangerous to have such a trap in the garden and that he intended to fill it up soon. A mound of earth was now piled up high beside the well, no doubt having been brought there by the gardeners, to whom I had suggested only a few days ago that they fill up the hole on this very day.

I crouched down, hiding myself in the shrubbery, and waited

calmly, expecting at any moment to hear my brother's footsteps, for it was his custom to take a stroll in the garden every morning after his toilet. As I waited, I felt cold beads of sweat run down along my arms from my armpits. How long I waited I do not recall, except that time seemed to stand completely still. Perhaps it was about three hours later – hours which seemed more like years – when I at last heard the clatter of his clogs. My first impulse was to run away – to escape from the horror of my own devilish scheme; but somehow my legs seemed to have grown roots in the ground, and I couldn't move.

Before I knew it, my long-awaited victim had arrived just in front of the shrubbery in which I was concealed, and I realized with a start that my time had come. With amazing agility, I suddenly sprang out and wound the rope which I had prepared around my brother's neck – and then I slowly proceeded to strangle him.

[. . .] Had there been a witness to the scene, he would certainly have thought it nothing but a bad nightmare. Just imagined – he would have seen one man strangling another wearing the same clothes, possessing the same figure and even the same face.

EDO SAWA RAMPO

from The Off Season

IT happened so fast he didn't know what happened, *all of it,* first came his identical twin brother by one hour, then him, and in the first grade he whacked a boy on the skull with the long wooden window pole – he didn't like the boy's freckles, too disorganized – and the teacher made him don a dunce cap, and cover the blackboard with *I will behave myself*s, then stand in the corner, nose pushed pug against the wall, and still she asked his mother to come in; yet his mother loved him more than his identical twin brother, his contemptible twin brother whose hand always shot up before the teacher's question was even out of her mouth, his despicable twin brother who at age seven was already clinking out sad nocturnes on the piano, his nauseating twin brother who helped younger children, and the blind, and the lame, negotiate crossroads, yes, his mother loved him more even though he once swiped her dentures from the nightstand jar and put on a ventriloquist show with them in the boys' room during lunch hour, sticking a cigar between those floating incorporeal teeth and making them blow triple smoke rings to cries of *bravo! bully! well doné!*, even though he once pocketed the magnifying glass his good twin brother had won for his science fair project on how to breed fatter prairie chickens and then used that magnifying glass to ignite those chickens, what squawking! [. . .] At the age of eighty-six, the years at last starting to show, finding himself penniless, realizing he'd sold the last of the jewels, exhausted the last of the cash from the bank accounts, ran through the last of just about everything, he went into town, picked up a rock, and chucked it through the window of the public library – hang the expense! – then sat on the curbstone and waited for the police who pulled up fifteen minutes later – those fifteen minutes passed with excruciating slowness, time crept and crawled, it dragged its slow length along, it came to a complete halt. Then the police arrived and once again it proceeded, and do you think they arrested him on charges of damaging public property? creating a public nuisance? disturbing the peace? vagrancy? loitering? riotous behavior? and so on and so forth, and ran a fingerprint check and discovered he'd escaped from prison forty years ago, and slaughtered his family ten years ago? no, they felt sorry for the old codger and accepted the fable of fake identification papers he'd been using so long the papers had become real, and saw to it he got placed in a charitable local geriatrics ward; and so he had a roof over his head, was fed, clothed, etc., etc., and a pleasant not uncomfortable year later, reasonably content in this old-age home nestled in the wooded foothills, he picked up a magazine and lo and behold! there was his brother, as despicable as ever, living in the prairies near the town where they'd grown up, he'd just received some public service award for breeding a new fatter prairie chicken – still up to his old tricks! – his identical twin brother who was living out the last years on a farm he owned, surrounded by endless expanses of rolling wheat fields beneath impossibly blue skies in a large house set amid oak and maple trees that turned red and gold in the fall, and with a windbreak of pines lining the main approach – yes, he could just picture it – so he mulled it over for a few months then wrote his brother giving some crafty reason for his new name and saying how much he missed him, and his brother promptly wrote back slopping over with enthusiasm and wouldn't he like to spend the last years on his long-lost brother's farm? it's only right that family should forgive – *forgive what?* – and pull together in the twilight years, and he wasn't jealous anymore about the way Mother – may she rest in peace – had always liked him better even though he was bad in school, and used to steal her dentures, and put dead plucked chickens under her pillow – he'd forgotten that one – anyway, the old age home was more than happy to let his brother assume responsibility, and they put a ticket in his fist and sent him on his way, but while the train clattered east his older brother suffered a massive coronary – and did he pull through? did he recuperate? did the younger brother arrive in time to nurse him back to health and vigor? – of course not, he died after twenty minutes of thost excruciating pain imaginable – we're not even going to go into it – his last coherent thought was, *What I do to deserve this?* (nothing, of course, so much for doppelgängers), and he arrived to find he'd inherited a hefty sum of money and the farm with the out-sized chickens, which he roasted one by one with garlic and rosemary and peppers, and the next two decades passed in a dream, he spent most of the time sitting on the screened porch, rocking peacefully back and forth in the great black oaken rocker that his brother – may he rot in hell – had banged together himself, and he'd rock there in the fading light, puffing on pipe, chuckling softly at the way things turn out, watching the wheat toss in the cool twilight breeze, no restlessness, no regret, no painful preoccupation or introspection tinged with autumnal melancholy, no, just an implacable calm, an imperturbable feeling of contentment – there's no justice anywhere.

MICHAEL COVINO

---

from Three Tales

[*QUARRELSOME twin sisters, Jeanie and Ellen are at war even in death. A tradition in their part of Scotland holds that the last person buried in the local graveyard has to keep watch over the other dead until the next burial occurs. No deaths are expected except for their own. Dying within a few hours of each other, each therefore is determined to be buried first. A race ensues between the supporters of the rival corpses.*]

[Jeanie] did not reach the graveyard first, but she reached it in time. As the men bore her in, there were lanterns and voices. The Macmillan party was there, with Ellen's coffin, standing by the open grave. Jeanie's grave was ready too, for it had been dug that afternoon, and the two mounds of earth stood side by side.

When the Macmillan party saw the others come, they were thunderstruck with astonishment. At the sight of them Hughie burst out into such rage that he took his shoulder from under the coffin, almost upsetting it, and rushed forward, foaming at the mouth, and shaking his huge fist. They shrank into a group for protection, and one of their men, glancing about him, picked up a spade. Ann, hopping behind a tombstone, held her breath.

Hughie's voice came out like the roar of a bull, hoarse and hollow at first, then finding its full strength. Beside himself, past all decency and care, he cursed and raged, denouncing their cunning and trickery, and reviling the dead.

That roused them. They began to mutter threateningly. The man with the spade made a movement. At once Hughie's party put down the coffin, and surged forward. Hughie's voice ended for want of breath, and there was a silence. What would have happened no one can tell, for at that moment a white-robed figure came striding down the path towards the two groups. It was Father Gallagher, the burly Irish priest, come to commit Ellen's body to the earth.

'Now then,' he barked angrily, 'what is the meaning of this disgraceful——'

He got no further, for with a rush both parties made for him. Murtagh seized one of his arms, Ellen's factor the other, and all began to shout at once, each urging that he should bury their corpse the first. Dumbfounded, the priest glared from one to another. His mouth opened once or twice, but if he said anything it could not be heard above the uproar. Before he knew what was happening they were pulling each at one of his arms, tugging him, jerking him, trying by main force to drag him to their own corpse. In their excitement they had lost all reverence, all fear.

At this crowning outrage, the priest recovered himself. His face went black in the moonlight, his eyes flashed, his cheeks blew out with rage. Plunging forward, he shook his right arm free, and with a swing of his fist gave Murtagh a backhander across the mouth that knocked him backwards over a gravestone . . .

Another plunge, and the priest swung out the other arm, but missed. Baffled, he paused, then pulled up his surplice and cassock and dealt the nearest man a terrific kick on the shins. With a yell, the unfortunate clasped his leg, hopped a few steps, and collapsed.

'What do you mean, ye sacrilegious blackguards!' roared the priest. 'How *dare* you lay your filthy hands on God's anointed priest? I declare I never—— What's come to ye all?' He faced round to the crowd. 'Is it mad you all are? . . . Faith, ye might all be atheists, or agnostics, or

Lutherans, or black heathen savages that had never heard of Christian behaviour!'

Ann stood frozen behind her stone. She was always terrified of Father Gallagher . . . Now, however, her terror was surmounted by admiration. He was a grand figure, standing there in his robes, one hand uplifted, denouncing both parties alike: and with the thrill that went through her, the child knew in her soul that Jeanie would have loved this scene, and wished no better farewell.

The priest had found his breath, now, and words flew out of him. He turned this way and that, and those whom he faced shrank back, feeling the words like a shower of stones. [. . .] By the time he had spoken for five minutes, the spirit had gone out of them all. They forgot their zeal and their partisanship: they forgot Jeanie and Ellen. They knew only that they were crawling worms, that their presence offended honest earth, and their sins stank to heaven worse than the knacker's cart.

'Now then,' said Father Gallagher at last. 'I want an explanation of this disgraceful scene. You——' He pointed to Ellen's factor. 'What have you to say?'

In a small, meek voice, the factor told him of Ellen's last written testament.

'Humph,' he snorted through his nose, at the end of it. He turned to Hughie. 'You?'

Hughie's voice was not so meek as the other man's, and warmth returned to it as his indignation at the trick revived.

'Humph,' said Father Gallagher again: and stood for a minute thinking, while all looked at him dumbly.

'A very unseemly business,' he said. 'Sharp practice, trickery, and malice. Disgraceful.'

He brooded for another minute. Then all saw, from the movement of his head, that he had reached a decision.

'Now I'll tell you what I'll do. There's been a deal too much barging and wrangling hereabouts, and these two dead women did not set the best example they might. I'm not going to say who was to blame. They were sisters, twin sisters at that, and they were at feud. That's enough. In the name of the Lord God' – his voice swelled suddenly – 'I'm going to make a lasting peace between them, and between you who followed them, from now till the Judgment Day. Holy Church can give no countenance to feuds and rivalries and superstitions.' He turned to the coffins. 'Into the ground they shall go, side by side, and at the same time: and I will read the one service over the two of them.'

So Jeanie and Ellen were laid in the earth together, and the service read, and the clods shovelled down on top of them. An hour later, there was no one in the churchyard. The voices had retreated, the priest had gone back to his house, and already the boats had set out and were beginning, like disconsolate beetles, to fumble their way homeward across the wide calm sea. The moon, serene and powerful, rode high above the land. [. . .] All sound departed. The shadows of the gravestones shortened; the lights in the cottages went out one by one: and at last there was nothing but the moonlight, as Jeanie and Ellen entered on their watch together.

L.A.G. STRONG

---

from The Day the Wall Came Down

I

We began as one
pram with two hoods
a secret language
a single dent in the bed.

At eleven plus
we failed at arithmetic
simple division
the test of love.

I thought you'd got all the heart
that I'd gobbled your brain.

To keep myself in
I had to keep you out:
our free air
hardened to glass
unscratchable.

The times were un-nourishing.
There was one too many:
it was you or me.

You thinned yourself
down to bone
broth. Your hair fell out.
Your toes and fingers turned blue.
I was white fat, pork belly
I was mash and grease.

Both of us
made ourselves scarce.
Our conjuring trick:
our disappearing needs.

Sometimes, from far away
I'd holler
into your silence, at
our sad milk.

2

Our date: astonishing November
near Euston
an oven-basement
where lunch
eats up the afternoon

and we chew over
the babies you've got
the baby I dreamed I'd steal

and you feed me advice fresh
and gritty as pepper, necessary
as salt

my sister in black and silver
your breath close, your
face flushed with wine

and we taste garlic, spaghetti
anchovies, broccoli
hot with red chillies

and what has divided us
comes down
the work of our mouths
desirous
eating, meeting.

3

Twins with our guards
torn down: now
we reclaim
each other's hidden city
as our own, the
other side of skin.

Foreign as freedom
on my new route back

to slip on the silvery
grease of pavements
smell the secret life of Camden
feel the electric blue
bruise of the evening sky
over the railway lines
of Kentish Town

where cafés offer honeycakes
the tick of dominoes
contact with strangers'
eyes idling by TV screens

and greengrocers' caves
are dark mouths, bearded
with cloths of grass
moustached by swags of brilliant
bulbs, pearl onions.

In my arms rustle papery
sheaths: inky irises
unfurl their blue fur tongues
anemones in mud-coloured ruffs
open their fat black eyes
a shout of purple.

All the way home
I listen to
the morse code of
woodpeckers

my sister calling for
me through the cold
years, the

tapping
of the axes
of love.

4

The pour of bodies.
The gap.

Memorial
to that which is still missing
all that which longs to be said.

MICHÈLE ROBERTS

———————

4

SEPARATION AND DEATH

❧&

A s I was contemplating, rather mournfully, writing this particular introduction, I saw, out of my attic window, a family much as we were fifty years ago, walking up the street. Father, small boy of four or so, and, running ahead and behind, two little girls in long white dresses, each with a sun hat, one red, one blue. They looked less than 2 years old; whether they were identical I could not see because of their floppy hats; but they were the same size as well as identically dressed; they might well have been. They did not act identically; one twin went more soberly, quietly than the other, who weaved giddily, stopped, started, waved her hands, had to be waited for. I wondered if the small boy in his baseball cap was as phased as our brother had been by this wearing, all too fascinating competition. (There are times I think that our brother, the centre of attention until our doubled appearance took his glory away, has never quite forgiven us for it, and with reason. I hope this other brother fares better.) But much more I wondered about the twins – different, yet so nearly the same; always together, imagining nothing else. What separations would they face – would they ache seeing other twins later as I ache seeing them, remembering all our separations; and now, with death, the irrevocable one?

And it makes me think, too, that perhaps the main problem for twins is, precisely, that whereas those born singly are reputed to be permanently seeking union with another, their other half, twins start out that way; and end up single – many of them anyway. And spend the rest of our lives in some way or other mourning and in need of those images the Yoruba make of dead twins to prevent their sibling missing them too much. Some twins of course stay very close. Some never leave each other, remain wedded totally, but since what is charming in 2- or even 12-year-olds is much less charming if not downright disgusting in identically dressed 60-year-olds, this seems a mistake; for psychic and physical survival, let alone growth, probably, twins need to separate at some point, alive or dead. Even if it is not necessary to be as brutal about it as one twin I met, who abandoned her sister for an enclosed order of nuns. (Not surprisingly, her twin wasn't exactly welcoming on her leaving the convent aged 50 or so.)

Most twin separations are more inadvertent. Our first one came when we were 8, and I contracted glandular TB. For three months of that I was at home, in bed, infectious, only able to talk to my fit sister through the bedroom window. Then, for another three months, I was away from home entirely, first in hospital having the gland removed, thereafter, since tubercular patients were thought to need fattening up on dairy products hard to obtain privately in post-war Britain, in a convalescent home. How much my desolation in both places related to my sister, I don't know; I didn't know then probably. All I could be sure of was that I was bereft of everything familiar. But since my sister always did seem to draw the short straw, I suspect, now, it was all much worse for her. After all, she was not, unlike me, the centre of attention. After all she had lost nothing except me. For her, unlike me, it must have been the paramount, obvious separation. Yet I wonder if the precise weight of her temporary, yet to a child seemingly endless, bereavement – or of her fear for me, perhaps, in my illness – had she thought I was going to die? – was apparent to anyone except her.

It was, I daresay, the reason for the greeting she gave me on my return. Luckily I was myself the well fatted calf – she made clear she was not going to provide one. I found her, I remember, upstairs, in our gloomy hallway. Her face glimmering whitely in the dusk, she did not smile, she barely spoke. 'Hullo', I think, was all I got. I remember the sinking feeling even now. If my feelings, too, were mixed on seeing her, I had not wanted, had not expected this. Yet I felt far too much of a stranger to take comfort from launching myself at her in our old fury; even though,

I suspect, it was by fighting in due course that we broke our mutual strangeness.

As time went on, of course, we drew further and further into different lives and likings. But she was still always there, as I was always there for her, until we were 17, the period before I went to Oxford, when we both departed for Europe to learn German, she to Austria, I to Munich. There, after three weeks of inflated adolescent exhilaration, I sank into a state of utter gloom and dislocation – madness, it felt like briefly. The world seemed to have stopped turning. Fleeing Munich, I did not return there until this year; and only then, walking in the Englischer Garten where I used to roam endlessly because it reminded me of home, did I understand at last that the loss I felt was more than anything that of twinness; bringing the realisation for the first time, perhaps, that, like everyone else, I was alone, finally, and liable to remain that way. I did not know it in my head, but wept for it in my body, undoubtedly. Thirty-eight years later, I knew exactly what I was weeping for. Still weeping, no longer caring how she would have raged against such sentimentality – I think she would – I lit a candle for my dead sister before a shrine to the Virgin Mary, in St Michael's Kirche.

Like I said, I was the survivor of the two of us, and usually the luckier and she was not. She suffered not only the ill-luck, therefore, but the resentment that followed. But how could she not have resented the final blow; the illness – breast cancer – that killed her in less than eighteen months, but that left me, then ten years beyond my encounter with it, still very much alive. The particular irony was – in most things to do with my sister, existentially speaking, there almost always were ironies – that she was happy, for nearly the first time in her life. Whether her remarriage would have continued to make her happy was a moot point; but it did then, one effect being to improve the up till that point ever-deteriorating relationship between me and her. As she got more ill, once again relations got worse. But the intention of both of us, I think, to spend time together in the final weeks of her life and try and mend relations for good, was negated by the brain tumour that removed her in one week flat. Again, typical. So I made my peace with her as best I could, without words, without explanations, by bathing her forehead through the worst of her headaches, sitting by her day after day as she sank into a coma; holding her right hand still while she died, while her daughter on the other side of the bed held her left, and we both whispered to her that we loved her; I think, I hope, she might have heard. And all the time I had this profound feeling that it was, yet wasn't, my flesh that was dying before my eyes, under my fingers; a feeling that had overwhelmed me from the first moment I heard about her illness. It was all the more disturbing and awful for our having seemed so far apart, so far from being, as now appeared, still as joined and one, as we had been in the womb, in our Moses basket, in our mother's arms. Yet when I heard of her mastectomy, I grieved and raged as if for the mutilation of my own flesh. During her months of chemotherapy I felt nauseated every time. As the tumours advanced – 'my lumps' she called them with a kind of horrible almost proprietory affection – they appalled me as if they had been my own. I had dreams of jumping into her open grave, and for months after she died was plagued by images of her rotting flesh, of worms, of the skeleton they would have been stripping bare. But as I began to emerge into the relief of understanding that I was not her, that I was still very much alive, along with gratitude and relief came a guilty yet deep exhilaration. It felt in a terrible, wonderful way as if I was, literally, feeding on, being given life by, her dead flesh. Too much life. I put on a stone and a half in a year – but the difficulty I've had shedding such excess weight is nothing to the mental difficulty of attempting to shed her.

After this, it was intriguing to find in almost all the material I encountered on the death of twins, whether written by twins or not, this same deep physicality. Corpses, tombs, connections to rotting flesh proliferate. The Marquez piece included here is particularly apt – 'Before, when they were both living their separate lives they were . . . simple and apart. But now, when rigidity . . . was climbing up his back . . . another body . . . was coming from beyond his, that had been sunken with him in the liquid night of the maternal womb . . .' My case entirely, even if I am much too English – and too inhibited by being a twin myself – to put it quite like that.

Though she and I were one, yet we were also two; and for the first time I felt the terror of uniqueness, of our being apart one day and lost to each other.

DAVID GARNETT, *Two by Two*

ANTIPHOLUS OF SYRACUSE He that commends me to mine own
   content,
Commends me to the thing I cannot get.
I to the world am like a drop of water
That in the ocean seeks another drop;
Who, failing there to find his fellow forth,
Unseen, inquisitive, confounds himself.

WILLIAM SHAKESPEARE, *The Comedy of Errors*

And though she had lived so close to Fan – in intimate contact with her for nine months before they were born and ever since – it was strange that she could not see into Fan's mind or Fan into hers. Wondering about the mystery which makes every individual, even an identical twin, a separate person, inscrutable to all others, she fell asleep.

DAVID GARNETT, *Two by Two*

The Wilbur twin was abashed and puzzled. The detail most impressing him seemed to be that having no longer a brother, he would cease to be a twin. His life long he had been made intensely conscious of being a twin – he was one of a pair – and now, suddenly, he gathered, he was something whole and complete in himself.

H.L. WHITTON, *The Wrong Twin*

from Those Extraordinary Twins

AT times, in his seasons of deepest depressions, Angelo almost wished that he and his brother might become segregated from each other and be separate individuals, like other men. But of course as soon as his mind cleared and these diseased imaginings passed away, he shuddered at the repulsive thought, and earnestly prayed that it might visit him no more. To be separate, and as other men are! How awkward it would seem; how unendurable. What would he do with his hands, his arms? How would his legs feel? How odd, and strange, and grotesque every action, attitude, movement, gesture would be. To sleep by himself, eat by himself, walk by himself – how lonely, how unspeakably lonely! No, no, any fate but that. In every way and from every point, the idea was revolting.

MARK TWAIN

from Twins

JESSIE AND BESSIE

It was difficult for Jessie and Bessie to stand being separated even for a few minutes.

At 2 years, when Jessie was taken into the garden and Bessie left upstairs, Jessie cried and called Bessie.

At 2 years, Jessie came into the nursery looking around for Bessie; she asked 'Bessie?' then went out again and looked for her in the bathroom. She returned to the nursery holding Bessie's hand, pointing at her and shouting with a happy face, 'Bessie, my Bessie.'

At 2 years Jessie had impetigo and spent most of the day in a pram in the garden. Bessie remaining upstairs in a cot because she had a cold. Bessie was very sad, did not play and sat quietly in the cot most of the time. When Jessie was brought upstairs, Bessie brightened up at once, laughed and played.

At 2 years the twins were separated because Bessie was ill. Bessie cried for Jessie in the shelter. She seemed so unhappy that she was taken to Jessie's bed. Bessie looked at Jessie, smiled at her and put her hand inside her shelter net and stroked Jessie's face, saying softly, 'Jessie, Jessie', then she went back to her bed and was soon asleep. [. . .]

A State of Mourning for the Missing Twin during a Separation of Seven Months

MARY AND MADGE

At 4 years 4 months Madge had to go to hospital with ringworm. Mary was desperately unhappy. She sat on the floor, rocked and cried, saying over and over again: 'My Madge, my Madge.' Later she asked: 'When will she come back?' 'I want her now.' She continually came and asked whether the nurse would go now and fetch Madge in the car.

Mary collected all sorts of things for Madge and saved them for her. On a walk all the children were each given a hazelnut. Mary said: 'You must not eat them, they belong to Madge; she must have them all because she is in hospital.'

Some days Mary cried off and on all day long. She was asked why she was so unhappy and she replied that she had been crying for her mummy and for Madge.

When Mary hurt herself or was cross she would cry in a continuous monotonous way and call 'my Madge, my Madge'.

Mary woke up screaming in the night; the night nurse could not comfort her. Finally she sent for her own nurse. When her own nurse came she told her she wanted 'my Madge'.

DOROTHY BURLINGHAM

---

from The Silent Twins

EARLY in March 1978, Cathy's pressure had its effect. Evan Davies rang her to say he would take one twin in his unit. Tim Thomas broke the news to the twins. He was nervous about what he had to say and blurted out: 'I'll come to the point at once. Things aren't going very well for you here and we've decided to separate you. One of you must go to Dr Davies's residential unit in Carmarthen. The other can stay with us. You can choose who does what.'

At first the girls remained still. Then, slowly, they began to move. Jennifer gave June a menacing glower. The muscles in her hands tightened. Both their bodies began to arch and tense, their eyes fixed on each other. There was something malevolent in their postures, like cats about to strike. There was a scream, then a series of unintelligible shouts as Jennifer lunged forward and dug her long nails into June's cheek, just below the eye, drawing blood. June replied by clutching her sister's head with such ferocity that chunks of wiry black hair fell to the floor. Before Tim Thomas could react, they were out of the room, chasing each other. Their screams grew louder and edged with anguish. Tim Thomas rushed out and prised the girls apart. The forces locking the two together disturbed him. In combat, the girls possessed remarkable strength, but once separated, that strength fell away, leaving them as limp as two rag dolls in his hands.

News of the separation triggered a new round of telephone harassment. Members of the Eastgate staff began to receive calls from phone boxes and listened again and again to the pathetic stammered message: 'We p-p-p-promise to talk if we c-c-c-can b-both stay at Eastgate.' (The origin of the stammer is interesting. Ann Treharne had detected no stammer when she first started to treat the children. She believes that they 'picked it up' from other children while waiting for her in the speech therapy clinic and used it later for effect.)

On 13th March 1978 the separation plan was carried through. Tim Thomas picked up Jennifer to take her to Eastgate, and some time later Cathy Arthur called for June and drove her to St David's Adolescent Unit in Carmarthen. Cathy's diary records that June was 'very frightened and crying'.

The timing of the separation could not have been worse, for four days after June was admitted the Easter holidays started and she was home again. The whole holiday the twins spent their time threatening and cajoling the Eastgate staff to end the separation. But no-one would help them and on 10th April, the day before their birthday, they were separated again. June retreated into a state of anguish from which no-one at the residential unit could rescue her. 'Everybody tried to offer her warmth and understanding but she would stand on her own, an isolated, tragic figure,' says Vivian Hughes, the teacher in charge. June's fifteenth birthday was the worst day of her life. She ignored the cards and presents. She almost ceased to move at all, holding herself rigid like a small animal under threat. Evan Davies came into the ward in the morning and found her still lying in bed. 'I tried to jolly her up by saying that I would have to lift her out personally. But the joke was on me. It took two of us to lift her out and then we had to prop her against the wall like a plank.'

'I shared a room with two other girls,' recalls June in a diary she wrote some years later.

> Ah, the loneliness. For I would not talk. Mentally alone . . .
> Hungry. Bitter. Angry. J. was in Eastgate. Enjoying her life.
> The joy of going home to her own bed; seeing her own family.
> Eating familiar food. I had to suffer the torment of listening
> to strange conversations; eating strange food. And even then I
> would have agony to eat it. For I would not eat with people at
> the table.

June attended the special school for disturbed adolescents, a rickety old house at the entrance to the main hospital. She walked each day from the ward to the school but would just stand in the doorway when she arrived. Vivian Hughes or some of the boys who developed protective feelings towards her would have to take her arms and lift her in. They would remove her coat and then very slowly, staring straight ahead, she would lower herself into a chair where she sat motionless until the end of the morning lessons. What distressed everyone at St David's were the tears that flowed silently down her cheeks. She made no sound of crying, nor any effort to wipe them away. The staff and schoolchildren used to carry boxes of tissues with them to dry her cheeks and nose but she seemed oblivious to their gestures.

June showed signs of life only at lunchtime when Cathy Arthur allowed Jennifer to telephone her. She chatted away in her fluttering speech, smiling and giggling. The phone call over, she would return to her lifeless pose. 'What struck me about her was the strength of will which lay behind her stillness,' says Vivian Hughes, who has spent his working life dealing with disturbed children. 'It seemed she was on a leash to Jennifer. There was something almost mystic about their relationship, like black magic. I felt June could have been a normal, popular young girl if she had been released from her sister.'

During the following weeks June's grief continued unabated. She began to refuse all food. After the fifth week, she did not turn up at the unit after a weekend at home. The same day Jennifer absconded from Eastgate. To Evan Davies's relief, on Monday 8th May 1978 the separation was officially abandoned. He was not prepared to force-feed June or to watch such suffering. June returned to Eastgate for the remainder of the term.

By now their physical appearance had deteriorated to reflect their inner gloom. They were no longer chubby, identically dressed school

girls but arrived each day, their faces drab and drawn, wearing
shapeless yellowed khaki sweaters which hung over their protruding
shoulder blades like rags on a row of pegs. Gloria had given up
her half-hour's labour every morning plaiting their hair, which was
now held back in untidy chunks with anything from curling tongs
to paperclips. Their underclothes, too, were a mass of ironmongery,
held together by bits of metal, rope and wire.

MARJORIE WALLACE

---

from The Wrong Twin

THEY went out in the porch, going down the path. The listener
stepped lightly to a window and became also a watcher. Ahead
walked Patricia Whipple and her new brother. The stepmother and
Mrs Penniman followed. Then came Winona with the suit-case, which
was of wicker. Judge Penniman lumbered ponderously behind. At the
hitching post in front was the pony cart and the fat pony of sickening
memory. Merle was politely helping the stepmother to the driver's
seat. It was over. But the watcher suddenly recalled something.

In swift silence, descending the stairs, he entered the parlour. On
a stand beneath the powerful picture of the lion behind real bars was
a frosted cake of rare beauty. Three pieces were gone and two more
were cut. On top of each piece was the half of a walnut. He tenderly
seized one of these and stole through the deserted house, through
kitchen and wood-shed, out to the free air again. At the back of the
wood-shed he sat down on the hard bare ground, his back to the wall,
looking into the garden where Judge Penniman, in the intervals of
his suffering, raised a few vegetables. It was safe seclusion for the
pleasant task in hand. He gloated rapturously over the cake, eating
first the half of a walnut, which he carefully removed. But he thought
it didn't taste right.

He now regarded the cake itself uncertainly. It was surely perfect
cake. He broke a fragment from the thin edge and tasted it almost
fearfully. It wasn't going right. He persisted with a larger fragment,
but upon this he was like to choke; his mouth was dry and, curiously,
no place for even the choicest cake. He wondered about it in something
like panic, staring at it in puzzled consternation. There was the choice
thing and he couldn't eat it. Then he became aware that his eyes were

hot, the lids burning, and there came a choking, even though he no longer had any cake in his mouth. Suddenly he knew that he couldn't eat the cake because he had lost his brother – his brother who had passed on. He gulped alarmingly as the full knowledge overwhelmed him. He was wishing that Merle had kept the knife, even if it wasn't such a good knife, so he would have something to remember him by. Now he would have nothing. He would always remember Merle, even if he was no longer a twin, but Merle would surely forget him. He had passed on.

Over by the little house he heard the bark of Frank, the dog. Frank's voice was changing, and his bark was now a promising baritone. His owner tried to whistle, but made poor work of this, so he called, 'Here, Frank! Here, Frank!' reckless of betraying his own whereabouts. His voice was not clear, it still choked, but it carried; Frank came bounding to him. He had a dog left anyway – a good fighting dog. His eyes still burned, but they were no longer dry, and his gulps were periodic, threatening a catastrophe of the most dreadful sort.

Frank, the dog, swallowed the cake hungrily, eating it with a terrible ease, as he was wont to eat enemy dogs.

H. L. WHITTON

---

from The Tuppenny Twins

'HERE, you barbed-wire entanglement,' he said on the morning of the expected arrival. 'I've got a surprise for you. It'll be coming any day now, and you've got to like it; the first birthday present I've ever given you.'

Timothy, incredulous of anything good coming to him from such a source, asked for further information.

'You wait, my dove-tailed duckling,' he replied. 'It hasn't been made to measure, but you're only a little one; creep into it and you'll be safe.'

Thus he roused Timothy's curiosity, and at last even his hopes. 'You notice,' said Titus, 'I've left off drinking?'

Timothy had noticed.

'To-morrow,' he went on, 'if you say the word (so long as it's the *right* word) I'll take the pledge; I'll go to church with you. I'll say my prayers, I'll do anything.'

Timothy began to sit up; this sounded almost like conversion; and when later in the day a huge package arrived addressed to Titus – a queer shapeless bundle stitched up in an old tarpaulin – his interest in the undoing of it was as great as, and his curiosity much greater than that of Titus.

Seeing his look of wistful eagerness, Titus played him artfully, and delayed disclosure of the contents while by way of good counsel he gave Timothy a further piece of his mind:

'See here,' he said. 'I'm reasonable if I'm reasonably treated. "Live and let live" is my motto – pity it hasn't been yours. I don't want to hurt your feelings as long as you don't hurt mine: so here's a proposition for you, and a present to go with it. I saw it advertised second-hand. "Why, that's just the thing that we want!" says I to myself; and if you can think of anything better, say so.'

He undid the package as he spoke, and after a lengthy process of untying and unwinding, revealed a small size diving-suit, of the lighter kind intended only for shallow water, all rubber, with head-piece and glass eye-sockets complete.

'There,' he said. 'What do you think of that, for a separator?'

'I don't know what you mean,' said Timothy bewildered.

'Sheep from goat's what I mean,' replied Titus; 'you being the sheep.'

'But what is it?'

'A container, Timothy, my boy: patent moral life-preserving air-tight compartment, sentry-box, refrigerator, incubator – call it what you like. Point is, when you get into it, you are all by yourself, and what goes on outside doesn't concern you. Whenever I'm for doing anything you don't want to know about, get in there – I've had the eyes blacked out for you – and then you needn't know anything: you'll be as if you were in another world. Well, that's the proposition; what have you to say to it? You agree to it, and you shall have a quiet life from now on. I'll be a reformed character – in every other respect, that is to say.'

Timothy looked at him doubtfully, as the implications of the proposition gradually penetrated his rather obtuse mind.

'Try it on!' said Titus encouragingly.

There was no harm in trying it on, thought Timothy; that committed him to nothing. Trying it on did not necessarily mean consent. So with Titus's ready assistance the thing was tried on. The interlocked arm required a split seam, and a certain amount of readjustment afterwards; otherwise the try-on presented no difficulty.

'Fits you like a glove!' exclaimed Titus; and when Timothy had put on the helmet and joined it to the shoulder-pieces he was as much out of action as a candle under an extinguisher: he could not see out through the blackened glasses, and when Titus spoke to him he could not hear.

But it was undeniably stuffy and uncomfortable. 'I don't like it,' said Timothy, and began to take it off again.

Just then (how accurately Titus had timed it!) there came a discreet and thrice-repeated knock at the door. Titus recognizing the signal became masterful, 'Now you jugged tortoise,' he cried, 'get back into your shell!'

Pushing the helmet on again, he clamped it down, and Timothy meekly submitted. The moral separator was in operation; the *modus vivendi* had been established.

'Come in!' called Titus.

LAURENCE HOUSMAN

---

from Castor and Polydeucês

They with alternate change for one day keep
   By their dear father Zeus; the next they lie
Far-sunk beneath Therapnê's valleys deep
   In earth, fulfilling thus one destiny
For each alike; for Polydeucês chose
      To share the grave's repose
And not himself alone in Heaven to dwell
   In full eternity of life divine,
Since in the strife his brother Castor fell,
   When Îdas haply for his raided kine
Was angered sore, and through his body sheer
      Drove the bronze-pointed spear.

For gazing from Tâÿgetus' far height,
   Lynceus espied them where they lay reclined
Within an hollow oak, for keener sight
   Had he than all the rest of humankind;
And thither straight on lightning feet he hied
      With Îdas at his side,

And they together planned the monstrous deed.
　　Yet dreadful retribution fell anon
On both Apháreus' sons, as Zeus decreed,
　　When swiftly on their track came Lêda's son,
And face to face they stood, anigh the ground
　　　　Of their sire's burial-mound.

　　From thence a carven stone, that bore
　　The glory of the dead, they tore,
　　　　And flung it at the breast
　　Of Polydeucês; but it failed
　　To crush him, and he still assailed,
　　　　And forward hotly pressed,
　　And through the side of Lynceus sped
　　His flying javelin's brazen head,
　　　　While Zeus on Îdas threw
　　His bolt of fire; and there the two
　　Perished forlorn, for hard it is to fight
With those that be of stronger might.

Then quickly to his brother's manly frame
　　Back Polydeucês went. Not yet had Death
Quite mastered him, but from his throat there came
　　The shuddering gasps of his departing breath.
And while he moaned and the hot teardrops shed,
　　　　He cried aloud and said:
'O Father, Son of Cronus, what can fall
　　To save me from my grief? O let me die,
Let me too die with him, great Lord of All!
　　The glory of life departeth utterly
When dear ones leave us, and of all mankind
　　　　In sorrow we shall find

Few only we may trust to share our woe.'
　　He spake; then Zeus himself before him stood
And uttered thus his voice: 'Full well I know
　　Thou art my son, whereas thy brother's blood
Flowed through thy mother from her lord on earth
　　　　After thy Heavenly birth.
But now, behold, this choice I offer thee.
　　If thou thyself would'st never more be vowed
To death and hateful age, but dwell with me,

And with Athênê, and with Arês proud,
The dark spear's lord, upon our Mount Divine,
    That portion shall be thine.

But if for thy dear brother slain
Thou pleadest, and thyself art fain
    To share with him thy doom,
Then may'st thou draw the living breath
For half thy time where after death
    He lies in nether gloom,
And half thy time abide on high
In golden mansions of the sky.'
    Then, hearing the god's voice,
The other stayed not in his choice;
And straightway Zeus unsealed the lips and eyes
    Of Castor in his bronzen guise.

                    PINDAR, trs. C. J. Billson

'And what is the name of the youngest boy here?' Charles
Dublin asked.
    'Fatty,' said Fatty Rampart.
    'But surely that's not your given name?'
    'Andifax,' said five year old Fatty.
    'Ah well, Andifax, Fatty, are you a kidder too?'
    'He's getting better at it, Mr Dublin,' Mary Mabel said. 'He
was a twin till last week. His twin was named Skinny. Mama left
Skinny unguarded while she was out tippling, and there were
wild dogs in the neighbourhood. Do you know what was left of
Skinny? Two neckbones and an anklebone. That was all.'
    'Poor Skinny,' Dublin said.

                    R.A. LAFFERTY, *Narrow Valley*, 1966

[*Achille Geremicca invents an imaginary twin soul, Amile, then discovers
he had a twin died at birth.*]

And so, all of a sudden . . . my heart received a great shock from which

239

it did not recover for many years. Amile was no longer someone to be with in the future, no longer a desire, a hope, but a sorrow and a bereavement. My mind held no memory of my lost companion, but my heart did . . . Now I know why I was weak and timid and overcome by my enemies even before fighting them. From the day of my birth I was but a poor surviver, a remaining soul, a mutilated life, a mere half which, by itself, is as sad as a ruin. Twins are made in such a way that two make a perfect creature. The one who survives the death of his brother is a yearning heart that cannot be healed because it can never be joined to another.

ACHILLE GEREMICCA, *I fantasmi della mia vita*
(translated by L. Gedda)

We are twins . . . two shoots from one stem which has been broken and half lies in the ground and half sits at the head of this table.

ANDREW LANG, *Boys with the Golden Stars*

from The Solid Mandala

BECAUSE at first Arthur was so upset. Waldo could feel rather than hear his brother gibbering and blubbing. Waldo did not want to hear.

Finally, from behind his eyelids, he could sense Arthur subsiding.

Arthur asked: 'Did they give you oxygen, Waldo, on the way?'

'There was no need,' Waldo replied.

At least that was the answer it was decided he should give always from behind those merciful walls, his eyelids.

'If you were to die,' Arthur was saying, 'I know how to fry myself eggs. There's always the bread. I could live on bread-and-milk. I have my job, haven't I? Haven't I, Waldo?'

'Yes,' said Waldo.

'I might get a dog or two for company.'

Arthur's anxiety began, it seemed, to heave again.

'But who'll put the notice in the paper?' he gasped. 'The *death* notice!'

'Nobody to read it,' Waldo suggested.

'But you gotta put it,' Arthur said. 'I know! I'll ask Dulcie Dulcie'll do it!'

So relieved to find himself saved.

When the sister came and led Arthur away Waldo knew from the passage of air and the gap which was left. His eyelids no longer protected him. He was crying for Dulcie he would have liked to think, only it would not have been true. He was crying for Arthur, for Arthur or himself.

'That time you almost died,' said Arthur.

They were struggling against the Barranugli Road.

'When you might have, but didn't,' Arthur gulped.

'No! The point is: I didn't, I didn't!'

Waldo had perhaps shrieked. The two blue dogs sank their heads between their shoulders.

Waldo had shrunk inside his oilskin, which was so stiff it could have continued standing on its own.

'People die,' he said, 'usually in one of two ways. They are either removed against their will, or their will removes them.'

'What about our father?'

Waldo did not want to think about that.

'That was certainly different,' he admitted. 'In the past,' he stammered, 'I think some people simply died.'

'Oh dear, this walk is pointless!' Arthur began to mutter. 'Can't you see? What are we doing? Can't we turn?'

'Yes,' said Waldo. 'It is pointless.'

So they turned, and the two old dogs were at once joyful. They tossed their sterns in the air, and cavorted a little. Their tongues lolled on their grinning teeth. One of the dogs farted, and turned to smell whether it was he.

The two brothers walking hand in hand back back up along the Barranugli Road did not pause to consider who was who. They took it for granted it had been decided for them at birth, and at least Waldo had begun to suspect it might not be possible for one of them to die without the other.

PATRICK WHITE

from Autobiography

IMAGINE two young girls, of what exact age I really do not know, but apparently from twelve to fourteen, twins, remarkably plain in person and features, unhealthy, and obscurely reputed to be idiots. Whether they really were such was more than I knew, or could devise any plan for learning. Without dreaming of anything unkind or uncourteous, my original impulse had been to say, 'If you please, are you idiots?' But I felt that such a question had an air of coarseness about it, though, for my own part, I had long reconciled myself to being called an idiot by my brother. There was, however, a further difficulty: breathed as a gentle, murmuring whisper, the question might possibly be reconciled to an indulgent ear as confidential and tender. Even to take a liberty with those you love, is to show your trust in their affection; but, alas! these poor girls were deaf; and to have shouted out, 'Are you idiots, if you please?' in a voice that would have rung down three flights of stairs, promised (as I felt, without exactly seeing why) a dreadful exaggeration to whatever incivility might, at any rate, attach to the question; and some *did* attach, that was clear even if warbled through an air of Cherubini's, and accompanied on the flute. Perhaps they were *not* idiots, and only seemed to be such from the slowness of apprehension naturally connected with deafness. That I saw them but seldom, arose from their peculiar position in the family. Their father had no private fortune; his income from the church was very slender; and, though considerably increased by the allowance made for us, his two pupils, still, in a great town, and with so large a family, it left him little room for luxuries. Consequently, he never had more than two servants, and at times only one. Upon this plea rose the scheme of the mother for employing these two young girls in menial offices of the household economy. One reason for that was, that she thus indulged her dislike for them, which she took no pains to conceal; and thus, also, she withdrew them from the notice of strangers. In this way, it happened that I saw them myself but at uncertain intervals. Gradually, however, I came to be aware of their forlorn condition, to pity them, and to love them. The poor twins were undoubtedly plain, to the degree which is called, by unfeeling people, ugliness They were also deaf, as I have said, and they were scrofulous; one of them was disfigured by the small-pox; they had glimmering eyes, red, like the eyes of ferrets, and scarcely half-open; and they did not walk so much as stumble along. There, you have the worst of them. Now, hear something on the other side.

What first won my pity was, their affection for each other, united to their constant sadness; secondly, a notion which had crept into my head, probably derived from something said in my presence by elder people, that they were destined to an early death; and, lastly, the incessant persecutions of their mother. This lady belonged, by birth, to a more elevated rank than that of her husband, and she was remarkably well-bred as regarded her manners. But she had probably a weak understanding: she was shrewish in her temper; was a severe economist; a merciless exactor of what she viewed as duty; and, in persecuting her two unhappy daughters, though she yielded blindly to her unconscious dislike of them, as creatures that disgraced her, she was not aware, perhaps, of ever having put forth more expressions of anger and severity than were absolutely required to rouse the constitutional torpor of her daughters' nature; and where disgust has once rooted itself, and been habitually expressed in tones of harshness, the mere sight of the hateful object mechanically calls forth the eternal tones of anger, without distinct consciousness or separate intention in the speaker. Loud speaking, besides, or even shouting, was required by the deafness of the two girls. From anger so constantly discharging its thunders, naturally they did not show open signs of recoiling; but that they felt it deeply, may be presumed from their sensibility to kindness. My own experience showed *that*; for, as often as I met them, we exchanged kisses; and my wish had always been to beg them, if they really *were* idiots, not to mind it, since I should not like them the less on that account. This wish of mine never came to utterance; but not the less they were aware, by my manner of salutation, that one person at least, amongst those who might be considered strangers, did not find anything repulsive about them; and the pleasure they felt was expressed broadly upon their kindly faces.

Such was the outline of their position; and, that being explained, what I saw was simply this; it composed a silent and symbolic scene, a momentary interlude in dumb show, which interpreted itself and settled for ever in my recollection, as if it had prophesied and interpreted the event which soon followed. They were resting from toil, and both sitting down. This had lasted for perhaps ten or fifteen minutes. Suddenly from below-stairs the voice of angry summons rang up to their ears. Both rose in an instant, as if the echoing scourge of some avenging Tisiphone were uplifted above their heads; both opened their arms; flung them round each other's necks; and then, unclasping them, parted to their separate labours.

This was my last rememberable interview with the two sisters; in a week both were corpses. They had died, I believe, of scarlatina, and very nearly at the same moment.

THOMAS DE QUINCY

———————

from The Twins

Three years old when their mother died
in what my grandmother called
accouchement, my father labour,
they heard the neighbours intone
'A mercy the child went with her.'

Their father raised them somehow.
No one could tell them apart.
At seven they sat in school
in their rightful place, at the top
of the class, the first to respond
with raised arm and finger-flick.

When one gave the answer, her sister
repeated it under her breath.
An inspector accused them of cheating,
but later, in front of the class,

declared himself sorry, and taught us
a marvellous word: *telepathic.*

On Fridays, the story went,
they slept in the shed, barred in
from their father's rage as he drank
his dead wife back to his house.
For the rest of the week he was sober
and proud. My grandmother gave them
a basket of fruit. He returned it.
'We manage. We don't need help.'

They could wash their own hair, skin rabbits,
milk the cow, make porridge, clean boots.

Unlike most of the class I had shoes,
clean handkerchiefs, ribbons, a toothbrush.
We all shared the schoolsores and nits
and the language I learned to forget
at the gate of my welcoming home.

One day as I sat on the fence
my pinafore goffered, my hair
still crisp from the curlers, the twins
came by. I scuttled away
so I should not have to share
my Saturday sweets. My mother
saw me, and slapped me, and offered
the bag to the twins, who replied
one aloud and one sotto voce,
'No thank you. We don't like lollies.'

They lied in their greenish teeth
as they knew, and we knew.
Good angel
give me that morning again
and let me share, and spare me
the shame of my parents' rebuke.
If there are multiple worlds
then let there be one with an ending
quite other than theirs: leaving school
too early and coming to grief.

Or if this is our one life sentence,
hold them in innocence, writing
Our Father which art in Heaven
in copperplate, or drawing
(their work being done) the same picture
on the backs of their slates: a foursquare
house where a smiling woman
winged like an angel welcomes
two children home from school.

                                        GWEN HARWOOD

----

from The Corsican Brothers

LUCIEN'S appearance created quite a sensation in consequence of his remarkable likeness to his brother.

The news of Louis' death had gone abroad – not perhaps, in all its details, but it was known, and Lucien's appearance astonished many.

I requested a private room, saying that we were expecting the Baron Giordano, and we got a room at the end.

Lucien began to read the papers carelessly, as if he were oblivious of everything.

While we were seated at breakfast Giordano arrived.

The two young men had not met for four or five years, nevertheless, a firm clasp of the hand was the only demonstration they permitted themselves.

'Well, everything is settled,' he said.

'Then M. de Chateau Renaud has accepted?'

'Yes, on condition, however, that after he has fought you he shall be left in peace.'

'Oh, he may be quite easy; I am the last of the de Franchi. Have you seen him, or his seconds?'

'I saw him; he will notify MM. de Boissy and de Chateaugrand. The weapons, the hour and the place will be the same.'

'Capital, sit down and have some breakfast.'

The Baron seated himself, and we spoke on indifferent topics.

After breakfast Lucien begged us to introduce him to the Commissioner of Police, who had sealed up his brother's property, and to the proprietors of the house at which his brother had lived, for he wished to sleep that night, the last night that separated him from his vengeance, in Louis' room.

All these arrangements took up time, so it was not till five o'clock that Lucien entered his brother's apartment. Respecting his grief, we left him there alone.

We had arranged to meet him again next morning at eight o'clock, and he begged me to bring the same pistols, and to buy them if they were for sale.

I went to Devismes and purchased the weapons. Next morning, at eight o'clock I was with Lucien.

When I entered, he was seated writing at the same table, where his brother had sat writing. He smiled when he saw me, but he was very pale.

'Good morning,' he said, 'I am writing to my mother.'

'I hope you will be able to write her a less doleful letter than poor Louis wrote eight days ago.'

'I have told her that she may rest happy, for her son is avenged.'

'How are you able to speak with such certainty?'

'Did not my brother announce to you his own approaching death? Well, then, I announce to you the death of M. de Chateau Renaud.'

He rose as he spoke, and touching me on the temple, said –

'There, that's where I shall put my bullet.'

'And yourself.'

'I shall not be touched.'

'But, at least, wait for the issue of the duel, before you send your letter.'

'It would be perfectly useless.'

He rang, the servant appeared.

'Joseph,' said he, 'take this letter to the post.'

'But have you seen your dead brother?'

'Yes,' he answered.

It is a very strange thing the occurrence of these two duels so close together, and in each of which one of the two combatants was doomed. While we were talking the Baron Giordano arrived. It was eight o'clock, so we started.

Lucien was very anxious to arrive first, so we were on the field ten minutes before the hour.

Our adversaries arrived at nine o'clock punctually. They came on horseback, followed by a groom also on horseback.

M. de Chateau Renaud had his hand in the breast of his coat. I at first thought he was carrying his arm in a sling.

The gentlemen dismounted twenty paces from us, and gave their bridles to the groom.

Monsieur de Chateau Renaud remained apart, but looked stead-fastly at Lucien, and I thought he became paler. He turned aside and amused himself knocking off the little flowers with his riding whip.

'Well, gentlemen, here we are!' said MM. de Chateaugrand and de Boissy, 'but you know our conditions. This duel is to be the last, and no matter what the issue may be, M. de Chateau Renaud shall not have to answer to any one for the double result.'

'That is understood,' we replied. Then Lucien bowed assent.

'You have the weapons, gentlemen?' said the Viscount.

'Here are the same pistols.'

'And they are unknown to M. de Franchi?'

'Less known to him than to M. de Chateau Renaud who has already used them once. M. de Franchi has not even seen them.'

'That is sufficient, gentlemen. Come, Chateau Renaud!'

We immediately entered the wood, and each one felt, as he revisited the fatal spot, that a tragedy more terrible still was about to be enacted.

We soon arrived in the little dell.

M. de Chateau Renaud, thanks to his great self-command, appeared quite calm, but those who had seen both encounters could appreciate the difference.

From time to time he glanced under his lids at Lucien, and his furtive looks denoted a disquietude approaching to fear.

Perhaps it was the great resemblance between the brothers that struck him, and he thought he saw in Lucien the avenging shade of Louis.

While they were loading the pistols I saw him draw his hand from the breast of his coat. The fingers were enveloped in a handkerchief as if to prevent their twitching.

Lucien waited calmly, like a man who was sure of his vengeance.

Without being told, Lucien walked to the place his brother had occupied, which compelled Chateau Renaud to take up his position as before.

Lucien received his weapon with a joyous smile.

When Chateau Renaud took his pistol he became deadly pale. Then he passed his hand between his cravat and his neck as if he were suffocating.

No one can conceive with what feelings of terror I regarded this young man, handsome, rich, and elegant, who but yesterday believed he had many years still before him, and who to-day, with the sweat on his brow and agony at his heart, felt he was condemned.

'Are you ready, gentlemen?' asked M. de Chateaugrand.

'Yes,' replied Lucien.

M. de Chateau Renaud made a sign in the affirmative.

As for me I was obliged to turn away, not daring to look upon the scene.

I heard the two successive clappings of the hands, and at the third the simultaneous reports of the pistols. I turned round.

Chateau Renaud was lying on the ground, stark dead; he had not uttered a sound nor made a movement.

I approached the body, impelled by that invincible curiosity which compels one to see the end of a catastrophe.

The bullet had entered the dead man's temple, at the very spot that Lucien had indicated to me previously.

I ran to him, he was calm and motionless, but seeing me coming towards him he let fall the pistol, and threw himself into my arms.

'Ah, my brother, my poor brother!' he cried as he burst into a passion of sobs.

These were the first tears that the young man had shed.

ALEXANDRE DUMAS

---

from The Suicide and his Brother

Amadeo was fully aware that Benito's unhappiness would grow in step with his own. Little by little, Benito would participate in his suffering, claiming, so to speak, his portion, in the same way that, in other times, they had transferred to each other night-fears, laughter, and even erotic desires.

Amadeo was a good man and he swore to sever the matter at the roots. He decided to disappear from the orbit of his brother, his uniovular brother. He imagined inventing an artistic vocation for himself, or perhaps a religious one. He imagined going far away from the town, emigrating, like any peon without spiritual employment. He imagined disillusioning Benito, he imagined offending him! In the cafe, while he played cards, or in his room, alone, surrounded by programs of the Fiesta and bottles of whisky, he pondered, he pondered incessantly.

People were murmuring, 'What's happening to Amadeo?' Herminia, the old servant, starched only his white shirts. Without knowing why, the good woman attributed curative properties, of resurrection, to the color white.

But this was not resolving the problem. Amadeo decided to leave, to run away, although he wondered if his doing so would not add to the feeling of fraternal rupture, of failure, which had seized Benito.

However, he was in no hurry, since it was not a matter a desperate outburst but the fruit of a methodical and painful mental operation. Thus, he chose to take his leave of the town, of things, slowly, so as to keep Benito from guessing his intention.

It didn't matter what direction he took, as long as he wound up far away. Any day now he would rise, say 'to-day,' and head for the open road. How captivating all his surroundings now appeared! He gazed at the buildings, the houses, thinking, 'Perhaps this is the last time.' He became a glutton, a glutton for trees, for boats, for shop windows, for objects. In the middle of his forehead a Third Eye had grown, thanks to which he discovered a secret universe in the town, previously buried by routine. He would never have imagined that the nets laid out on the beach could be so beautiful and that the smack of the corks among themselves could sound so pleasant.

In this manner, with his cane, his light-footed dog, and the so-white shirts that Herminia pressed for him, he was sipping the postponement he had conceded himself. Benito, his brother, observed him cautiously, and continued aging.

Never again did he say to him, 'Amadeo, you hate me.' On the contrary, he continued inviting him to lunch, 'We'll be waiting for you on Sunday, you know,' and every morning, coinciding as always at the factory door, he exclaimed, 'Hello, Amadeo! You go in first.'

It was precisely a Sunday when Amadeo decided, 'to-day.' It was windy, a cold wind that ruffled the sea and, a little, the temper of men. Amadeo looked out the window. Materials clashed with each other and the world had bolted the shutters securely. Not a single cloud in the sky. The sun was king.

Amadeo took his leave of Herminia and the dog. 'Thank you Herminia, you're very good.' 'Thank you pooch, you're very faithful.' In the street he took leave of the balconies and the sidewalks, 'Good-bye, good-bye.' Then he entered a pastry shop and bought pastries and champagne. 'Benito likes pastries,' he said to himself, 'and his wife also. And the little one.'

This was the farewell that moved him most: the one that took place at his brother's house. They received him gaily and Benito's wife, seeing him arrive with those presents, conceived the hope that Amadeo might have regained his good humor. The child played with the champagne bottle until the cork that crowned it popped. Benito joked, 'A cork from our house! Manufactured by the Gandol brothers!'

The lunch took place as though there were no walls in the house, as though the crazy wind stirred the tableware, the glasses, and the four hearts at its pleasure. No sooner were they all united into a single heart, transformed into flame, than a frozen gust would overtake and numb them. Amadeo led the conversation and he did it with skill; although using somewhat exaggerated adjectives, from time to time.

His sister-in-law looked into his eyes. Could something be happening? At the moment of toasting, Amadeo lifted his glass and offering it to all said dryly, 'Until forever.'

After the coffee, Amadeo lit a cigar and stood up on the pretext of an appointment.

'I have to go. They're waiting for me.'

'Where?' asked Benito.

Amadeo hesitated. 'In the chapel of San Telmo,' he answered.

They all accompanied him to the door. And it was there, in the last instant, that the fugitive was on the verge of losing his serenity. First he kissed the boy, on the cheeks; then his sister-in-law, on the forehead; then he offered his hand to Benito, his brother, who gripped it with such unexpected strength that Amadeo winced.

It was the key moment. Without a doubt, Benito intuitively felt that Amadeo's 'Until forever' hid a secret and he wanted to assure him that he was on his side. It could have been that the gripping of hands transfused half his warm blood. 'Here, Amadeo,' he seemed to say to him, 'all this for you.'

Amadeo experienced a soothing sensation in his veins, almost of strength. He looked fixedly at Benito, whose eyes were interrogating. He got away as best he could, took his cane and, making a pirouette, which was not his habit, turned and ran down the stairs.

The Boardwalk was deserted. Only the boats; and the clashing of materials, especially of wood and iron. Amadeo saw, on the left, the port, the breakwater and the lighthouse. Behind the lighthouse, the open sea. Then he saw, up there on the right, the chapel of San Telmo presiding over the mountain. Behind the mountain, the sea, even more free.

He branched off toward the cemetery, which was not far away, with the thought of bidding farewell to his parents. The gate was latched and he had to push it, making it creak. Soon he was surrounded by cypresses and crosses. His parents were there as always, photographed, waiting. He heard a noise and turned. He thought perhaps that the hunchbacked man or the woman who rubbed her wrists with alcohol might be about the place. But, apart from the crosses and the cypresses, there was no one.

Then a profound depression invaded Amadeo. The niche with his parents inside was the last barrier opposing his departure. Amadeo asked himself if running away would serve a purpose. Probably not. Wherever he went he would be he, Amadeo Gandol, with his jealousies, with his solitude, with his hostile emotions.

He looked at his parents as though accusing them of having brought him into the world together with another being, a twin being. And in that precise instant he understood that the only escape for his anguish was to remain there, in the cemetery.

The idea of suicide penetrated him with such force that he shook his cane, thinking that by breaking it in two he could form a cross. Then, without knowing why, he stammered, 'Forgive me.' Whom was he asking? Then he shuddered and felt in his pockets as though looking for something.

Moments passed. Finally, Amadeo decided. He did it with strange calm, as though death were very familiar to him. He considered it unnecessary to write a few words for Benito; everything was very clear. He looked at the trees, tall, and again searched in his pockets.

Just then, he again heard a noise and immediately afterward a bark: he recognized his dog. How was it possible? Yes, there was his dog, light-footed, black and white, with his tongue hanging out.

Amadeo was stunned. He was going toward the dog when he saw Herminia, the old servant, appear from among the monuments, with her hands in a gesture of supplication.

Amadeo, his breath stilled, waited motionless for the old woman to come up to him.

'Señor, señor!'

'Why have you come? What's the matter?'

'Your brother . . .!'

'My brother? What's happened?'

'Oh, señor! He's committed suicide.'

JOSÉ MARIA GIRONDELLA, trs. Terry Brock

---

from Balin And Balan

THAT weird yell,
Unearthlier than all shriek of bird or beast, Thrill'd thro' the woods; and Balan lurking there—
His quest was unaccomplish'd – heard and thought
'The scream of that wood-devil I came to quell!'
Then nearing: 'Lo! he hath slain some brother-knight,
And tramples on the goodly shield to show
His loathing of our Order and the Queen.

My quest, meseems, is here. Or devil or man,
Guard thou thine head.' Sir Balin spake not word,
But snatch'd a sudden buckler from the squire,
And vaulted on his horse, and so they crash'd
In onset, and King Pellam's holy spear,
Reputed to be red with sinless blood,
Redden'd at once with sinful, for the point
Across the maiden shield of Balan prick'd
The hauberk to the flesh; and Balin's horse
Was wearied to the death, and, when they clash'd,
Rolling back upon Balin, crush'd the man
Inward, and either fell and swoon'd away.

Then to her squire mutter'd the damsel: 'Fools!
This fellow hath wrought some foulness with his Queen;
Else never had he borne her crown, nor raved
And thus foam'd over at a rival name.
But thou, Sir Chick, that scarce hast broken shell,
Art yet half-yolk, not even come to down—
Who never sawest Caerleon upon Usk—
And yet hast often pleaded for my love—
See what I see, be thou where I have been,
Or else, Sir Chick – dismount and loose their casques;
I fain would know what manner of men they be.'
And when the squire had loosed them, 'Goodly! – look!
They might have cropt the myriad flower of May,
And butt each other here, like brainless bulls,
Dead for one heifer!'

    Then the gentle squire:
'I hold them happy, so they died for love;
And, Vivien, tho'ye beat me like your dog,
I too could die, as now I live, for thee.'

    'Live on, Sir Boy,' she cried; 'I better prize
The living dog than the dead lion. Away!
I cannot brook to gaze upon the dead.'
Then leapt her palfrey o'er the fallen oak,
And bounding forward, 'Leave them to the wolves.'

    But when their foreheads felt the cooling air,
Balin first woke, and seeing that true face,
Familiar up from cradle-time, so wan,

Crawl'd slowly with low moans to where he lay,
And on his dying brother cast himself
Dying; and *he* lifted faint eyes; he felt
One near him; all at once they found the world,
Staring wild-wide; then with a childlike wail,
And drawing down the dim disastrous brow
That o'er him hung, he kiss'd it, moan'd, and spake:

   'O Balin, Balin, I that fain had died
To save they life, have brought thee to thy death.
Why had ye not the shield I knew? and why
Trampled ye thus on that which bare the crown?'

Then Balin told him brokenly and in gasps
All that had chanced, and Balan moan'd again:

   'Brother, I dwelt a day in Pellam's hall;
This Garlon mock'd me, but I heeded not.
And one said, "Eat in peace! a liar is he,
And hates thee for the tribute!" This good knight
Told me that twice a wanton damsel came,
And sought for Garlon at the castle-gates,
Whom Pellam drove away with holy heat.
I well believe this damsel, and the one
Who stood beside thee even now, the same.
"She dwells among the woods," he said, "and meets
And dallies with him in the Mouth of Hell."
Foul are their lives, foul are their lips; they lied.
Pure as our own true mother is our Queen.'

   'O brother,' answer'd Balin, 'woe is me!
My madness all thy life has been thy doom,
Thy curse, and darken'd all thy day; and now
The night has come. I scarce can see thee now.
Good night! for we shall never bid again
Good morrow – Dark my doom was here, and dark
It will be there. I see thee now no more.
I would not mine again should darken thine;
Good night, true brother.'

     Balan answer'd low,
'Good night, true brother, here! good morrow there!
We two were born together, and we die

Together by one doom:' and while he spoke
Closed his death-drowsing eyes, and slept the sleep
With Balin, either lock'd in either's arm.

ALFRED, LORD TENNYSON

---

from The Dualitists

[*TWO boys dual with equal objects; assaying which survives better the other's onslaught. They have progressed from the inanimate – cutlery etc, to live – rabbits. But now what?*]

Hand in hand Zacariah and Zerubbabel advanced from the back door; they had escaped from their nurses, and with the exploring instinct of humanity, advanced boldly into the great world – the *terra incognita*, the *ultima Thule* of the paternal domain.

In the course of time they approached the hedge of poplars, from behind which the anxious eyes of Harry and Tommy looked for their approach, for the boys knew that where the twins were the nurses were accustomed to be gathered together, and they feared discovery if their retreat should be cut off.

It was a touching sight, these lovely babes, alike in form, feature, size, expression, and dress; in fact, so like each other that one 'might not have told either from which'. When the startling similarity was recognized by Harry and Tommy, each suddenly turned, and, grasping the other by the shoulder, spoke in a keen whisper: 'Hack! They are exactly equal! This is the very apotheosis of our art!'

With excited faces and trembling hands they laid their plans to lure the unsuspecting babes within the precincts of their charnel house, and they were so successful in their efforts that in a little time the twins had toddled behind the hedge and were lost to the sight of the parental mansion.

Harry and Tommy were not famed for gentleness within the immediate precincts of their respective homes, but it would have delighted the heart of any philanthropist to see the kindly manner in which they arranged for the pleasures of the helpless babes. With smiling faces and playful words and gentle wiles they led them within the arbour, and then, under pretence of giving them some of those sudden jumps in which infants rejoice, they raised them from the

255

ground. Tommy held Zacariah across his arm with his baby moonface smiling up at the cobwebs on the arbour roof, and Harry, with a mighty effort, raised the cherubic Zerubbabel aloft.

Each nerved himself for a great endeavour, Harry to give, Tommy to endure a shock, and then the form of Zerubbabel was seen whirling through the air round Harry's glowing and determined face. There was a sickening crash and the arm of Tommy yielded visibly.

The pasty face of Zerubbabel had fallen fair on that of Zacariah, for Tommy and Harry were by this time artists of too great experience to miss so simple a mark. The putty-like noses collapsed, the putty-like cheeks became for a moment flattened, and when in an instant more they parted, the faces of both were dabbled in gore. Immediately the firmament was rent with a series of such yells as might have awakened the dead. Forthwith from the house of Bubb came the echoes in parental cries and footsteps. As the sounds of scurrying feet rang through the mansion, Harry cried to Tommy: 'They will be on us soon. Let us cut to the roof of the stable and draw up the ladder.'

Tommy answered by a nod, and the two boys, regardless of consequences, and bearing each a twin, ascended to the roof of the stable by means of a ladder which usually stood against the wall, and which they pulled up after them.

As Ephraim Bubb issued from his house in pursuit of his lost darlings, the sight which met his gaze froze his very soul. There, on the coping of the stable roof, stood Harry and Tommy renewing their game. They seemed like two young demons forging some diabolical implement, for each in turn the twins were lifted high in air and let fall with stunning force on the supine form of its fellow. How Ephraim felt none but a tender and imaginative father can conceive. It would be enough to wring the heart of even a callous parent to see his children, the darlings of his old age – his own beloved twins – being sacrificed to the brutal pleasure of unregenerate youths, without being made unconsciously and helplessly guilty of the crime of fratricide.

Loudly did Ephraim and also Sophonisba, who, with dishevelled locks, had now appeared upon the scene, bewail their unhappy lot and shriek in vain for aid; but by rare ill-chance no eyes save their own saw the work of butchery or heard the shrieks of anguish and despair. Wildly did Ephraim, mounting on the shoulders of his spouse, strive, but in vain, to scale the stable wall.

Baffled in every effort, he rushed into the house and appeared in a moment bearing in his hands a double-barrelled gun, into which he poured the contents of a shot pouch as he ran. He came anigh the stable and hailed the murderous youths: 'Drop them twins and come down here or I'll shoot you like a brace of dogs.'

'Never!' exclaimed the heroic two with one impulse, and continued their awful pastime with a zest tenfold as they knew that the agonized eyes of parents wept at the cause of their joy.

'Then die!' shrieked Ephraim, as he fired both barrels, right – left, at the hackers.

But, alas! love for his darlings shook the hand that never shook before. As the smoke cleared off and Ephraim recovered from the kick of his gun, he heard a loud twofold laugh of triumph and saw Harry and Tommy, all unhurt, waving in the air the trunks of the twins – the fond father had blown the heads completely off his own offspring.

BRAM STOKER

---

from The Nazi Doctors

THE more sinister side of Mengele's twin research emerged in his elaborate arrangements for pathological examination of corpses. For Dr Miklos Nyiszli, his main prisoner pathologist, Mengele prepared a special dissection room, including a 'dissecting table of polished marble,' a basin with 'nickel taps' and 'three porcelain sinks,' and windows 'with green metal screens to keep out flies and mosquitoes.' The adjoining working room had a large table, 'comfortable arm chairs,' three microscopes and 'a well-stocked library, which contained the most recent editions.' The overall arrangement, as Nyiszli later wrote, was 'the exact replica of any large city's institute of pathology.'

Nyiszli's earler deposition (made in July 1945) reveals Mengele to be a direct murderer of his twins:

In the work room next to the dissecting room, fourteen Gypsy twins were waiting [about midnight one night], guarded by SS men, and crying bitterly. Dr Mengele didn't say a single word to us, and prepared a 10 cc. and 5 cc. syringe. From a box he took evipan, and from another box he took chloroform, which was in 20 cubic-centimeter glass containers, and put these on the operating table. After that, the first twin was brought in,

. . . a fourteen-year-old girl. Dr Mengele ordered me to undress the girl and put her on the dissecting table. Then he injected the evipan into her right arm intravenously. After the child had fallen asleep, he felt for the left ventricle of the heart and injected 10 cc. of chloroform. After one little twitch the child was dead, whereupon Dr Mengele had it taken into the morgue. In this manner, all fourteen twins were killed during the night.

ROBERT JAY LIFTON

---

from The Siamese Twins

FOR many years Chang and Eng Bunker lived in North Carolina, where they were married, and raised large families of children, Chang being the father of ten, Eng of nine. Dr Joseph Hollingsworth, to whom we are indebted for the information given in this article as to their habits of life and the circumstances of their death, states that he has known them as residents in the neighborhood of Mount Airy, North Carolina, for some twenty years, during which time he has acted as their family physician. Chang, who is said to have derived his name from the Siamese word for 'left,' was the left of the pair, and was much smaller and more feeble than his brother Eng, whose name signifies 'right.' Their habits were very active: during the latter part of their life they and their families lived in two houses, about a mile and a half apart, and it was an inflexible rule that they should pass three days alternately at each house. So determinedly was this alternation maintained that sickness and death in one family had no effect upon the movements of the father, and a dying or dead child was on one occasion left in obedience to it: indeed, Dr Hollingsworth is very positively of the opinion that the death of the twins themselves was the result of this rule, or, at least, was materially hastened thereby. This will be made apparent hereafter.

The evidences during life that the twins were physiologically distinct entities were very numerous and apparent. They were different in form, tastes, and disposition; all their physical functions were performed separately and unconnectedly. What Chang liked to eat, Eng detested. Eng was very good-natured, Chang cross and irritable. The sickness of one had no effect upon the other, so that while one would be suffering from fever the pulse of the other would beat at its natural rate. The twins not rarely suffered from bilious attacks, but one never suffered at the same time as the other; a circumstance which seems somewhat singular in view of the close connection which the post-mortem has shown to exist between the livers of the pair. Chang drank pretty heavily, – at times getting drunk; but Eng never felt any influence from the debauch of his brother, – a seemingly conclusive proof that there was no free interchange in their circulations.

The twins often quarrelled; and of course, under the circumstances, their quarrels were bitter. They sometimes came to blows, and on one occasion came under the jurisdiction of the courts. After one of these difficulties Chang and Eng applied to Dr Hollingsworth to separate them, stating that they could not live longer together. Eng affirmed that Chang was so bad that he could live no longer with him; and Chang stated that he was satisfied to be separated, only asking that he be given an equal chance with his brother, and that the band be cut exactly in the middle. But as Dr Hollingsworth advised very decidedly against this, and declined to interfere, cooler counsels prevailed.

In August, 1870, Chang suffered from a paralytic stroke, from which he never fully recovered; and during the last year of his life he several times said to Dr Hollingsworth, '*We* can't live long.'

On the Thursday evening preceding their death, the time having arrived for their departure from the house at which they were staying, the twins rode a mile and a half in an open wagon. The weather was very cold, – the night being the severest of the winter. Chang had been complaining for some days of cough, with distress and actual pain in the chest. He was so unwell that his wife thought he would be unable to bear the trip; but he finally went. On Friday morning Chang reported that he felt better, but that in the night he had had such severe pain in the chest, and so much distress, that he thought he should have died.

The twins slept in a room by themselves or with only a very young child present; and some time in the course of Friday night they got up and sat by the fire. As they were accustomed to do this frequently, nothing was thought of it by those of the family who saw them, even though they heard Eng saying he was sleepy and wanted to retire, and Chang insisting on remaining up, stating that his breathing was so bad that it would kill him to lie down. Finally, however, the couple went to bed again, and after an hour or so the family heard some one call. No one went to the twins for some little time, and, when they did go, Chang was dead, and Eng was awake.

[. . .] When Eng saw his wife after learning that Chang was dead, he said, 'I am dying,' but did not speak of his brother's death. He soon afterwards expressed a desire to defecate, and this continued for half an hour. He rubbed his upper extremities, raised them restlessly, and complained of a choking sensation. The only notice he took of Chang was to move him nearer. His last words were, 'May the Lord have mercy on my soul!'

The Death Of Enkidu

'Hear me, great ones of Uruk,
I weep for Enkidu, my friend,
Bitterly moaning like a woman mourning
I weep for my brother.
O Enkidu, my brother,
You were the axe at my side;
My hand's strength, the sword in my belt,
The shield before me,
A glorious robe, my fairest ornament;
An evil Fate has robbed me.
The wild ass and the gazelle
That were father and mother,
All long-tailed creatures that nourished you
Weep for you,
All the wild things of the plain and pastures;
The paths that you loved in the forest of cedars
Night and day murmur.
Let the great ones of strong-walled Uruk
Weep for you;
Let the finger of blessing
Be stretched out in mourning;
Enkidu, young brother. Hark,
There is an echo through all the country
Like a mother mourning.
Weep all the paths where we walked together;
And the beasts we hunted, the bear and hyena,
Tiger and panther, leopard and lion,
The stag and the ibex, the bull and the doe.
The river along whose banks we used to walk,
Weeps for you,
Ula of Elam and dear Euphrates
Where once we drew water for the water-skins.

The mountain we climbed where we slew the Watchman,
Weeps for you.
The warriors of strong-walled Uruk
Where the Bull of Heaven was killed,
Weep for you.
All the people of Eridu
Weep for you Enkidu.
Those who brought grain for your eating
Mourn for you now;
Who rubbed oil on your back
Mourn for you now;
Who poured beer for your drinking
Mourn for you now.
The harlot who anointed you with fragrant ointment
Laments for you now;
The women of the palace, who brought you a wife,
A chosen ring of good advice,
Lament for you now.
And the young men your brothers
As though they were women
Go long-haired in mourning.
What is this sleep which holds you now?
You are lost in the dark and cannot hear me.'

from *The Epic of Gilgamesh*, trans. by N K Sanders

---

from My Twin Sister Erika

MOTHER spoke first.

'Inge,' she said, 'last night angels came and took Erika from us.'

'I know . . . I heard their wings,' I whispered.

Father stroked my hair and said, 'You are the only one now, the only one.'

'The only one,' I said, and a strange feeling came over me. Not so much of loneliness as of importance. The only one, I repeated in my mind, over and over. And each time I thought, *I am Inge and I am alive.*

'May I see Erika?' I asked Mother after I had dressed.

'No, dear. You can't enter that room. If you do, you might catch what made Erika so sick.'

What was I to do today, I wondered. I wanted to see Erika. I was truly curious. I wanted to see what she looked like.

'Does Erika still look like me?' I asked Grandmother.

'She looks like she is asleep,' Grandmother answered.

This made me even more curious. What would happen if I would climb into bed next to Erika, lie down and hold my breath? Would I look dead or would Erika look alive? I had to find out.

Against all orders I crept into the room. The curtains were drawn. My eyes had to get used to the darkness, and I was too excited to really look at Erika. Then I heard footsteps. I quickly climbed into Erika's bed, slipped under the linen sheet, and folded my hands on my chest the way Erika's were folded. The footsteps came closer. Who would find us there? Mother? Grandmother? Father? I thought my heart would burst or stop beating.

The footsteps passed. I heard another door open and shut, and the next second I found myself outside the room. Alone and alive. I trembled so much, I had to sit down.

Who are you, I asked myself. Are you Erika or are you Inge? I didn't know what to answer. Are you Inge or Erika, I asked once more. And instead of an answer, there came tears. That was how Mother found me – weeping at the door.

She sat down on the floor next to me and cradled me in her arms. 'You are all I have now,' she said, 'all I have.'

ISE-MARGARET VOGEL

————

from God My Exceeding Joy

I WAS summoned here by telegram. I need not dwell on how I feel, for by your letter you seem to have grapsed the situation. But for the prospect of the tender love which welcomed me here yesterday (Nov. 5th) and tenacious grip of the hand which keeps me captive at her side being resumed one day above, this would be an unbearable trial. Yet in it all God upholds! On entering her room in the early morning, she at once seizes my hand and says, 'Promise me you will not leave me; pray me to sleep.' The way she drops off so trustfully makes her the literal expression of, '*He giveth His beloved sleep.*' To look at her she is like a child with the flush of youth on its cheek.

On arrival I found she would have been the better of an air pillow or hot water bed, and got one. Her limbs were cold and stiff, and I chafed them with warm water and spirits. The comfort of the air bed and chafing was such that she frequently exclaimed, 'Darling Margaret a thousand times over! You will get your reward for this! etc.' I felt it to be such an honour to be ministering to one who made the glory of God and good of souls the first, yea the only thing worth living for. I only wish I had known earlier she was so hopelessly ill. A letter which should have reached me two days before I received the telegram was only delivered two days after my arrival. All were kind to her, yea devoted – the frequent calls, cards, and loving inquiries and bunches of violets are echoes of the use God made of her in that place, but as she said herself, 'There is nothing like having one's own flesh and blood near one after all' – at a time like this. She was perfectly clear and collected, and acted as naturally as when quite well. At once she impressed upon me that all expenses connected with the sick-room, etc., were advanced to a penny, and that I was to have no anxiety. All personal matters received careful attention just as if the end was anticipated.

One morning she said, 'Margaret dear, I am quite happy.' Latterly, she was not able to recognize me, and she would on seizing my hand say 'Are you bone of my bone and flesh of my flesh?' On feeling reassured that such was the case she would say, 'Margaret dear, bind me with you. Are you ready? You go first, but don't shut the gates,' etc.

Latterly the graciousness was much reduced by the more frequent intervals of pain and exhaustion . . . finally the spirit took its flight like a bird eagerly longing to roam through space. The glory which threw a halo round her life and this was all we had from the 20th to the 25th . . . she has now got what she longed for.

MARGARET MCMILLAN

A 4-year-old recently bereaved of her identical twin, is scolded for climbing up to look at herself in the mirror over the fireplace. She answers, in bewilderment. 'But mayn't I look at Gracie?'

story reported to author

263

from The Godhunters

THE place he was seeking was there, and so was the man who did the sewing, expecting him, averring that he'd have recognized Aubrey anywhere as Arnie's twin brother, and leading Aubrey in, apologizing as he went, saying that he'd scarcely begun, that he'd be working all night to make the eight o'clock plane to Seattle, that he'd seen them come and he'd seen them clawed but that Arnie was the worst and what kind of an animal was that bear anyway, half of a lion? And this stitchman was old, older than his craft, his face rubescent and epispastically scarred, his voice a moan from a pox-stricken sail loft, his eyes like those of the needles through which no man might pass or be passed, and his body like coarse thread, wound and wound on no spine at all, so that he was a circlet without a spool, a fleshy cycle without a cylinder, a spinning without a spindle, and he seemed to unravel as he walked.

His voice warmed to death talk as they went deeper and deeper into the place, as the smell became more and more defeating. And the stitchman rattled on and on until Aubrey, gagging, could answer him no longer. And his eyes flashed on Aubrey with the true pride of the unsqueamish as, swiftly, he turned from closing a final door, plucked up nimbly the edges of a tabled and mounded sheet, and, deliberately but quickly, drew it down to the belly pit of all that remained of Arnie.

Aubrey went back from the sight like a spitting cat, drawing all the air his lungs could contain up and in through his open mouth in one horrified gasp. And he clawed for the doorknob behind him with one hand and covered his eyes almost at once with the other. But too late: for he had seen the gape-mouthed, slug-white, nail-hackled horror that was there – the canescent, dreadfully torn, naked trunk of his brother – all cross-stitched clumsily in blue like a cartographer's marks for an antic railroad all up and down a whited desert; had seen, too, the cold blue flaps of flesh as yet unsewed; had seen what looked like a wad of white fish-paper stuffed in the hole in the pit of the stomach; had seen, most horribly, Arnie's face, the head lolled toward him, the jaw ghastly slack, the teeth slightly bared in a grin of last, indescribable agony, and the near eye, the left eye, wide open and staring – a living, surprised, pleading eye, fixed upon Aubrey leperlike, asking only not to be loathed.

And heard then, in the silence – a silence that obtained only because Aubrey was unable to reverse the gasping intake of his breath and scream – was the stitchman, saying, 'That's him, isn't it? That your brother?'

'No, no, no! You butcher!' Aubrey screeched, turned away now, releasing his swollen lungs, grappling with the doorknob with both hands, the valves of his heart sucking at and welcoming a sudden, engulfing tidal surge of that black blood that his will had so recently turned back. 'You stinking, foul, bastard of a butcher! May God damn you to hell!'

And he wrenched open that door and left it banging and echoing behind him, and tore at the next door and the next of that carrion place, and went howling and cursing down its decayed corridors, and screamed piercingly when some hag, some decomposing, friable, grave-haired victim of zoothapsis, suddenly appeared in his way, grinning hideously. He charged her desperately, still shouting, and knocked her back into a wall, and felt that arm and shoulder which had brushed against her immediately die and grow rigid, but went on and out and out, and flew into the street, dancing for his life, too terrified and stark of lung to scream any more, and ran again, taking on the driving rain as an engine takes on water, and revived enough to begin to see his way, to remember and retrace the startled streets back to the hotel – other pedestrians turning at ten feet hearing the lump of him, and then at thirty and more feet (as he revived enough to shout and howl Arnie's name again) hearing the anguished voice of him, and scattering before his onrush like seals to their rocks – and came down the last fifty yards and into the hotel lobby in full sprint, came up short in front of the newsstand against the immovable bulk of Kunkel, bounced away, stood speechless for a moment, then put all that remained between the bare survival and utter collapse of his lungs into one despairing howl of summation: 'Kunkel, Kunkel, Jesus Christ! You took him to a goddamned taxidermist!'

WILLIAM KELLEY

---

from The Inseparable Twins

AT that moment he saw Sashka.

Kolka's heart gave a bound of joy: Sashka was standing at the very end of the street, leaning against a fence and staring hard

265

at something – perhaps at the crows which were circling around near by.

Kolka put two fingers into his mouth and whistled.

Anyone familiar with the twins' habits could have told them apart by the way they whistled. Kolka only used two fingers, but he could make a sound capable of intricate modulations. Sashka, on the other hand, employed four fingers, two from each hand, and he could whistle louder than Kolka, so loud that it made your ears ring, but only on one note.

Now Kolka whistled and grinned to himself. 'Aha! Sashka must have gone deaf – he can't hear me whistling! He's standing there like a statue.'

Kolka ran along the village street, straight towards Sashka, thinking what fun it would be to creep up on Sashka while his brother was still watching the crows; he had done this before – he would creep alongside the fence and then bark at the top of his voice, 'Hands up – I'm a Chechen!'

But as he came nearer, he slowed his pace involuntarily: there was something very strange about Sashka, but at first Kolka could not make out what it was.

Either Sashka had grown taller, or he was standing in an awkward attitude – what's more, the fact that he hadn't moved for so long was beginning to seem suspicious.

Kolka took a few more hesitant steps and stopped.

Suddenly he felt cold all over and sick and short of breath. His body froze, down to the very tips of his fingers and toes. His legs gave way under him and he dropped down to the grass, though without taking his gaze off Sashka, his eyes wide with horror.

Sashka was not standing; he was hanging, impaled through his armpits on the spikes of the fence, and from his stomach there protruded a yellow corn-cob, its silky 'floss' waving in the breeze.

The other half of the corn-cob had been rammed into Sashka's mouth, its thick end sticking out, giving Sashka's face a silly, even stupid, expression.

Kolka remained sitting on the ground, overcome by a strange feeling of aloofness, as though he were not in his own body but was nevertheless seeing and remembering everything. He saw, for instance, that the flock of crows, perched on a nearby tree, was watching his every movement; he saw some nimble grey sparrows taking a dust-bath; and he saw an ugly chicken leap out from behind the fence, chased by a hungry, feral cat.

Kolka made an effort to stand up, and succeeded. Walking forward, he did not go to Sashka but around him, without going either nearer or further away.

Now, standing directly opposite his brother he saw that Sashka had no eyes; the crows had pecked them out. They had also pecked at his right cheek and ear, but not so hard. Below his stomach and below the the corn-cob and tufts of grass that had been stuffed into it, Sashka's intestines – black with clotted blood – were hanging out down his trousers, and had also been pecked by the crows. Clearly the blood had also run down his legs, which were so oddly raised above ground level; it was hanging in large clots from the soles of his feet and from Sashka's dirty toes, while the grass under his feet was a single, jelly-like mass.

[*Kolka takes his brother down puts him in a handcart*]

[. . .] The train was drawing nearer. The dull click of the wheels could already be heard, reflected back from the hills on the far side of the line.

Kolka jumped up and set off at a run across the field, pulling his brother in the handcart behind him. They reached the railway line at the very moment when the train braked sharply and stopped, with a hissing sound from under the carriages.

Kolka left the cart among a clump of burdock at the foot of the embankment, then ran along the line of carriages looking for one with an underslung luggage-box. Neither the first nor the second carriage was fitted with one of these boxes, but he found one under the third carriage.

He opened the steel lid and felt inside the box to make sure there were no passengers in it already. Then he ran back, pulled the handcart along the embankment to the third carriage and untied the leather strap. He spread out the quilted jacket on the bottom of the box then gripped Sashka under the armpits, praying that the train would not move off. Sashka was now so stiff that none of his limbs would bend, but he seemed lighter than before.

Panting with exertion, Kolka heaved Sashka up and tipped him into the luggage-box, face upward. He arranged the sacks along his sides and on top of him, so that he wouldn't be cold; the box, after all was only made of thin metal and wasn't heated.

He kicked the handcart with its rope down the embankment and into the long grass. It had done its job; they had no more need of it.

As the train still hadn't started to move, Kolka went back to the luggage-box, squatted down in front of it on his haunches, and said to Sasha through a hole in its side, 'Well, you'll be off soon . . . you wanted to go to the mountains, didn't you? . . . But I'll stay here a while. I would've gone with you, but Regina Petrovna . . . would be left alone. Don't worry, Sashka, I'll be thinking about you all the time.'

Kolka tapped on the box so that Sashka shouldn't feel lonely and frightened.

As he was walking away, he saw the guard jump down from one of the carriages. The man was just about to walk past Kolka, when he stopped. 'Aha! Hallo there!' he shouted, showing all his teeth in a wide grin.

Kolka looked closer: it was Ilya. 'Hallo!' he replied. 'Weren't you burned up with your house?'

Ilya laughed. 'Ha! I don't burn! Non-inflammable, that's me! I'd already guessed what sort of trouble was on the way, so I went back to work on the railway. I'm on this train now, as you can see. I'll take you wherever you like to go.'

'No,' said Kolka. 'I can't go.'

'Which one are you? Are you Kolka or Sashka?'

After a moment's pause Kolka said, 'I'm both.'

At that moment the engine whistled.

Ilya shouted, 'Ah! We're off. You'd do better to come with me and get away from all this trouble, wouldn't you?' He ran back to his carriage and jumped up on to the steps.

'Yes, perhaps I would,' Kolka nodded with a sigh. Ilya could no longer hear him. The train started with a jerk and a clanking of buffers, then picked up speed as it moved off towards the still-invisible mountains. And Sashka went off with it, leaving Kolka alone on the dark embankment.

ANATOLY PRISTAVKIN, trs. M. Glennie

---

from The Duchess Of Malfi

FERD. Is she dead?

BOS. She is what
  You'd have her. But here begin your pity:
                              [*Shows the Children strangled*]
  Alas, how have these offended?

FERD. The death
  Of young wolves is never to be pitied.

BOS. Fix your eye here.

FERD. Constantly.

BOS. Do you not weep?
　　Other sins only speak; murder shrieks out:
　　The element of water moistens the earth,
　　But blood flies upwards and bedews the heavens.

FERD. Cover her face; mine eyes dazzle: she died young.

BOS. I think not so; her infelicity
　　Seem'd to have years too many.

FERD. She and I were twins;
　　And should I die this instant, I had liv'd
　　Her time to a minute.

BOS. It seems she was born first:
　　You have bloodily approv'd the ancient truth,
　　That kindred commonly do worse agree
　　Than remote strangers.

FERD. Let me see her face
　　Again.

JOHN WEBSTER

---

from The Fall of the House of Usher

NO sooner had these syllables passed my lips, than – as if a shield of brass had . . . at the moment, fallen heavily upon a floor of silver – I became aware of a distinct, hollow, metallic, and clangorous, yet apparently muffled reverberation. Completely unnerved, I leaped to my feet; but the measured rocking movement of Usher was undisturbed. I rushed to the chair in which he sat. His eyes were bent fixedly before him, and throughout his whole countenance there reigned a stony rigidity. But, as I placed my hand upon his shoulder, there came a strong shudder over his whole person; a sickly smile quivered about his lips; and I saw that he spoke in a low, hurried, and gibbering murmur, as if unconscious of my presence. Bending closely over him, I at length drank in the hideous import of his words.

'Not hear it? – yes, I hear it, and *have* heard it. Long – long – long – many minutes, many hours, many days, have I heard it – yet I dared not – oh, pity me, miserable wretch that I am! – I dared not – I *dared* not speak! *We have put her living in the tomb!* Said I not that my senses were acute? I *now* tell you that I heard her first feeble movements in the hollow coffin. I heard them – many, many days ago – yet I dared not – *I dared not speak!* And now – to-night – Ethelred – ha! ha! – the breaking of the hermit's door, and the death-cry of the dragon, and the clangour of the shield! – say, rather, the rending of her coffin, and the grating of the iron hinges of her prison, and her struggles within the coppered archway of the vault! Oh whither shall I fly? Will she not be here anon? Is she not hurrying to upbraid me for my haste? Have I not heard her footstep on the stair? Do I not distinguish that heavy and horrible beating of her heart? MADMAN!' here he sprang furiously to his feet, and shrieked out his syllables, as if in the effort he were giving up his soul – 'MADMAN! I TELL YOU THAT SHE NOW STANDS WITHOUT THE DOOR!'

As if in the superhuman energy of his utterance there had been found the potency of a spell – the huge antique panels to which the speaker pointed, threw slowly back, upon the instant, their ponderous and ebony jaws. It was the work of the rushing gust – but then without those doors there DID stand the lofty and enshrouded figure of the Lady Madeline of Usher. There was blood upon her white robes, and the evidence of some bitter struggle upon every portion of her emaciated frame. For a moment she remained trembling and reeling to and fro upon the threshold, then, with a low moaning cry, fell heavily inward upon the person of her brother, and in her violent and now final death-agonies, bore him to the floor a corpse, and a victim to the terrors he had anticipated.

From that chamber, and from that mansion, I fled aghast.

EDGAR ALLAN POE

---

from The Other Side of Death

HE wasn't exactly sure how long he'd been like that, between the noble surface of dreams and realities, but he did remember that suddenly, as if his throat had been cut by the slash of a knife, he'd given a start in bed and felt that his twin brother, his dead brother, was sitting on the edge of the bed.

Again, as before, his heart was a fist that rose up into his mouth and pushed him into a leap. The dawning light, the cricket that continued grinding the solitude with its little out-of-tune hand organ, the cool air that came up from the garden's universe, everything contributed to make him return to the real world once more. But this time he could understand what had caused his start. During the brief minutes of his dozing, and – I can see it now – during the whole night, when he had thought he'd had a peaceful, simple sleep, *with no thoughts*, his memory had been fixed on one single, constant, invariable image, an *autonomous* image that imposed itself on his thought in spite of the will and the resistance of the thought itself. Yes. Almost without his noticing it, 'that' thought had been overpowering him, filling him, completely inhabiting him, turning into a backdrop that was fixed there behind the other thoughts, giving support, the definitive vertebrae to the mental drama of his day and night. The idea of his twin brother's corpse had been firmly stuck in the whole centre of his life. And now that they had left him there, in his parcel of land now, his eyelids fluttered by the rain, now *he was afraid* of him.

He never thought the blow would have been so strong. Through the partly opened window the smell entered again, mixed in now with a different smell, of damp earth, submerged bones, and his sense of smell came out to meet it joyfully, with the tremendous happiness of a bestial man. Many hours had already passed since the moment in which *he saw* it twisting like a badly wounded dog under the sheets, howling, biting out that last shout that filled his throat with salt, using his nails to try to break the pain that was climbing up *him*, along his back, to the roots of the tumour. He couldn't forget *his* thrashing like a dying animal, rebellious at the truth that had stopped in front of *him*, that had clasped *his* body with tenacity, with imperturbable constancy, something definitive, like death itself. He saw *him* during the last moments of *his* barbarous death throes. When he broke *his* nails against the walls, clawing at the last piece of life which was slipping away through his fingers, bleeding *him*, while the gangrene *was getting into him* through the side like an implacable woman. Then he saw *him* fall on to the messy bed, with a touch of resigned fatigue, sweating, as his froth-covered teeth drew a horrible, monstrous smile for the world out of him and death began to flow through his bones like a river of ashes.

It was then that I thought about the tumour that had ceased to pain in his stomach. I imagined it as round – now he felt the same sensation – swelling like an interior sun, unbearable like a yellow insect extending its vicious filaments towards the depths of the intestines. (He felt that his viscera had become dislocated inside him as before the imminence of a physiological necessity.) Maybe I'll have a tumour like his some day. At first it will be a small but growing sphere that will branch out, growing larger in my stomach like a foetus. I will probably feel it when it starts to take on motion, moving inwards, with the fury of a sleepwalking child, travelling through my intestines blindly – he put his hands on his stomach to contain the sharp pain – its anxious hands held out towards the shadows, looking for the warm matrix, the hospitable uterus that it is never to find; while its hundred feet of a fantastic animal will go on wrapping themselves up into a long and yellow umbilical cord. Yes. Maybe I – the stomach – like this brother who has just died, have a tumour at the root of my viscera. The smell that the garden had sent was returning now, strong, repugnant, enveloped in a nauseating stench. Time seemed to have stopped on the edge of dawn. The morning star had jelled on the glass while the neighbouring room, where the corpse had been all the night before, was still exuding its strong formaldehyde message. It was, certainly, a different smell from that of the garden. This was a more anguished, a more specific smell than that mingled smell of unequal flowers. A smell that always, once it was known, was related to corpses. It was the glacial and exuberant smell left with him from the formic aldehyde of amphitheatres. He thought about the laboratory. He remembered the viscera preserved in absolute alcohol; the dissected birds. A rabbit saturated with formaldehyde has its flesh harden, it becomes dehydrated and loses its docile elasticity until it changes into a perpetual, eternalized rabbit. Formaldehyde. Where is this smell coming from? *The only way to contain rot.* If we men *had* formaldehyde in our veins *we would be* like the anatomical specimens submerged in absolute alcohol.

There outside he heard the beating of the increasing rain as it came hammering on the glass of the partly open window. A cool, joyful, and new air came in, loaded with dampness. The cold of his hands intensified, making him feel the presence of the formaldehyde in his arteries; as if the dampness of the courtyard had come into him down to the bones. Dampness. There's a lot of dampness 'there'. With a certain displeasure he thought about the winter nights when the rain will pass through the grass and the dampness will come to rest on his brother's side, circulate through his body like a concrete current. It seemed to him that the dead had need of a different circulatory system that hurled them towards another irremediable and final death. At that moment he didn't want it to rain any more, he wanted summer to be an eternal, dominant season. Because of his thoughts, he was displeased by the persistence of that damp clatter on the grass. He wanted the clay of cemeteries to be dry, always dry, because it made him restless to think that after two weeks, when the dampness begins to run through the marrow, there would no longer be another man equal, exactly equal to him under the ground.

Yes. *They* were twin brothers, exact, whom no one could distinguish at first sight. Before, when they both were living their separate lives, they were nothing but *two twin brothers*, simple and apart like two different men. *Spiritually* there was no common factor between them. But now, when rigidity, the terrible reality, was climbing up along his back like an invertebrate animal, something had dissolved in his integral atmosphere, something that sounded like an emptiness, as if a precipice had opened up at his side, or as if his body had suddenly been sliced in two by an axe; not that exact, anatomical body under a perfect geometrical definition; not that physical body that now felt fear; another body, rather, that was coming from beyond his, that had been sunken with him in the liquid night of the maternal womb and was climbing up with him through the branches of an ancient genealogy; that was with him in the blood of his four pairs of great-grandparents and that came from way back, from the beginning of the world, sustaining with its weight, with its mysterious presence, the whole universal balance. It might be that he had been in the blood of Isaac and Rebecca, that it was his other brother who had been born shackled to his heel and who came tumbling along generation after generation, night after night, from kiss to kiss, from love to love, descending through arteries and testicles until he arrived, as on a night voyage at the womb of his recent mother. The mysterious ancestral itinerary was being presented to him now as painful and true, now that the equilibrium had been broken and the equation definitively solved. He knew that something was lacking for his personal harmony, his formal and everyday integrity: *Jacob had been irremediably freed from his ankles!*

During the days when his brother was ill he hadn't had this feeling, because the emaciated face, transfigured by fever and pain, with the grown beard, had been quite different from his.

Once he was motionless, lying out on top of his total death, a barber was called to 'arrange' the corpse. He was present, leaning tightly against the wall, when the man dressed in white arrived bearing the clean instruments of his profession . . . With the precision of a master he covered the dead man's beard with lather – the frothy mouth: that was how I saw him before he died – and slowly, as one who goes about revealing a tremendous secret, he began to shave him. It was then that he was assaulted by 'that' terrible idea. As the pale and earthen face of his twin brother emerged under the passage of the razor, he had the feeling that the corpse there was not a *thing* that was alien to him but was made from his same earthy substance, that it was his own repetition . . . He had the strange feeling that his kin had extracted his image from the mirror, the one he saw reflected in the glass when he shaved. Now that image, which used to respond to every movement of his, had gained independence. He had watched it being shaved other times, every morning. But now he was witnessing the dramatic experience of another man's taking the beard off the image in his mirror, his own physical presence unneeded. He had the certainty, the assurance, that if he had gone over to a mirror at that moment he would have found it blank, even though physics had no precise explanation for the phenomenon. It was an awareness of splitting in two! His double was a corpse! Desperate, trying to react, he touched the firm wall that rose up in him by touch, a kind of current of security. The barber finished his work and with the tip of his scissors closed the corpse's eyelids. Night left him trembling inside, with the irrevocable solitude of the plucked corpse. That was how exact they were. Two identical brothers, disquietingly repeated.

GABRIEL GARCIA MARQUEZ

---

from A Shadow of Light

AT the front of our house there were two front parlors, with the hall and stairway between them. The one on the north, opening into the dining room, was the nicest, and the one least used. The ceilings were high, the front windows came down almost to the floor, an ornamental plaster cove molding graced the ceiling line, and on the north wall was a plain, but very beautiful, white marble fireplace and mantel. The casket was placed in this room near the opened doors to the dining room. I wanted very much to go into the parlor and be alone with my twin brother, to look at him, to think, and to wonder, why? So, when no one was around, and mother was busy in the kitchen, I slipped quietly into the parlor and stood by the head of the casket near the mantel on which I rested my hand, in loneliness and sadness. Why was I left? We were so much alike, it seemed that whatever happened to one must also happen to the other. It had been so with most things in our life; now it could be that way no more. On the playground, we had most often been called 'Twin' because it was so much easier for the kids. Now, I would be known by my own name, which mother always used. As I looked at him with my eyes blurred with tears, I touched his forehead with my finger, and drew back quickly in shock and surprise as a little child would do when his curiosity had caused him to touch a hot stove. It was the same temperature as the marble mantel at my side, although softer, as if someone had pulled a piece of satin tightly over it.

No two bodies had ever lived together more closely, nor shared more intimately the warmth, coziness, and joy of living than he and I.

[. . .] We had snuggled close together, deep in the featherbed on cold winter nights, and, when finally warm, had turned from each other and gone to sleep. Now we must sleep alone, and yet not wholly alone, for often before I go to sleep at night, or in the dead of night, having wakened, he comes to me. You might say that I am restless and cannot sleep, but that is not true. I do not wish to sleep. Far better to be with him and dry my eyes on my pillow. We are together again, as when we were kids. But now there is no such thing as age. We move about in a world where there is no language, where speech is not heard, where words are futile, in a world in which feelings, emotions, understanding, and love reign. Anyone might think me sad, but this is because sorrow and joy are often expressed in identical ways. The sound of laughter may be much like the sound of sobbing. The tears on one's cheek – who can say whether they are tears of jubilance or of grief? Sorrow and joy, they, too, are twins.

RALPH W. THOMPSON

---

from The Silent Twins

NINE days before their release, when I visited them, Jennifer told me: 'I am going to die . . .'

'Don't be silly,' I replied. 'You are so young. There is no reason.' 'I just know,' she replied, 'I just know.'

In her diary and in a poem she wrote for June she described her presentiment:

> 'That was our laughing,
> That too was our smiling.
> And now I am dead
> And that too is your crying.'

On March 9, 10 minutes after the twins had climbed into a minibus taking them out of Broadmoor for the last time, Jennifer said: 'Thank heavens we are out of here at last,' before slumping on her sister's shoulder. Throughout the journey she remained limp and silent, apparently asleep but with her eyes open. When they arrived at the Caswell Clinic in South Wales she was lifted onto a bed, still unable to speak and barely recognising her twin. Four hours later, following the results of a blood test, she was rushed to hospital. By 6.15 pm she was dead.

The verdict at Jennifer's inquest was accidental death. The pathology reports showed that she died from acute myocarditis, an inflammation of the heart muscle that can be triggered by a host of causes, from a viral infection to drugs, poison, sudden exercise, malnutrition or even stress.

June reached the hospital minutes after her twin's heart had given out. Her reaction was one of deep grief and mourning, mixed with anger that Jennifer had spoiled their 'big day'. As she recalls in one of the many letters she wrote to Jennifer after her death: 'Why did you have to die, Jenny? Why did you choose to die on such a glorious day? Our glory; our dream. We left Broadmoor. Now I am alone. You are gone like a passing breeze, swept away like a fairy on a flower. I saw those daffodils in your room and I smelled death. I saw those daffodils swaying their heads as if to mock me . . . and on your chest was a Bible opened with a single red rose on top. You looked peaceful. I wept.'

When I visited June a few days after Jennifer's death, she expressed the same conflict of emotions. 'In some ways it was a sweet release,' she said. 'We were war weary. It had been a long battle. Someone had to break the vicious circle.' She asked me if I could float a banner across the skies of Haverfordwest a month after Jennifer's funeral. 'What would it say?' I asked. 'June is alive and well and has at last come into her own,' she replied.

She was convinced then, as she is now, that Jennifer sacrificed her life to set her twin free. But the profound love she feels for her liberator vies with jealousy and fear for the sister she still regards as her captor. Even from her grave Jennifer exerts an uncanny influence. 'Part of me wants to hug her more. I keep saying, if only I'd demonstrated my love to her more. I'd hold her now and say, "Jennifer, always remember that I love you no matter what." She had the devil in her, but she was an angel in disguise and she gave me back my life and I must thank her for that.'

$\star$ $\star$ $\star$

We are standing at Jennifer's grave on the slopes of the municipal cemetery, a short walk from June's family home. She places a bunch of tulips (she had vehemently rejected daffodils) and together we plant a blue pansy that shivers in the gusts of wind blowing across the hill from the Irish Sea. A headstone now stands in black marble, the words chosen by June and carved in gold. They were adapted from a magazine article she read quoting an inscription the writer Izaak Walton had commissioned for the wedding chest he gave his first wife:

> *We once were two*
> *We two made one*
> *We no more two*
> *Through life be one.*

June is not anxious to follow her sister into the grave. 'She is calling me. Calling me slowly,' she says. 'But I don't want to share the same grave. It would be like our old bunk beds. And unless she's changed she might grab me and say "Gotcha! You're dead now. I died before you, but you're with me, and we're even now." And she would laugh. She robbed me of sunlight. And she stole into my personality. If she were alive now she would still be stealing it from me.'

The sun breaks through, but June zips her jacket against the chill of these unwelcome thoughts. As we crouch together, wiping the fork and trowel and collecting bits of paper that have blown across the grave, June continues her explanation of the mystery of the silent twins.

'Jennifer was the one who gave me mental illness,' she says. 'It was Jennifer's mind making me mentally sick. She poisoned my mind. If she were alive we would still be fighting like cat and dog and she would be part of me. When she died, after a few months I came into my own. Not straight away, but about five months later. She let go of me and I got my life back. I was born again.'

'Don't you feel guilty when you come here and think these things?' I ask. June shrugs. She won the battle for survival. But she believes Jennifer's prediction that the victory will be short-lived and she will die five years later. 'I don't feel guilty,' she says. 'I feel better now. I've missed out on years. All this twin business. We should have been separated years ago, at birth. If we were living together now, back home, it wouldn't work, would it? I say to myself, she's dead now.

She's given life to me. I should be happy that I am alive, that I wake up every morning safe and sound and breathing.'

MARJORIE WALLACE, JULY 1994

---

from Euripides

HELEN Electra, will you – please – do something that I ask?
ELECTRA I would – but I am not free; I must stay with my brother.
HELEN Will you go for me, Electra, to my sister's grave?
ELECTRA You mean – my mother's grave? What for?
HELEN To pour out wine,
　And to lay on the mound an offering of my hair.
ELECTRA What law prevents *you* visiting your sister's grave?
HELEN I shrink from being seen in Argos.
ELECTRA Good: it's time
　You felt some shame for leaving home the way you did.
HELEN What you have said is just, Electra, but not kind.
ELECTRA What is this shame you feel before the citizens?
HELEN I am afraid of the men whose sons were killed at Troy.
ELECTRA You may well be; your name is execrated here.
HELEN So, save me from this fear; do for me what I ask.
ELECTRA To stand and see my mother's grave – I could not do it.
HELEN To send these gifts by servants would show disrespect.
ELECTRA Then why do you not send your daughter Hermione?
HELEN A young girl should not walk alone through crowded streets.
ELECTRA But she could pay the gifts due for her bringing-up.
HELEN You are quite right, Electra. I'll do as you say.—
　Hermione! Come out here, my dear.
[Enter HERMIONE]
Now take this jar
　For a libation, and these locks cut from my hair,
　And go and stand by Clytemnestra's tomb, and pour
　Round it this honey mixed with milk and bubbling wine;
　Then climb the mound and say these words: Your sister Helen
　Sends this libation as a gift, being herself
　Afraid to approach your monument, through terror of
　The Argive citizens. Beg her to have kindly thoughts
　For me, and you, and for my husband, and for these

278

Two unhappy children, whom Apollo has destroyed.
And speak my promise that I will discharge in full
All gifts and ceremonies due to a sister dead.
Go quickly, dear child, and when you have paid these rites
Over the grave, remember, come straight home again.

ORESTES

---

from My Sister and her Visit West

MY twin sister died in the same town where she was born, raised, and married within the borders of the upper class. It is one of those towns rich in fine houses and very green lawns, big mimosa trees and lots of rain to keep the well-kept rose gardens watered and thriving. I was also born and raised within these same borders, but I left when I was seventeen, I have no roses, and I have never married, even way out here, as far west and south as one can go on the desert.

She died on a Tuesday. I knew the end was near those few days before because of urgent notes from back home requesting my return. I did not return. Instead, on one of those last nights, I dreamed my sister came to visit me.

My sister never visited me. She never left the immediate vicinity of that same lush town, never saw sand that wasn't beach, or trees with thorns for leaves, or a sky that could glide by for days without a single cloud interrupting it.

I never encouraged her to visit. I do not believe I ever invited her to come west.

I had not seen my sister in twelve years when she died. We spoke on the phone now and then, usually about estate matters, or someone's wedding, or someone else's funeral. I never told her, or anyone back home, about my success – my serene adobe home on the edge of the desert, my dress studio and clients. I wanted the details of my western life to be mysterious and hardly known. The vast space between my dry, dusty patio and their wet, lacquered verandas meant I was – heart, soul, and way of thinking – a different species of person from what I was born into.

After my sister became ill, I called home more often, although we did not enjoy one another's conversation anymore than before, nor find a new depth to our relationship after the illness became permanent. I called home because a tightness moved into my stomach while I was trying to work in my studio – a tightness that solidified my feelings about illness and a sister's impending death, about the years between me and the past coming to nothing.

The dream was one of those that takes just enough of the natural elements, the real environment of one's thinking, to fool the dreamer of her dream. I lay on my bed in the dream, in my bedroom, every detail just as it is when I am awake: huge windows facing west, the end of the patio wall seen through thin, white curtains. Even the bureau with my carved jewelry box, the ceiling made of split cedar branches, forever dusty because I have not yet found a cleaning lady who will climb up and wipe them off with a cloth after a dust storm – all were in my dream just as in life.

My sister floated into my bedroom through the large western windows. Her body blocked my view of the western sky which was just then the most perfect peach as dusk came to me from the desert of my dream.

I know the sky well from this place in my room. I wanted the color of the sky to fill my room, and although I was enchanted at the sight of my frail, naked sister, a wispy cloud floating in from the patio, I was annoyed that she was here, uninvited, in my western life at all.

She smelled like the old rose garden our mother tended with the servants back home, and she hummed a song just enough out of tune to be irritating. I had disliked her humming and the smell of that garden – both reminded me of old women. And now my sister, forty years later, had brought it all back: roses and servants and a song of old women in my western bedroom.

I left the bed in an effort to look past her out the windows, but I could not see around her. I began to reach for her, hoping to pull her down; I jumped at her body, now rising towards the ceiling, swinging my arms in an effort to hit her. But she was out of my reach.

My sister stretched out a thin, transparent hand and examined the dust on the ceiling wood. She inspected my room. She touched each object as she floated past, felt the plaster of the old adobe walls, the cloth of the curtains, the skirts hanging in the closet. And then she turned and drifted back out the window, dissolving into the now gray sky, the soft and lovely peach of only a moment before gone. My sister dissolved into the desert air as if she had always known it, as if it were all hers for the asking.

I woke crying in the early dawn.

I called her the morning after the dream on what was to be the day before she died. I knew she was about to go – a telegram from her doctor and her husband both had come at breakfast. I called before beginning work. We immediately fell into the conversation we had had last time – about the garden and how difficult it was to get good help these days, someone who really knows roses, who didn't complain or steal.

Back home just wasn't the same, she told me again. I did not say it seemed very much the same to me.

I wanted to tell her, just as she began to relate the redecorating plans for the living room, that I was nothing like her and that I detested her garden and her yellow carpeted bathroom. But then I remembered the dream and the way she had drifted over the desert, a little cloud, my twin sister, a lovely mute breeze lifting the curtains of my favorite windows. I drawled something about the summer ending, the heat almost over, the dry air lifting, instead.

I said goodbye without once pursuing the paths that were our lives, the rhythm of our thoughts that had nothing and everything to do with being twin sisters. I sat in the studio thinking how I hated her garden and how I wished she would not die because it threatened to age my idea of myself; to change my belief in my own immortality.

After I left home I went west – far away where I sought unpaved streets and houses without grass between them and the road, and people who were proud of their differences. I was determined to like everything about this new home – not only the wide open beauty of the blue sky and the rose color of the sand at sundown; but the sandstorms of early spring, too, and the loud, repetitious and somewhat off-key music that beat incessantly from every bar and apartment window on a Saturday night in town. Even the plastic flowers bought at five and dime stores used to adorn the graves at the local cemetery: I even learned to like those flowers, although I could never quite imagine my own headstone covered with them.

I could never quite imagine my own headstone.

My sister died on a Tuesday and I did not go home. I sent flowers. I thought about sending something that would tell them all back home how different I was – like a huge wreath of those fake flowers, a real prize in the eyes of my neighbors. But I sent a standard bouquet of roses and a card embossed with silver, nothing that spoke of deserts or sandstorms or ceilings made of cedar branches.

It had been a predictable dream in content and emotion. I figured it was a textbook example of a dream about a sibling's death. Even so, after all the telephone calls and wires and letters to and from home, after all the death stuff was finally exhausted, the sister of the dream changed her mind and, instead of drifting out into the desert, turned around and came to my house as a visitor.

My sister came to visit me.

LESLEY POLING-KEMPES

———————

5

FREAKS: OR TWINS
AS CURIOSITIES

ﮩ&

ALL OF us twins are freaks. We twins don't have to be Siamese or
conjoined twins to be freakish. In a world where the normal are
born singly, are physically, mentally unique, all of us are freaks. It's
as freak show we make the eyes of the world light up – the showman
sees us a means of making money, the doctors, the psychologists,
the geneticists, as research material. Arguments about nature versus
nurture; about whether this disease or that is transmitted genetically
– about whether this quality or characteristic has a genetic basis, oh
yes, what would they do without us. And of course we play up to it,
we even enjoy it. Some of us make money out of twinship, Angela
Carter's showbiz twins, for instance; the twins of Twins Restaurant;
or the Dionne quints who came doubled twice over – but reading that
appalling story, who would want to be like them? And even without the
cash, the rest of us are glad enough of the attention we attract. We're
glamour, aren't we; people point at us, whisper 'the twins', want to
know us, particularly when we're the only twins in sight – there were
no other twins in either of the schools we went to. The problem is
that you get to rely on that attention, get to identify yourself with it.
Which makes it all the harder, when you're thrown into the world on
your own, to find no one is interested in you any more; for it's only as
twins, a look-alike, dress-alike, charming pair of pages, bridesmaids,

283

pantomime babes or fairies, that you know how to attract attention. There's momentary interest, of course, if you confess your twinship – but without the twin to back the claim it doesn't last long, especially when you have to confess you're not identical, not as freakish as all that. Maybe I became a writer, it occurs to me, to reclaim that attention.

In our early thirties, briefly, my sister and I reanimated our twin credentials; her first marriage broke down and she and her two children took shelter with me and my family. The first time we had lived together since we were 18, it felt good to me – despite her problems, I think it felt good to her, too. I look back with a fond ache on our rediscovery of the pleasure of going to parties together, and chorusing oh yes, we're twins, and seeing the interest that generated. It felt altogether familiar and comfortable just having her around – for me at that time it more than made up for the vagaries of my own increasingly difficult marriage. So much did we revert to twinship, that we even agreed to take part in the twin study at the Institute of Psychiatry in London, thereby encountering that other aspect of twin freakdom, twins as scientifically useful. We spent a morning or two finding out what it must feel like to be a rat having its intelligence tested by this obstacle course or that. One test of dexterity, I remember, involved looking in a mirror and tracing out a kind of hand-sized maze with an electrified probe, which beeped when your hand slipped and met its metal sides. Thereafter, for years, until long after she'd moved out, endless questionnaires came through the post, getting longer and seemingly more irrelevant as time went on. We gave up, I think, on one that compared our reaction to dirty jokes. On the other hand, we earned £100 each for keeping a detailed diary of our contacts with each other over a whole month – the first time I was paid for being a twin, if not the last. (How angry it would make my sister, I think, to find me making part of my living by editing a book about twinship, and so writing about her.) Recently I contacted the Institute to find out what had happened to the material gathered during the study, and found that, since it all pre-dated computers, none of it had been entered, not much analysed, and very little written up. Not an uncommon fate of scientific studies, perhaps. Even if the basis for it was sounder than Dr Mengele's twin researches in Auschwitz, it was quite as useless, if by comparison benign.

But as for the twins experimented on by Dr Mengele; their double bind was that twinship could mean agonising death at his hands in pursuit of some crazy theory; but it could also mean survival; whereas to be a single child meant certain death. Freakdom indeed has its uses

– uses exploited by non-twins sometimes, like one of Mengele's boys who was mistaken for a twin and by going along with that falsehood saved his life; like Sarah Orne Jowett's old woman who lived for and on a gentle fantasy of being Queen Victoria's twin; like the man in another story, which I haven't found room for here, who invented a twin in order to be able to marry each of a pair of twin sisters; like Sinclair Lewis's bank clerk who successfully robbed a bank by inventing a twin brother, but then became trapped in his double persona, which real twins might regard as a paradigm of what happens to them if they're not careful, without their having had to invent anyone.

As it happens I have my own experience of a twin invented for psychology – or psychopathic – reasons. My twin's second husband changed his name and claimed to be a twin; she, alas, believed him – despite the fact that he called himself Kaine, and his twin, guess what, Abel. I suspect that her twinship was one reason he was attracted to her. (As I do not think it wholly coincidental that my husband's mother has a twin brother. Or that my editor come to that, is the daughter of identical twin brothers.) Presumably the invented twin helps counter loneliness, as with the Queen's twin; or is the literal expression of the double self, the sense of psychic if not clinical schizophrenia.

It is an illusion, of course. Those who invent twins for themselves remain, in reality, single. After all, even genuine twins appear to be single, to ape normalcy, when walking alone. Often they become single through death or separation, whether they like it or not. Without surgery, conjoined twins have no such option; this is where freakdom becomes serious; where compassion can break down – to be replaced by curiosity, the pointing finger; and by fear, prejudice, lest, by contamination, such seeming monsters turn us monstrous too. Martin Luther, for one, said that Siamese twins were the work of the devil; had no souls. But curiosity itself produces monsters – monsters of uncompassion. For compassion needs empathy. And if Leslie Fiedler is right in suggesting that the fascination of us physically normal with the abnormal arises from our seeing – fearing to see – in those we designate monstrous some deep yet fundamental image of themselves, such empathy draws us too close to what we fear; is dangerous. At the same time, perhaps, it accounts for the fascination that crops up in the most literary of sources, with the sex life of Siamese twins; do they, can they, make love? They can and do, obviously; Chang and Eng the original Siamese twins produced families. But then, of course, given the physical anomalies, how exactly do they do it? Some twins after all share sexual organs; and even if not, what happens to the twin who is not then having sex; is the other one watching? Then, the thrill of curiosity turns voyeuristic, besides.

From such all too common prurience it is a relief to turn to compassion and the compassionate; to those who write about conjoined or otherwise freakish twins, in bed or out, as real individuals who happen to be joined. Mark Twain almost managed it despite the jokiness. Donald Newlove certainly does – while Oliver Sachs, writing about mentally rather than physically conjoined twins sees their mathematical union as a profound even holy genius to be cherished and admired. As for Montaigne, bless him, at the other end of the century in which Martin Luther denied the humanity of those from monster births, he proclaimed them as the creation of God no less than the rest of us; thereby suggesting like Blake later, that everything made by God – everything that lives – is holy.

TWINS AS CURIOSITIES

Don't Worry If You See Double
Don't Worry If You See Double

PUT Lisa Ganz next to her identical twin sister Debbie and heads turn. 'We're like a freak show,' says Lisa Ganz.

The 27-year-old Ganzes were working separately in the restaurant business when they decided to capitalize on people's fascination with twins. This week they're opening Twins, a Manhattan bar and restaurant that will be staffed by some two dozen sets of identical twins – wearing identical clothes and working identical hours.

In addition to the look-alike serving staff, there is a model of the World Trade Center's twin towers behind the bar, two doorknobs for each restroom and such dishes as Pate Duke Platter (two kinds of pate) and Twin Peaks Nachos (two mounds of chips) on the menu. Most items cost less than $10.

But the Ganzes may be doubling their work. First they had to locate enough twins, through newspaper ads and word of mouth. 'It was difficult, but it wasn't desperate,' says Lisa Ganz.

Both twins had to be qualified – making it especially tough to find bartenders. And when one twin is sick – well, they're in this together. Each pair must find another pair to substitute for them. At least they're easy to reach – most of them live together.

Scheduling is already a worry for Juanita and Chenita Townsend. Juanita attends Brooklyn College, but Chenita is taking time off. 'If she can't work, I can't work,' says Chenita.

Many of the twins have already waited tables together. Customers at a restaurant where Carla and Karen Prepon once worked used to think they were one super-waitress. And Susan Lydon collected tips she didn't deserve, until people saw her twin across the room.

Twins' General Manager Carlo Bruno plans to emphasize team-work and to issue directives to both twins at once. His one worry: accountability. 'People will not be able to tell who their waiter is,' he says. Neither will he.

Some down time is expected because of customers' inevitable requests to see the twins side by side. But 'we have to make business sense,' says Lisa Ganz. She is still undecided about how to fit the staff to the crowd. If six waiters are too many and four not enough, do the Ganz twins violate their theme and risk a lone fifth?

That's why they're on the lookout for triplets.

JOYCE COHEN, *Wall Street Journal*, November 1994

'No, I won't come there now, I won't come to you at all. Why should I? I shall go to some good people . . . Good people live honestly, good people live without any faking and they never come double . . . Yes sir, they never come in twos, and they're not an offence to God and honest people . . .'

FYODOR DOSTOEVSKY, *The Double*

---

from Notes of an Anatomist

IN all these examples, asymmetry is wrought by the violence of prenatal strife, and of two prospective equals one emerges victorious, the other dead, vanquished, or maimed. Brotherly union, for once, results in weakness. 'Together we are weaker' is the conjoined twin's motto. Some say that this physical fusion has been advantageous, but their stories are simply incredible. Regnault, with all the respectability of a cleric, wrote that the hunting party that accompanied Louis XIV in the forest of Compiègne, captured a wild goat with two heads, which nonetheless pranced and grazed with all the vigor of its single-headed congeners. And across the Rhine, another king is said to have come across an even more admirable animal. A conjoined hare was so formed as to exhibit a double set of limbs and heads. The fusion, according to the chronicler, had taken place along the dorsal plane in such a way that when one set of legs was resting on the ground, the second set was lifted toward the sky. This 'Double Hare of Germany' astounded its persecutors by being able to run for long distances without showing signs of fatigue. The reason, in the quaint account, was that through periodic rolling on the ground the ingenious hare managed to alternate the use of each set of limbs and was on each turn carried by limbs that had been previously resting!

Twin fusion is, of course, compatible with longevity. This we know by the stories, always engrossing, of conjoined twins: the Biddenden Maids, fused at the arms; the Hungarian Sisters, joined at the pelvis; the conjoined twins of Bohemia; and the most famous of all, the Siamese twins, 'stuck' to each other by a bridge going from abdomen to abdomen. Fusion was only partial and did not hamper the development of separate identities. Thus we hear that, of the Siamese twins, Chang was outspoken and Chen quiet; this one timid, that one arrogant. Forced to subordinate all their activities to the inalterable fact of their physical togetherness, they learned to coordinate their steps while walking and, having married, scrupulously respected for many years the convenant to spend three days in the house of each one's spouse, in alternation. All of which did not stop an altercation when, on a certain day, Chang wished to take a bath and Chen did not. There were witnesses to the shouting of insults, and it is reported that they came to blows, for apparently physical pain was experienced by each onc individually, although, if one contracted an infection, fever was manifested by both.

Of the Hungarian sisters, joined at the pelvis, medical reports say that they had a common rectum, a single external genital area, but two wombs and two birth canals. These are the only conjoined twins ever to have conceived. In times of Victorian prudishness, the two sisters appeared in the emergency room of a hospital, A's abdomen swollen, B's flat. Questioned about their sexual history, A adamantly denied, and B consistently supported her, even if, in the graphic pun of their biographer, 'she should have been in a position to know.' After A was delivered of a healthy baby, there was plenty of sassy commentary, although not without troubling religiophilosophical undertones. Given the described anatomical arrangement, it was asked, should they have one or two husbands? In like manner friars of early Spanish America argued over whether the holy rites of the Catholic Church should be administered once or twice to a pair of dying conjoined twins. This problem was solved, in this case, by an autopsy that showed that the liver was the only shared organ. Now, the liver was never seriously thought in theological circles to be the site of residence of the soul; therefore the case was firmly settled in favor of duality. This may be said to be a little known instance of a contribution of pathology to Christian theology.

An even more difficult quandary was posed by abnormal twins born in Medina-Sidonia on February 29, 1793. The conceptus had two heads, two necks, and four upper extremities, but only two legs. Parturition was difficult, and one foot was delivered first. As it became clear that the infant would soon die, the baptism and last rites were administered to the part – the foot – of the expected singleton. Upon delivery of the entire body, the problem was stated thus: assuming the existence of two immortal souls, which of the two had been baptized? This was the problem presented to Father Feijoo, the learned Jesuit who was to earn a place of distinction in Spanish literature. Feijoo's answer was dressed up in the most rigorous logic. Firstly, the existence of the soul could not be denied. The site of residence of the soul was a matter of debate; contending parties favored either the heart or the brain. Now, since all major viscera were duplicated, there could be no doubt that two independent souls were involved. Secondly, everyone wished to believe that both had been baptized because Christian piety moves us to feel sorry for those who are deprived of the sovereign benefit of baptism. However, our desires count for little in front of the heavenly tribunal, and charitable wishes cannot repair the damage that is done. The search for truth must take precedence over our wistful expectations. Thirdly, a priest who baptizes performs an act that extends to a subject previously apprehended by the understanding. The words used, *ego te baptizo*, refer to a single individual. No willful act can be extended to any other subject than that apprehended by the mind preceding, or accompanying, the act of volition, according to the formula: *nihil volitum, quin praecognitum*. Now, the baptizing priest had no idea that the foot on which he sprinkled holy water was, in effect, shared by two separate souls. Therefore, his understanding apprehended a single one, and by a volitional act he performed a ceremony that confers regenerative grace upon a single individual. Therefore, he used the wrong formula. Therefore, the ceremony was invalid. Therefore, none was baptized.

There is yet one more step. The binomial becomes AA, the 'monster' of perfect symmetry; some call it Janus, pathologists cranio-thoraco-pagus. Imagine two profiles meeting on a median plane of fusion, as if two lovers would have wished to fuse while they embraced and their wish had been granted. The foreheads are fused, the noses have blended. Viewed frontally, two eyes can be seen, although each one is actually in profile. And this strange face repeats itself in the back – or is it the front? – of Janus. The necks are fused into one, and so are the chest and abdomen. There are two hearts, but they are joined by a common aorta. Two mouths, but the intestines are shared. Human beings are supposed to have a front and a back, a top and a bottom. But when the front is also the back and the left is as much left as it is right, can we say that there is top and bottom? The duality of Janus is more than startling: it is impossible. Three centuries ago Sir Thomas Browne denied the existence of amphisbaena, the snake with a head at each end, on theoretical grounds, 'for the senses being placed at both extreams doth make both ends anterior, which is impossible.' But a pathologist, who has seen Janus, chimera, cyclops, acardius, and mermaid (sirenomelia), no longer doubts the existence of the impossible. Instead, he will concede the truth in this statement of Borges: 'The zoology of dreams is far poorer than the zoology of the Maker.'

F. CRUSSI-GONZALEZ

---

from Gemini

THAT Jean-Paul was a monster was demonstrated by what between ourselves we called the 'circus.' This depressing business, which repeated itself every time we had a visitor, would start with exclamations of surprise at how alike we were and go on to the game of comparing, substituting and confusing. In fact, Maria-Barbara was the only person in the world who could tell us apart – except, as she admitted to us, when we were asleep, because then sleep erased all differences between us, as the rising tide obliterates all traces left by children on the sand at the end of the day. By Edouard, we were treated to a little piece of playacting – at least that is how I interpret his behavior today, for at the time it was painful and hurt us and, if we had had the heart to talk about it, we would have used a harsher word, lies or cheating. Edouard never could tell us apart, nor would he ever try to. One day he decided, half seriously, half as a joke: 'One twin each. Maria-Barbara, you have Jean, since he is your favorite. For myself, I'll choose Paul.' Now Maria-Barbara's favorite was me, at that very moment my mother was cuddling me in her arms, and it was Jean whom Edouard scooped up, startled and rather cross, from off the ground and pretended to carry off with him. After that, it became an established ritual and whenever either of us came within his reach, Edouard would seize hold of him indiscriminately, calling him 'his' twin, his favorite, dandling him, giving him piggybacks, and having mock fights with him. The thing looked all right, because we were each of us his 'favorite' in turn, but although he had sensibly given up calling us by our own names, and said Jean-Paul like everyone else, there was something fraudulent in his behavior that cut us to the quick. It was, naturally, when visitors were present that the pretense was especially upsetting. Because then he would display his assumed knowledge with complete confidence, confounding the baffled newcomer with assurances which half the time were wrong. At such times neither Maria-Barbara nor Jean-Paul would have dared give him away, but our discomfort must have been obvious.

'Monster' comes from the Latin *monstrare*. A monster is a creature that is demonstrated, put on show in circuses, fairs and so on, and we were not to escape this fate. We were spared the fair and the circus, but not the cinema, and in its most trivial form the advertising film. We must have been about eight years old when a summer visitor from Paris noticed us playing on the little beach at Quatre Vaux, which is where the Quinteux brook comes out. He came up to us, got us chattering, asking us how old we were, what we were called and where we lived, then went straight up the little stairway of eighty-five steps to La Cassine, whose roof was visible at the top of the cliff. Had he come by the road, he would have had to deal with a hostile Méline, who would undoubtedly have sent him packing. Emerging directly into the garden, he came upon Maria-Barbara surrounded by her 'encampment' of deck chair, workbox, books, basket of fruit, spectacles, shawl, rugs, etc. As always when she was embarrassed or bothered, Maman concentrated on her work, paying only the slightest attention and returning evasive answers.

[. . .] Edouard, who had seen from a distance, by Maria-Barbara's attitude, that she was stuck with an unwelcome visitor, came striding up to intervene. What the stranger had to say astonished him so much at first that he was temporarily speechless. The man's name was Ned Steward and he worked for a film publicity agency called Kinotop, whose business was mostly in making short advertising films put on in cinemas between the main features. He had noticed Jean-Paul on the beach and was asking permission to use him in one of his films. Edouard was highly indignant and let it show in his face, which always reflected whatever he was feeling as though on a screen. Steward made matters worse by mentioning the considerable rewards that we would certainly reap from the 'performance,' a word Edouard was to take up and produce ever after as though in quotation marks on the end of a pair of forceps. But Steward was shrewd and persistent and probably had some experience in such negotiations. He retrieved what seemed to be a hopeless situation by two masterstrokes. First, he offered to double the proposed sum and present it to St Brigitte's. Secondly, he explained what kind of advertising he wanted to use us for. It was not, of course, for some commonplace product like shoe polish, salad oil, or puncture-proof tires. No indeed, the purpose he had in mind for us was a noble one, one for which we seemed, moreover, to be framed by destiny. Just before the holidays he had been put in charge of an advertising campaign for a brand of marine binoculars called Gemini. This was why he had been roaming along the North Sea coast in search of an idea. Well, he had found his idea. Why not put Gemini's reputation in the hands of twin brothers? There is a particular combination of silliness, humor and obtuseness by which Edouard was easily disarmed. I know it well because I am fairly susceptible to it myself. He saw in this business the germ of a good after-dinner story to tell his friends in Paris. Moreover, reading in his paper about the Dionne family in Canada and their quints who seemed to be a fairly profitable source of income, he had more than once teasingly asked Jean-Paul when he was going to settle down and make the family fortune. So he shut himself up with Steward and argued inch by inch the details of a contract according to which we were to make three short, two-minute films for Gemini binoculars.

The shooting took more than a fortnight – the whole of our Easter holidays – and left us with an absolute horror of such 'performances.' I seem to remember that what we disliked most about it was a kind of absurdity which we felt very strongly, without being able to put it into words. They made us go over and over the same words, the same actions, the same short scenes ad nauseam, each time imploring us to be more *natural* than in the take before. Well, it seemed to us that we were more likely to be less and less *natural* because we were getting more tired, more irritable and more and more caught up in a meaningless rigmarole. At eight years old we were to be forgiven for not knowing that naturalism – especially in matters artistic, and in this context we were actors playing a part – is something that can be acquired, worked up to, and is in fact nothing but the height of artifice.

MICHEL TOURNIER

---

from The Dionne Years

THE turn-off road was heavy with automobiles. On peak days they formed themselves into a metallic snake, two and a half miles long, winding from Callander to the Dafoe Hospital. In one sixteen-hour period, in July, 1936, an observer clocked 1,956 cars on the turn-off – a rate of two cars a minute. They rumbled along through rough, inhospitable country, an unkempt mélange of dense brush and craggy outcrops interspersed with ragged hay fields. Except for a small sign, TO THE DIONNE QUINTUPLETS, there was no hint of anything unusual. But then, as the roadway rose to the crest of a low hill, each newcomer encountered a swirl of dust and was treated to a spectacle he could never forget.

Directly ahead a small community had been carved out of forest, swamp, and rock. Each summer morning and afternoon, seven days a week, it vibrated with people. The road spread out into a macadamized plaza, choked with parked cars and ringed with buildings and signs. At the far end, where the road curved, stood an ungainly frame structure on which were emblazoned the words MADAM LEGROS AND MADAM LEBEL MIDWIVES OF THE QUINTUPLETS BID YOU WELCOME! In the foreground, to the right, was the birthplace of the Quints, an unpainted farmhouse and a cluster of barns. Beyond it lay Oliva Dionne's two souvenir stands, with his name in gigantic letters and the words SOUVENIRS – REFRESHMENTS – OPERATED BY PARENTS OF THE WORLD´S MOST FAMOUS BABIES. Behind these were a parking lot for a thousand cars and a large log rest room.

On the left side of the plaza were more buildings: the nursery in the foreground, a neat, squat structure with a red roof and stained log walls, flanked by a staff house and a guardhouse. Beyond it lay the horseshoe-shaped playground building and observation gallery. The entire complex was surrounded by a seven-foot fence of meshed wire, like that of some minor correctional institution. Uniformed policemen stood guard at the gates.

There were people everywhere, pouring out of cars and buses, and spending money – buying souvenir postcards, pamphlets about the birth, binoculars at inflated prices, British woollens and china, candy, pop, hot dogs, and, for a quarter, Oliva Dionne's own autograph.

They came as early as six in the morning. By the time the first observation period began at 9:30, the queue could stretch back for half a mile or more. As the people moved forward they passed a long trough labelled STONES FROM THE QUINTUPLETS' PLAYGROUND. These were the famous 'fertility stones,' gathered each morning from the shores of Lake Nipissing in the trucks of the Ontario highways department and widely believed to be a boon to barren women. Everybody took one; like the view of the Quints, they were free.

The visitors were allowed to enter the gallery in groups of one hundred, peeling off in two directions, some moving counterclockwise and some in the opposite direction. No one was allowed to bring a camera. Only one man could take pictures: Fred Davis, late of the *Toronto Star* and now the representative of an American picture syndicate. Oliva Dionne himself could not photograph his own children.

The playground was surrounded on three sides by a U-shaped roofed passageway with windows facing inward and fitted with a silvery screen of wire mesh so closely woven that a pin could not be thrust through the opening. From this dark tunnel the five toddlers could be seen, playing on swings and tricycles or splashing in their shallow pool, apparently oblivious of the unseen thousands shuffling silently past them.

Few could resist a gasp on first seeing the Quints. By 1936, when the new playground was first opened, the two-year-olds were glowing with health, cheeks pink, enormous eyes framed by long lashes, hair in soft curls. The contrast between that spectacle and the memory of the early photographs, which had shown them as tiny inhuman creatures – 'like skinned rabbits,' as one report put it – was one reason why the sight of them was almost magical. To add to the fantasy, each was a carbon copy of the others. Which one was Cécile? Which Yvonne? Which Marie? Was that one Annette – or was it Emilie? In the gloom of the gallery people whispered those questions, but it was not possible to tell them apart.

The magic is still remembered. Those who saw the quintuplets at their cutest can never forget the spectacle. Forty years later, when other events have faded from memory, the enchantment of that moment remains. For many, such as Margaret Bennett of Windsor, who was eight years old when she saw the quintuplets in 1936, it was the thrill of their lives.

My memories of that trip are very strong – despite childhood visits to Banff, Yellowstone, and Quebec City during those same years – so it must have been a real milestone. The fact that both my parents were teachers in Windsor probably predisposed us all to an interest in children, yet I think we were, like all the other thousands of tourists, drawn by the fact that we were seeing a curiosity, a 'wonder of the world,' something we would never see again or hear of in our lifetime. It was really VERY exciting. That first sight of the five lovely baby girls playing innocently in an enclosed playground absolutely overwhelmed me. They were so adorable; it was like seeing a miracle.

When I returned to school that fall I boasted to teachers and classmates alike that I had seen the Quints that summer, and they were terribly impressed. In other summers, coming back from long family camping trips to the Rockies or down East, there was no point in telling anyone except the teachers where I had been because most of the kids didn't know enough geography to be impressed. So you can see, it was a real highlight in everyone's life to see the Quints.

[. . .] A later generation, surfeited with a steady diet of TV glamour, might well ask: What was all the fuss about? Why did these five girls cause such a commotion? Why did millions leave their homes, in the depths of the century's worst depression, to drive hundreds of miles into the back country of Ontario just to watch a group of children playing together?

It is not easy to recapture in words the public's infatuation with the Dionne quintuplets. They were international stars of the first magnitude – greater than Garbo or Barrymore or Harlow. Nobody, with the possible exception of Roosevelt, enjoyed a higher visibility. No week went by without the newspapers carrying a picture layout of the five babies. A quintuplets scrapbook – and tens of thousands kept quintuplets scrapbooks in the Thirties – became an anthology of photographic clichés. Every season, feast day, and national holiday was marked by photographs of the famous five, dressed in witches costumes for Hallowe'en, ogling turkeys at Thanksgiving, lighting candles at Christmas (with Dafoe as Santa Claus), emerging from giant valentines on February 14, patting bunnies at Easter, ushering in winter with toboggans, skis, snowshoes, and skates, spring with new bonnets, summer with identical bathing suits. When, in 1937, all five had their tonsils removed, it was front-page news everywhere.

[. . .] As public favourites they had several advantages over the other big names of the period. They were beautiful babies – so cute, so chubby, so cuddly that one longed to pick them up and hug them. In this area, only Shirley Temple could compete with the Quints. But there was only one Shirley Temple; there were five Dionnes, absolutely identical to the untutored eye. *That* was the real marvel. Until 1934, the word 'quintuplet' was all but unknown. For the rest of the decade it was synonymous with the Dionnes.

Finally, there was the near certainty of being able to see them in the flesh. One might visit Hollywood and never catch a glimpse of a movie star. But you could drive to Callander knowing that twice a day the quintuplets would be on display. The bulk of the North American population, living north of the Mason–Dixon line and east of the Mississippi, could easily manage the trip within the confines of a two-week summer vacation – a vacation which, as an added bonus, took the visitors into the much-touted scenic wilderness that Hollywood labelled 'the north woods.' The Quints were fashionable. In the mid-Thirties, a visit to the Dafoe Hospital became The Thing to Do.

This helps to explain why the decision to display the quintuplets could not have been reversed. The public on both sides of the border would never have stood for it. Indeed, it is probable that if the babies had not been displayed at the outset, thousands would have arrived anyway and demanded that they be shown.

The quintuplets could not see the people lining up four abreast an hour and a half or more before each showing. But they must have heard 'a sort of dull, rhapsodic hum [that] fills the air from early morning until nightfall.' They were taken from the nursery porch and conducted to the play area along a pathway that was hidden from the road by a high white screen. As they grew older, they realized that they were on display. Years later, Annette recalled the day when Marie, at the age of five, held up a toy monkey, and Emilie, who was always making comical remarks, said to her: 'You'd better drop that monkey or they'll think there are *six* of us.' They also sensed that they were special. As one of their nurses, Cécile Michaud, discovered, they knew that they were the Quints.

They could hear the sounds of children and crying babies in the audience. They couldn't see them, but they began to realize as they got older that these people had come to see the Quints. They'd say that in French: that people were coming to see the Quints. They knew that they were the Quints. But they weren't excited about it. I don't think they realized how important 'Quints' meant.

PIERRE BERTON

---

from The Young Gentlemen

'COME!' said Mrs Durant in a resolute tone; and again I followed her.

She led the way into a large pantry, airy, orderly, well-stocked with china and glass. That too was empty; and two doors opened from it. Mrs Durant passed through the one on the right, and we found ourselves, not, as I had expected, in the kitchen, but in a kind of vague unfurnished anteroom. The quarrelling voices had meanwhile died out; we seemed once more to have the mysterious place to ourselves. Suddenly, beyond another closed door, we heard a shrill crowing laugh. Mrs Durant dashed at this last door and it let us into a large high-studded room. We paused and looked about us. Evidently we were in what Cranch had always described as the lumber room on the ground floor of the wing. But there was no lumber in it now. It was scrupulously neat, and fitted up like a big and rather bare nursery; and in the middle of the floor, on a square of drugget, stood a great rearing black-and-white animal: my Aunt Lucilla's hobbyhorse . . .

I gasped at the sight; but in spite of its strangeness it did not detain me long, for at the farther end of the room, before a fire protected by a tall nursery fender, I had seen something stranger still. Two little boys in old-fashioned round jackets and knickerbockers knelt by the hearth, absorbed in the building of a house of blocks. Mrs Durant saw them at the same moment. She caught my arm as if she were about to fall, and uttered a faint cry.

The sound, low as it was, produced a terrifying effect on the two children. Both of them dropped their blocks, turned around as if to dart at us, and then stopped short, holding each other by the hand, and staring and trembling as if we had been ghosts.

At the opposite end of the room, we stood staring and trembling also; for it was they who were the ghosts to our terrified eyes. It must have been Mrs Durant who spoke first.

'Oh . . . the poor things . . .' she said in a low choking voice.

The little boys stood there, motionless and far off, among the ruins of their house of blocks. But, as my eyes grew used to the faint light – there was only one lamp in the big room – and as my shaken nerves adjusted themselves to the strangeness of the scene, I perceived the meaning of Mrs Durant's cry.

The children before us were not children; they were two tiny withered men, with frowning foreheads under their baby curls, and heavy-shouldered middle-aged bodies. The sight was horrible, and rendered more so by the sameness of their size and by their old-fashioned childish dress. I recoiled; but Mrs Durant had let my arm go, and was moving softly forward. Her own arms outstretched, she advanced toward the two strange beings. 'You poor poor things, you,' she repeated, the tears running down her face.

EDITH WHARTON

---

from Twins on Twins

'IN 1923, when we were five years old, Siamese twins came to the local vaudeville theatre in Brooklyn and were presented as an act. The Brooklyn *Daily Eagle* advertised that any twins could enter the theater free. We were taken by a friend of the family. I remember that the red velvet curtains opened and we saw these twins dressed in red velvet costumes trimmed with gold braid. They were attached at the hips; they were at an angle to each other and couldn't sit straight forward. I didn't know what I was seeing. It never occurred to me that such a joining could be possible. No one had ever explained it to us.

'Between them was a red velvet tablecloth with a gold fringe. Whatever tissue or membrane bound them was covered with this red velvet cloth . . . They were young women with breasts and they spoke with a foreign accent of some kind. I don't remember what the act was about. I just remember two pretty ladies on the stage. After the act, we were taken backstage. I don't know why. When we were taken into their dressing rooms, it hit me. I realized that these two lovely looking ladies couldn't get up and walk. They seemed to be in an invalid situation and I realized that something was very, very wrong. A feeling of horror came over me because, by that time, we were very aware that we, too, were twins, and that one of us could run down the street and the other run up the block. But here were two people bound to each other who couldn't run. I didn't know how they were tied to each other, but I knew it was something more than the red velvet material and that something was horribly wrong. I wondered what was under the red velvet because, obviously, we didn't have anything like that.

'We thought the Siamese twins might have been under a spell of some kind, or had a curse put on them. At home we acted it all out. I remember getting safety pins from the sewing box next to grandma's bed and then joining together our knee-length dresses with the pins. We walked around and finally tore the dresses. It was terribly confining. At that time, life was much simpler than now without television and radio – we acted out many, many things which was very healthy. I think we acted it out enough to get the trauma out of our systems.'

K. L. ABBE AND F. M. GILL

In our time the double man Lyddae has been born, he has two heads, four hands, one belly and two feet.

ST JEROME, writing to Vitale

A brief selection from the many terms used to describe the many ways in which Siamese Twins may be joined

Xaphopagous	pigopagi
ischiopagi	pygothoracipagi
xyphodymi	tetratodymi
craniopagos	xiphodymus

from A Letter From an Eminent Merchant in Ostend

Containing an Account Of a Strange and Monstrous Birth hapned there, A Woman being brought to Bed of two Children, which are joined together by the Crowns of their Heads. He being an Eye-Witness thereof.

Dated May 7. *Old Stile.*

HAVING for some Days resided in this City, I came to understand that there happened a Strange and wonderful Birth, about an hour and a half, or a *Dutch* Mile, from this place, in a Dorp called *Clems,* or rather *Clements Churth.* Yesterday I walked thither in Company with several others, and found it answerable to the Relation I heard, viz. That they are two Daughters, well Shap'd and perfect in all their Members, onely they are joyned together, at the top of the head, and so fast that it seems to be but one head. Yet it is apparent both heads have their perfect faculties: and a partition may be easily felt, which I felt my self yesterday: But yet several Doctors and Chyrurgeons from *Bridges,* haveing been there, to see whether the Children might be parted without danger of death, find no probability. The Father is called *Roelan Voyoen,* being by Trade a Wagonmaker, of about 23 Years of age: The Mothers name is *Maria Castelmans,* about 19 Years old. She was delivered of these two Children (being her first-born on the sixth of this Moneth, being Ascension day (so called) about two a Clock in the Morning: they are both baptized, and the one named *Pieternella,* the other *Barbara.* That they are distinct in life, soul and brains, appear plainly from the actions which they have, both together, and sometimes apart: for the one often sleeps, while the other is awake, Cryes and eats: and they are ofenttimes both awake, and both eating: I have seen them both asleep, and both awake, and one asleep, and the other awake. The Heads are so united together, that when that which is awake turns it self, the Neck of the other turns also: They will never be able to go, sit, or stand: for if the one should sit, or stand upright, the other must stand on her Head, with the Heels upward: Their Face, Nose, and Eyes, are not directly opposite to one another, but somewhat sideways, so as that one looks toward you, and the other from you. Many People come daily to see them, and give 3 *Stivers* apiece: Their Parents are offered a great Sum of Money for them to be carried about: They told us, they did intend (after the

Holy Days, so called) to carry their Children to *Bridges*, and it may be from thence to the Cities of *Holland*.

London, Printed for *F. Stans*, and Sold by *R. Faneway*, 1682.

---

from Mr Bolton on the United Siamese Twins

THESE youths are both of the same height, namely, five feet two inches; and their united weight is one hundred and eighty pounds. They are much shorter, and appear less advanced in puberty, than youths of this country at the age of eighteen years; but the average stature of their countrymen is less than that of Europeans. Many of our ordinary twins bear a stronger resemblance to each other in countenance than is observed in these youths. Their bodies and limbs are well formed, but the spine of CHANG, who habitually holds his arm over the shoulder of ENG, is considerably curved laterally, an effect which is apparently the result of this long continued habit. They have not the broad and flat forehead so characteristic of the Chinese race, but resemble the lower class of the people of Canton in the colour of their skins, and in the forms of their noses, lips, eyes, and ears. The left eye of CHANG is weaker than the right; but this is reversed in the case of ENG, so that each sees best with the eye nearest his brother. Their bodies are much paler now than they were on their first arrival in England. Their genital organs are, like all their other external parts, regularly formed; but the youths are naturally modest, and evince a strong repugnance to any close investigation on this subject.

The band of union is formed in the following manner. – At the lowest part of the sternum of each boy, the ensiform cartilage is bent upwards and forwards, meeting the other in the middle of the upper part of the band, where moveable joints exist, which admit of vertical as well as lateral motion; each junction appearing to be connected by ligamentous structures. It is difficult to define precisely where the respective cartilages from each body meet, and whether a slip from one of the cartilages of the false ribs enters into the structure of these parts; but it is certain that the ensiform cartilages have assumed an extended and altered figure. This cartilaginous portion occupies the upper region of the band. The outline of the band is convex above, and arched below. Under the cartilage, while they stand in their ordinary posture, are large hernial sacs opening into each abdomen,

302

and into which, on coughing, congenital herniæ are forced; probably, in each boy formed by a portion of the transverse arch of the colon: generally, however, and under ordinary circumstances, these herniæ are not apparent. Whether there is a communication between the two abdominal cavities, or a distinct peritoneal sac belonging to each hernia, is by no means obvious; and this is a point of vital importance, if ever, by their mutual desire, a surgical separation should be contemplated. If, however, any such operation hereafter be strongly requested by both the youths, when arrived at years of discretion, and after they have been fully apprised of its danger, it will be essential that some preliminary steps be taken to provide against the exposure of either or both of the abdominal cavities.

When these herniæ protrude, their respective contents are pushed forwards as far as the middle of the band. The entire band is covered with common integument; and when the boys face each other, its length at the upper edge is one inch and three quarters, and at the lower, not quite three inches. From above downwards, it is three inches and a quarter, and its greatest thickness is one inch and five-eighths. In the centre of the lower part of this band, which presents a thin edge, formed only by skin and cellular substance, there is the cicatrix of a single navel, showing where the umbilical cords or cord had entered, and which I have no doubt contained two sets of vessels. Small blood-vessels and nerves must of course traverse the substance of the band, but no pulsation can be detected in it.

Captain COFFIN and Mr HUNTER were informed by the mother of the twins, that soon after their birth, and during the period of infancy, this band was much larger in proportion to the size of their bodies than it is at the present time: it had then no hard cartilaginous feel at its upper margin; it was also larger in circumference, and the bodies of the twins were nearer in contact; but from continued stretching it has become elongated, and its circumference has diminished. In their own country they were employed to row a boat, for which purpose both stood at the stern, each using a one-handed oar, an exercise which must have assisted greatly in stretching the band. It is now remarkably strong, and possesses little sensibility; for they have been formerly pulled by a rope fastened to it, without complaining of pain, or expressing any uneasiness. In the month of February last one of them fell out of bed while asleep, and hung by the band for some time, and when both awoke, they alike stated, that they experienced no pain in the band from this accident. Mr HALE, their constant attendant, has lifted one of them from the ground, allowing the other to hang by the band with his feet raised from the floor; yet the whole weight of one of the boys thus suspended did not occasion pain to either, or even excite their displeasure. The circumstance of the small degree of sensibility possessed by the band, tends to corroborate the opinion I entertain of the possibility of effecting a separation of the twins by a surgical operation.

To the ordinary touch there is not any middle line where the sense of feeling common to both the boys terminates; but it is difficult to ascertain the precise point where the inosculation of the one individual with the other takes place: and this is not discoverable by making punctures with a needle, for each boy shrinks from a puncture whenever it is made in any part of a vertical line drawn down the middle of the band. It is therefore obvious, that the nerves of the common skin covering the band maintain a sensitive communication with each of the two youths; and it is reasonable to infer, that a similar communication subsists between the small arteries and veins, which mutually nourish the middle portion of the band. If, however, slight punctures be made at the distance of half an inch from the centre of the band, then the sensation is only felt by the individual belonging to the side punctured.

From these evidences it may be concluded, that the united twins would be subject to certain distempers in common, although each possesses a distinct existence, and even different constitutional peculiarities.

On the suggestion of Doctor ROGET, a silver teaspoon was placed on the tongue of one of the twins, and a disk of zinc on the tongue of his brother: when the metals thus placed were brought into contact, the youths both cried out 'Sour, sour.' This experiment was repeated several times with the same result, and was reversed by exchanging the positions of the metals, when a similar effect was produced.

These experiments prove that the galvanic influence passes from one individual to the other, through the band which connects their bodies, and thus establishes a galvanic circuit with the metals when these are brought into contact.

They habitually face in one direction, and place themselves side by side, ENG to the right and CHANG on the left, but are able to turn and remain in the opposite position. They always walk in the posture first described, although there is no other reason for this than established habit, as they are physically able to move in a reverse direction. Their united strength is great, for they can with perfect ease throw down a powerful man. At Philadelphia they also carried without inconvenience a person weighing rather more than twenty stone for a considerable distance. Their activity is remarkable; they run with great swiftness, and elude pursuit so admirably, that in sportive exercises they can with great difficulty be caught by a single person. They have each the power to bend their bodies in all directions, and turn their heels over their shoulders. They also often playfully tumble head over heels while on their bed, without occasioning the slightest pain or inconvenience in the band. The same degree of personal dexterity is evinced by each youth when playing at battledore and shuttlecock; and in all the bodily actions common to both, such as running and jumping, a remarkable consent or agreement is displayed without any apparent conference. These concurrences appear to be the necessary result of long continued and extraordinary intimacy.

In their respective physical constitutions, however, several differences occur. The boy on the left, CHANG, possesses the more vigorous bodily health of the two; but their intellectual abilities appear equal, for they are alike proficients in the games of chess and draughts, although they object to compete with each other. In the game of whist, however, they rather prefer not to be partners.

The tongue of ENG is at all times whiter than that of CHANG, and his digestion is more easily deranged by unsuitable diet. I have never heard that CHANG has passed a single day without alimentary discharges, but the contrary has often occurred to ENG. In general they both obey the calls of nature at the same time, and this happens even when these result from the operation of medicines.

It having occurred to me, that the odour given by asparagus to the urine would be a test of the extent of the circulation of the blood through both the twins, on the 22nd of March I gave that vegetable to CHANG with his dinner, not allowing any to be given to his brother. On examining their urine four hours after this meal, that of CHANG had distinctly the peculiar asparagus smell, but the urine of his brother was not influenced by it. The next day this experiment was reversed, and therefore with reversed results. These trials sufficiently prove a fact which was otherwise apparent, – that the sanguineous communication between the united twins is very limited.

By GEORGE BUCKLEY BOLTON, ESQ., Member of the Royal College of Surgeons, and of the Medical and Chirurgical Society of London

from Those Extraordinary Twins

AT last a cold little shudder quivered along down the widow's meager frame and she said in a weak voice:

'Ugh, it was awful – just the mere look of that phillipene!'

Rowena did not answer. Her faculties were still caked, she had not yet found her voice. Presently the widow said, a little resentfully:

'Always been *used* to sleeping together – in fact, *prefer* it. And I was thinking it was to accommodate me. I thought it was very good of them, whereas a person situated as that young man is – '

'Ma, you oughtn't to begin by getting up a prejudice against him. I'm sure he is good-hearted and means well. Both of his faces show it.'

'I'm not so certain about that. The one on the left – I mean the one on *its* left – hasn't near as good a face, in my opinion, as its brother.'

'That's Luigi.'

'Yes, Luigi; anyway it's the dark-skinned one; the one that was west of his brother when they stood in the door. Up to all kinds of mischief and disobedience when he was a boy, I'll be bound. I lay his mother had trouble to lay her hand on him when she wanted him. But the one on the right is as good as gold, I can see that.'

'That's Angelo.'

'Yes, Angelo, I reckon, though I can't tell t' other from which by their names, yet awhile. But it's the right-hand one – the blonde one. He has such kind blue eyes, and curly copper hair and fresh complexion – '

'And such a noble face! – oh, it *is* a noble face, ma, just royal, you may say! And beautiful – deary me, how beautiful! But both are that; the dark one's as beautiful as a picture. There's no such wonderful faces and handsome heads in this town – none that even begin. And such hands – especially Angelo's – so shapely and – '

'Stuff, how could you tell which they belonged to? – they had gloves on.'

'Why, didn't I see them take off their hats?'

'That don't signify. They might have taken off each other's hats. Nobody could tell. There was just a wormy squirming of arms in the air – seemed to be a couple of dozen of them, all writhing at once, and it just made me dizzy to see them go.'

'Why, ma, I hadn't any difficulty. There's two arms on each shoulder – '

'There, now. One arm on each shoulder belongs to each of the creatures, don't it? For a person to have two arms on one shoulder wouldn't do him any good, would it? Of course not. Each has an arm on each shoulder. Now then, you tell me which of them belongs to which, if you can. *They* don't know, themselves – they just work whichever arm comes handy. Of course they do; especially if they are in a hurry and can't stop to think which belongs to which.'

The mother seemed to have the rights of the argument, so the daughter abandoned the struggle. Presently the widow rose with a yawn and said:

'Poor thing, I hope it won't catch cold; it was powerful wet, just drenched, you may say. I hope it has left its boots outside, so they can be dried.' Then she gave a little start, and looked perplexed. 'Now I remember I heard one of them ask Joe to call him at half after seven – I think it was the one on the left – no, it was the one to the east of the other one – but I didn't hear the other one say anything. I wonder if he wants to be called too. Do you reckon it's too late to ask?'

'Why, ma, it's not necessary. Calling one is calling both. If one gets up, the other's *got* to.'

MARK TWAIN

In joined twins the confusion of self and other, substance and shadow, ego and other; is more terrifyingly confounded than when the child first perceives face to face in the mirror an image moving as he moves, though clearly in another world.

LESLIE FIEDLER, *Freaks*

Siamese twins: one, maddened by
The other's moral bigotry,
Resolved at length to misbehave
And drink them both into the grave.

ROBERT GRAVES

---

from The Break

LIKE freak Texan sisters
joined at the hip
playing saxophone duets in vaudeville,
we slept leaning, back to back.
When, more and more, our silences deepened,
a new perfume, a phone bill in her padlocked diary
were props on a stage inside my head
where I woke, sweat-drenched, alone.
Now she's gone I seem to crowd myself;
it takes a second soul to hear the soul,
a third to hear the second. They keep coming;
angels many armed, heraldic chimeras,
two-headed monsters at the map's edge screaming.

Inseparable sisters, I watch you every night
from my half-world, my single mattress.
You are smoking out back between shows
wearing the teal silk double cocktail dress.
You never speak. You pass the smoke
and the silence between you is a lake on the moon.
Daisy, Violet, you are a girl at a dance
resting, for a moment, against a mirror.

MICHAEL DONAGHY

---

from Freaks

IN our ancestors' awareness of Siamese Twins, the myth of the double merged with that of the multiple monster to create a myth of the Monstrous Self and an identically Monstrous Other *joined together till death do them part*. And this myth created a *frisson* no longer available to us, alas, even when confronting those who have chosen not to be separated. Recalling older show Freaks, however, who still felt themselves 'chained for life,' we can almost, *almost* re-create the original thrill. I myself think first of Daisy and Violet Hilton, who made a film with that grim title, and were perhaps for that reason chosen to represent their kind in Todd Browning's *Freaks*. THE STORY OF THE

LOVE LIFE OF THE SIDESHOW, its publicity posters were headed, and the first question which followed, taking precedence over 'Can a full grown woman love a midget?' and 'What sex is the half man half woman?' was 'Do Siamese twins make love?'

LESLIE FIEDLER

———————

from We So Seldom Look on Love

IT's a long drive back to the hotel, the taxi is caught in rush-hour traffic. 'Two legs do not add up to a human being,' she says to herself. The night before last John said, 'Just keep telling yourself that.' He said, 'There is no Sue.'

They were in a restaurant, drinking champagne to celebrate the future her. When she repeated 'There is no Sue,' he kissed the tips of each of her fingers, then presented her with the diamond-and-gold watch. Afterward, crossing the parking lot, he stopped and pressed her against a wall, pressing his hips against her little legs, and kissed her on the mouth.

On the drive home Sylvie's little legs started to twitch, but after a minute they settled into slow, rhythmic kicks under her skirt. It made her feel languid to hold her little knees. She and John didn't speak, except once she said, 'Oh, look!' at the ovations of fireflies glittering along her side of the road. She thought of the fireflies she had caught and preserved in her first scrapbook – a page of them. Until her mother said, 'They have to be alive, stupid,' she had turned to that page every night, wondering where the lights were.

John was nervous. He held her hand too tightly as they walked from the car to the door of his house. Sylvie *wasn't* nervous, she didn't know why. She tried to startle herself by thinking, 'In a few minutes I will be in his bedroom,' but once they were inside the house John didn't take her upstairs, he took her into his office. He threw the cushions off the sofa and pulled it out into a bed. Then he turned to her and began to kiss her on the mouth while undoing her blouse. His hands shook, reminding her of when he gave the tea and also that he was no surgeon. Since there were a lot of buttons (she was wearing a high-necked Victorian blouse), she started undoing some herself. She wanted him to know that she was willing. He started clawing at his own clothes as if they were on fire.

As soon as he was naked he resumed helping her, pulling her stockings over her ankles, yanking down her skirt before it was undone. Popping a button. They still didn't speak. He was out of breath. He drew the combs from her hair and let them drop on the floor.

And then he stopped. On his knees in front of her, his hands on her knees, he stopped.

Sylvie closed her eyes. 'Do you call ten dollars a bargain?' her mother shouted. 'Sure,' her father shrugged, backing away, 'bargain.' 'Ten dollars?' her mother shouted. 'Ten dollars?'

'God.' That was outside her head, that was John. He yanked down Sue's underpants, pulling off her stockings and shoes at the same time.

A great tremor went through her little legs, which then began to clasp his thighs and kick out, clasp and kick out. The moment of pain was nothing compared to the spectacular relief. Sylvie felt as if her little vagina were a yards-long sucking tube, and he was heading right out the back and into her own vagina. She felt a second sharp pain at what she imagined was the point of entry into her own vagina, and after that she felt him as a lightning rod conducting heat and pleasure from Sue to herself.

When he began to ejaculate, he dug his hands under her hips and lifted her, crushing her little groin into his and bringing on her first orgasm. The waves of the orgasm rolled up his lightning-rod penis into her own vagina and along to her own clitoris, where she had another, more luxurious orgasm.

For a few seconds longer, her little legs went on kicking. He seemed to wait them out. Then he withdrew and rolled onto his back. She ran her hand up and down the goosebumps on her little thigh.

'God,' he said. 'Oh, Sylvie, God.' He sounded stricken.

Her hand stopped moving. 'What?' she said.

'We got carried away,' he said.

'Yes,' she said uncertainly.

'I had no idea,' he said.

She waited, frightened.

'Of course,' he said, as if hitting upon some comfort, 'this presents a whole new angle.'

Doors slammed in her mind. He didn't want to marry her. He couldn't let her have the operation, not now, and unless she had the operation, he wouldn't marry her.

'New territory,' he said. 'New data.'

Her feet were cold, sunk in mud at the edge of the duck pond. Her little feet were tucked in the folds of her flannel nightgown. There were crickets.

'But perhaps I'm being presumptuous,' he said. He paused. 'Tell me, did . . . did what I think happened, happen?'

She turned her head to look at him. 'Did what happen?'

He kept his eyes on the ceiling. 'Did you experience orgasm with your . . .'

She looked down at his left hand. He was rubbing his thumb and forefinger together so hard, he was making the noise that, for a second, she had thought she was hearing in her memory spell, a noise at the pond. 'Two,' she said quietly. 'I had two, I think. I mean, I know I did.'

'Two?'

'One in each place.'

He reached for her hand and squeezed it but kept his eyes on the ceiling. After a moment he said, 'We can pretend it never happened, you know. You see, technically speaking, you have not had intercourse. By you I mean you the autosite, the host body.'

'Nothing has changed,' she said, but it was a question.

'No, no,' he said. 'Not as far as you're concerned.'

BARBARA GOWDY

---

from The Man Who Mistook His Wife For a Hat

COULD the twins, who seemed to have a peculiar passion and grasp of numbers – could these twins who had seen '111-ness' at a glance, perhaps see in their minds a numerical 'vine', with all the number-leaves, number-tendrils, number-fruit, that made it up? A strange, perhaps absurd, almost impossible thought – but what they had already shown me was so strange as to be almost beyond comprehension. And it was, for all I knew, the merest hint of what they might do.

I thought about the matter, but it hardly bore thinking about. And then I forgot it. Forgot it until a second, spontaneous scene, a magical scene, which I blundered into, completely by chance.

This second time they were seated in a corner together, with a mysterious, secret smile on their faces, a smile I had never seen before, enjoying the strange pleasure and peace they now seemed to have. I crept up quietly, so as not to disturb them. They seemed to be locked in a singular, purely numerical, converse. John would say a number – a six-figure number. Michael would catch the number, nod, smile and seem to savour it. Then he, in turn, would say another six-figure number, and now it was John who received, and appreciated it richly. They looked, at first, like two connoisseurs wine-tasting, sharing rare tastes, rare appreciations. I sat still, unseen by them, mesmerised, bewildered.

What were they doing? What on earth was going on? I could make nothing of it. It was perhaps a sort of game, but it had a gravity and an intensity, a sort of serene and meditative and almost holy intensity which I had never seen in any ordinary game before, and which I certainly had never seen before in the usually agitated and distracted twins. I contented myself with noting down the numbers they uttered – the numbers that manifestly gave them such delight, and which they 'contemplated', savoured, shared, in communion.

Had the numbers any meaning, I wondered on the way home, had they any 'real' or universal sense, or (if any at all) a merely whimsical or private sense, like the secret and silly 'languages' brothers and sisters sometimes work out for themselves? And, as I drove home, I thought of Luria's twins – Liosha and Yura – brain-damaged, speech-damaged identical twins, and how they would play and prattle with each other, in a primitive, babble-like language of their own. John and Michael were not even using words or half-words – simply throwing numbers at each other. Were these 'Borgesian' or 'Funesian' numbers, mere numeric vines, or pony manes, or constellations, private number-forms – a sort of number argot – known to the twins alone?

As soon as I got home I pulled out tables of powers, factors, logarithms and primes – mementos and relics of an odd, isolated period in my own childhood, when I too was something of a number brooder, a number 'see-er', and had a peculiar passion for numbers. I already had a hunch – and now I confirmed it. *All the numbers, the six figure numbers, which the twins had exchanged, were primes* – i.e., numbers that could be evenly divided by no other whole number than itself or one. Had they somehow seen or possessed such a book as mine – or were they, in some unimaginable way, themselves 'seeing' primes, in somewhat the same way as they had 'seen' 111-ness, or triple 37-ness? Certainly they could not be *calculating* them – they could calculate nothing.

I returned to the ward the next day, carrying the precious book of primes with me. I again found them closeted in their numerical communion, but this time, without saying anything, I quietly joined them. They were taken aback at first, but when I made no interruption, they resumed their 'game' of six-figure primes. After a few minutes I decided to join in, and ventured a number, an eight-figure prime. They both turned towards me, then suddenly became still, with a look of intense concentration and perhaps wonder on their faces. There was a long pause – the longest I had ever known them to make, it must have lasted a half-minute or more – and then suddenly, simultaneously, they both broke into smiles.

They had, after some unimaginable internal process of testing, suddenly seen my own eight-digit number as a prime – and this was manifestly a great joy, a double joy, to them: first because I had introduced a delightful new plaything, a prime of an order they had never previously encountered; and, secondly, because it was evident that I had seen what they were doing, that I liked it, that I admired it, and that I could join in myself.

They drew apart slightly, making room for me, a new number playmate, a third in their world. Then John, who always took the lead, thought for a very long time – it must have been at least five minutes, though I dared not move, and scarcely breathed – and brought out a nine-figure number; and after a similar time his twin Michael responded with a similar one. And then I, in my turn, after a surreptitious look in my book, added my own rather dishonest contribution, a ten-figure prime I found in my book.

There was again, and for even longer, a wondering, still silence; and then John, after a prodigious internal contemplation, brought out a twelve-figure number. I had no way of checking this, and could not respond, because my own book – which, as far as I knew, was unique of its kind – did not go beyond ten-figure primes. But Michael was up to it, though it took him five minutes – and an hour later the twins were swapping twenty-figure primes, at least I assume this was so, for I had no way of checking it. Nor was there any easy way, in 1966, unless one had the use of a sophisticated computer. And even then, it would have been difficult, for whether one uses Eratosthenes' sieve, or any other algorithm, there *is* no simple method of calculating primes. *There is no simple method, for primes of this order – and yet the twins were doing it.*

It is strange to compare these moron twins to an intellect, a spirit, like that of Bertrand Russell. And yet it is not, I think, so far-fetched. The twins live exclusively in a thought-world of numbers. They have no interest in the stars shining, or the hearts of men. And yet numbers for them, I believe, are not 'just' numbers, but significances, signifiers whose 'significand' is the world.

They do not approach numbers lightly, as most calculators do. They are not interested in, have no capacity for, cannot comprehend, calculations. They are, rather, serene contemplators of number – and approach numbers with a sense of reverence and awe. Numbers for them are holy, fraught with significance. This is their way – as music is Martin's way – of apprehending the First Composer.

But numbers are not just awesome for them, they are friends too – perhaps the only friends they have known in their isolated, autistic lives.

[. . .] I believe the twins, seemingly so isolated, live in a world full of friends, that they have millions, billions, of numbers to which they say 'Hi!' and which, I am sure, say 'Hi!' back. But none of the numbers is arbitrary – like 62 squared – nor (and this is the mystery) is it arrived at by any of the usual methods, or any method so far as I can make out. The twins seem to employ a direct cognition – like angels. They see, directly, a universe and heaven of numbers. And this, however singular, however bizarre – but what right have we to call it 'pathological'? – provides a singular self-sufficiency and serenity to their lives, and one which it might be tragic to interfere with, or break.

This serenity, was, in fact, interrupted and broken up ten years later, when it was felt that the twins should be separated – 'for their own good', to prevent their 'unhealthy communication together', and in order that they could 'come out and face the world . . . in an appropriate, socially acceptable way' (as the medical and sociological jargon had it). They were separated, then, in 1977, with results that might be considered as either gratifying or dire. Both have been moved now into 'halfway houses', and do menial jobs, for pocket money, under close supervision. They are able to take buses, if carefully directed and given a token, and to keep themselves moderately presentable and clean, though their moronic and psychotic character is still recognisable at a glance.

This is the positive side – but there is a negative side too (not mentioned in their charts, because it was never recognised in the first place). Deprived of their numerical 'communion' with each other, and of time and opportunity for any 'contemplation' or 'communion' at all – they are always being hurried and jostled from one job to another – they seem to have lost their strange numerical power, and with this the chief joy and sense of their lives. But this is considered a small price to pay, no doubt, for their having become quasi-independent and 'socially acceptable'.

OLIVER SACKS

---

from Slapstick

THUS did Eliza and I destroy our Paradise – our nation of two.

We arose the next morning before our parents did, before the servants could come to dress us. We sensed no danger. We supposed ourselves still to be in Paradise as we dressed ourselves.

I chose to wear a conservative blue, pinstripe, three-piece suit, I remember. Eliza chose to wear a cashmere sweater, a tweed skirt, and pearls.

We agreed that Eliza should be our spokesman at first, since she had a rich alto voice. My voice did not have the authority to announce calmingly but convincingly that, in effect, the world had just turned upside down.

Remember, please, that almost all that anyone had ever heard us say up to then was 'Buh' and 'Duh', and so on.

Now we encountered Oveta Cooper, our practical nurse, in the colonnaded green marble foyer. She was startled to see us up and dressed.

Before she could comment on this, though, Eliza and I leaned our heads together, put them in actual contact, just above our ears. The single genius we composed thereby then spoke to Oveta in Eliza's voice, which was as lovely as a viola.

This is what the voice said:

'Good morning, Oveta. A new life begins for all of us today. As you can see and hear, Wilbur and I are no longer idiots. A miracle has taken place overnight. Our parents' dreams have come true. We are healed.

'As for you, Oveta: You will keep your apartment and your color television, and perhaps even receive a salary increase – as a reward for all you did to make this miracle come to pass. No one on the staff will experience any change, except for this one: Life here will become even easier and more pleasant than it was before.'

315

Oveta, a bleak, Yankee dumpling, was hypnotized – like a rabbit who has met a rattlesnake. But Eliza and I were not a rattlesnake. With our heads together, we were one of the gentlest geniuses the world has ever known.

'We will not be using the tiled diningroom any more,' said Eliza's voice. 'We have lovely manners, as you shall see. Please have our breakfast served in the solarium, and notify us when Mater and Pater are up and around. It would be very nice if, from now on, you would address my brother and me as 'Master Wilbur' and 'Mistress Eliza'.

'You may go now, and tell the others about the miracle.'

Oveta remained transfixed. I at last had to snap my fingers under her nose to wake her up.

She curtseyed. 'As you wish, Mistress Eliza,' she said. And she went to spread the news.

As we settled ourselves in the solarium, the rest of the staff straggled in humbly – to have a look at the young master and the young mistress we had become.

We greeted them by their full names. We asked them friendly questions which indicated that we had a detailed understanding of their lives. We apologized for having perhaps shocked some of them for changing so quickly.

'We simply did not realize,' Eliza said, 'that anybody *wanted* us to be intelligent.'

We were by then so in charge of things that I, too, dared to speak of important matters. My high voice wouldn't be silly any more.

'With your cooperation,' I said, 'we will make this mansion famous for intelligence as it has been infamous for idiocy in days gone by. Let the fences come down.'

'Are there any questions?' said Eliza.

Somebody called Dr Mott.

Our mother did not come down to breakfast. She remained in bed – petrified.

Father came down alone. He was wearing his nightclothes. He had not shaved. Young as he was, he was palsied and drawn.

Eliza and I were puzzled that he did not look happier. We hailed him not only in English, but in several other languages we knew.

It was to one of these foreign salutations that he responded at last. 'Bonjour,' he said.

'Sit thee doon! Sit thee doon!' said Eliza merrily.

The poor man sat.

He was sick with guilt, of course, over having allowed intelligent human beings, his own flesh and blood, to be treated like idiots for so long.

Worse: His conscience and his advisors had told him before that it was all right if he could not love us, since we were incapable of deep feelings, and since there was nothing about us, objectively, that anyone in his right mind *could* love. But now it was his *duty* to love us, and he did not think he could do it.

He was horrified to discover what our mother knew she would discover, if she came downstairs: That intelligence and sensitivity in monstrous bodies like Eliza's and mine merely made us more repulsive.

This was not Father's fault or Mother's fault. It was not anybody's fault. It was as natural as breathing to all human beings, and to all warm-blooded creatures, for that matter, to wish quick deaths for monsters. This was an instinct. And now Eliza and I had raised that instinct to intolerable tragedy.

Without knowing what we were doing, Eliza and I were putting the traditional curse of monsters on normal creatures. We were asking for respect.

KURT VONNEGUT

---

from On a Monster Child

THOSE which we call monsters are not so with God, who in the immensitie of his worke seeth the infinitie of formes therein contained. And it may be thought, that any figure [which] doth amaze us, hath relation unto some other figure of the same kinde, although unknown unto man. *From out his all seeing wisedome proceedeth nothing but good, common, regular and orderly; but we neither see the sorting, nor conceive the relation. Quod crebrô videt, non miratur, etiam si, cur fiat, nescit. Quod antè non vidit, id, si evenerit, ostentum esse censet* (CIC. *Divin.* ii.). *That which he often seeth, he doth not wonder at, though he know not why it is done; But if that happen, which he never saw before, he thinkes it some portentuous wonder.* Wee call that against nature, which commeth against custome. There is nothing, whatsoever it be, that is not according to hir. Let therefore this universall and naturall reason, chase from us the error, and expell the astonishment, which noveltie breedeth, and strangenes causeth in us.

MONTAIGNE trs. John Florio, 1603

In the first few moments of meeting the twins, you may wonder why they have not been separated; but before long it's likely you'll agree with the parents. . . . 'Why should we do it?' asks Mike. 'They're perfectly put together, perfect in their own way.'

Observer, 27 August 1995

TWINS AS USEFUL

'I've often wished we were one person and not two. But actually as things turned out we are damned lucky to be twins,' said Fan.

'How so?' asked Niss in a supercilious tone which would ordinarily have infuriated Fan. But she took no notice, because she was explaining the thought which had just come to her.

'If we hadn't been two, we should never have got into the ark. We had to be a pair to be let in. If we had been one person we should have been drowned long before now.'

'That's true,' said Niss nodding her head. 'That makes up for a lot.'

DAVID GARNETT, *Two by Two*

She relives the fateful moment when the handsome Doctor Mengele stepped up to ask her the question that both saved and damned her; was she a twin . . .

'As I clutched my mother's hand, an SS man hurried by shouting. 'Twins! Twins!' He stopped to look at us. Miriam and I looked very much alike. We were wearing similar clothes.

'Are they twins? he asked my mother. 'Is that good?' she replied. He nodded yes. 'They are twins,' she said.

LUCETTE MATALON LAGNADO, SHEILA COHN DEKEL, from *Children of the Flames*

When he found identical twins in any transport . . . 'Mengele

319

beamed – he was happy . . . in a kind of trance.' When deprived of possible twins – as on one occasion when he was not notified about the arrival of a transport – he was observed to become enraged and threatening.

ROBERT JAY LIFTON, *The Nazi Doctors*

———————

The Stoic, Diogenes, grants that the Chaldeans possess the power of foreseeing certain events . . . but he denies that the other things they profess can possibly be known. For instance, two twins may resemble each other in appearance, yet their lives and fortunes be entirely dissimilar. Procles and Eurysthemese, Kings of the Lacedemonions, were twin brothers, but they did not live the same number of years, for Procles died a year before his brother and much excelled him in the glory of his actions . . . Need I press the argument that those who are born at one and the same moment are dissimiliar in their nature, their lives and their circumstances?

CICERO, inveighing against astrology

———————

In man the phenomenon of twins is, as it were, a kind of natural experiment which permits us to distinguish between the influences of heredity and environment.

GALTON

———————

from The Language of the Genes

THERE are several ways in which twins could be used to study nature and nurture. Apparently the simplest (but by far the least common) is to find identical twins separated at birth and brought up in different households. If a character is under genetic control the twins should stay the same in spite of their differing circumstances. If the environment is more important each twin should grow to resemble the family with which they spent their childhood.

This simple plot is the basis of a great deal of fiction, in science as much as in literature. In the early days, many studies claimed to show that identical twins reared apart were similar in size, weight or sexual orientation. Much of this work had problems. Often, the adoptive families were similar in class and social position. Sometimes, the twins even knew each other as they grew up. Twins who believed themselves to be identical turned out to be fraternal when blood tests were used. Even worse, there have been persistent accusations of fraud, particularly where intelligence testing is involved. All this means that most of the older research on twins reared apart has been discarded. However, there is the beginning of a new study of this kind which shows quite convincingly that some traits of personality – aggressiveness, introversion and so on – have a genetic component. This does not, of course, imply that nurture can be disregarded. An intrinsically aggressive man may be calm until he is given a chance to express his genotype by joining the army.

There is a more subtle way of using twins. It involves comparing the similarity of identical twins with that of fraternals. The argument is that, as both kinds of twins are brought up within their own family, the degree to which they share an environment is the same. Any greater resemblance of identical twins to each other must show that genes are involved. This approach could be powerful but has its own problems, particularly where studies of behaviour are involved. Although both types of twin are brought up together, identicals may copy each other's behaviour on purpose, making them appear more similar for reasons quite unconnected with their biology. The very fact of being identical twins – perhaps called Rosy and Posy and dressed in identical clothes – may predispose to mental disease. Twins often have a poor environment before birth as they share a placenta. This happens more in identicals so that their similarity may be due more to a shared environment than at first appears.

Nevertheless, this approach has had its successes. Members of a pair of identical twins are twice as likely to suffer from coronary heart disease than are those of a pair of fraternal twins: and five times as likely to have diabetes. Even tuberculosis is more commonly shared between identical than fraternal twins, suggesting that there may be an inherited basis for susceptibility. Other characters, such as schizophrenia or the age when a baby first sits up are more similar for identical than for fraternal twins.

STEVE JONES

———————

TWINS INVENTED

from The Queen's Twin

MRS Martin was looking straight in my eyes to see if I showed any genuine interest in the most interesting person in the world.

'Oh, I am very glad you saw the Queen,' I hastened to say. 'Mrs Todd has told me that you and she were born the very same day.'

'We were indeed, dear!' said Mrs Martin, and she leaned back comfortably and smiled as she had not smiled before. Mrs Todd gave a satisfied nod and glance, as if to say that things were going on as well as possible in this anxious moment.

'Yes,' said Mrs Martin again, drawing her chair a little nearer, ''t was a very remarkable thing; we were born the same day, and at exactly the same hour, after you allowed for all the difference in time. My father figured it out sea-fashion. Her Royal Majesty and I opened our eyes upon this world together; say what you may, 't is a bond between us.'

Mrs Todd assented with an air of triumph, and untied her hat-strings and threw them back over her shoulders with a gallant air.

'And I married a man by the name of Albert, just the same as she did, and all by chance, for I didn't get the news that she had an Albert too till a fortnight afterward; news was slower coming then than it is now. My first baby was a girl, and I called her Victoria after my mate; but the next one was a boy, and my husband wanted the right to name him, and took his own name and his brother Edward's, and pretty soon I saw in the paper that the little Prince o' Wales had been christened just the same. After that I made excuse to wait till I knew what she'd named her children. I didn't want to break the chain, so I had an Alfred, and my darling Alice that I lost long before she lost hers, and there I stopped. If I'd only had a dear daughter to stay at home with me, same's her youngest one, I should have been so

323

thankful! But if only one of us could have a little Beatrice, I'm glad 't was the Queen; we've both seen trouble, but she's had the most care.' [. . .] Mrs Martin began to speak in a lower tone. 'One day I got thinkin' so about my dear Queen,' she said, 'an' livin' so in my thoughts, that I went to work an' got all ready for her, just as if she was really comin'. I never told this to a livin' soul before, but I feel you'll understand. I put my best fine sheets and blankets I spun an' wove myself on the bed, and I picked some pretty flowers and put 'em all round the house, an' I worked as hard an' happy as I could all day, and had as nice a supper ready as I could get, sort of telling myself a story all the time. She was comin' an' I was goin' to see her again, an' I kep' it up until nightfall; an' when I see the dark an' it come to me I was all alone, the dream left me, an' I sat down on the doorstep an' felt all foolish an' tired. An', if you'll believe it, I heard steps comin', an' an old cousin o' mine come wanderin' along, one I was apt to be shy of. She wasn't all there, as folks used to say, but harmless enough and a kind of poor old talking body. And I went right to meet her when I first heard her call, 'stead o' hidin' as I sometimes did, an' she come in dreadful willin', an' we sat down to supper together; 't was a supper I should have had no heart to eat alone.'

'I don't believe she ever had such a splendid time in her life as she did then. I heard her tell all about it afterwards,' exclaimed Mrs Todd compassionately. 'There, now I hear all this it seems just as if the Queen might have known and couldn't come herself, so she sent that poor old creatur' that was always in need!'

Mrs Martin looked timidly at Mrs Todd and then at me. ''T was childish o' me to go an' get supper,' she confessed.

'I guess you wa'n't the first one to do that,' said Mrs Todd. 'No, I guess you wa'n't the first one who's got supper that way, Abby,' and then for a moment she could say no more.

Mrs Todd and Mrs Martin had moved their chairs a little so that they faced each other, and I, at one side, could see them both.

'No, you never told me o' that before, Abby,' said Mrs Todd gently. 'Don't it show that for folks that have any fancy in 'em, such beautiful dreams is the real part o' life? But to most folks the common things that happens outside 'em is all in all.'

Mrs Martin did not appear to understand at first, strange to say, when the secret of her heart was put into words; then a glow of pleasure and comprehension shone upon her face. 'Why, I believe you're right, Almira!' she said, and turned to me.

'Wouldn't you like to look at my pictures of the Queen?' she asked, and we rose and went into the best room.

SARAH ORNE JEWETT

---

from The Willow Walk

IT was midnight when he returned to his house.

Before it he gasped. The front door was open. He chuckled with relief as he remembered that he had not closed it. He sauntered in. He was passing the door of the living room, going directly up to his bedroom, when his foot struck an object the size of a book, but hollow sounding. He picked it up. It was one of the booklike candy boxes. And it was quite empty. Frightened, he listened. There was no sound. He crept into the living room and lighted the lamp.

The doors of the bookcase had been wrenched open. Every book had been pulled out on the floor. All of the candy boxes, which that evening had contained almost ninety-six thousand dollars, were in a pile, and all of them were empty. He searched for ten minutes, but the only money he found was one five-dollar bill, which had fluttered under the table. In his pocket he had one dollar and sixteen cents. John Holt had six dollars and sixteen cents, no job, no friends – and no identity.

When the president of the Lumber National Bank was informed that John Holt was waiting to see him he scowled.

'Lord, I'd forgotten that minor plague! Must be a year since he's been here. Oh, let him – No, hanged if I will! Tell him I'm too busy to see him. That is, unless he's got some news about Jasper. Pump him, and find out.'

The president's secretary sweetly confided to John:

'I'm so sorry, but the president is in conference just now. What was it you wanted to see him about? Is there any news about – uh – about your brother?'

'There is not, miss. I am here to see the president on the business of the Lord.'

'Oh! If that's all I'm afraid I can't disturb him.'

'I will wait.'

Wait he did, through all the morning, through the lunch hour –

325

when the president hastened out past him – then into the afternoon, till the president was unable to work with the thought of that scarecrow out there, and sent for him.

'Well, well! What is it this time, John? I'm pretty busy. No news about Jasper, eh?'

'No news, sir, but – Jasper himself! I am Jasper Holt! His sin is my sin.'

'Yes, yes, I know all that stuff – twin brothers, twin souls, share responsibility—'

'You don't understand. There isn't any twin brother. There isn't any John Holt. I am Jasper, I invented an imaginary brother, and disguised myself – Why, don't you recognize my voice?'

While John leaned over the desk, his two hands upon it, and smiled wistfully, the president shook his head and soothed: 'No, I'm afraid I don't. Sounds like good old religious John to me! Jasper was a cheerful, efficient sort of crook. Why, his laugh—'

'But I can laugh!' The dreadful croak which John uttered was the cry of an evil bird of the swamps. The president shuddered. Under the edge of the desk his fingers crept toward the buzzer by which he summoned his secretary.

They stopped as John urged: 'Look – this wig – it's a wig. See, I am Jasper!'

He had snatched off the brown thatch. He stood expectant, a little afraid.

The president was startled, but he shook his head and sighed.

'You poor devil! Wig, all right. But I wouldn't say that hair was much like Jasper's!'

He motioned toward the mirror in the corner of the room.

John wavered to it. And indeed he saw that his hair had turned from Jasper's thin sleek blackness to a straggle of damp gray locks writhing over a yellow skull.

He begged pitifully: 'Oh, can't you see I am Jasper? I stole ninety-seven thousand dollars from the bank. I want to be punished! I want to do anything to prove – Why, I've been at your house. Your wife's name is Evelyn. My salary here was—'

'My dear boy, don't you suppose that Jasper might have told you all these interesting facts? I'm afraid the worry of this has – pardon me if I'm frank, but I'm afraid it's turned your head a little, John.'

'There isn't any John! There isn't! There isn't!'

'I'd believe that a little more easily if I hadn't met you before Jasper disappeared.'

'Give me a piece of paper. You know my writing—'

With clutching claws John seized a sheet of bank stationery and tried to write in the round script of Jasper. During the past year and a half he had filled thousands of pages with the small finicky hand of John. Now, though he tried to prevent it, after he had traced two or three words in large but shaky letters the writing became smaller, more pinched, less legible.

Even while John wrote the president looked at the sheet and said easily: 'Afraid it's no use. That isn't Jasper's fist. See here, I want you to get away from Rosebank – go to some farm – work outdoors – cut out this fuming and fussing – get some fresh air in your lungs.' The president rose and purred: 'Now, I'm afraid I have some work to do.'

He paused, waiting for John to go.

John fiercely crumpled the sheet and hurled it away. Tears were in his weary eyes.

He wailed: 'Is there nothing I can do to prove I am Jasper?'

'Why, certainly! You can produce what's left of the ninety-seven thousand!'

John took from his ragged waistcoat pocket a five-dollar bill and some change. 'Here's all there is. Ninety-six thousand of it was stolen from my house last night.'

Sorry though he was for the madman, the president could not help laughing. Then he tried to look sympathetic, and he comforted: 'Well, that's hard luck, old man. Uh, let's see. You might produce some parents or relatives or somebody to prove that Jasper never did have a twin brother.'

'My parents are dead, and I've lost track of their kin – I was born in England – Father came over when I was six. There might be some cousins or some old neighbors, but I don't know. Probably impossible to find out, in these wartimes, without going over there.'

'Well, I guess we'll have to let it go, old man.' The president was pressing the buzzer for his secretary and gently bidding her: 'Show Mr Holt out, please.'

From the door John desperately tried to add: 'You will find my car sunk—'

The door had closed behind him. The president had not listened.

The president gave orders that never, for any reason, was John Holt to be admitted to his office again. He telephoned to the bonding company that John Holt had now gone crazy; that they would save trouble by refusing to admit him.

John did not try to see them. He went to the county jail. He entered the keeper's office and said quietly: 'I have stolen a lot of money, but I can't prove it. Will you put me in jail?'

The keeper shouted: 'Get out of here! You hoboes always spring that when you want a good warm lodging for the winter! Why the devil don't you go to work with a shovel in the sand pits? They're paying two-seventy-five a day.'

'Yes, sir,' said John timorously. 'Where are they?'

SINCLAIR LEWIS

---

from Brave New World

'BOKANOVSKY'S Process,' repeated the Director, and the students underlined the words in their little note books.

One egg, one embryo, one adult – normality. But a bokanovskified egg will bud, will proliferate, will divide. From eight to ninety-six buds, and every bud will grow into a perfectly formed embryo, and every embryo into a full-sized adult. Making ninety-six human beings grow where only one grew before. Progress.

'Essentially,' the D.H.C. concluded, 'bokanovskification consists of a series of arrests of development. We check the normal growth and, paradoxically enough, the egg responds by budding.'

Responds by budding. The pencils were busy.

He pointed. On a very slowly moving band a rack-full of test-tubes was entering a large metal box, another rack-full was emerging. Machinery faintly purred. It took eight minutes for the tubes to go through, he told them. Eight minutes of hard X-rays being about as much as an egg can stand. A few died; of the rest, the least susceptible divided into two; most put out four buds; some eight; all were returned to the incubators, where the buds began to develop; then, after two days, were suddenly chilled, chilled and checked. Two, four, eight, the buds in their turn budded; and having budded were dosed almost to death with alcohol; consequently burgeoned again and having budded – bud out of bud out of bud were thereafter – further arrest being generally fatal – left to develop in peace. By which time the original egg was in a fair way to becoming anything from eight to ninety-six embryos – a prodigious improvement, you will agree, on nature. Identical twins – but not in piddling twos and threes as in the old viviparous days, when an egg would sometimes accidentally divide; actually by dozens, by scores at a time.

'Scores,' the Director repeated and flung out his arms, as though he were distributing largesse. 'Scores.'

But one of the students was fool enough to ask where the advantage lay.

'My good boy!' The Director wheeled sharply round on him. 'Can't you see? Can't you *see*?' He raised a hand; his expression was solemn. 'Bokanovsky's Process is one of the major instruments of social stability!'

Major instruments of social stability.

Standard men and women; in uniform batches. The whole of a small factory staffed with the products of a single bokanovskified egg.

'Ninety-six identical twins working ninety-six identical machines!' The voice was almost tremulous with enthusiasm. 'You really know where you are. For the first time in history.'

ALDOUS HUXLEY

6

THE MYTH OF THE TWIN

୬&

W ITH MYTH, the particular experience of twins begins to feed itself into common experience. For though twins both feel and see the myth of twinship acted out in their own lives, on their own bodies, the feelings and images their lives and bodies evoke in others do not belong to them, only. The unease, the fascination, the longing, is common to us all. Thus as real, unmythical twins, we belong to everyone, by virtue of our embodying the myth.

Not least, mythically and actually, we reflect the unease of division within and between people – and the possibility of healing. Hence . . . they don't call you by your given name; they call you 'twin'. (The headmistress at our first school had to announce at prayers that in future only our actual names were to be used.) Hence . . . if you're twins, why do you dress differently? And so forth. The myth here, of course, is the myth not just of doubleness but likeness; or sameness – a peculiarly western twin obsession, if Lévi-Strauss is right (see the piece quoted in Part Two, pp. 84). Elsewhere, traditions are less uncomfortable with two being other, dissonant, different; differences defining twinship, not likeness. But the origins of the distinction are the same everywhere – in all societies what makes twin birth seem uncanny isn't likeness or unlikeness, it's doubleness; in our species to be normal is to come single. Hence the seemingly universal need to give twins a special status, special rituals, mental or actual, in order to reintegrate the society that their very otherness divides. Thus they are declared holy and worshipped or even, as among the Dogon, declared the norm – only most people's twins do not survive the womb. (An interesting variant given the recent theory that behind up to 20 per cent of single births lie twin conceptions, where one of the pair vanishes *in utero*.) Alternatively they are abhorred, eliminated, taboo.

The origin of all of this is of course the number two; the first true number, you could say, because if, by definition, multiplicity is the defining quality of number, one, which by its nature is single and cannot be split is not a number. In consequence, the difference between one and two is infinitely greater than that between two and three – or two and two hundred and three, come to that. One is the number of God; of precreation. Two is the number of creation – the point where the creator splits her-/himself to make the universe and in due course its inhabitants. But within the split lies the possibility not only of good, but also evil. The medieval church deeply distrusted the number two – it was the number of woman; who divides man. It was the number of the devil, likewise. This distrust could lie behind the Western obsession with sameness; and, too, behind its obsession with that other contrary kind of sameness, dichotomy; or opposites. Such perfect oppositions, such absolute division between, in particular, good/evil – here, good twin/bad twin – but also night/day, wet/dry, open/shut, and so forth, do not heal the divisions: on the contrary they emphasise them; but they at least set them within a recognisable structure; or alternatively allow the possibility of creating unity by eliminating the unfavoured half. It could even be that the origins of such thinking go still deeper, are built into the very structure of the human brain, the way the double helix lies at the heart of all biological creation. There is a form of epileptic seizure which manifests itself as an obsession with dichotomies; evidence that, neurologically speaking, we might indeed be programmed to think in binary terms.

Polarities which set oppositions at either end of one axis rather than splitting them absolutely, are subtler than dichotomies, and therefore altogether more interesting. Polarities, too, exist in Western myth. There's a Christian tradition which sees Thomas – Doubting Thomas – as the twin of Jesus; dark twin against light. While in the Celtic tradition of the Year Kings who each rule for half a year, Llew Llaw the sun god succeeds his twin brother Dylan, the fish, that is the water or moon twin. The point of these is that there is no absolute division: Thomas was not the son of God, but nor was he the epitome of evil against the absolute good that was Jesus; Llew Llaw *was* his twin Dylan under a different name. For, the fact that different qualities can co-exist within polarity means that they *can* shift – what twin has not groaned like us, at having A. A. Milne's poem about two bears recited to them for the umpteenth time ('And then quite suddenly, just like us one of them got better and the other got wuss'). Much more interesting and subtle is the comment made by a fraternal twin of 14 looking at a yin-yang image – that is, black and white figures coiled into each other to make up a whole. If M (his twin) died, he said, I would be one of those; I don't know which yet. But I couldn't be both. Yes. For there *we* were, right-hand sister, left-hand sister, only put together could we make a whole. On the other hand, her qualities, long disregarded in me as mine in her, could in fact co-exist with mine; and vice versa. Though I was the 'artistic' one, my sister later in life became a very good photographer – just as I, the unpractical one, the cared-for, took on her role and turned family carer. The patterns die hard. But the point is they are not immutable; within each polarity all possibilities exist – poles swing and turn other way about; North to South and South to North. Thus, to go beyond the personal, back to myth, in non-Western twin traditions the trickster twin can by turns be both destroyer and creator; the creator can be both good and evil; the twins can be water and warrior, or water then warrior. Whatever.

And then there is that other myth of twinship, the one that connects to the deepest of all yearnings; the myth of the twin soul. Plato's version might be the first one we Westerners think of. But others knew it too – in Hawaiian creation myth when first man is called to earth, only half of him is sent, meaning that he cannot regain his whole self till the end of the world. In much the same way, Plato, and after him Swedenborg, suggested that half man was always seeking his male or female other half. It's a paradigm of the divided self if you like. But more literally it's made actual in twins – people see us as enviable because we are born with our soulmates, who never have to go looking to be made whole like everybody else. Obligingly, twins demonstrate such unity; they fall down in a faint at the same moment, they read each other's thoughts, they break the same bones in the same way. Even I, the fraternal twin, can lay claim to the odd coincidence – which could be just coincidence, but is strange, all the same. For instance: neither my twin nor I broke a single bone till we were 37, whereupon she broke her left knee and I my right within six months of each other. (Our ailments always mirrored our handedness.) Again, I've been trekking in Nepal, twice. The first time, at altitude, I had a dream she was grievously ill, and agitated all the way back to Kathmandu and a not very convenient telephone which told me she was not sick; of course. Seven years later I trekked dreamlessly. But was rung the night we got home to say my sister had had her mastectomy. Odd, that. As well as awful.

That twins do not find their perfect soul companion in their twin, after all, is too often the case, alas. See Jennifer Gibbon's longing for the true twin her sister June wasn't. My twin as must be clear wasn't my true twin in that sense either, no matter the longing there might have been in either case. The failure to reach the ideal togetherness was, no doubt, one potent – if not the most potent – source of our anger with each other. A photograph taken in the registry office during my second wedding sums it up. In the foreground my new husband and I are kissing each other. In the background sits my sister, frowning, light reflected on her glasses hiding an expression I do not need to see, can read perfectly well from what she's wearing, the way she sits, from the fixed horizontal of her mouth. Acting out not only what she was, but what I projected on her, she demonstrates that myth of otherness, of jealousy, twisted love and hate found in European myth as in non-European myth quite as much as the other kind; the tragedy of which is that the twin souls are there, longed for just the same. If only, I thought then, angrily, my Esau could have enjoyed her Jacob's good fortune just this once. But now I have to forgive her. Here was a woman in whom the world brought out the best – two hundred people with whom she worked as probation officer, drug counsellor came to her memorial service; and all I, her opposite, polarity, twin soul, other half, all I could do was bring out the worst in her; just as, too often, she brought out the worst in me. In too many twinships I fear, it is the same. The myth of the twin to which we are subject both creates and defines what is for us a double reality, in which any single mythical and real quality can point to, or even contain, its equally mythical, equally real opposite. And in that our whole problem lies.

The Myth of the Twin

Say it moved when you moved:
a softness that rose in the ground
when you walked, or a give in your step,
the substance that Virgil saw
in the shadows under our feet;

and say it was out there, out in the snow,
meshed with the birdsong and light
the way things are real: a blackbird, a scribble of thorns,
a quickening into the moment, the present tense,

and the way that a stumbling or sudden
rooting in authenticity is not
the revelation of a foreign place,
but emptiness, a stillness in the frost,
the silence that stands in the birchwoods, the common soul.

JOHN BURNSIDE

Everything in the universe is double; there is male light and
female darkness, just as there is also full and empty, yes and
no, hot and cold, sympathy and antipathy. But each demon is
countered by an angel.
Quoted by RENÉ ZAZZO, from *Journal d'Harvey* Jean Hamburger,
(translated by Penelope Farmer)

Twins are a species of the uncanny, of phenomena that lie
in the region between the familiar and the unfamiliar, the
revealed and the hidden – ambiguous phenomena which provoke
apprehension. . . . Elsewhere even twin rivalries illustrate an
innate tendency to contrast/echo/balance oppositions. . . . As
Isis, Osiris, Dogons, etc., suggest a once broken embryonic unity
seeking reconstitution.

TED WOLNER, *Parallels*

In the duality of their union, twins may embody the socratic dialogues which occur within each of us, dialogues of a self which questions and a self which answers . . . Twins seem in fact to be surreal disfigurations, strange identical dream figures who appear before us as if in the half life of the unreal, messenger from out of the subconscious, bearing us some needed, even dreaded knowledge of ourselves.

IBID.

. . .There is more difference between one and two than between one and any other number. Because two can be divided into two halves . . . in effect one each again – and so on, ad infinitum. Such mechanical reproduction flouts our assumption that each and everyone of us is unique.

From CARL JUNG, *Psychology of Religion*

from Psychology and Religion: West

THE number one claims an exceptional position, which we meet again in the natural philosophy of the Middle Ages. According to this, one is not a number at all; the first number is two. Two is the first number because, with it, separation and multiplication begin, which alone make counting possible. With the appearance of the number two, *another* appears alongside the one, a happening which is so striking that in many languages 'the other' and 'the second' are expressed by the same word. Also associated with the number two is the idea of right and left and remarkably enough, of favourable and unfavourable, good and bad. The 'other' can have a 'sinister' significance – or one feels it, at least, as something opposite and alien. Therefore, argues a medieval alchemist, God did not praise the second day of creation, because on this day (Monday, the day of the moon) the *binarius*, alias the devil, came into existence. Two implies a one which is different and distinct from the 'numberless' One. In other words, as soon as the number two appears, a unit is produced out of the original unity, and this

336

unit is none other than that same unity split into two and turned into a 'number.'

CARL JUNG

---

from The Mystery of Numbers

Die Zwei ist Zweifel, Zwist, ist Zwietracht, Zwiespalt, Zwitter,
Die Zwei is Zwillingsfrucht am Zweige, süß and bitter.

(Two is doubt, disunion, discord, dissension, hermaphrodite,
Two is the twin fruit on the twig, both sweet and bitter.)

RÜCKERT invented this ingenious wordplay to allude to many negative characteristics of the number 2. In religious traditions, 2 means disunion, the falling apart of the absolute divine unity, and is therefore the number connected with the world of creation: 'creature is twofold in itself,' as Valentin Weigel said in the sixteenth century.

[. . .] Islamic Sufis have discovered an allusion to the created world in the second letter of the alphabet, *b*, which in both Hebrew and Arabic has the numerical value of 2. And just as the Bible begins with *b'reshit*, 'In the beginning . . .,' the first words of the Quran are *Bismillāh*, 'In the name of God . . .,' so that in both cases the first letter of the holy book is the letter of creation, the *b*.

A beautiful symbol of the duality that appears through creation was invented by the great Persian mystical poet Jalaladdin Rumi, who compares God's creative word *kun* (written in Arabic *KN*) with a twisted rope of 2 threads (which in English is called *twine*, in German *Zwirn*, both words derived from the root 'two'). This twisted yarn appears in all manifestations of creation but dupes only the ignorant, who are led to believe in multiplicity, while the wise know that the world of unity is hidden behind the apparent contrasts.

Perhaps the most ingenious way to show the fundamental polarity on which life rests is found in the yin and yang of the Chinese religion, by which active and passive, male and female, begetter and begotten, fire and water, day and night, and whatever complementary relations exist are expressed. These relations are extremely subtle and appear in both cosmic and human relations. Thus the highest celestial being and the highest ruler appear in the yang principle, while the moon, the water, and the empress are related to the yin principle. Yin and yang are omnipresent and inseparable, for it is impossible to make either one absolute: the mention of 'woman' includes involuntarily the idea of 'man,' just as 'health' presupposes the existence of 'illness.'

It is therefore not astonishing that in many religious traditions primordial man is imagined as androgynous.

[. . .] Such a state, seen as one of higher perfection, is alluded to in an agraphon of Jesus: 'Then Salome asked Jesus: 'When shall thy kingdom come?' And the Lord spoke: 'When two have become one, when the male has become female and when there is no female any more', In other words, the kingdom of God will return once duality has been overcome. For duality appeared, as the Torah and later the Cabala hold, because man ate from the tree of knowledge and thus became aware of the existence of good and evil and of life and death, as well as of sexuality.

The Christian church also had negative interpretations of the number 2, seen as a deviation from unity, from the first good. Is it not written in the Bible that 2 unclean animals from each race were taken into the ark? Furthermore, 2 is the number associated with heretics, those who are *duplex cor*, having two hearts, and thus do not follow the Gospel wholeheartedly.

In fact, the link between 2 and unreliability is known to most cultures, beginning with the double-faced Janus in ancient Rome. In Persian, *two-faced* means 'false' and *two-colored*, 'hypocritical,' while the Arabs call a hypocrite 'father of two tongues,' or 'double tongued,' like the German *doppelzüngig*. Things ambivalent and ambiguous belong, as the root *ambi* ('both') shows, to the same sphere of uncertainty (or *twi*light) as the *di*-lemma.

ANNEMARIE SCHIMMEL

---

from A Note on Twins

IN Laguna, N. M., twins are considered a misfortune. So much so in fact, that a woman is not told she is giving birth to twins for fear she might in some way interfere with the birth of the second child.

It is believed that twins are due to some evil person – a witch – with whom the prospective mother might unwittingly have quarrelled or whom she had offended in some way, during pregnancy. As soon as the twins are born, *kcurna wawa*, a root, is burned constantly in the middle of the room. The smoke from this will drive away the witch.

To further counteract the evil influence of the witch, the twins are taken to the medicine man (*tcaiyani*). He gives each twin a teaspoonful of the urine of their mother that has been preserved for a week. Unless this is administered the twins will continue to be an evil influence in the community— 'they will know all and become witches themselves.'

From *American Anthropologist*, 1921

from The Sacrifice of the Twins

TOKUBO finished bathing the children and she dressed them up in new clothes. She then persuaded Omote to go and bathe and prepare herself for the ceremony. While Omote was bathing and getting ready, Tokubo prepared the pot. She put some clothes into it, so as to make it comfortable, and she tied young, white palm fronds around its neck. The palm fronds were to show people that those in the pot were dead or as good as dead.

About three or four hours after daybreak, people began to gather in front of Okoro's house. Okoro and his wife stood on either side of their door. They faced the crowd. Many people avoided their eyes because they could not bear to look at such unhappiness. Suddenly the crowd parted and a figure stepped into the space between the crowd and the house. This was the high priest of the god of the village. He was strangely dressed. He wore a raffia skirt, and charms were tied round his arms and legs. His eyes were painted round with chalk while the rest of his face was painted black. In his right hand he held a rattle.

Looking straight at Okoro and Omote, he shook his rattle at them three times before he began to speak. The crowd was silent and Omote and Okoro looked at the ground.

'Okoro,' he shouted, 'you and your wife have soiled our land. Omote, you have delivered animals. The village is no longer clean. It cannot be clean until the animals have been thrown out. When the animals have been thrown out, you must prepare to clean the village.

Are you ready? Are you ready to remove the evil you have brought into this village?'

There was a long silence.

'Are you ready?' the chief priest shouted.

'Yes, we are ready,' replied Okoro quietly.

'Then, where are they?'

Okoro turned to his wife, who seemed to be unaware of what was going on.

'Omote,' he whispered, 'they are waiting for you.'

He touched her gently, and she jerked away. With a cry of anguish, she rushed into the house.

Tokubo was inside, ready to help her. Quickly, she began to undress Omote, until only the red skirt – called *obuluku* – which she wore underneath remained. Tokubo crushed some chalk in her palm and rubbed some of it around each of Omote's eyes. Then she used the remainder to draw short, thick lines down her friend's and her own forehead.

The twins were crying inside the pot. Tokubo was weeping and Omote was sobbing. But they were waiting outside for her.

Tokubo made a pad from some old cloth in the house. Then she put it on Omote's head and placed the pot on it. She had to keep a hand on the pot, while she forced her friend to hold it. When Omote finally gripped the pot with both hands, Tokubo pushed her gently but firmly towards the door.

Omote staggered out, and the crowd drew back in awe. She stood in front of the door swaying from side to side. Okoro stood quite still, looking at the crowd, but seeing no one. Someone from the back of the crowd began to beat a drum. The chief priest stepped beside Omote and motioned Okoro to the other side. The three of them moved forward. The crowd parted to give the strange trio way, and then it closed behind and followed them.

Omote was slow and she staggered a great deal. Okoro was slow also but he did not stagger. The priest was deliberately slow, to keep pace with husband and wife. The twins were silent throughout the walk, until they reached the edge of the river. At the river bank, Omote put down the pot and knelt by it, more because she wanted a last look at her children than because it was part of the ritual.

Along the edge of the river people stood quietly looking on. The drum had stopped. The priest was making some incantations. When he finished he poured some local gin into the river and some on the land. He shared what was left among himself, Okoro and Omote.

Omote was then asked to take the pot and wade into the river until the water came to her chest. There she was to put the pot on the river and return.

As Omote moved forward to obey, it appeared as though something had happened to her. She no longer wept. She did not even need help. Without hesitation she carried the pot and began to wade into the river. As she moved farther away from the bank, the water rose up her body higher and higher, until it touched her naked chest. Here she stopped, and gently lowered the pot on to the river. She took one long look at the children and then turned. But she could not turn her back on her own babies. So she turned again, and waded backwards until she slipped and fell. A sigh rose from the bank as she splashed and staggered against the muddy river bed and then fell backwards, away from the pot. Nearly all the women on the shore were crying. The men maintained a strong silence.

CHRISTIANA EDO OBO

Our being identical twins led to some curious encounters. When we were in France in 1940, an elderly man suddenly knelt at our feet as paying homage, and a curious crowd gathered. Embarrassed, we did not know what we were expected to do until someone explained that a local superstition held that seeing identical twins was a lucky event.

ALEC BEDSER, *Twin Ambitions*

---

from Conversations with Ogotemmêli

ACTUALLY the birth of twins [among the Dogon] is a notable event. It recalls the fabulous past, when all beings came into existence in twos, symbols of the balance between the human and the divine. It repeats the child-birth of the first woman and the transformation of her clitoris into a scorpion. The scorpion with his eight feet is a symbol of two new-born infants with their sum of eight arms and legs. He is also their protector: no one dares touch them for fear of his sting.

A twin-birth initiates a series of practices and rites of an exceptional character. It is not till eight weeks after the event – eight is the number of twins – that the mother emerges from her seclusion. At the first-fruits festival which follows, the children are shaved by adult twins, and the relatives put special jars on the family altar; for from their earliest days, these children will be the objects of a cult forming part of the cult of the family's ancestors.

This cult seemed to show that some special quality was attributed to the ancestry of twins. It was a popular belief that their mother had been 'touched' during pregnancy by a Spirit – it would never be called a Nummo, for that was too dangerous a name, too much for a human mouth to utter. The children of such a mother would therefore be essentially different from other children.

But all this was common knowledge, and the European had no desire to discuss all the different forms of ritual celebrated in such cases. Earlier enquiries had established all the details that could be desired, and he was anxious to find out what Ogotemmêli had to say about something which seemed to him to be highly significant – namely the special earthenware reserved for twins. These objects have a peculiar shape: each consists of two shallow round cups, five to six centimetres in diameter, joined together at the edge like a wide open oyster-shell. There was something of this sort in the celestial granary, at the top of the pyramid of superimposed jars placed at the point of intersection of the lower interior partitions. It covered the small container which held toilet perfumes and which formed the lid of the pot of oil, symbol of the foetus, which itself was set on top of the large jar symbolizing the womb. In this position it was placed in a context of generation: it was an invocation to creation by pairs, of which it was also a symbol.

'The two cups joined side by side,' said Ogotemmêli, 'are, like twins, of the same shape and size.'

On the day when the children are shaved, the father procures four double cups, which he places on the family altar, and two small trapezium-shaped pieces of leather, on each of which eight cowries are sewn. These objects are consecrated by a blood sacrifice of eight fowls, and are then made into pendants, which the children wear round their necks as a sign of their quality. The earthenware cups receive regular offerings from the relatives, and later from the twins themselves.

'The double cup,' said Ogotemmêli, 'is the symbol of twins – the same shape, same size, same words; and, just as the cups are equal to one another, so the twins are interchangeable, and therefore,' he added, 'trade began with twins.'

MARCEL GRIAULE

GEMINI: positive house of Mercury, 21 May to 20 June

The dual nature of the Twins is reflected in the nature of the Geminean. Brilliant, charming and imaginative, they are at the same time elusive, materialist and almost stolid. They have a great love of intellectual pursuits, although their knowledge is more likely to have been gained by superficial means; although they may concentrate on studies for a short time, they prefer to pick the brains of others.

For themselves, Gemineans are cunning, very clever and not over-scrupulous. A combination of Sun in Gemini with Moon in Aries, Leo or Sagittarius is one to watch: the nature may tend to extremes, with instability, financial rashness, fickleness and all two-faced qualities accentuated. In general, Gemineans are eloquent speakers, delight in telling stories, and make excellent actors and diplomats.

The ascendant in Gemini indicates a constitution that is not very strong: the health rapidly breaks down under strain, and catarrh, bronchitis and pneumonia should be guarded against. The body is tall, thin and upright, with a long face and colourful features; if the complexion is dark the eyes are usually hazel, big and piercing. Movements are quick and active.

---

from The Manuscript Found in Saragossa

EVENTUALLY Semiamas, Prince of the Grigori, came and told me that it was time to begin. I emerged from my cave and formed my star-spangled scarf into a circle, opened my book and spoke aloud the terrible formulae which I had until then only dared read silently to myself. As you will appreciate, Señor Alphonse, I cannot tell you what happened next. In any case, you would not understand. All I will tell you is that I acquired some considerable power over spirits and that I was taught how to contact the heavenly twins. At about the same time my brother succeeded in seeing the tips of the feet of Solomon's daughters. I waited for the sun to enter the sign of Gemini and performed my operations in turn. On that day, or rather night, I worked prodigiously hard and in the end was overcome by sleep and forced to give in to it.

The next morning Zulica brought my mirror and in it I caught sight of two human forms which seemed to be behind me. I turned round and saw nothing. I looked back in the mirror and saw them again. I should add that this apparition was in no way frightening. I saw two young men who were slightly taller than human beings. Their shoulders were a little broader and were rounded in the way women's shoulders are. Their torso was also feminine in form but they did not have breasts. Their arms, plump and perfectly shaped, were resting at their sides in the posture that Egyptian statues have. The heavy curls of their blue and gold hair fell down to their shoulders. I will not describe their faces to you. You can well imagine how handsome demi-gods are for these were indeed the heavenly twins. I recognized them by the little flames which burned above their heads.

'How were these demi-gods dressed?' I asked Rebecca.

'They wore nothing at all,' she replied. 'Each one had four wings, two lying on their shoulders and two folded and crossed around their waists. These wings were actually as transparent as those of a fly, but woven through with gold and blue veins which hid from sight anything which might have shocked my modesty.'

'So here they are,' I said to myself, 'the heavenly spouses to whom I am promised.' I could not help privately comparing them to the young mulatto who adored Zulica. But I was ashamed of the thought. I looked in the mirror and thought that I saw two demi-gods looking severely at me, as though they had been able to read my mind and had taken offence at the involuntary comparison I had made.

JAN POTOCKI

344

from The Story of Romulus

THE Vestal was forcibly violated and gave birth to twins. She named Mars as their father, either because she really believed it, or because the fault might appear less heinous if a deity were the cause of it. But neither gods nor men sheltered her or her babes from the king's cruelty; the priestess was thrown into prison, the boys were ordered to be thrown into the river. By a heaven-sent chance it happened that the Tiber was then overflowing its banks, and stretches of standing water prevented any approach to the main channel. Those who were carrying the children expected that this stagnant water would be sufficient to drown them, so under the impression that they were carrying out the king's orders they exposed the boys at the nearest point of the overflow, where the Ficus Ruminalis (said to have been formerly called Romularis) now stands. The locality was then a wild solitude. The tradition goes on to say that after the floating cradle in which the boys had been exposed had been left by the retreating water on dry land, a thirsty she-wolf from the surrounding hills, attracted by the crying of the children, came to them, gave them her teats to suck and was so gentle towards them that the king's flock-master found her licking the boys with her tongue. According to the story, his name was Faustulus. He took the children to his hut and gave them to his wife Larentia to bring up . . .

As soon as the boys, thus born and thus brought up, grew to be young men they did not neglect their pastoral duties, but their special delight was roaming through the woods on hunting expeditions. As their strength and courage were thus developed, they used not only to lie in wait for fierce beasts of prey, but they even attacked brigands when loaded with plunder. They distributed what they took amongst the shepherds, with whom, surrounded by a continually increasing body of young men, they associated themselves in their serious undertakings and in their sports and pastimes.

It is said that the festival of the Lupercalia, which is still observed, was even in those days celebrated on the Palatine hill. [. . .] The existence of this festival was widely recognised, and it was while the two brothers were engaged in it that the brigands, enraged at losing their plunder, ambushed them. Romulus successfully defended himself, but Remus was taken prisoner and brought before Amulius, his captors impudently accusing him of their own crimes. The principal charge brought against them was that of invading Numitor's lands with a body of young men whom they had got together, and carrying off plunder as though in regular warfare. Remus accordingly was handed over to Numitor for punishment.

Faustulus had from the beginning suspected that it was royal offspring that he was bringing up, for he was aware that the boys had been exposed at the king's command and the time at which he had taken them away exactly corresponded with that of their exposure. He had, however, refused to divulge the matter prematurely, until either a fitting opportunity occurred or necessity demanded its disclosure. The necessity came first. Alarmed for the safety of Remus he revealed the state of the case to Romulus. It so happened that Numitor also, who had Remus in his custody, on hearing that he and his brother were twins, and comparing their ages, and the character and bearing so unlike that of one in a servile condition, began to recall the memory of his grandchildren, and further inquiries brought him to the same conclusion as Faustulus; nothing was wanting to the recognition of Remus. So the king Amulius was being enmeshed on all sides by hostile purposes. Romulus shrunk from a direct attack with his body of shepherds, for he was no match for the king in open fight. They were instructed to approach the palace by different routes and meet there at a given time, whilst from Numitor's house Remus lent his assistance with a second band he had collected. The attack succeeded and the king was killed.

At the beginning of the fray, Numitor gave out that an enemy had entered the City and was attacking the palace, in order to draw off the Alban soldiery to the citadel, to defend it. When he saw the young men coming to congratulate him after the assassination, he at once called a council of his people and explained his brother's infamous conduct towards him, the story of his grandsons, their parentage and bringing up, and how he recognised them. Then he proceeded to inform them of the tyrant's death and his responsibility for it. The young men marched in order through the midst of the assembly and saluted their grandfather as king; their action was approved by the whole population, who with one voice ratified the title and sovereignty of the king.

After the government of Alba was thus transferred to Numitor, Romulus and Remus were seized with the desire of building a city in the locality where they had been exposed. There was the superfluous population of the Alban and Latin towns, to these were added the shepherds: it was natural to hope that with all these Alba would be small and Lavinium small in comparison with the city which was to be founded.

These pleasant anticipations were disturbed by the ancestral curse – ambition – which led to a deplorable quarrel over what was at first a trivial matter. As they were twins and no claim to precedence could be based on seniority, they decided to consult the tutelary deities of the place by means of augury as to who was to give his name to the new city, and who was to rule it after it had been founded. Romulus accordingly selected the Palatine as his station for observation, Remus the Aventine.

Remus is said to have been the first to receive an omen: six vultures appeared to him. The augury had just been announced to Romulus when double the number appeared to him. Each was saluted as king by his own party. The one side based their claim on the priority of the appearance, the other on the number of the birds. Then followed an angry altercation; heated passions led to bloodshed; in the tumult Remus was killed. The more common report is that Remus contemptuously jumped over the newly raised walls and was forthwith killed by the enraged Romulus, who exclaimed, 'So shall it be henceforth with every one who leaps over my walls.' Romulus thus became sole ruler, and the city was called after him, its founder.

LIVY

from Hindu Myths

TVAṢṬṚ had twin children, Saraṇyū and Triśiras ['Three-headed']. He himself gave Saraṇyū in marriage to Vivasvat. Then Yama and Yami were born of Saraṇyū and Vivasvat; these two also were twins, but Yama was the elder of the two. Without her husband's knowledge, Saraṇyū created a woman identical to herself; entrusting the twins to the latter, she became a mare and went away. But in ignorance of this, Vivasvat begat upon the woman a son, Manu, who became a royal sage with energy like that of Vivasvat. Then he became aware that Saraṇyū had departed in the form of a mare, and he went quickly after the daughter of Tvaṣṭṛ, having become a horse of the same qualities. And Saraṇyū, knowing that it was Vivasvat in the form of a horse, approached him for sexual intercourse, and he mounted her. But in their haste the semen fell on the ground, and the mare smelled that semen because she desired to become pregnant. From that semen that was inhaled two youths were born, called Nāsatya

347

['From-the-nose'] and Dasra ['Performing-wondrous-deeds'], famed
as the Aśvins.

WENDY DONIGER O′FLAHERTY

---

from The Two Brothers

WHEN absolutely nothing as yet existed, neither heaven, nor earth,
nor other creatures such as might be in heaven or upon earth – there
was one named Zurvan, which may be rendered 'fate' or 'fortune.'
For a thousand years he had offered sacrifice that he might perhaps
have a son who would be named Ohrmazd, and who would make the
heavens and the earth and all that they contain. He had thus offered
sacrifice for a thousand years when he began to reflect, saying: 'Of
what good use is this sacrifice which I am offering? Shall I have a son,
Ohrmazd? Or do I make these efforts in vain?' And as soon as he had
reflected thus, Ohrmazd and Ahriman were conceived in the womb of
their mother: Ohrmazd by virtue of the offered sacrifice, and Ahriman
by virtue of the aforesaid doubt. Then therefore, having taken account
of this, Zurvan said: 'Behold, there are two sons in the womb, and the
one of them, whichever he may be, who comes to me the sooner, him
will I make king.'

Ohrmazd, knowing the intentions of their father, revealed them to
Ahriman, saying: 'Zurvan our father has planned that whichever of us
comes to him the sooner shall be made king.' Ahriman having heard
this pierced through the womb, came forth, and presented himself
before his father.

And Zurvan, having seen him, knew not who he might be and
asked, 'You, who are you?' And he answered, 'I am your son.'
Zurvan said to him, 'My son is sweet smelling and radiant, and you,
you are benighted and stinking.' And when they had exchanged these
words, Ohrmazd was born at his time, radiant and sweet smelling, and
came and presented himself before Zurvan. And, having seen him,
Zurvan knew that this was his son Ohrmazd for whom he had offered
sacrifice. And taking the *barsom* [a bundle of twigs, being the scepter
of high priesthood] which he held in his hand and with which he had
offered sacrifice, he gave it to Ohrmazd saying, 'Until now it is I who
have offered sacrifice for you; henceforth it is you who will offer it
for me.'

And as soon as Zurvan had given the *barsom* to Ohrmazd and blessed him, Ahriman came before Zurvan and said to him, 'Have you not made the following vow: Whichever of my two sons comes to me the first, him I will make king?' And Zurvan, so as not to violate his word, said to Ahriman, 'O false and malicious one the kingdom shall be accorded to you for nine thousand years, but Ohrmazd I shall make king above you; and after nine thousand years Ohrmazd shall reign, and he shall do all that he wishes.'

Thereupon Ohrmazd and Ahriman set themselves to the making of creatures. And all that Ohrmazd created was good and right, but whatever Ahriman made was evil and twisted.

(translated by R. C. Zaehner)

---

from Parallels

OUR responses to looking at twins are described by the powers of the magical twins dreamed of by the mediaeval theologian Albertus Magnus: in one twin, the evil on his right side unlocked all bolted doors to the right, while the virtue in his twin's left side closed all *open* doors. Twins unleash a flood of associations, each of which triggers its converse . . . [They] induce a vertigo of the self: they are indisputably two, inescapably one, both and neither at once.

TED WOLNER

---

from Sisters: A Chapbook

LUCINDA and Dorothea were twin sisters, and so much like each other when they grew up, that it was difficult for anyone, not intimately acquainted with them, to know the one from the other when asunder. They were in person tall and genteel, their motions majestic and their countenance lovely as aurora: the roses and lilies were displayed on their cheeks; their skin was alabaster and their teeth ivory; in short, one could imagine, on viewing them, that Nature has exhausted all her skill in forming these lovely twins. Their parents dressed them alike, gave them the same education; and neither one nor the other had the least reason to complain of any particularity in either indulgences or corrections.

It would seem as though Nature took delight in sporting with her own works, and spoiling, by one single fault, the beauty of the whole. Though they were alike in their external form, they differed widely in the disposition of their minds. Lucinda was cheerful, affable and good-natured; and possessed all those internal accomplishments which set off beauty with the greatest lustre; Dorothea was gloomy, proud and ill-natured; and so proud of her charms as to look upon the rest of her sex with an eye of indifference and contempt. It is not, therefore, to be wondered at, that her bosom was the seat of hatred and revenge.

As they grew up, they engrossed the attention of all the gentry in the neighbourhood, from which they received frequent invitations. The behaviour of Lucinda procured for her the esteem and friendship of all she approached, while those of Dorothea gave only uneasiness and disgust. Lucinda, perceiving her reputation daily increased, while that of her sister diminished, she grew extremely uneasy for the consequences, and being alone one day with her sister, thus spoke to her; 'My dear Dorothea, it gives me inexpressible concern to see you fall in the opinion of the world. Why will you give way to the warmth of your temper, and not endeavour to curb that which distorts every feature in your lovely face? Why will you make those your enemies who would gladly be your best friends? My sister cannot but be sensible that I bear a part in, and feel much for, the disgraces she brings on herself'. Dorothea, instead of improving from this tender and wise admonition, fell in a rage, and asked what right she had to scrutinize her conduct.

From this time, Dorothea treated her sister with the utmost indifference: but the time soon approached when that indifference was changed into hatred and revenge. The virtues, and universal approbation of Lucinda, attracted the attention of a gentleman in the neighbourhood, who soon conceived for her the sincerest passion. Dorothea, perceiving the attention this gentleman paid her sister, made use of all her arts to rival her, but in vain. The day arrived, which united Lucinda to the most amiable of men: but their joy was dampened by the disappearance of Dorothea, who was nowhere to be found.

After some months had passed, a letter came, directed to Lucinda, in which she was informed, that a young lady, at a few miles distance, requested to speak with her immediately. Lucinda's carriage was ordered immediately: she set off, and found Dorothea almost expiring, who, on seeing Lucinda, endeavoured to recover her spirits, and uttered these last works. 'You see, Lucinda (for I will not dare to call you by the tender name of sister), a wretch, whose misery flows from your happiness. Unable to bear the prospect of your approaching marriage, I retired to this place, where I have been gradually declining ever since, preyed on by the worm of hatred and disappointed revenge. I die a just sacrifice to my own hateful crimes: may heaven and Lucinda forgive me!' Having uttered these words, she bid adieu to this vain world.

ANON., 1790

from The Sadeian Woman

THE life of Juliette exists in a dialectical relationship to that of her sister. The vision of the inevitable prosperity of vice, as shown in her triumphant career, and the vision of the inevitable misfortunes of virtue that Justine's life offers do not cancel one another out; rather, they mutually reflect and complement one another, like a pair of mirrors. Each story has the same moral, offered at many levels, which may be summed up as: the comfort of one class depends on the misery of another class. There is no room in Sade's impeccable logic for the well-upholstered wishful thinking that would like the poor to have more money if that did not mean we ourselves had less. To be a woman is to be automatically at a disadvantage in a man's world, just like being poor, but to be a woman is a more easily remedied condition. If she abandons the praxis of femininity, then it is easy enough to enter the class of the rich, the men, provided one enters it on the terms of that class.

The life of Juliette proposes a method of profane mastery of the instruments of power. She is a woman who acts according to the precepts and also the practice of a man's world and so she does not suffer. Instead, she causes suffering.

'It was no accident that the Marquis de Sade chose heroines and not heroes,' said Guillaume Apollinaire. 'Justine is woman as she has been until now, enslaved, miserable and less than human; her opposite, Juliette, represents the woman whose advent he anticipated, a figure of whom minds have as yet no conception, who is rising out of mankind, who will have wings and who will renew the world.' Seventy years ago, Apollinaire could equate Juliette with the New Woman; it is not so easy to do so today, although Juliette remains a model for women, in some ways. She is rationality personified and leaves no single cell of her brain unused. She will never obey the fallacious promptings of her heart. Her mind functions like a computer programmed to produce two results for herself – financial profit and libidinal gratification. By the use of her reason, an intellectual apparatus women themselves are still inclined to undervalue, she rids herself of some of the more crippling aspects of femininity; but she is a New Woman in the mode of irony.

She is, just as her sister is, a description of a type of female behaviour rather than a model of female behaviour and her triumph is just as ambivalent as is Justine's disaster. Justine is the thesis, Juliette the antithesis; both are without hope and neither pays any heed to a future in which might lie the possibility of a synthesis of their modes of being, neither submissive nor aggressive, capable of both thought and feeling.

ANGELA CARTER

DROMIO OF EPHESUS Methinks you are my glass, and not my brother:
I see by you I am a sweet-faced youth.
Will you walk into to see their gossiping?
DROMIO OF SYRACUSE Not I sir; you are my elder.
DROMIO OF EPHESUS That's a question: how shall we try it?
DROMIO OF SY. We'll draw cuts for the senior: till then lead thou first.
DROMIO OF EPH. Nay, then, thus:
We came into the world like brother and brother:
And now lets go hand in hand, not one before another.
WILLIAM SHAKESPEARE, *The Comedy of Errors*

---

from The Banquet

JUPITER, with some difficulty having desired silence, at length spoke. 'I think,' said he, 'I have contrived a method by which we may, by rendering the human race more feeble, quell the insolence which they

352

exercise, without proceeding to their utter destruction. I will cut each of them in half; and so they will at once be weaker and more useful on account of their numbers. They shall walk upright on two legs. If they show any more insolence, and will not keep quiet, I will cut them up in half again, so they shall go hopping on one leg.'

So saying, he cut human beings in half, as people cut eggs before they salt them, or as I have seen eggs cut with hairs. He ordered Apollo to take each one as he cut him, and turn his face and half his neck towards the operation, so that by contemplating it he might become more cautious and humble; and then, to cure him, Apollo turned the face round, and drawing the skin upon what we now call the belly, like a contracted pouch, and leaving one opening, that which is called the navel, tied it in the middle. He then smoothed many other wrinkles, and moulded the breast with much such an instrument as the leather-cutters use to smooth the skins upon the block. He left only a few wrinkles in the belly, near the navel, to serve as a record of its former adventure. Immediately after this division, as each desired to possess the other half of himself, these divided people threw their arms around and embraced each other, seeking to grow together; and from this resolution to do nothing without the other half, they died of hunger and weakness: when one half died and the other was left alive, that which was thus left sought the other and folded it to its bosom; whether that half were an entire woman (for we now call it a woman) or a man; and thus they perished. But Jupiter, pitying them, thought of another contrivance. In this manner is generation now produced, by the union of male and female; so that from the embrace of a man and woman the race is propagated.

From this period, mutual love has naturally existed between human beings, that reconciler and bond of union of their original nature, which seeks to make two one, and to heal the divided nature of man. Every one of us is thus the half of what may be properly termed a man, and like a pselta cut in two, is the imperfect portion of an entire whole, perpetually necessitated to seek the half belonging to him.

PLATO (translated by P. B. Shelley)

---

from On Love

THOU demandest what is love? It is that powerful attraction towards all that we conceive, or fear, or hope beyond ourselves, when we find within our own thoughts the chasm of an insufficient void, and seek to awaken in all things that are, a community with what we experience within ourselves. If we reason, we would be understood; if we imagine, we would that the airy children of our brain were born anew within another's; if we feel, we would that another's nerves should vibrate to our own, that the beams of their eyes should kindle at once and mix and melt into our own, that lips of motionless ice should not reply to lips quivering and burning with the heart's best blood. This is Love. This is the bond and the sanction which connects not only man with man, but with everything which exists. We are born into the world, and there is something within us which, from the instant that we live, more and more thirsts after its likeness. It is probably in correspondence with this law that the infant drains milk from the bosom of its mother; this propensity develops itself with the development of our nature. We dimly see within our intellectual nature a miniature as it were of our entire self, yet deprived of all that we condemn or despise, the ideal prototype of everything excellent or lovely that we are capable of conceiving as belonging to the nature of man. Not only the portrait of our external being, but an assemblage of the minutest particles of which our nature is composed; a mirror whose surface reflects only the forms of purity and brightness; a soul within our soul that describes a circle around its proper paradise, which pain, and sorrow, and evil dare not overleap. To this we eagerly refer all sensations, thirsting that they should resemble or correspond with it. The discovery of its antitype; the meeting with an understanding capable of clearly estimating our own; an imagination which should enter into and seize upon the subtle and delicate peculiarities which we have delighted to cherish and unfold in secret; with a frame whose nerves, like the chords of two exquisite lyres, strung to the accompaniment of one delightful voice, vibrate with the vibrations of our own; and of a combination of all these in such proportion as the type within demands; this is the invisible and unattainable point to which Love tends; and to attain which, it urges forth the powers of man to arrest the faintest shadow of that, without the possession of which there is no rest nor respite to the heart over which it rules.

PERCY BYSSHE SHELLEY

The fact is that the ordinary child, born without a twin, the single child, cannot get over his loneliness ... The single adolescent breaks out of the family circle and seeks a partner with whom to try to form the couple it dreams of ... but ... germinate adolescence ... is, to a great extent the opposite of the non-twin's adolescence. Because while the single adolescent seeks fumblingly, far from home, right across the world for this imperfect partner, the twin finds him face to face from the start in the person of his twin brother.

MICHEL TOURNIER, *Gemini*

A DOUBLE ACT BUT DEFINITELY NOT A CIRCUS TURN

There is one problem ... which I must admit is of our own making; in our adult lives we expect of our friends and partners what we receive from each other, a relationship that is more profound than between parents and children, most siblings and probably many couples.

EDWARD WELSH, *Weekend Telegraph*, 5 February 1994

from The Twin Brothers

I was shearing in a field adjoining my uncle's dwelling when a dizziness seized me. My body was enervated; my faculties refused to perform their functions; and to all appearances the soul had forsaken its tenement of clay. In a moment, mirth was changed to sadness, my mind which was at the instant of affliction anxiously occupied in study, was for a space annihilated, and every feature wore the semblance of death. My length was measured upon the earth; one hand clenched the sickle, the other the cut grain; and over me my fellow labourers stood weeping and sorrowing ... In about an hour, however, I awoke ... to the great joy of my friends; and I felt not and showed not the least remains of a visitation so unaccountable.

Some readers may perhaps say there is nothing extraordinary in the above occurrence; they may say . . . that it was a fainting fit . . . or be inclined to give it some other names. But what will such people divine when I inform them that my brother-twin during the same afternoon when we were 15 miles asunder was afflicted in exactly the same manner?

JOHN DIXON, 1826

---

from Charles Maurice and Edward Julius Detmold

THE Detmold twins were born in Putney in 1883, at the home of an uncle. Shortly afterwards the twins and their parents moved to Hampstead with this uncle, Dr Edward Barton Shuldham, in whose home they were brought up.

[. . .] They started drawing at a very early age and soon showed a precocious talent. Apart from six months at the Hampstead Conservatoire they were to receive no formal training. Frequent visits to the zoo and the Natural History Museum helped to give their drawing a direction and by the time they were eleven it was obvious that their futures lay in the field of natural history illustration.

[. . .] In 1897 Edward Burne Jones, an old schoolfriend of Dr Shuldham, met the twins and later wrote about them;

I've met with two geniuses. Of course there's no knowing whether anything may come of it, but they might be a great comfort in the future. They're English, they're boys of fourteen. One has painted a stag beetle quite perfectly. Every hair is done, and the light upon it and the shadows cast on it and all the flatnesses and every kind of shape of it.

They are twins, and one's called Teddy and the other Maurice. And one's an idealist and the other's a realist.

They can't bear to read, won't read if they can help it, it gives them no pleasure, which is quite right, but seeing they can't have enough of, they can't look at a thing long enough. That's all good isn't it?

They were such funny little fellows, being twins they both do just the same things and use just the same words.

One of their drawings was of a brass pot, and all the room reflected in it, and the little chap himself drawing at the table, and very like him too.

There's no knowing where this gift comes from, it's very wonderful. They've got every equipment for being very great artists indeed.

They bought a printing press and started producing their own work, a portfolio of eight proof etchings was quickly sold out. They exhibited at the Royal Institute of Painters in Watercolour, the English Art Club and the International Exhibition in Kensington.

In his article in the 'Print Collectors Quarterly', art critic Campbell Dodgson wrote of their work;

> The etchings had always been the separate work of one or other of the twins, though, in several cases, Edward had etched a plate after a drawing by Maurice and vice versa. But in 1899 began what is the most curious and interesting phenomenon in their joint career, the collaboration of both brothers in producing a single plate . . . and their joint labour resulted, in some of the later and more accomplished plates, in an effect so completely finished and harmonious, that it would be almost incredible, but for their direct assurance, that more than one brain should have conceived, or one hand executed, a work so completely at unity with itself . . . The 'Long-Eared Bat' . . . in technical execution the finest and most wonderful of all. It was drawn in pencil by Edward, etched chiefly by Maurice, and bitten-in by Edward. No reproduction could render successfully the wonderful lightness of the thin lines, so subtly adapted to every variety of texture, bone, fur, and skin.

. . . I do not remember in the History of Art another case in which twin brothers, sharing an equal talent, lived and worked together in close companionship as two young Englishmen, Charles Maurice and Edward Julius did till a few years ago. They seemed as one soul divided between two bodies, inspired by the same ideal, using the same means of expression, possessing the same deftness of eye and quickness of hand . . . In conversation it was curious to notice how one brother would begin one sentence and the other finish it, as if even in thought they were nearer to one another than two ordinary beings and one mind knew instinctively the working of the other. The normal opening of a sentence with them was 'we' not 'I.'

NEIL GIBSON

[*Both brothers committed suicide; more than fifty years apart*]

If you take two watches with similar cases and similar works, then you can take the wheel out of one and exchange it for the other and the watches will go on ticking in just the same harmony. And it is the same way with twins.

CHARLES CRAILL, My Twin Joe

from On the Black Hill

THE twins' first memory – a shared memory which both remembered equally well – was of the day they were stung by the wasp.

They were perched on high-chairs at the tea-table. It must have been teatime because the sun was streaming in from the west, bouncing off the table-cloth and making them blink. It must have been late in the year, perhaps as late as October, when wasps are drowsy. Outside the window, a magpie hung from the sky, and bunches of red rowanberries thrashed in the gale. Inside, the slabs of bread-and-butter glistened the colour of primroses. Mary was spooning egg-yolk into Lewis's mouth and Benjamin, in a fit of jealousy, was waving his hands to attract attention when his left hand hit the wasp, and was stung.

Mary rummaged in the medicine cupboard for cotton-wool and ammonia, dabbed the hand and, as it swelled and turned scarlet, said soothingly, 'Be brave, little man! Be brave!'

But Benjamin did not cry. He simply pursed his mouth and turned his sad grey eyes on his brother. For it was Lewis, not he, who was whimpering with pain, and stroking his own left hand as if it were a wounded bird.

BRUCE CHATWIN

from Cassandra at the Wedding

I got my thumbnail under the tape and released one side of the lid and folded it back. Inside there was a sea of white tissue paper, systematically crumpled around the edges, and with a pretty pink sales slip on top. I picked up the slip, folded it and pushed it down along the edge of the box, out of sight, because I didn't want anybody's opinion of the dress to be influenced by what it cost. Then I broke a seal and unfolded the paper. The dress lay there quietly and unobtrusively white against the white paper, but with extreme elegance and style. Easily the best dress I'd had since the seventh grade.

I think I was expecting Judith to whistle and granny to chirp, but neither one of them made any sound at all; so I took hold of the shoulders and lifted it out of the box and told them it was the kind of dress that doesn't give the best account of itself lying in a box. Or hanging on a hanger, for that matter. The way it fits is the thing. And the way it's made.

'This back pleat, for instance,' I said. I turned it over and showed granny the beautiful tailor's tacks that held the pleat at the top and the bottom, and granny looked and didn't say a thing.

'Pure silk,' I said, 'feel the weight of it. It crunches.'

I was beginning to feel like a saleswoman making a hard sale to an unconvinced customer. Two unconvinced customers. And when I looked away from the dress I saw them looking at each other in a way that was hard to interpret. It was as if they were sharing a private joke. And they were, of course, but I had no idea what it was. All I could tell was that something was wrong with either me or my choice.

'It's obvious enough you don't like it,' I said, and Jude sat there looking first at the dress and then at gran with this puzzled and puzzling look on her face, a sort of combination of astonishment and dismay.

'I didn't say I didn't like it,' she said in a rather low, unemphatic voice. 'I'm crazy about it. I was crazy about it before I ever saw yours.'

She stopped and sat there looking somehow baffled, and then looked at gran and said: 'Go ahead, Granny, you tell her.'

Granny didn't look baffled. I hadn't seen her look so excited in years.

'Oh Cassie, this is rich,' she said, 'after all these years of you two refusing to dress alike.'

I stopped breathing, and then started again. By rich, our grandmother usually means side-splittingly amusing. She says it where other people say this will kill you, and I got the idea clearly enough, what I'd done wrong, and where my gross error lay, without letting myself consciously believe it. I let everything get vague, the dress, the voice, the voices, and I sat there sullen in my tied-together tank suit and considered the part chance plays in a life, or two lives, and how little control can be brought to it. I also thought about brandy.

'Let's leave God out of this,' I heard Jude say, and I sat up straighter and asked her what she'd been talking about.

'Where've you been?' Jude said, and I told her here, but not listening, and then she told me that granny had been saying it all went to prove that God had meant us to dress alike all the time. How else after twenty-four years of carefully avoiding any duplication in clothes could we have come up with the same dress, in two separate cities, all independently? And for the same occasion.

Granny was sitting at the foot of my bed now, across from Jude, looking truly triumphant. And vindicated.

'Goodness knows *I* always wanted to dress you alike, and I never could understand what Jane had against it. Or Jim either.'

'I believe,' I said, quite stiffly and slowly, so that she'd listen, 'they were concerned to have us become individuals, each of us in our own right, and not be confused in ourselves, nor confusing to other people.'

'That's right,' Judith said, like an amen.

'Oh I've heard them explain it a hundred times,' gran said, and she sighed. 'I used to bring you the dearest outfits, everything alike right down to the little socks and panties, and every time I'd do it they'd make me send them right back.'

She sighed again, and I felt a light twinge in an old war wound. I could still remember having to say goodbye to some very pretty presents, and crying with Jude after they'd been sent back.

We looked at each other now while granny went on with variations on her theme – ending where it began, with how rich it was for us to have chosen, separately, the very same wedding dresses.

DOROTHY BAKER

---

from My Twin and I

I sat on, while she went off into a biting exposition of the wickedness and folly of spiritualists . . . The true life of man was on this earth. Men and women did not return to earth in the spirit to console their friends, but in the flesh, to continue the evolution and expansion of their race until it filled the Universe and the Creator of Mankind was merged in the Creator of All Things. To this end, a great many Hierarchs walked the world *incognito*, recognised only by those who were, as one might say, working their passages to join the Hierarchy [. . .] It was towards this end that Roz had been ordered by her Hierarch to come to Paris. Departing for Athens, where she was to undertake an intensive course of development, she would leave behind her a nucleus of intellectuals from whom would spread further nuclei in the acceptance of the truth.

Her audience purred, enjoying the word 'intellectuals'. How, somebody inquired, did Hierarchs communicate with one another? Did they enjoy superhuman powers? They had powers of clairvoyance and of magnetism, Roz replied, but to no greater degree than many other highly-evolved human beings, which, after all, was what they were. They communicated with one another and with their pupils by means of telepathy.

Roz stood to one side of the stage in her dramatic get-up, her hands clasped under her chin, earnestly searching her audience from eye-sockets made huge by the strange lighting. She had, she said immediate proof of her mentor's telepathic powers. As some of her audience knew, she possessed a sister, a twin sister . . .

Every muscle in me went into a state of cold refusal. Roz could not have seen me, sitting towards the back in this dim light, but she knew I was there, and she intended to make capital of her knowledge. Someone had observed the resemblance between us – the woman in the brown monk's robe, who had looked at me so curiously, spoken to me and gone away? Well, I should have to go with what dignity I could through whatever farcical sister-act Roz now intended to stage. Her oddly-lit face, which seemed to have huge cheek-bones and no chin, was full of tender yearning, confound her! I sat there.

A twin sister, continued Roz seductively, whom she had not seen for a long time. (Liar!) She had longed to see this sister, but she had been told by her mentor that she must not go to England. She had implored him to bring about a meeting, and he had promised that if her sister had a mind open to receive his messages, she should be here. And here – here, indeed, she was!

Roz made an appealing gesture somewhat in my direction, she looked somewhat towards me. I knew she could not see me, but heads were beginning to turn, there was a buzz of anticipation and excitement, and there seemed nothing for it but to stand up.

'Well, Roz,' I said dryly. 'I am here, you see.' I could at the moment willingly have killed her for taking this mean advantage of what I temporarily chose to see as my affection for her.

'*Ronnie!*' she cried with histrionic ecstasy, and held out both her bare, strong arms.

IANTHE JERROLD

Somewhere I have a real twin in this world. J can't be my real twin. My real twin was born the exact same time as me, has my rising sign, my looks, my ways, my dreams, my ambitions. He or she will have my weaknesses, failures, opinions. All this makes a twin – no differences. I can't stand differences.

JENNIFER GIBBONS. Quoted in: Marjorie Wallace,
The Silent Twins

Nothing in the world is single,
All things by a law divine
With one another's being mingle
Then why not I with thine?

PERCY BYSSHE SHELLEY

There is an electricity of magnetism between persons of congenial tastes and studies which sometimes declares itself with the suddenness of the lightning flash and this occurred between Mr Rameses and me. We understood each other at the first exchange of looks, even before words gave expression to the ideas which prompted them.

Is it not a reasonable and encouraging thought that souls may be allotted to one another in pairs for mutual love and helping on their long pilgrimage?

ANON., *Twin Souls; or the strange experiences of Mr Rameses*, 1887

---

from The Epic of Gilgamesh

NOW Gilgamesh got up to tell his dream to his mother, Ninsun, one of the wise gods. 'Mother, last night I had a dream. I was full of joy, the young heroes were round me and I walked through the night under the stars of the firmament, and one, a meteor of the stuff of Anu, fell down from heaven. I tried to lift it but it proved too heavy. All the people of Uruk came round to see it, the common people jostled and the nobles thronged to kiss its feet; and to me its attraction was like the love of woman. They helped me, I braced my forehead and I raised it with thongs and brought it to you, and you yourself pronounced it my brother.'

Then Ninsun, who is well-beloved and wise, said to Gilgamesh, 'This star of heaven which descended like a meteor from the sky; which you tried to lift, but found too heavy, when you tried to move it it would not budge, and so you brought it to my feet; I made it for you, a goad and spur, and you were drawn as though to a woman. This is the strong comrade, the one who brings help to his friend in his need. He is the strongest of wild creatures, the stuff of Anu; born in the grass-lands and the wild hills reared him; when you see him you will be glad; you will love him as a woman and he will never forsake you. This is the meaning of the dream.'

Gilgamesh said, 'Mother, I dreamed a second dream. In the streets of strong-walled Uruk there lay an axe; the shape of it was strange and the people thronged round. I saw it and was glad. I bent down, deeply drawn towards it; I loved it like a woman and wore it at my side.' Ninsun answered, 'That axe, which you saw, which drew you so powerfully like love of a woman, that is the comrade whom I give you, and he will come in his strength like one of the host of heaven. He is the brave companion who rescues his friend in necessity.' Gilgamesh said to his mother, 'A friend, a counsellor has come to me from Enlil, and now I shall befriend and counsel him.' So Gilgamesh told his dreams; and the harlot retold them to Enkidu.

ANON., trs. N. K. Sanders

363

from Finding One's Twin

BEGINNING in the fall of 1983, I lived for fourteen months in Iragbiji, Osun State, Nigeria, with the support of a Fulbright research grant. My time was divided between becoming familiar with the Yoruba culture and completing a body of sculptural work.

My original plan had been to be in Oshogbo, but it turned out not to suit my needs, as the artists I had arranged to work with there regarded me as an art collector rather than as an art maker. I was interested in bridging the gap that exists in my own Western culture between art and everyday life, and I had come to Nigeria to learn from the Yoruba, who make less of a distinction between life and art. I knew no one in Iragbiji, but I recognized that this place retained the spirit of that interplay.

Soon after my arrival, I met Adeleke Sangoyoyin, whom everyone there knew as 'Sango.' Later, he described our meeting this way.

> We first met in Nigeria just like saying 'Ekabo' (good morning). No one introduced ourselves to ourselves. One morning I went out of my door and I saw him turning at the front of my house in his car. I said to myself, 'What is this? It's a white man.' So I said hello and he said hello. Then we greeted ourselves and I introduced myself as a farmer and artist and he introduced himself as an artist. This is how we met.

In Sango, I had found an individual who considered the myths, folklore, and everyday vocabulary of his people of equal importance to his formal artistic tradition.

Within the first twenty-four hours. Sango took me to visit Iyalode Ajibola, a town elder and head priestess of the cult of the orisha Obaluaye. Sango had spent over ten years with her studying traditional practices. He introduced me and asked her to consult Obaluaye about the nature of our relationship. Her interpretation at that time was that we were 'brothers.'

There is a Yoruba proverb which says, in effect, 'Wherever you go, there you are.' We all carry with us a personal history. Mine has included the untimely accidental drowning of my only younger brother.

My brother and I were born one year apart. Having lived in a rural area with few peers, we were both best friends and rivals. Our personalities were a contrast. He tended to be impulsive while I approached life more cautiously. When we grew up, my brother wanted to be a fireman; I was undecided.

When I was ten, my brother and I had been participating in a summer swim program. One afternoon, I had playfully dared him to swim in the deep end of the pool. An hour later, his body was found on the pool's bottom. In my young mind, I blamed myself for his having drowned. Over the years I have struggled with the guilt of being responsible for his death. Unavoidably, I brought to Iragbiji this long-buried pain.

Over time Iyalode Ajibola, the Obaluaye priestess, modified her interpretation and identified us as 'twins.' In Yoruba tradition, everyone is considered to have a double in heaven, and the birth of twins is seen as earthly evidence of this spiritual double. Each twin is attributed contrasting personalities. The first to be born is referred to as 'Taiwo.' He or she is considered to be quick-witted and impatient, a risk taker. The second born, 'Kehinde,' moves more slowly and with more wisdom. The first born is considered the junior to the second born.

According to Sango, 'Ibeji is an orisha in our place. If you have twins, you should worship them as orisha. It's a big gift. You have to do special things for them.' Among the Yoruba, the incidence of twin births is high. If one or both of the twins die, the mother is expected to have the local carver make a wood surrogate (*ere ibeji*). This carving is then clothed, washed, and fed much as would be a living infant. The duration of this care is determined through divination. The Obaluaye priestess told us, 'Everyone has a spirit twin. When you meet yourself, you will be happy all the time. The two of you have met yourselves.' She identified me as 'Taiwo,' the junior, and Sango as 'Kehinde,' the senior.

In naming Sango as my twin, I was being invited to consider him my spiritual mirror image. Sango embodies a gentle spirit. He approaches life in a slow, deliberate manner. His typical refrain to me is, 'You have a good idea, but let us think about it for some time.' I, on the other hand, usually want to do things immediately. Surprisingly, my adopted Yoruba community had recognized in me qualities I had always attributed to my brother. The emotional search for reunion that had been set in motion with the death of my brother was being reflected in my emerging relationship with Sango.

Sango and I grew close. I helped him cultivate his fields, hunt, and carry water. He assisted me in gathering materials for my sculptures and acquainting me in the ways of his culture. Toward the end of my stay, we decided to collaborate. Our first sculptures were made of indigenous natural materials we found in and around Iragbiji. More recently, working in my studio in Chicago during one of Sango's visits, we have begun to incorporate industrial materials. Our latest projects have been paired objects that reflect our twinship. Neither of us dictates the design but we work in a collaborative process of continuous give and take. The eagerness and spontaneity of 'Taiwo' is balanced by the wisdom and carefulness of 'Kehinde.'

Twinship is a mirror. The gift of the twin is to reveal aspects of ourselves that have gone unseen. In Sango was reflected my relationship to my brother and the forgotten richness of fraternal love. In finding Sango, I am reminded of myself.

JAMES ELNISKI

---

from Twin Souls

'AH! doubtless, but it is of our present, this current life, I want to talk. I am not so much in the clouds, or, I should say, not so often in the skies, as you are. You have passed through just twenty-three years as Dorothy Verity. I want you to promise me you will change your name to Unite on the tenth of April, in the very next year to come.'

An ecstatic thrill, such as can be experienced by certain lovers only, passed through both, as the magnetic circuit was completed by her right hand, lying loosely in his left, being pressed by him. This transporting elevation of mutual altruism is possible only to those of different sexes. It is the touch of the ethereal male and female polarities, unsullied by the least alloy of selfishness. Although, whilst we are in the flesh, everything that arises becomes cognizant to us only by the media of our mechanical structure, there are many who will recognize that the exquisite consciousness has not all to do with the chemical organism. The temporary rapture has its origin in the unseen forces, and, although it passes, it is not without an abiding influence. The male and female principles form a trinity together with a higher dimension.

'Is it not premature to make an appointment so long in advance?'
remonstrated Dorothy.

ANON., 1906

'Some may be disposed to fight shy of the idea of Twin Souls,
lest it should be made a screen for attractions which were rather
of the flesh than of the spirit.'

ANON., *Duality Eternal*, 1927

The Mathematics of Encounter

Two never-ever-will-be
lovers each
Thatched in a thicket of one-
liness, huddled in onlyhood,
teach eye to perilous eye and contract
in an absolute gaze, in a clasping
of I's, a wedding. In that (ah marginal)
marrying of marrows, flesh blooms and bells,
blood shimmers and arrows, bones melt
and meld, loins lock.
In that look's-lasting love is resolved
in one-plus-one, dissolved again in two, these two absolved,
and the equation solved.

ISABELLA GARDNER

from A Valediction Forbidding Mourning

Our two soules therefore, which are one,
Though I must goe, endure not yet

A breach but an expansion,
Like gold to ayery thinnesse beate.

If they be two, they are two so
As stiffe twin compassess are two,
Thy soule the fixt foot, makes no show
To move, but doth if the other doe.

And though it in the center sit,
Yet when the other far doth rome,
It leanes and hearkens after it,
And grows erect, as that comes home . . .

JOHN DONNE

———————

7

SHADOWS, REFLECTIONS
AND OTHER DOUBLES

ও&

C ONTEMPLATING THE vexed ambiguities of shadows, reflections, doubles, I went to the Tate Gallery in London and
re-explored that unsettling painting reproduced on the cover of
this book; *The Cholmondley Ladies*. Dating from the early seventeenth
century, it is a picture at once straightforward and weird. Two
apparently identical women sit stiffly upright in bed, swaddled babies
held in their right arms. Each is wearing, at first glance, identical
lace-edged head-dresses, ruffs, hooped sleeves, made of some kind of
whitish stuff. Twins, you'd think. But the inscription confirms no such
perception. Two ladies of the Cholmondley family, it says, who were
born the same day, married the same day, brought to bed of the same
day. The word 'sisters' appears nowhere, let alone the word 'twin'. In
any case, born the same day but not twins, they couldn't have been
sisters, only cousins. Nor could they have been identical twins; the
one on the left and her baby have blue eyes; the one on the right
and her baby brown. Once you notice that difference, you begin to
notice others; the women wear different jewellery; the patterns of the
lace edgings on ruff and bonnet are different; the embroidered silk of
their bodices is different; above all, the expressions on their faces are
different – the brown-eyed one is much grimmer than the other. It is
hard for me not to be solipsistic in the face of such images, and yet

again, sighing this time, I am reminded of me and my sister. Yet, the existence of such differences within likeness, has far wider significance. Not all doubles – or doubles so-called – are twins. As these two may well not be twins. Doubled, however, they demonstrate that there is no such thing as perfect doubleness. In the seemingly identical the differences are quite as significant – and in some ways more telling – than the likenesses.

Attempts by twins, of course, to use such differences to make separate identities are not always successful; they may result merely in a distorted reflection of that other self. (I think, sadly, how my early taste for listening to classical music led my sister to turn her back on her own talent for performing it.) Even when differences are not so stressed, the tension between like and unlike remains, as with any doubled image of anything which is and is not what it relates to. A shadow, for instance, is the person who casts it, but at the same time by definition different – Hans Anderson's story, *The Shadow* – inspired by an early nineteenth-century story, Albert Chamisso's *Peter Schlemihl* – is based on such a premise. It is different according to the time of day; at times it is invisible. Its possessor forgets she or he possesses such a thing – unless the shadow is figurative and takes the form of a twin, in which case it is harder to forget; though when the shadow is a twin and elsewhere, others may be fooled into thinking there is none, just as they may never suspect the presence of the internal self-shadow harboured within so many breasts. Yet everybody has a shadow of sorts. Two shadows, in fact – the one seen in sunlight, the one felt within the psyche. Here again twin experience shades into common experience.

Still more to the point are reflections – self-images also common to everyone. Identical twins, though, not only have mirror images like the rest of us, they see themselves reflected in another person. This has interesting implications for their sense of identity, as Dorothy Burlingham's researches show. Stories of twins seeing a mirror image and mistaking it for their twin – or vice versa – abound. It makes them come up with depressingly cute yet sometimes touching statements of their own, reinforcing the stereotype the world so adores: the most common version of which is – I don't need to look in the mirror to see what I look like; I only have to look at my twin. But the fact is that, here again, absolute identity between image and reflection is not only a myth but a false one; mirror images are not identical, by definition. Moreover, the differences are actually dangerous – or would be if met with in the same universe, since in terms of physics, right-hand universe opposes left-hand universe on the other side of the glass. If Alice really had gone through her looking glass, matter thereby meeting anti-matter, the ensuing explosion would have been the equivalent, weight for weight, of the dropping of a hydrogen bomb. On a mundane level, too, the image of ourselves in the mirror is different from our non-reflected ones in ways at once so odd and so indefinable that the experience of seeing the mirrored image of someone we are familiar with in the flesh can be deeply uncomfortable (a fact capitalised on by writers of ghost and horror stories!).

Lacan in his convoluted way sums it up; the mirror image, he says, 'Symbolises mental permanence of the I, at the same time as it prefigures its alienating destination.' By which he means, I think, that, while seeing oneself in the mirror identifies the onlooker to her- or himself, at the same time, by splitting the self into reflector and reflection it prefigures the self-division that can lead to psychic disintegration. A similar perception must lie behind the reluctance of the Chinese to let children see themselves in the mirror until they are old enough to have a true sense of themselves. My 'twin instinct' feels that probably they are right. For the twin ambiguities – that which unifies also divides while divided identity makes it hard to define any identity at all – is precisely the paradox that twins embody. All of which sets me wondering, too, on the psychic effects of our being so surrounded by mirrors: is anorexia nervosa merely the pathological end of general dis-ease? Mirrorless, on long trekking holidays, I note a definite decrease in physical self-consciousness. And think how differently we must see ourselves, compared to those who so rarely encountered their reflected selves that they could imagine, like Narcissus, that their reflection was another person rather than an image of themselves.

Whatever the truth, stories of doubles, other selves, have proliferated since the late eighteenth century. The word *doppelgänger* itself was coined by Jean Paul Richter, a writer of fictions riddled with doubleness of all kinds, from twins to doubles to mirror images. As were the fictions of E. T. A. Hoffman, whose *New Year's Eve Adventure* turns round the psychic disintegration of a man who sells his reflection for the sake of love, much as Faust sold his soul for youth. In all such tales, as in the relations between twins, the dynamic, the motor force, is the interesting but dangerous tension between like and unlike, sameness and difference, unity and disintegration.

The doubles can be actual doubles; not only in stories, but in real life – Mary Flanagan's double, for instance. Or they can be figments of the self – as with Goethe's encounter with himself – or with those encounters, well known in folklore and prefiguring death, which neurologists call heutoscopy and put down to a form of epileptic seizure. They can be psychic alter egos made flesh; self-created ones like Jekyll's wicked Hyde, or Frankenstein's monster; or involuntary ones, like Edgar Allan Poe's doubled William Wilson or indeed Dostoevsky's poor doubled Golyadkin – though *his* double appears at first to be a separate person, a literal look-alike. They can be animal others. Alternatively the second self can be a physically split-off bodily part – as in Gogol's story, *The Nose*. This last is an interesting reflection of early myths in which the trickster hero's body is still composed of parts that can act quite independently. The anthropologist, Mary Douglas, has suggested that Coyote's progressive incorporation of his bodily parts in the stories collected by Paul Radin is a mythic reflection of mankind's progressive defining of its separate self and of its psychic, social and physical bounds. In the light of which, I find myself wondering what the outburst of such fictional disintegrations portended. Did it mean that we had grown mature or sophisticated enough to take the psyche apart (or the body in Gogol's story) thereby creating a subtler image of ourselves and society without destroying ourselves? Had society grown so complicated we needed to start understanding ourselves in such ways in order to survive? It is certainly true that the fiction of the double prefigured in some ways the Freudian revolutions – the exploration of the divided self. And it's probably significant that since William James, since Freud, the fiction of the double has much diminished, indeed all but disappeared: writers are busy exploring internal divisions now in quite other ways. Or is it a sign of some kind of psychic sickness, lying behind, presaging the disintegration of society so many see – or claim to see?

So back to nature's actual prototype; twins; who by comparison are not ambiguous for once, no figments of anyone's imagination. We exist. And in many forms. My sister for instance, was not my mirror image, by definition (though I was intrigued to read recently of the man with seemingly unlike fraternal twin daughters, who held one up to a mirror and in it recognised the other) rather she was my alter ego. Sitting alongside me like the grimmer of the Cholmondley women, she often seemed like my shadow, too – no doubt to her I seemed hers. Thomas Shapcott sums it up; having stated that one twin of any pair was always the shadow, his spokesman adds: '. . . we called them all "shadow" in the end.'

SHADOWS

Just as my spontaneity gives pleasure to people, so there is this shadow, this dark side, which has to follow.

ERIC CANTONA, footballer, banned for six months
for attacking a spectator

FERDINAND . . . Look, what's that follows me?

MALATESTI. Nothing, my lord.

FERD. Yes.

MAL. 'Tis your shadow.

FRED. Stay it. Let it not haunt me.

MAL. Impossible if you move, and the sun shine.

FERD. I will throttle it. [*Throws himself down on his shadow*]

MAL. Oh, my lord, you are angry with nothing.

FERD. You are a fool: how is't possible I should catch my shadow, unless I fall upon't?

JOHN WEBSTER, *The Duchess of Malfi*

Now everything is 3-dimensional reality, has shadows, don't you see; even the most ordinary ant patiently carries his shadow round on his back like a twin.

ORHAN PAMUK, *White Castle*

A man who is possessed by his shadow is always standing in his own light and falling into his own traps.

CARL JUNG, *Archetypes of the Collective Subconscious*

We had two lots of twins in my class at school. Each case was the same. One was the boss, the other was always the trick one. You know: suddenly out of the blue would get punch drunk; or get sneaky, or get all independent like it was pathetic. Because that was always the shadow one. The offkick. Though the boss one, too, would get sort of lost, like, if his shadow wasn't around. Shadow, we called them all 'shadow' in the end.

THOMAS SHAPCOTT, *The Birthday Present*

---

from The Shadow

ONE evening the stranger was sitting on his balcony, and as a light was burning behind him in the room, it was quite natural that his Shadow should fall upon the opposite wall. Yes, there it sat on the balcony among the flowers; and when the stranger moved it moved too, for that is the habit of Shadows.

'I firmly believe my Shadow is the only living thing opposite there!' the learned man said. 'Just see how nicely it sits amongst the flowers; and now, if it had sense, as the window is open, it would just slip in, and look about it, and when it came back tell me what it had seen. You should make yourself useful,' he said jokingly. 'Pray have the kindness to go in there. Well, are you going?' He nodded to his Shadow, and the Shadow nodded also. 'Go, then, but do not stop away altogether.' The stranger then got up, and the Shadow on the opposite balcony did the same; the stranger turned round, and the Shadow turned round also; and if any one had paid particular attention, he would have seen clearly that the Shadow went into the half-open window of the opposite house just as the stranger stepped into his room, and drew the curtain after him.

The next morning the learned man went out to drink his coffee and read the newspaper. 'How is this?' he exclaimed, when he got into the sunshine. 'I have no Shadow! So it really did go away last night, and has not returned! That is exceedingly unpleasant!'

He was considerably annoyed, not so much that his Shadow was gone, but because there was a story of a man who had lost his shadow, which every one in his own country knew.

[. . .] Vexatious it certainly was, but in warm countries everything grows very fast, so that after a week's time he noticed, to his great joy, that a new Shadow was sprouting out from the feet when he got into the sunshine, the roots of the old one having no doubt remained. In the course of three weeks he had a very respectable-sized Shadow, which increased more and more on his way to the northern countries, so that at last it grew so long and so big, that half of it would have been quite enough.

Well, the learned man reached home, and he wrote books about truth, goodness, and beauty, and thus many years passed by.

He was sitting one evening in his room when there was a gentle knock at the door.

'Come in!' he said, but no one came, so he opened the door himself, and there stood such a wonderfully thin man, that quite a strange feeling crept over him.

'Whom have I the honour of addressing?' he asked.

'Ah, that is just what I expected!' the thin man said, 'that you would not know me. I have become so thoroughly flesh and blood, and covered with clothes too, and, no doubt, you never expected to see me so well off. Do you not know your old Shadow? You never thought that I should come back. Everything has prospered wonderfully with me since I was with you, and in every way I have become rich, so that if it is necessary I should purchase my freedom, I can do it.' As he said this he jingled a bunch of valuable seals which hung from his watch, and his fingers played with the massive gold chain he wore round his neck. How all his fingers glittered with diamond rings, all of the purest water!

'What does all this mean?' the learned man cried. 'I cannot get over my surprise!'

'Well, it is not commonplace,' the Shadow said; 'but then you are something out of the common yourself, and you know that from your childhood up I have always trodden in your footsteps. As soon as I found that I could make my way alone in the world I started for myself, and a brilliant position I have gained; but then an irresistible longing came over me to see you once more before you die, for you know that die you must. I wanted to see this country again as well, for one always must love the land of one's birth. I know that you have another Shadow; and if I have to pay it or you anything, pray have the goodness to tell me so.'

'And is it really you?' the learned man said. 'It is most extraordinary! and never would I have believed that an old Shadow could return as a man!'

[. . .] It was quite extraordinary how thoroughly human the Shadow was; he was dressed all in black, of the very finest cloth, had patent leather boots and a crush-hat; and then there were the seals, the chain, and the diamond rings which we know of already. He was remarkably well dressed.

[*Soon after, he left.*]

A year passed by and the Shadow returned.

'How does the world treat you?' he asked.

'Oh!' the learned man said, 'I write about truth, goodness, and beauty, but no one cares to hear about them, and I am in despair; I take it so to heart.'

'I do not take anything to heart!' the Shadow said, 'and I am growing fat, as one ought to be. You are not fit for the world. You will get quite ill. You must travel. This summer I am going on a journey; will you go with me? I should like a travelling companion: will you go as my shadow? I shall be very happy to take you with me, and will pay your expenses.'

'That is madness!' the learned man said.

'That depends entirely upon how one looks upon it!' the Shadow said. 'Such is the world, and such it will remain!'

[. . .] So they started, the Shadow as master, and the master as shadow. They drove together, they rode together, and they walked together, side by side; before and after one another, according to the position of the sun. The Shadow chose his place and acted as master in everything; the learned man making no difficulty about it, for he was an easy, good-natured man.

Thus they reached the baths, where there were many strangers, and amongst these the beautiful daughter of a king, whose malady was that she saw too clearly, which was highly distressing.

She saw at once that the new arrival was quite a different man to others. 'It is said that he is here for the growth of his beard, but I know the real reason – he cannot cast a shadow.'

Her curiosity was excited, and she therefore at once entered into conversation with the stranger. Being a king's daughter she had not to stand upon much ceremony, so she said, 'Your illness is, that you cannot cast a shadow.'

'Your Royal Highness must have improved considerably in your health!' the Shadow said. 'I know that your illness was seeing too clearly, but that defect has evidently left you, and you are cured. I have not only a shadow, but a most extraordinary one. Other people have only a common shadow, but I do not like what is common. People give their servants finer clothes than they wear themselves, and I have made my shadow human. Do you not see the person who always accompanies me? He is my shadow; and you may observe that I have even given him a shadow of his own. I like what is out of the common way.'

[. . .] The Princess went up to the shadow and spoke with him about the sun and moon, and about man physically and morally, and he answered everything with great learning.

'What an extraordinary man that must be, to have so learned a shadow!' she thought. 'It would be a real blessing for my subjects if I chose him as a husband. I will do so!'

All was soon arranged between them, but no one was to know anything about it till she got back to her own country.

'No one, not even my shadow!' the Shadow said, and he formed projects of his own.

Then they went to the country where the Princess ruled, when she was at home.

'Now attend to me, my good friend!' the Shadow said to the learned man. 'I am now very happy, and have become as powerful as any one can be, so that now I intend to do something extraordinary for you. You shall always live with me in the palace, and drive with me in my state-carriage, and have ten thousand pounds a year; but then you must allow yourself to be called shadow by every one, and not say that you have ever been a man; besides which, once a year when I sit on the balcony and show myself to the people, you must lie at my feet, as it becomes a shadow to do. I will now tell you that I am going to marry the Princess. This evening the wedding takes place.'

'That is too great a piece of madness!' the learned man cried; 'I cannot, and will not, do it; that would be deceiving the whole country, as well as the Princess. I will tell all! That I am a man, and that you are only a Shadow dressed up!'

'No one will believe you!' the Shadow said. 'Be sensible, or I call the guard.'

'I will go straight to the Princess!' the learned man said. 'But I will go first!' the Shadow said, 'and you shall be placed under arrest!' and so it was, for the guards obeyed him, knowing he was to marry the Princess.

'You are trembling!' the Princess said, when the Shadow appeared before her: 'what has happened? You must not be taken ill just when we are going to be married!'

'Oh, the most dreadful occurrence has taken place!' the Shadow said. 'Only imagine! – oh, that poor shadow's brain cannot bear much! just imagine – my shadow has gone mad! he fancies he is a man, and that I – just imagine – that I am his shadow!'

'That is dreadful!' the Princess said; 'I hope he is in confinement?'

'Yes, he is! and I fear he will never recover!'

'Poor shadow!' the Princess said. 'He is very unhappy, and it would be a real blessing to release him from his sufferings, and I think it will be necessary to get rid of him privately!'

'That is really hard,' the Shadow said, 'for he has been a faithful servant!' and he pretended to sigh.

'You are a noble character!' the Princess cried.

That night the whole town was illuminated and the cannon were fired, 'Boom!' and the soliders presented arms. That was a wedding! The Princess and the Shadow went on to the balcony to show themselves to the people and to receive one more hurrah.

The learned man heard nothing of all that, for he had been put to death.

HANS CHRISTIAN ANDERSEN

———

PROSPERO. This thing of darkness I
    Acknowledge mine . . .

WILLIAM SHAKESPEARE, The Tempest

———

The meeting with oneself is, at first, the meeting with one's own shadow. The shadow is a tight passage, a narrow door whose painful constriction noone is spared who goes down into the deep well. For what comes after the door is, surprisingly enough, a boundless expanse full of unprecedented uncertainty with apparently no inside and no outside, no above and no below, no mine and no thine, no good and no bad.

CARL JUNG, *Collected Works*, vol. 9

———————

MIRRORS: REFLECTIONS

Reflection: the action of a mirror or other polished surface in exhibiting or producing the image of an object.

O.E.D.

Mirror, mirror on the wall,
Who is the fairest of them all?

---

from The Mirror Stage

THE conception of the mirror stage that I introduced at our last congress, thirteen years ago, has since become more or less established in the practice of the French group. However, I think it worthwhile to bring it again to your attention, especially today, for the light it sheds on the formation of the *I* as we experience it in psychoanalysis. It is an experience that leads us to oppose any philosophy directly issuing from the *Cogito*.

Some of you may recall that this conception originated in a feature of human behaviour illuminated by a fact of comparative psychology. The child, at an age when he is for a time, however short, outdone by the chimpanzee in instrumental intelligence, can nevertheless already recognize as such his own image in a mirror . . .

This act, far from exhausting itself, as in the case of the monkey, once the image has been mastered and found empty, immediately rebounds in the case of the child in a series of gestures in which he experiences in play the relation between the movements assumed in the image and the reflected environment, and between this virtual complex and the reality it reduplicates – the child's own body, and the persons and things, around him.

This event can take place, as we have known since Baldwin, from the age of six months, and its repetition has often made me reflect upon the startling spectacle of the infant in front of the mirror. Unable as yet to walk, or even to stand up, and held tightly as he is by some support, human or artificial (what, in France, we call a *'trotte-bébé'*), he nevertheless overcomes, in a flutter of jubilant activity, the obstructions of his support and, fixing his attitude in a slightly leaning-forward position, in order to hold it in his gaze, brings back an instantaneous aspect of the image.

[. . .] We have only to understand the mirror stage *as an identification*, in the full sense that analysis gives to the term: namely, the transformation that takes place in the subject when he assumes an image – whose predestination to this phase-effect is sufficiently indicated by the use, in analytic theory, of the ancient term *imago*.

This jubilant assumption of his specular image by the child at the *infans* stage, still sunk in his motor incapacity and nursling dependence, would seem to exhibit in an exemplary situation the symbolic matrix in which the *I* is precipitated in a primordial form, before it is objectified in the dialectic of identification with the other, and before language restores to it, in the universal, its function as subject.

This form would have to be called the Ideal-I, if we wished to incorporate it into our usual register, in the sense that it will also be the source of secondary identifications, under which term I would place the functions of libidinal normalization. But the important point is that this form situates the agency of the ego, before its social determination, in a fictional direction, which will always remain irreducible for the individual alone, or rather, which will only rejoin the coming-into-being (*le devenir*) of the subject asymptotically, whatever the success of the dialectical syntheses by which he must resolve as *I* his discordance with his own reality.

The fact is that the total form of the body by which the subject anticipates in a mirage the maturation of his power is given to him only as *Gestalt*, that is to say, in an exteriority in which this form is certainly more constituent than constituted, but in which it appears to him above all in a contrasting size (*un relief de stature*) that fixes it and in a symmetry that inverts it, in contrast with the turbulent movements that the subject feels are animating him. Thus, this *Gestalt* – whose pregnancy should be regarded as bound up with the species, though its motor style remains scarcely recognizable – by these two aspects of its appearance, symbolizes the mental permanence of the *I*, at the same time as it prefigures its alienating destination; it is still pregnant with the correspondences that unite the *I* with the statue in which man projects himself, with the phantoms that dominate him, or with the automation in which, in an ambiguous relation, the world of his own making tends to find completion.

Indeed, for the *imagos* – whose veiled faces it is our privilege to see in outline in our daily experience and in the penumbra of symbolic efficacity – the mirror-image would seem to be the threshold of the visible world, if we go by the mirror disposition that the *image of one's own body* presents in hallucinations or dreams, whether it concerns its individual features, or even its infirmities, or its object-projections; or if we observe the role of the mirror apparatus in the appearances of the *double*, in which psychical realities, however heterogeneous, are manifested.

JACQUES LACAN

---

from Twins

The Mirror Image as a Source of Comfort.

IN the Junior Department of the Hampstead Nurseries there was ample opportunity to watch the behaviour of all the children towards their mirror image. When children under 2 were shown their reflection in the mirror, at first they usually said 'baby' as if they did not recognize themselves. Some children showed great pleasure and affection towards the mirror image and tried to kiss it. Children from 2–3 years were often noticed talking to the mirror image. When some children were shown photographs of their playmates they recognized them at once, but they did not recognize themselves. Some characteristic examples of such behaviour are the following:

Larry, 20 months, was shown a photograph of himself with his sister; he pointed to his sister and named her, but when he was told to look at himself he did not appear to know his photograph.

Lilian, 2 years 7 months, was shown photographs of nursery

382

children; she recognized them at once, showed pleasure and named each one. She never recognized herself; she either did not react to her own picture at all, as if the photograph were of a perfect stranger, or she named a certain boy in her own place. Soon afterwards Lilian and other children were all looking in the mirror. Lilian pointed at the reflection of her playmates and called them by name, to her own image she named the same boy she had mistaken for herself on the photograph.

[. . .] The twins followed the pattern of the other children in the Nursery in not recognizing the mirror image as that of themselves, but they took the image to be that of their twin. The twins must have been far more familiar with each other than with themselves, and the mirror situation appeared to them as the most ordinary and familiar day-to-day experience. This was made clear by many of their actions before they could speak, and received confirmation once they were able to express their thoughts in words. For instance, Bill at 2 years 5 months called Bert, 'other one Bill' and used the same expression for Jessie: 'other one Bessie'. And he made use of the same words when seeing his own reflection in the lavatory mirror when urinating: 'other one Bill do wee-wee'.

DOROTHY BURLINGHAM

In a library once I met this old man, who said to me suddenly, 'You know I was born an identical twin . . . But my twin died when we were eleven months old.' He paused; then added, 'You know what they did? They pickled him. I still have him in a jar. That's good, you know, it means if I want to know what I looked like at eleven months old, all I have to do is go and look at him.'
Personal Communication to Penelope Farmer.

'I look at one and then the other,' she said. 'Mom? I get to thinking one of 'em is inside a mirror . . . It's Levi trapped in there and he can't get out! It's so creepy.'
VIRGINA HAMILTON, *Justice and her Brothers*

from Gemini

I was trying on a navy blue cloth cap in Conchon-Quinette's shop. I can still see the shop with its glass-fronted shelves, the heavy table piled with lengths of cloth and a brass-based measuring rod made of light wood standing on it. The cap seemed to suit me but I was trying not very successfully to make out my reflection in the glass cupboard doors. The shopkeeper noticed and invited me to go into a fitting room, where a triple mirror with the side panels moving on hinges let you see yourself full face and from both sides. I walked forward unsuspectingly into the trap and instantly its reflecting jaws closed on me and mangled me so cruelly that I shall carry the marks with me always. I felt an instant's shock. Someone was there, reflected three times over in that tiny space. Who? No sooner was the question framed than the answer came back thunderously: *Paul!* That rather pale boy, seen full face, from the right and from the left, fixed in that threefold photograph, was my twin brother, come there by what means I knew not, but undeniably there. And at the same time, a terrible emptiness grew within me and I was chilled by a deathly fear. For if Paul was there, living within the triptych, then I, Jean, was nowhere, I no longer existed.

MICHEL TOURNIER

from Enigma

TO penetrate the mirror, as Alice did when she went through the looking glass and as Orphée did when Cocteau took him by the hand of Death and plunged him through mercury into a limbo peopled by men who carried on their backs great sheets of glass, is an act of exploration. It is also a mystery mirrored in the flesh by mirror twins.

The implications of this enigma would be more familiar to us if we were not subject to a poetic mistranslation of I Corinthians, 13, 12, which would have us understand that St Paul wrote: 'Now we see through a glass darkly,' whereas, in the Vulgate, St Paul's Latin reads: *Videmus nunc per speculum in aenigmate* which, literally translated, means: 'Now we see in an enigma by means of a mirror.' Certainly *Tunc autem facia ad faciem* precisely means 'But then face to face', which establishes the temporal balance of St Paul's memorable pronouncement, but what if the enigma involves mirror twins and the mirror itself is both reflective and translucent?

It seems that, between six and nine months old, a single child will invariably be fascinated by his image, his *alter ego*, striving to touch and communicate with it in the glass. It also seems that identical twins, subject to tests with mirrors and also with sheets of plain glass placed between them, are indifferent to such effects and do not respond to such tests, but whether, at that age, each knows that his image is shown in his brother, or believes that he *is* his brother, or that his brother is his image, is not yet known.

Identical twins share not only identical blood, they share similar, although not identical patterns in the prints of their fingers, the palms of their hands and the soles of their feet. Even the shapes of their ears are alike and, beyond these visible similarities, they share more mysterious affinities.

There are, moreover, identical twins who are not identical, although they share all these similarities, because they are mirror images of one another. These unusual twins exhibit reversed particularities in such *minutiae* as the whorl of hair on the crown of the head; which will run clockwise in one twin and counter-clockwise in the other; the tilt of the mouth will be reversed, the slight discrepancy in the size of one eye will mirror the brother's and even, in rare cases, certain internal organs may be reversed from the norm in one twin, as one twin will be left-handed and the other right-handed. This phenomenon, which takes place in the blastic state of the cell when the cell mass is disposed, is evidence of the strange manipulation of mankind by the gods and, in one instance, of the divine manipulation of the divine.

MICHAEL AYRTON

---

from The Image in the Mirror

'WHEN I was about seven or eight I should think, she took me with her to see a thing – I remember the name now – *The Student of Prague*, it was called. I've forgotten the story, but it was a costume piece, about a young fellow at the university who sold himself to the devil, and one day his reflection came stalking out of the mirror on its own, and went about committing dreadful crimes, so that everybody thought it was him. At least, I think it was that, but I forget the details, it's so long ago. But what I shan't forget in a hurry is the fright it gave me to see that dretful figure come out of the mirror. It was that ghastly to see it, I cried and yelled, and after a time mother had to take me out.

'For months and years after that I used to dream of it. I'd dream I was looking in a great long glass, same as the student in the picture, and after a bit I'd see my reflection smiling at me and I'd walk up to the mirror holding out my left hand, it might be, and seeing myself walking to meet me with its right hand out. And just as it came up to me, it would suddenly – that was the awful moment – turn its back on me and walk away into the mirror again, grinning over its shoulder, and suddenly I'd know that *it* was the real person and *I* was only the reflection, and I'd make a dash after it into the mirror, and then everything would go grey and misty round me and with the horror of it I'd wake up all of a perspiration.'

'Uncommonly disagreeable,' said Wimsey. 'That legend of the *Doppelgänger*, it's one of the oldest and the most widespread and never fails to terrify me.

[. . .] The little man nodded thoughtfully.

'Well,' he went on, 'about that time the nightmare came back. At first it was only at intervals, you know, but it grew on me. At last it started coming every night. I hadn't closed my eyes before there was the long mirror and the thing coming grinning along, always with its hand out as if it meant to catch hold of me and pull me through the glass. Sometimes I'd wake up with the shock, but sometimes the dream went on, and I'd be stumbling for hours through a queer sort of world – all mist and half-lights, and the walls would be all crooked, like they are in that picture of "Dr Caligari." Lunatic, that's what it was. Many's the time I've sat up all night for fear of going to sleep. I didn't know, you see. I used to lock the bedroom door and hide the key for fear – you see, I didn't know what I might be doing. But then I read in a book that sleepwalkers can remember the places where they've hidden things when they were awake. So that was no use.'

'Why didn't you get someone to share the room with you?'

'Well, I did.' He hesitated. 'I got a woman – she was a good kid. The dream went away then. I had blessed peace for three years. I was fond of that girl. Damned fond of her. Then she died.'

He gulped down the last of his whisky and blinked.

'Influenza, it was. Pneumonia. It kind of broke me up. Pretty she was, too . . .

'After that, I was alone again. I felt bad about it. I couldn't – I didn't like – but the dreams came back. Worse. I dreamed about doing things – well! That doesn't matter now.

'And one day it came in broad daylight . . .

'I was going along Holborn at lunch-time. I was still at Crichton's. Head of the packing department I was then, and doing pretty well. It was a wet beast of a day, I remember – dark and drizzling. I wanted a hair-cut. There's a barber's shop on the south side, about half-way along – one of those places where you go down a passage and there's a door at the end with a mirror and the name written across it in gold letters. You know what I mean.

'I went in there. There was a light in the passage, so I could see quite plainly. As I got up to the mirror I could see my reflection coming to meet me, and all of a sudden the awful dream-feeling came over me. I told myself it was all nonsense and put my hand out to the door-handle – my left hand, because the handle was that side and I was still apt to be left-handed when I didn't think about it.

'The reflection, of course, put out its right hand – that was all right, of course – and I saw my own figure in my old squash hat and burberry – but the face – oh, my God! It was grinning at me – and then just like in the dream, it suddenly turned its back and walked away from me, looking over its shoulder—

'I had my hand on the door, and it opened, and I felt myself stumbling and falling over the threshold.

'After that, I don't remember anything more. I woke up in my own bed and there was a doctor with me. He told me I had fainted in the street, and they'd found some letters on me with my address and taken me home.'

[. . .] 'Of course,' said Wimsey to Chief-Inspector Parker a few days later, 'the whole thing was quite obvious when one had heard about the reversal of friend Duckworthy's interior economy.'

'No doubt, no doubt,' said Parker. 'Nothing could be simpler. But all the same, you are aching to tell me how you deduced it and I am willing to be instructed. Are all twins wrong-sided? And are all wrong-sided people twins?'

'Yes. No. Or rather, no, yes. Dissimilar twins and some kinds of similar twins may both be quite normal. But the kind of similar twins that result from the splitting of a single cell *may* come out as looking-glass twins. It depends on the line of fission in the original cell. You can do it artificially with tadpoles and a bit of horsehair.'

'I will make a note to do it at once,' said Parker gravely.

'In fact, I've read somewhere that a person with a reversed inside practically always turns out to be one of a pair of similar twins. So you see, while poor old R. D. was burbling on about the *Student of Prague* and the fourth dimension, I was expecting the twin-brother.'

DOROTHY L. SAYERS

---

from Melmoth the Wanderer

'AND you live here alone,' he said, 'and you have lived in this beautiful place without a companion?' – 'Oh no!' said Immalee, 'I have a companion more beautiful than all the flowers in the isle. There is not a rose-leaf that drops in the river so bright as its cheek. My friend lives under the water, but its colours are so bright. It kisses me too, but its lips are very cold; and when I kiss it, it seems to dance, and its beauty is all broken into a thousand faces, that come smiling at me like little stars. But, though my friend has a thousand faces, and I have but one, still there is one thing that troubles me. There is but one stream where it meets me, and that is where there are no shadows from the trees – and I never can catch it but when the sun is bright. Then when I catch it in the stream, I kiss it on my knees; but my friend has grown so tall; that sometimes I wish it were smaller. Its lips spread so much wider, that I give it a thousand kisses for one that I get.' 'Is your friend male or female,' said the stranger. – 'What is that?' answered Immalee. – 'I mean, of what sex is your friend?'

'But to this question he could obtain no satisfactory answer; and it was not till his return the next day, when he revisited the isle, that he discovered Immalee's friend was what he suspected. He found this innocent and lovely being bending over a stream that reflected her image, and wooing it with a thousand wild and graceful attitudes of joyful fondness.

CHARLES MATURIN

---

from Metamorphoses

THERE stands a Fountain in a darksom Wood,
Nor stain'd with falling Leaves nor rising Mud,
Untroubled by the Breath of Winds it rests,
Unsully'd by the Touch of Men or Beasts;
High Bow'rs of shady Trees above it grow,
And rising Grass and chearful Greens below.
Pleas'd with the Form and Coolness of the Place,
And over-heated by the Morning Chace,
Narcissus on the grassie Verdure lyes:
But whilst within the Chrystal Fount he tries
To quench his Heat, he feels new Heats arise.
For as his own bright Image he survey'd,
He fell in Love with the fantastick Shade;
And o'er the fair Resemblance hung unmov'd,
Nor knew, fond Youth! it was himself he lov'd.
The well-turn'd Neck and Shoulders he descries,
The spacious Forehead, and the sparkling Eyes;
The Hands that *Bacchus* might not scorn to show,
And Hair that round *Apollo*'s Head might flow;
With all the Purple Youthfulness of Face,
That gently blushes in the wat'ry Glass.
By his own Flames consum'd the Lover lyes,
And gives himself the Wound by which he dies.
To the cold Water oft he joins his Lips,
Oft catching at the beauteous Shade he dips
His Arms, as often from himself he slips.
Nor knows he who it is his Arms pursue
With eager Clasps, but loves he knows not who.
    What could, fond Youth, this helpless Passion move?
What kindled in thee this unpity'd Love?
Thy own warm Blush within the Water glows,
With thee the colour'd Shadow comes and goes,

Its empty Being on thy self relies;
Step thou aside, and the frail Charmer dies.

OVID, trs. by John Dryden

Reflection on the mode, operation or faculty by which the mind has knowledge of itself and its operations.

JOHN LOCKE, 1690

[On Edith] The broad high mirrors showed her, at full length, a woman with a noble quality, yet dwelling in her nature, who was too false to her better self, and too debased and lost to save herself.

CHARLES DICKENS, *Dombey and Son*

One of my patients – I suspect she'd been abused as a child, but she wasn't remembering it – she had this thing about mirrors. She would have an absolute compulsion sometimes to go and look into a mirror; and when she did, when she saw her reflection, it seemed like someone quite other than herself – she always referred to the reflection as 'she' as 'her', for instance. The woman in the mirror would accuse her of being a whore, dirty, a slut; very soon she'd be as compelled to run away from the mirror, as she'd been compelled to look into it in the first place . . .

Conversation with a psychologist, Personal Communication to
Penelope Farmer

I think there has to be a moment of . . . recognition. Acceptance.

There has to be a moment when you look in the mirror and say, yes, this too is myself.

PAT BARKER, *The Eye in the Door*

---

from A New Year's Eve Adventure

THE thought of leaving Giuletta threw Erasmus into pain and sorrow. 'Let me stay here,' he cried. 'I'm willing to die. Dying is better than living without you.'

But suddenly it seemed to him as if a soft, distant voice was calling his name painfully. It was the voice of his wife at home. Erasmus was stricken dumb. Strangely enough, Giuletta asked him, 'Are you thinking of your wife? Ah, Erasmus, you will forget me only too soon!'

'If I could only remain yours forever and ever,' said Erasmus. They were standing directly in front of the beautiful wide mirror, which was set in the wall, and on the sides of it tapers were burning brightly. More firmly, more closely, Giuletta pressed Erasmus to her, while she murmured softly in his ear, 'Leave me your reflection, my beloved; it will be mine and will remain with me forever.'

'Giuletta,' cried Erasmus in amazement. 'What do you mean? My reflection?' He looked in the mirror, which showed him himself and Giuletta in sweet, close embrace. 'How can you keep my reflection? It is part of me. It springs out to meet me from every clear body of water or polished surface.'

'Aren't you willing to give me even this dream of your ego? Even though you say you want to be mine, body and soul? Won't you even give me this trivial thing, so that after you leave, it can accompany me in the loveless, pleasureless life that is left to me?'

Hot tears started from Giuletta's beautiful dark eyes.

At this point Erasmus, mad with pain and passion, cried, 'Do I have to leave? If I have to, my reflection will be yours forever and a day. No power – not even the Devil – can take it away from you until you own me, body and soul.'

Giuletta's kisses burned like fire on his mouth as he said this, and then she released him and stretched out her arms longingly to the mirror. Erasmus saw his image step forward independent of his movements, glide into Giuletta's arms, and disappear with her in

391

a strange vapor. Then Erasmus heard all sorts of hideous voices bleating and laughing in demoniac scorn, and, seized with a spasm of terror, he sank to the floor. But his horror and fear aroused him, and in thick dense darkness he stumbled out the door and down the steps. In front of the house he was seized and lifted into a carriage, which rolled away with him rapidly.

'Things have changed somewhat, it seems,' said a man in German, who had taken a seat beside him. 'Nevertheless, everything will be all right if you give yourself over to me completely. Dear Giuletta has done her share, and has recommended you to me. You are a fine, pleasant young man and you have a strong inclination to pleasant pranks and jokes – which please Giuletta and me nicely. That was a real nice German kick in the neck. Did you see how Amoroso's tongue protruded – purple and swollen – it was a fine sight and the strangling noises and groans – ha, ha, ha.' The man's voice was so repellent in its mockery, his chatter so gruesomely unpleasant, that his words felt like dagger blows in Erasmus's chest.

'Whoever you are,' he said, 'don't say any more about it. I regret it bitterly.'

'Regret? Regret?' replied the unknown man. 'I'll be bound that you probably regret knowing Giuletta and winning her love.'

'Ah, Giuletta, Giuletta!' sighed Spikher.

'Now,' said the man, 'you are being childish. Everything will run smoothly. It is horrible that you have to leave her, I know, but if you were to remain here, I could keep your enemies' daggers away from you, and even the authorities.'

The thought of being able to stay with Giuletta appealed strongly to Erasmus. 'How, how can that be?'

'I know a magical way to strike your enemies with blindness, in short; that you will always appear to them with a different face, and they will never recognize you again. Since it is getting on toward daylight, perhaps you will be good enough to look long and attentively into any mirror. I shall then perform certain operations upon your reflection, without damaging it in the least, and you will be hidden and can live forever with Giuletta. As happy as can be; no danger at all.'

'Oh, God,' screamed Erasmus.

'Why call upon God, my most worthy friend,' asked the stranger with a sneer.

'I – I have . . .' began Erasmus.

'Left your reflection behind – with Giuletta—' interrupted the other. 'Fine. Bravissimo, my dear sir. And now you course through floods and forests, cities and towns, until you find your wife and little Rasmus, and become a paterfamilias again. No reflection, of course – though this really shouldn't bother your wife since she has you physically. Even though Giuletta will eternally own your dream-ego.'

A torch procession of singers drew near at this moment, and the light the torches cast into the carriage revealed to Erasmus the sneering visage of Dr Dapertutto. Erasmus leaped out of the carriage and ran toward the procession, for he had recognized Friedrich's resounding bass voice among the singers. It was his friends returning from a party in the countryside. Erasmus breathlessly told Friedrich everything that had happened, only withholding mention of the loss of his reflection. Friedrich hurried with him into the city, and arrangements were made so rapidly that when dawn broke, Erasmus, mounted on a fast horse, had already left Florence far behind.

Spikher set down in his manuscript the many adventures that befell him upon his journey. Among the most remarkable is the incident which first caused him to appreciate the loss of his reflection. He had stopped over in a large town, since his tired horse needed a rest, and he had sat down without thinking at a well-filled inn table, not noticing that a fine clear mirror hung before him. A devil of a waiter, who stood behind his chair, noticed that the chair seemed to be empty in the reflection and did not show the person who was sitting in it. He shared his observation with Erasmus's neighbor, who in turn called it to the attention of his. A murmuring and whispering thereupon ran all around the table, and the guests first stared at Erasmus, then at the mirror. Erasmus, however, was unaware that the disturbance concerned him, until a grave gentleman stood up, took Erasmus to the mirror, looked in, and then turning to the company, cried out loudly, "Struth. He's not there. He doesn't reflect.'

'What? No reflection? He's not in the mirror?' everyone cried in confusion. 'He's a *mauvais sujet*, a *homo nefas*. Kick him out the door!'

Raging and filled with shame, Erasmus fled to his room, but he had hardly gotten there when he was informed by the police that he must either appear with full, complete, impeccably accurate reflection before the magistrate within one hour or leave the town. He rushed away, followed by the idle mob, tormented by street urchins, who called after him, 'There he goes. He sold his reflection to the Devil. There he goes!' Finally he escaped. And from then on, under the pretext of having a phobia against mirrors, he insisted on having them covered. For this reason he was nicknamed General Suvarov, since Suvarov acted the same way.

When he finally reached his home city and his house, his wife and child received him with joy, and he began to think that calm, peaceful domesticity would heal the pain of his lost reflection. One day, however, it happened that Spikher, who had now put Giuletta completely out of his mind, was playing with little Rasmus. Rasmus's little hands were covered with soot from the stove, and he dragged his fingers across his father's face. 'Daddy! I've turned you black. Look, look!' cried the child, and before Spikher could prevent it or avoid it, the little boy held a mirror in front of him, looking into it at the same time. The child dropped the mirror with a scream of terror and ran away to his room.

Spikher's wife soon came to him, astonishment and terror plainly on her face. 'What has Rasmus told me—' she began. 'Perhaps that I don't have a reflection, dear,' interrupted Spikher with a forced smile, and he feverishly tried to prove that the story was too foolish to believe, that one could not lose a reflection, but if one did, since a mirror image was only an illusion, it didn't matter much, that staring into a mirror led to vanity, and pseudo-philosophical nonsense about the reflection dividing the ego into truth and dream. While he was declaiming, his wife removed the covering from a mirror that hung in the room and looked into it. She fell to the floor as if struck by lightning. Spikher lifted her up, but when she regained consciousness, she pushed him away with horror. 'Leave me, get away from me, you demon! You are not my husband. No! You are a demon from Hell, who wants to destroy my chance of heaven, who wants to corrupt me. Away! Leave me alone! You have no power over me, damned spirit!'

E.T.A. HOFFMAN

---

from Nature's Numbers

ONE of the more puzzling types of symmetry in nature is mirror symmetry, symmetry with respect to a reflection. Mirror symmetries of three-dimensional objects cannot be realized by turning the objects in space – a left shoe cannot be turned into a right shoe by rotating it. However, the laws of physics are very nearly mirror-symmetric, the exceptions being certain interactions of subatomic particles. As a result, any molecule that is not mirror-symmetric potentially exists in two different forms – left- and right-handed, so to speak. On Earth, life has selected a particular molecular handedness: for example, for amino acids. Where does this particular handedness of terrestrial life come from? It could have been just an accident – primeval chance propagated by the mass-production techniques of replication. If so, we might imagine that on some distant planet, creatures exist whose molecules are mirror images of ours. On the other hand, there may be a deep reason for life everywhere to choose the same direction. Physicists currently recognize four fundamental forces in nature: gravity, electromagnetism, and the strong and weak nuclear interactions. It is known that the weak force violates mirror symmetry – that is, it behaves differently in left- or right-handed versions of the same physical problem. As the Austrian-born physicist Wolfgang Pauli put it, 'The Lord is a weak left-hander.' One remarkable consequence of this violation of mirror symmetry is the fact that the energy levels of molecules and that of their mirror images are not exactly equal.

IAN STEWART

—————

DOUBLES AND
ALTER EGOS

Any one of us could be the man who encounters his double.

FRIEDRICH DÜRRENMATT

─────────

The double stands at the start of that cultivation of uncertainty by which the literature of the modern world has come to be distinguished.

KARL MILLER

─────────

I thought I was losing my senses when I saw myself two, and for a long time, I treated my other self as an imposter; but he compelled me in the end to recognise myself.

MOLIÈRE, *Amphytrion*

─────────

Tonight I heard a bell again –
Outside it was the same mist of fine rain,
The lamps just lighted down the long, dim street,
  Noone for me – I think it is myself I go to meet:
  I do not care: some day I *shall* not think; I shall not *be*!

CHARLOTTE MEW

─────────

The double is an ambassador of the absent self; its shadow rather than its substance.

PAUL COATES, *The Double and the Other*

The Heavy Bear

THE heavy bear who goes with me,
A manifold honey to smear his face,
Clumsy and lumbering here and there,
The central ton of every place,
The hungry beating brutish one
In love with candy, anger, and sleep,
Crazy factotum, dishevelling all,
Climbs the building, kicks the football,
Boxes his brother in the hate-ridden city.
Breathing at my side, that heavy animal,
That heavy bear who sleeps with me,
Howls in his sleep for a world of sugar,
A sweetness intimate as the water's clasp,
Howls in his sleep because the tight-rope
Trembles and shows the darkness beneath
– The strutting show-off is terrified,
Dressed in his dress-suit, bulging his pants
Trembles to think that his quivering meat
Must finally wince to nothing at all.

That inescapable animal walks with me,
Has followed me since the black womb held,
Moves where I move, distorting my gesture,
A caricature, a swollen shadow,
A stupid clown of the spirit's motive,
Perplexes and affronts with his own darkness,
The secret life of belly and bone,
Opaque, too near, my private, yet unknown,
Stretches to embrace the very dear
With whom I would walk without him near,
Touches her grossly, although a word
Would bare my heart and make me clear,

Stumbles, flounders, and strives to be fed
Dragging me with him in his mouthing care,
Amid the hundred million of his kind,
The scrimmage of appetite everywhere.

DELMORE SCHWARTZ

----

from The Twin

NO need to say, that after I moved in, Swanilda lost no time in introducing me to the young lady artist, who was now my next door neighbour. I hesitate to say that she introduced me to her owner, not only because as everyone knows, no one ever really owns a creature as independent as a cat but also, because the girl, Leila and Swanilda the cat, were on terms of such close companionship that there was no hint of ownership in it but only of the greatest, mutual affection.

Leila would sometimes ask me in, on a Sunday afternoon or evening, for a drink of hot chocolate topped with whipped cream of which she was very fond and we would sip it slowly and talk or listen to gramophone records of which she had a great number, especially of ballet music. If we were not out on the balcony, she would usually sit curled up on the divan, with her slim, pink-lipped fingers buried in Swanilda's soft, silky fur.

One evening as we sat talking, she put her face down close to the cat, so that her pale, spun-gold hair mingled with its fur and asked me: 'Don't you think we look alike? Don't you?' She narrowed her forget-me-not blue eyes in just the way Swanilda did sometimes and I was suddenly aware, that there was indeed a great resemblance between them. Their eyes were the same colour and Swanilda's pink nose was the same pink as Leila's small mouth but it was when I remembered, how Leila stretched her arms or legs, her light, springy walk, her air of cool aloofness, her steady scrutinizing gaze, the head sometimes slightly to one side, that their alikeness suddenly struck me as staggering.

'Swanilda is my twin . . .' Leila continued '. . . that is why we love each other so much.' She picked the cat up in her arms and pressed it against her breast. The cat's white fur blended with her white sweater and it was difficult to see, where cat ended and girl began . . .

'How long have you had her?' I asked.

'We have been together for seven years.'

'Seven! . . . How . . . how . . .' I was not sure how it would be best to express my question.

'Our meeting was rather interesting. Rather strange – naturally.'

'In what way?'

'I went down to Cornwall for my summer holidays, to stay with a rather ancient aunt. I was in my first year at the Art School and was most anxious to do some really interesting holiday work. Every day I would set off on my bicycle with a sketchbook and lunch in the basket. I wanted to do some fairy tale illustrations and was looking for interesting trees, cottages, flowers . . . anything that could be fitted into a fairy story picture. One day, turning down a small lane off the main road, I suddenly came to a cottage, that simply *asked* to be sketched. It had a tall chimney-stack, lattice windows and an enormous hydrangea bush, that nearly reached the roof. I sat down on a heap of stones and started sketching. After a few minutes' work, I saw Swanilda standing at the garden gate . . . She came up and spoke to me . . .'

'Spoke?' I inquired incredulously.

'I always understand what she says,' replied Leila, a little primly, '. . . a few minutes later, she climbed up on my lap and I knew instantly, that this was a being I would always love. A woman with dark, piercing eyes and gypsy-black hair came out to put an empty milk bottle on the doorstep and looked at us.

'The cat knows you,' she said.

'It's a lovely cat . . .' I answered, '. . . how I wish she were mine . . .'

'You can have her,' replied the woman.

'You cannot really mean that . . .'

'I've got three more kittens coming up from the farm . . . and this cat is yours. I knew that as soon as I saw you together. We know these things in Cornwall . . . we are different, you see . . .'

'I expressed my amazed gratitude and asked, when I could call for the cat.

'Take her now. She wants to go and I know you will be happy together.

'I thanked the woman once more, popped Swanilda into the bicycle basket – she was only a slim kitten in those days – and off we went. Needless to say, my aunt took to her immediately and Swanilda made herself at home in no time. A few days later, I thought it would be nice to go and see the woman again and tell her how well the cat had settled down, but do you know? Although I am sure I cycled over half Cornwall in my efforts, I never found that cottage again . . .'

'Really . . .? But then you know what country lanes are like . . . one always turns down the wrong one . . .'

'Explain it in any way you like, but the woman was right . . . things are different in Cornwall.' For a moment she stared fixedly ahead and her pupils seemed to dilate like those of a cat, then she smiled and tossed back her hair. This awoke Swanilda and, sliding out of her grasp, she started 'performing' as we called it, on the divan. This meant, that she turned over first on one side, then on the other, then on to her back, exposing her soft, furry 'tummy' and looking at us through half-shut eyes, waiting for our admiration and caresses. I tickled her under the 'arm' and she immediately twisted herself into another position, then rolled right over and curled up into a circle of fur with delicate, semi-transparent ears slightly twitching.

Leila looked on approvingly.

One night I came in late after an evening assignment for my paper and was surprised to see the light still burning in Leila's room. Usually, she firmly believed in 'early to bed.' I had just opened the door of my room, when she came out of hers and I saw that she looked pale and worried.

'Hullo, Leila – not in bed yet? It's late . . .'

'I know – David, Swanilda is *so* ill.'

For half the night, we sat up with the cat, wrapping her in blankets and changing hot water bottles, until at last she stopped shivering and being sick and went to sleep.

In the morning, before going to the office, I knocked softly on Leila's door to ask after Swanilda. She weakly called out 'come in' and I found that she too, was now in bed with the same symptoms as the cat. I suggested calling a doctor but she waved my suggestion away – 'I will be all right – as long as Swanilda is all right. We are always ill together. It's our affinity . . . I told you we were twins . . .'

She looked so exquisitely lovely in her pale-blue bed jacket, with her delicate, pathetic little face, that I suddenly felt a great urge to take her in my arms. I restrained myself however, just as I restrained myself from suggesting that being sick together might only mean that they had both eaten the same thing, which disagreed with them – they were always sharing tins of salmon, sardines or even lobster. This suggestion however, would have cast doubt on Leila's twin theory and hurt her feelings and I would not hurt her for the world.

From that moment I realised, as I had not done before, not

consciously anyway, that the one thing I wanted and I had never wanted anything so much in the whole of my life, was to marry Leila and to be with her always.

[. . .] She did not agree to the proposal all at once and for some reason, Swanilda also, was not very keen on the idea at first. Eventually however, she seems to have signified her approval and even became sufficiently friendly to wait for me outside when I returned from work.

'She had always liked you really, you know,' said Leila, '. . . after all, if you remember, she brought you to me.'

It was now getting towards the end of August and I suggested either September or October for our wedding. Leila agreed readily, if a little dreamily. She often appeared to be thinking of something else, or not even thinking at all, or anyway not listening and I was relieved to get a definite answer. I asked her what sort of an engagement ring, she would like.

'Not a ring,' she said quickly, 'Swanilda does not like rings, they catch in her fur. Give me something else.'

For a moment I wanted to remonstrate against Swanilda's likes and dislikes and a slight misgiving about our proposed 'ménage à trois' assailed me but one look at Leila's adorable face so close to mine, chased away doubt and warmed my heart. I kissed her cool, soft mouth and started my search.

[. . .] After a few days, I found what I thought she might like. It was a turquoise bracelet in the shape of a snake, not stiff like a bangle but beautifully flexible and of a perfect, delicate blue. It went twice round the wrist and then the snake's head snapped shut in any chosen place, thus making it suitable for any size of arm or wrist.

Leila was not a person who ever displayed great enthusiasm but the bracelet fascinated her.

'I think it is the loveliest thing that I have ever seen. I shall always wear it, David. Do you hear? Always.' I put it on for her and took her in my arms. She felt both cool and warm and her body was as soft and pliable as a cat's. Yes, I, too was beginning to make those comparisons, although I smiled half-amusedly, when Leila held forth on the subject.

A little while later, I was coming back from work on a lovely warm Saturday afternoon, to find both Leila and Swanilda waiting for me. Leila was on the balcony wearing a gay, orange-coloured wrapper, her pale hair falling loose on her shoulders and my bracelet on her wrist. As promised, she always wore it and even from a distance I thought how effective that touch of blue looked against the orange of her wrap. Swanilda waited for me on the side of the road, which was opposite the house. I always walked on this opposite side, because it enabled me to see Leila's balcony much sooner than if I walked on the same side as the house, where it was obscured from view by other balconies and trees. Leila waved to me and I blew her a kiss, then bent down and stroked Swanilda. She arched her back with pleasure and then slipping away from under my hand, set off across the road. At that moment, with a terrific roar and clatter, a low sports car, appearing seemingly from nowhere, flashed by at breakneck speed and above the roar of its engine I suddenly heard a shriek, a wild unhuman shriek, which for a moment froze my blood and rooted me to the spot. Before I could properly collect my thoughts again, the car had raced past me towards the main road and disappeared, while in the middle of the road lay a small, pathetic bundle of white fur. I rushed towards it, quickly glancing at the balcony at the same time, and saw that it was empty. I picked up the cat's body, soft and limp and still warm and walked towards the house. At any moment, I expected to see Leila running to meet us but there was no sign of her and after the infernal noise of the car and the dreadful shriek, there seemed to be a most eerie, deathly silence in the air. I wondered if Leila had fainted and started to walk rather more quickly. That agonized, inhuman, almost unearthly shriek, still sounded in my ears, a premonition of some dreadful disaster filled my mind and I felt almost numbed with fear, a fear of I hardly knew what, as I half-walked, half-stumbled up the stairs. The door of the room was ajar as usual, I pushed it open farther with my foot and holding the dead cat still firmly in my arms, went in and looked round. There was no sign of Leila. Perhaps she has fainted somewhere on the floor, flashed through my mind and at that moment, I caught sight of her orange wrapper, flung carelessly over a chair, half of it on the arm and half trailing on the floor by the divan. I quickly walked up to the divan and there, curled up amongst the cushions and looking at me with eyes of forget-me-not blue, was a white cat, identical with the one whose body I held in my arms. For a moment, I could hardly believe my eyes and as I walked up closer to look at it, it turned its head slightly and I saw that round its neck it wore a turquoise bracelet, shaped like a snake . . .

VERA LARINA

from Snake Twin and Other Stories

WITH the abundance of snakes in that island, Ariston thought, the percentage of the existence of snake twins there should be higher than in Negros. Joaquin Kintanar, the herpetologist who had told him about the sea snakes congregated like spaghetti in Siquijor's underwater caves, accepted the possibility, no matter how remote, of a snake lying alongside a baby in a crib, but ruled that baby and snake coming out of the same womb was biologically inconceivable.

Ariston asked Gabriel Duhaylungsod, a Siquijodnon, to stay after his class in differential calculus. In the graduate class of seven more-than-average students, Ariston rated him number three. Duhaylungsod's mouth, just a thin line above an insufficient chin, seemed to belie a certain churliness in the man: he had a habit of saying so little, though you had the feeling he knew much more.

'Dr Kintanar tells me the snake population in Siquijor is probably bigger than in any other island its size in the country.'

The abrupt statement did not register any reaction on the man's flint-like face.

'Are there snake twins of humans in Siquijor?'

His brows knitted and then he nodded slightly.

'Do you personally know of any in Siquijor?'

He nodded again.

'Where does he live?'

'She is a woman. In San Isidro. Silvestra Tulabing.'

'How old is she?'

'Sixty. No more than sixty-five.'

'There was no hospital in Siquijor sixty years ago, was there?'

He shook his head.

'So we can't check any records, Gabriel. Did the snake come out with her when she was born?'

'The snake was on her bed when she was born.'

'Does that mean they came out of the womb together?'

'She said the snake was on her bed when she was born.'

'Sixty years ago in rural areas – this would include Siquijor – lots of people didn't sleep on beds but on mats spread on the floor. Mats – of *pandanus* or hemp – were either folded or rolled up when not in use. It's possible a snake might have laid eggs in the folded or rolled mat. It's possible that when Silvestra was born a stray snake egg was hatched on the bed – or in the blanket – used by the mother and the baby. Is that scenario possible?'

The slow nod of Duhaylungsod and the way he looked at Ariston indicated his recognition of the teacher's intelligence.

'Does she have siblings?'

'The only begotten.'

'Either of her parents still living?'

'Almost mathematically impossible considering.'

'Considering what?'

'Lifespan in Siquijor, especially in the past, is not long. Her parents died when she was in her twenties.'

'Does she have a family of her own?'

'None. She's still a virgin.'

'How do you know that?'

'No man would ever propose to her despite her property.'

'Anything wrong with her?'

'Her legs are wide parentheses. A German shepherd can walk between her legs.'

'You mentioned property.'

'She is the richest woman in Siquijor. She owns three of the seven jeepneys running on the island. She also owns the biggest nipa swamp.'

'Does she admit she is the twin of a snake?'

'She is open about it.'

'Have you seen the snake yourself?'

He shook his head. 'Lazi, my town, is eight kilometers from San Isidro. Silvestra is a second cousin of my grandmother, who has seen the snake. When I was a boy I told Silvestra – I call her Lola – I wanted to see the snake. You cannot see it, she said, it was not good for me.'

'You say she speaks openly about her twin. I'd like to go to Siquijor with you one weekend. To talk to your Lola Silvestra.'

He nodded. 'I usually go home Friday. The last trip is 4:00 p.m.'

As Duhaylungsod was about to leave the room his solemn face broke into what looked like a smile. 'By the way. Lola Silvestra has a peculiar way of talking. I'm preparing you. She hisses.'

'What do you mean?'

He clamped his teeth together and expelled his breath three times by way of demonstration.

EDILBERTO K. TIEMPO

———

from The Trickster

In the midst of all these operations suddenly his left arm grabbed the buffalo. 'Give that back to me, it is mine! Stop that or I will use my knife on you!' So spoke the right arm. 'I will cut you to pieces, that is what I will do to you,' continued the right arm. Thereupon the left arm released its hold. But shortly after, the left arm again grabbed hold of the right arm . . . again and again this was repeated. In this manner did Trickster make both his arms quarrel. That quarrel soon turned into a vicious fight and the left arm was badly cut up . . .

In another story Trickster treats his own anus as if it could act as an independent agent and ally. He had killed some ducks and before going to sleep he tells his anus to keep guard over the meat. While he is asleep some foxes draw near:

'When they came close, much to their surprise however, gas was expelled from somewhere. "Pooh" was the sound made. "Be careful! He must be awake" so they ran back. After a while one of them said, "Well, I guess he is asleep now. That was only a bluff. He is always up to some tricks." So again they approached the fire. Again gas was expelled and again they ran back. Three times this happened . . . Then louder, still louder, was the sound of gas expelled. "Pooh! Pooh! Pooh!" Yet they did not run away. On the contrary they now began to eat the roasted pieces of duck . . .'

When Trickster woke up and saw the duck gone:

'. . . "Oh, you too, you despicable object, what about your behaviour? Did I not tell you to watch this fire? You shall remember this! As a punishment for your remissness, I will burn your mouth so that you will not be able to use it!" So he took a piece of burning wood and burned the mouth of his anus . . . and cried out of pain he was inflicting on himself.'
PAUL RADIN, quoted in *Mary Douglas: Purity and Danger*

---

from The Nose

COLLEGIATE assessor Kovalev awoke comparatively early and made the sound, b-r-r-r-r with his lips, which he always did on waking, although he himself did not know the reason for it. Kovalev stretched himself and called to his servant to give him a mirror which was standing on the table. He wanted to look at a pimple which had suddenly appeared on his nose the night before, but, to his great amazement, he saw that there was a completely smooth place instead of the nose. Kovalev grew frightened and shouted for some water. He rubbed his eyes with a towel – still no nose! He began to feel his face with his hand, and pinched himself to find out whether he was asleep or not – apparently he was not. Collegiate assessor Kovalev jumped out of bed, shook himself – still no nose! He immediately ordered his clothes to be brought to him, and rushed off straight to the Chief of Police.

But in the meantime I should say something about Kovalev, so that the reader may see what kind of a collegiate assessor he was.

[. . . He] was a Caucasian collegiate assessor. He had held this rank for only two years, and therefore could not forget it for a moment, and, in order to add more nobility and importance to himself, he never called himself just a collegiate assessor, but always a major. 'Listen, little pigeon,' he would say on meeting a woman in the street who was selling shirt-fronts, 'call at my place, my flat is on the Sadovaja. You just ask 'Does Major Kovalev live here?' – anybody will direct you.' If, however, he met a comely woman, he would, in addition, give her certain secret instructions, adding, 'Darling, you ask for Major Kovalev's flat.' Therefore, we too, shall in future call him a major.

Major Kovalev was in the habit of strolling along the Nevsky Prospect every day. The collar of his shirt-front was always extremely clean and well starched. His side whiskers were of the kind which are still to be seen on government and district land surveyors, on architects and regimental doctors, also on those performing various duties and, generally speaking, on all those men who have fat, rosy cheeks and are good boston players. These side whiskers grow along the very middle of the cheek and go straight up to the nose. Major Kovalev carried a multitude of little carnelian seals, some with coats of arms and some on which were engraved 'Wednesday,' 'Thursday,' 'Monday,' etc. Major Kovalev had come up to Petersburg on business, namely, to find an employment worthy of his profession.

[. . .] Therefore, reader, you may judge for yourself what the Major's predicament was when, instead of a nose, not uncomely but of reasonable proportions, he saw a very silly plain and smooth place.

As bad luck would have it, not one cab driver showed himself in the street, and he had to walk, having wrapped himself in his cloak and covered his face with a handkerchief, as if his nose was bleeding.

'But perhaps I only imagined it – it is impossible that a nose should so stupidly disappear,' he thought, and entered a pastry shop, where he intended to look at himself in a mirror.

Fortunately, there was nobody there. The boys were sweeping the rooms and replacing the chairs: some of them, with sleepy eyes, were carrying trays of hot pies. Yesterday's papers, wet with coffee, were scattered on tables and chairs.

'Well, thank Heaven, nobody's here,' Kovalev muttered, 'I can have a look now.' He timidly approached the mirror and looked into it.

'The Devil take it – what a filthy mess,' he said and spat. 'If there were only something in its place – but no, simply nothing there!'

He bit his lips in his grief and, on leaving the pastry shop, he decided, against his usual wont, not to look or smile at anybody.

Suddenly, as if thunderstruck, he stopped in front of a house. He beheld an inexplicable apparition. A coach stopped at the house entrance; the door opened and a gentleman in uniform jumped out and ran up the steps. How great was Kovalev's horror and at the same time his amazement when he recognised who it was – his very own nose! It seemed to him, witnessing this unusual sight, that everything swayed before him. He could hardly stand, but decided, whatever happened, to await the return of the nose to the coach. He was trembling as if with ague.

After two minutes the nose actually reappeared. It was in a uniform embroidered with gold and was wearing a stiff collar and suede breeches. A sword hung at its side. Judging by the plume on its hat, it held the rank of a State Councillor. Everything pointed to the fact that it was going to visit somebody. It looked around and, calling to the driver, 'Let's go,' sat down and was driven away.

Poor Kovalev nearly went mad. He did not know what to think of such a strange occurrence. How could the nose, which was yesterday on his face and could neither ride nor walk, wear a uniform? He ran after the coach, which, fortunately, did not go far and stopped in front of the bazaar. He hurried there, threading his way among a row of old beggar women, with bandaged faces and two holes for eyes, at whom he used to laugh. The crowd was not large. Kovalev was in such a bad state that he could not decide anything, and his eyes were searching for the gentleman in all the corners. Finally, he saw it standing in front of a shop. The nose's face was completely hidden in the large military collar and it was examining some merchandise with deep attention.

'How is the nose to be approached?' thought Kovalev. 'Judging by everything – the uniform and the hat – it is obvious that it is a State Councillor. The Devil knows how it is to be done!'

Drawing nearer, Kovalev coughed, but the nose did not change its posture for a moment.

'Sir,' said Kovalev, inwardly forcing himself to some courage, 'dear sir . . .'

'What is it you wish?' answered the nose, turning round.

'It is strange, dear sir . . . it seems to me . . . you ought to know your place. And suddenly I find you – and where? You will agree . . .'

'Forgive me, but I do not understand what you wish to say. Will you kindly explain?'

'How shall I explain it?' thought Kovalev, and, gathering courage, he began, 'Of course, I . . . by the way, I am a major. You will agree that it is unseemly for me to walk about without a nose. Some beggar woman selling peeled oranges on the Voskresenski Bridge may sit there without a nose, but I have prospects of obtaining . . . and in addition, being acquainted with ladies in many households – Mrs. Chechatiroeva, State Councillor's wife, and others . . . judge for yourself. I do not know, dear sir' (at this Major Kovalev shrugged his shoulders), 'forgive me, whether this is in accordance with the rules of honour and duty. You yourself will understand . . .'

'I do not understand anything at all,' answered the nose. 'Kindly explain more clearly.'

'My dear sir,' said Kovalev, full of dignity, 'I do not know how to interpret your words. It seems to me that the whole matter is quite obvious . . . or do you want . . .? After all, you are my own nose!'

The nose looked at the major and raised its eyebrows slightly.

'You are mistaken, sir, I am myself. Besides, there can be no close relationship between us. Judging by the buttons on your uniform, you are serving in a different department.' Having said this, the nose turned away.

GOGOL

* * *

Superficially, doubles are among the most facile and less reputable devices of fiction.

RALPH TYMMS, *The Double in Literature*

---

from Siebenkaes

THERE has seldom been a case of a royal alliance between two peculiar natures like that between these two. The same contempt for the childish nonsense held in this life to be noble matter, the same enmity to all pettiness and perfect indulgence to the little, the same indignation with dishonourable selfishness, the same delight in laughing in this lovely madhouse of an earth, the same deafness to the voice of the multitude, but not to that of honour; these are but some of the first at hand of the similarities which made of these two but one soul doing duty in two bodies. And the fact that they were also foster-brothers in their studies, having for nurses the same branches of knowledge, including the Law herself, I do not reckon among their chief resemblances; for it is often the case that the very identity of study becomes a dissolving decomponent of friendship. Indeed, it was not even the dissimilarity of their opposite poles which determined their mutual attraction for each other (Siebenkaes leant towards forgiving, Leibgeber towards punishing; the former was more a satire of Horace, the latter a street ballad of Aristophanes with unpoetic as well as poetic harshnesses). But, as two female friends are fond of being dressed alike, these two men's souls had put on just the same frock-coat and morning costume of life; I mean, two bodies of identical fashion, colour, button-holes, finishings, and cut. Both had the same flash of the eyes, the same earthy-coloured face, the same tallness, leanness, and everything. And indeed, the Nature freak of counterpart faces is commoner than we suppose, because we only notice it when some prince or great person casts a corporeal reflection.

For which reason I very much wish that Leibgeber had not had a slight limp, so that he might not have been thereby distinguishable from Siebenkaes, seeing, at least, that the latter had cleverly etched and dissolved away his own peculiar mark by causing a live toad to breathe its last above it. For there had been a pyramidal mole near his left ear, in the shape of a triangle, or of the zodiacal light, or a turned-up comet's tail, of an ass's ear in short. Partly from friendship, partly from the enjoyment they had in the scenes of absurdity which their being confounded with each other gave rise to in every-day life, they wished to carry the algebraic equation which existed between them yet a step further, by adopting the same Christian and surname. But on this point they had a friendly contest, as each wanted to be the other's namesake, till at length they settled the difference by *exchanging* names, thus following the example of the natives of Otaheite, among whom the lovers exchange names as well as hearts.

JEAN PAUL RICHTER

---

from The Double

'THAT is not what I wanted to say, Anton Antonovich,' went on Mr Golyadkin, staring hard at Anton Antonovich. The fact is, Anton Antonovich, I don't even know how to make you . . . mean to say, how to tackle the question, Anton Antonovich.'

'What? I advise you . . . you know . . . I confess I don't quite understand . . . You . . . look, explain yourself a bit more fully; what is it you find so difficult here?' said Anton Antonovich, who found it a little difficult himself, seeing that tears had started to Mr Golyadkin's eyes.

'Anton Antonovich, I . . . here . . . I'm an employee here, Anton Antonovich . . .'

'Well? I still don't understand.'

'I mean, Anton Antonovich, that there's a new employee here.'

'Yes, there is; his name's the same as yours.'

'What?' exclaimed Mr Golyadkin.

'I said his name's the same as yours; he's another Golyadkin. Is he your brother?'

'No, sir. Anton Antonovich, I . . .

'H'm! Then how is it . . . and I supposed he must be a close relative of yours. You know, there is some . . . what might be called family likeness.'

Mr Golyadkin was dumb with astonishment; for a time he simply could not speak. To treat such a shocking, such an unprecedented subject so lightly, a matter really unique of its kind, a matter that would have astonished even an indifferent bystander, to talk about a family likeness, when there was no more difference between them than if they were two peas in a pod!

'Do you know what my advice to you is, Yakov Petrovich?' went on Anton Antonovich. 'You just go to the doctor and ask him what he thinks. You know, you don't *look* at all well. You know, your eyes are peculiarly . . . you know, there's a special sort of expression in them.'

'No, Anton Antonovich, of course I feel . . . that is, I wanted to ask you, what is this new man?'

'What, sir?'

'I mean, Anton Antonovich, haven't you noticed something specially – something very striking about him?'

'You mean?'

'I mean, Anton Antonovich, what I meant was some very special likeness to somebody, for example, I mean to me, for example. Just now, Anton Antonovich, you talked of a family likeness, you made a passing reference. . . . You know, sometimes there are twins, I mean as like as two peas, so that you can't tell the difference. Well, that was what I meant.'

'Yes,' said Anton Antonovich, after a moment's thought, as if he had been struck by the idea for the first time, 'yes! you're quite right. The resemblance is indeed striking, and you are right, you really could take one of you for the other,' he continued, while his eyes grew rounder and rounder. 'And do you know, Yakov Petrovich, the resemblance is positively miraculous, it's fantastic, as people say; I mean he's exactly like you. . . . Have you noticed it, Yakov Petrovich? I was wanting to ask you myself if you could explain it; yes, I own I didn't pay it enough attention at first. Miraculous, really miraculous! And you know, Yakov Petrovich, your family isn't from here, I believe?'

'No.'

'He's not from here, either, you know. Perhaps he's from the same place as you. And really, it's absolutely marvellous,' went on the loquacious Anton Antonovich, for whom the opportunity of a good gossip was a real holiday, 'it really could attract attention; and, you know, how often you can walk past him, or brush against him, or bump into him, and not notice it! However, you mustn't be upset. These things happen. These things, you know – let me tell you about my aunt on my mother's side, the very same thing happened to her; she saw her double, too, just before she died . . .'

DOSTOEVSKY

from Confessions of a Justified Sinner

AS I thus wended my way, I beheld a young man of a mysterious appearance coming towards me. I tried to shun him, being bent on my own contemplations; but he cast himself in my way, so that I could not well avoid him; and more than that, I felt a sort of invisible power that drew me towards him, something like the force of enchantment, which I could not resist. As we approached each other, our eyes met, and I can never describe the strange sensations that thrilled through my whole frame at that impressive moment; a moment to me fraught with the most tremendous consequences; the beginning of a series of adventures which has puzzled myself, and will puzzle the world when I am no more in it. That time will now soon arrive, sooner than any one can devise who knows not the tumult of my thoughts, and the labour of my spirit; and when it hath come and passed over, – when my flesh and my bones are decayed, and my soul has passed to its everlasting home, then shall the sons of men ponder on the events of my life; wonder and tremble, and tremble and wonder how such things should be.

That stranger youth and I approached each other in silence, and slowly, with our eyes fixed on each other's eyes. We approached till not more than a yard intervened between us, and then stood still and gazed, measuring each other from head to foot. What was my astonishment, on perceiving that he was the same being as myself!

JAMES HOGG

---

from Amphitryon

SOSIA   No joke, Sir, I am speaking
in dead earnest, so do be good enough
to credit what I say. I swear to you
I left the camp a single soul, and arrived
in Thebes a double; that I stared with popping eyes
when I encountered my own self right here;
that this here I who's standing right in front
of you was dropping with fatigue and hunger when
the other one I'm telling you about
came out the palace door as fresh as he

could be, a bully boy if ever I
did see one; that these two rascals, emulous
each one to execute your orders, got
into an argument right off and I found
myself compelled to beat it back to camp
again, for being such a brainless brute. [. . .]

AMPHITRYON But how can anyone with all his wits
about him possibly believe it?

SOSIA   Goodness,
but the pain it cost me, just like you,
before I managed that! I was sure
I was possessed when I found my own self planted
here on the square and making a great
racket; I cursed myself a good long while
for playing knavish tricks on me. But I
was forced to recognize at last that he
was me with just as good a right as I.
As if the air had been a looking glass,
face to face with me he stood, a being
who resembled me in all respects, his manners
mine, his build – two drops of water aren't
more alike. And if he'd only been
the least bit friendly, instead of such
an ugly-tempered brute, I do believe
I would have liked him, honestly.

AMPHITRYON   The self-control
that I'm condemned to exercise! – But finally
you went inside the palace, didn't you?

SOSIA Inside the palace? That's a good one! How?
Would I allow it? Listen the least bit
to reason? Didn't I refuse myself
permission to go in, over and over, stubbornly?

AMPHITRYON What the devil are you saying? How—?

SOSIA How? With a thick stick is how, the marks
of which I've still got on my back.

AMPHITRYON   So someone
beat you.

SOSIA   Did he ever!

AMPHITRYON   Who? Who beat
You? Dared do that?

SOSIA   Me.

413

AMPHITRYON   You beat yourself?
SOSIA I did, for sure I did! Oh, not the one
   who's talking to you now, but that one, curse
   him, from the palace there, who stroked away
   on me like a whole rowing crew.
                          KLEIST, (translated by Martin Greenberg)

---

from Despair

LOOK, this is my nose; a big one of the northern type, with a hard bone somewhat arched and the fleshy part tipped up and almost rectangular. And that is his nose, a perfect replica of mine. Here are the two sharply drawn furrows on both sides of my mouth with lips so thin as to seem licked away. He has got them, too. Here are the cheekbones – but this is a passport list of facial features meaning nothing; an absurd convention. Somebody told me once that I looked like Amundsen, the Polar explorer. Well, Felix, too, looked like Amundsen. But it is not every person that can recall Amundsen's face. I myself recall it but faintly, nor am I sure whether there had not been some mix-up with Nansen. No, I can explain nothing.

VLADIMIR NABOKOV

My Doppelgänger

IN 1966 I bought a pair of of grey silk trousers. Flared, and size eight: I was thin. The next day another young woman walked into the same Manhattan boutique and attempted to purchase the same trousers. 'But you just bought these,' protested the sales assistant. The customer denied it; the puzzled woman insisted; the disagreement escalated in the New York manner and a tantrum ensued during which articles of clothing were thrown about and something shattered. The irate customer was Stella, friend of my youth and my *doppelgänger*.

We hadn't yet met. We'd been watching each other, though – I as she carried lobster and steak down the dangerous aisles of Max's

Kansas City, wearing red and white stockings, a tiny skirt and lots of attitude. She'd seen me waiting for my boyfriend, who was a bus boy in the same restaurant. 'I really like the way that girl looks,' she told him. He was the first to point out our resemblance, and suddenly everyone saw it, as if by naming it he had created it.

Stella and I became best friends. We were an act, capitalising shamelessly on our similarities – straight blond hair, prominent cheek bones, blue eyes with an Eskimo slant. Life as doubles was exciting, and we were quite reckless, charming ourselves with bad behaviour. I could never match her sauciness, however, or her self-assertion, especially with men, or the operatic petulance they adored.

We haunted art galleries, marched in Vietnam demos, hung around Max's until 5am, performed dance pieces in Bert Stern's loft. People stared at us, friends mixed us up when we weren't together. 'Mary,' someone said to Stella, 'what's happened? You look terrible.' We added to the confusion by swapping clothes and revelled in happy narcissism, twin Alices loose in an underground Wonderland.

Two years later, I left America. She married Jack, now a famous painter. From impoverished beginnings in an unheated loft full of dirty dishes and too many cats (one named Mary), they progressed to ever more lavish environments as the value of Jack's paintings soared. But they fought. She'd escape him with trips to India, then return to fight again. Drunken scenes ended with their being banned from favourite bars and restaurants. Friends called them Scott and Zelda. Finally they separated.

People we knew continued to be intrigued by our uncanny likeness. It was entering the realm of myth, partly because whenever I visited New York Stella wasn't around or it was impossible to find her, though I'd see Jack. There were sightings, messages that arrived too late, phones that rang in empty apartments. I did catch her once on the six o'clock news, outraged and in tears because the Bronx Zoo was refusing to return her pair of escaped fruit bats. And I dreamt of her (I still do, usually in times of crisis – dreams flooded with that atmosphere of unease which traditionally surrounds the *doppelgänger*). But I did not see her in the flesh again until I had an affair with her husband.

Perhaps Jack got confused or simply missed her. He certainly called me Stella more than once. It couldn't last. Suddenly she arrived in London with her 19-year-old boyfriend, appointed herself godmother to my toddler, then cornered me in our cramped kitchen, backed me up against the cooker and, well within earshot of her new godchild's father, demanded to know what I was doing with her husband.

I was scared. She's bigger than I am. 'I thought you didn't like him any more,' I stammered. But she was not prepared to liberate me from the cooker, which was set at 700 degrees. 'Please,' I said, 'the rice will burn.' I looked in her blazing eyes and saw my own.

The next day we declared a ceasefire which has held for 20 years, secured perhaps by the attractive young man I sent to her in New York.

We've never written each other a single letter, never planned our erratic meetings. We arrive unannounced. Sometimes, when I've stayed with her and Jack (since reunited) in one of their four houses, I've felt suffocated, like a poor relation. She's so tyrannical, I grumble, a 50-year-old brat. She deserves a good spanking. Yet I'm always beguiled by her lightning wit and the mad generosity she has never lost, operating on the principle that whoever is richest pays for everyone else. I marvel at what a good mother she is and how, unlike many of my Sixties friends, she has never abandoned her radical politics. It is one of the few ways in which we remain alike.

That and being late developers, she as a painter, I as a writer. The physical resemblance has gone, though occasionally a stranger will squint and inquire: 'You two sisters?' I'm darker now and she's fairer, my Celtic and her Anglo-Saxon chromosomes declaring themselves in middle-age. And she is sartorially eccentric, a post-punk in expensive rags, leopardskin beanie atop long white hair, flashy gold jewellery.

No longer twins, our features tell their stories. We look like what we've done and how we've lived, freed of that archetype which used to define us and which we shared so giddily. But what is left without the archetype?

I attempted to find out by basing a character in one of my novels on her. Various solutions emerged: Jungian theories of the divided self, reincarnation, two only children desperate for a sister, plain vanity. Her response to the book was: 'I don't recognise myself at all.' Well, she would say that, wouldn't she?

There are friends I like better who don't snap at me. But then friendship isn't necessarily decorous or even consoling. It endures because of the life that fills it, rising up fresh to meet you, at once mysterious and familiar.

As I'm typing this piece my phone rings. It's her, and she has three hours in London and what am I doing this afternoon?

'Funny,' I say, 'I was just thinking of you.'

MARY FLANAGAN, Observer, 1994

---

from Twins

THAT was the summer the strange thing happened that cut our lives in two. At the end of August, Father drove a carload of us to the state fair two hundred miles away because he'd got the idea from an advertisement he'd seen that his brother Les would be appearing there, with a troupe called the Monterey Ensemble. Mother thought it was a terrible idea; she seemed frightened of it. At first she didn't want to come along but then she said, yes, she'd better. She was worried about how Father would react when he didn't find Les but she worried too about what might happen if he *did* find him.

The state fair was gigantic, and the Monterey Ensemble was only one of numberless small attractions. We had a difficult time locating the shabby tent in which their performance was held, and as soon as we settled in our seats I knew we shouldn't have come. The atmosphere in the tent was rowdy – the audience was slow to settle down – it seemed the show was for children primarily, yet in some respects it seemed too sophisticated, or in any case too ironic, for children. Perhaps the performers were angry at their audience; the bleachers were only two thirds full. They strutted about in a peculiar swaggering manner, brash as adolescents. The youngest was about twenty years old and the oldest at least my father's age.

The first performers were jugglers, and they were very good, a man and a woman in bright spangled costumes who tossed Indian clubs and other odd-shaped items into the air with an extraordinary carelessness. My father was keyed up as I had never seen him, but absolutely still, watching the performers intently though it was immediately clear that the man wasn't his brother. He'd brought along a pint of bourbon in a paper bag and was sipping from it now and then.

Accompanying the performers was a clown musician playing drums, cymbals, horns, and other noisy instruments. He was bald and fat, with a bright lipsticked smile that never changed. I stared at him, dreading to think it might be Uncle Les but clearly it was

417

not; that man looked nothing like Father. I could see that Father was watching him too, anxiously, but he never turned into Uncle Les.

Father stared at the jugglers with such concentration he forgot to applaud at the end of the act.

Next were acrobats, then a mime with a seemingly elastic spine and long rubbery arms and legs, then a trio of clowns who made the audience roar with laughter, they were such crude buffoons, knocking one another down into the sawdust, kicking one another's rears. Shortly the entire troupe had introduced themselves. Was that all? None of the men resembled my father closely enough to have been his twin.

Unless it one of the clowns. Or the mime, made up grotesquely in white face, high arched eyebrows painted above his own eyebrows, small scarlet cupid's-bow mouth. Mother leaned over to Father and said, 'He isn't here!' with an air of vast relief but Father said nothing. He sipped from the pint bottle; he studied the performers. He was staring, staring. His eyes darted from place to place and tiny beads of perspiration stood out on his forehead. It was as if he knew Les was here but didn't know which person he was.

Of all the performers the clowns predictably drew the most laughter and applause. The mime drew the least, not because he wasn't good – he was very good – but because his routines went so swiftly, were so complex, it was difficult for the younger spectators to follow them. And there was that air about him of swagger and irony, a suggestion of mockery. He might have been anywhere between thirty and fifty years old. He wore black tights that emphasized his near-emaciated body – his ribs poked through the fabric – and an absurd curly black wig; his makeup was dead white, his eyes luridly outlined, How antic he was, even when his audience sat silent and baffled, how graceful his movements. As we stared at him it came to seem that he might resemble my father after all though he was probably years younger, and he was certainly smaller. If it was Uncle Les the flesh had melted away from his face, leaving it narrow and bony especially at the forehead. The man had a pinched, foxy look beneath his makeup that was disquieting to see.

After a few minutes Father whispered, 'That's him.'

The mime was climbing a flight of stairs, knocking on a door, opening the door to let himself in, kissing himself on the mouth, all very swiftly and it almost seemed naturally; it was remarkable how convincing his gestures were. He had an animated conversation, tossed himself downstairs, picked himself up from the sawdust floor, strode away in dignity. The audience was slow in responding so he stood with his hands on his hips in an arrogant posture, staring out at us. He did a somersault, bounced to his feet, stood again with his hands on his hips, head flung back, staring. Father broke into loud applause as if he meant to prod the audience into clapping. He got to his feet, raising his hands high so that the mime could see him. 'Bravo!' he called out.

Mother pulled him back down, greatly embarrassed. He was drunk, she said. And that wasn't Les.

'Yes, that's him,' Father said stubbornly. 'Which of the others can he be?'

'That man doesn't look anything like you,' Mother said. 'He's years younger.'

Father was on his feet again, applauding.

The mime bowed in his direction. Miming delight, gratitude, as if nothing pleased him more than Father's enthusiasm.

Mother tried to pull him down again but Father brushed her hands away. He was swaying drunk on his feet. In a stage whisper, cupping his hands to his mouth, he said, 'Hello, Les!' His gravelly whisper carried through the tent. 'Hello, Les – it's Lee. You can't fool me – it's Lee. Les? Hey? It's Lee! See who I am?'

The mime was staring at him blankly, showing no sign of recognition.

'Hey, Les – it's Lee! Your brother Lee! You can't fool me, Les!' Father said.

The mime's lips drew back from his teeth in a parody of a smile. A parody of recognition. He mimicked delight, rolling his eyes at the audience; he signaled for Father to join him in the ring. It *was* Uncle Les, wasn't it? Greatly changed and hideously made up, but wasn't it him? Father certainly thought so. He didn't hesitate a moment; he obeyed the mime's summons and stepped forward, staring, shambling, dazed as a man in a dream.

The mime lured him forward. And he obeyed. We all stared transfixed with misery: how could this be happening? Father drunk on his feet, a big man, graceless, stumbling, drawn forward to make a fool of himself before an audience of silly children. A savage blush mottled his neck and face; he'd sweated through his summer shirt. The mime mocked a friendly greeting, reaching out to shake hands with Father and then, as Father responded, drawing quickly back. He mocked Father's embarrassment and confusion. As in a mirror he aped Father's gestures. The audience exploded into laughter. As

Father stood flat-footed in the spotlights, smiling fatuously, the mime danced about him, rousing the audience to ever greater fits of laughter. He was quick as an eel, manic, sinister, funnier than any of the clowns; he lifted his wig as if it was a hat (beneath, his hair was gray-brown like Father's, cut brutally short), and so mesmerizing was the gesture you could see how close Father came to mimicking it.

A second time the mime tricked Father into reaching out to shake hands. He ducked under Father's arm, danced away behind him. It was the most humiliating sight I have ever witnessed. Father was surely aware of the audience of rowdy children laughing at him, he must have been aware of the mime, or of Les, mocking him, yet he couldn't seem to break away. He stood there dazed and clumsy, blinking into the lights. He spoke to the mime, who mocked his speech, he smiled at the mime, who mocked his smile as in a funhouse mirror. Adroitly the mime danced behind him to give him a quick kick in the seat of the pants – not hard, but hard enough to jolt him. Why didn't he fight back, I wondered, why didn't he kick the mime in return? It would have seemed natural, there in the spotlights. In the squalid little sawdust ring, with everybody laughing.

The comedy must have lasted no more than five minutes, though it seemed much longer. Then the mime relented, as if knowing he'd gone too far. Or maybe he suddenly felt sorry for his victim. He backed off, bowing low, and released Father from his spell. And one of the clowns escorted Father back to his seat.

And Father sat down heavily beside me, panting, soaked in sweat. I couldn't bear to look at him.

JOYCE CAROL OATES

---

from The Doubles

'THERE he is, look!' Newmore nodded towards a corner.

Peering hard Arben discerned a strange half opaque object, which looked like a vertical cloud the size of a man.

'The usual cyber-model, only based on anti-matter,' Newmore said, and gave Arben a nudge with his elbow. 'Don't be afraid, he is surrounded by a protective field. You must meet your future double after all.'

The cloud had a vague resemblance to a human figure. The arms he could only guess at were hanging listlessly down his sides, the head was hanging low. The wall could be seen through the body.

'Just an imitation of a human being. nothing more,' Newmore explained. 'A tribute to convention. I could endow Alva with any shape at all. But like this he will find it easier to mix with the crowd. Otherwise you will lose your freedom of movement.'

Arben fancied that the cloud gave a shudder every time Newmore pronounced the word Alva. Was he imagining it? Arben was deeply disturbed.

'I did not imagine him like this,' he said quietly.

'Oh, you think the double must resemble the original? He will when you enter into biological radio contact. In a month's time, when he launches forth into the world, so to speak, you will be as alike as two peas in a pod.'

'But he is transparent!'

'Small matter. I'll cover him with an opaque film. And I'll give him a suit of the best cut – but that of course will be a mere light effect. Or better still I shall give him the clothes you wear – beginning with this jacket and ending with crumpled pants. Let you be doubles in everything!'

'How fast can Alva move?'

'At any velocity at all. Without, of course, surpassing Einstein's light constant. It would be nothing to him to overtake a car or an airplane.'

'If he overtakes a car in the street, he will attract general attention,' Arben said with a worried air.

'Smart of you!' Newmore slapped Arben on the shoulder approvingly. 'I have already thought about it. We shall limit your brother's speed, so that he should not stand out in the street. Would three miles an hour be enough, what do you think?'

'Too much,' Arben answered curtly. He did not like the word 'brother' at all. A deadly brother was not such an enviable acquisition. But what could you do? Alva was the other side of the medal, and Newmore's proposition was extremely tempting.

[. . .] 'Your brother will have no difficulty in absorbing information coded in the cells,' Newmore said lighting up another cigarette.

'And what shall I be doing meanwhile?'

'You will be going about your own affairs peacefully. Peacefully is not just a figure of speech – you will feel more at peace than ever before. As soon as Alva is switched on, you will feel as though you have cast a heavy burden off your shoulders. Gradually Alva will relieve you of your nervous strain. Did you have a good look at yourself in the mirror? You look like death.'

'Then why did you have to get my agreement? You could do it all without it.'

'Here you are mistaken. It is very important for me that you should offer no inner resistance – it may distort the process of absorbing information.'

They had come to the door.

'What I shall do is to split your personality, as it were,' Newmore said in parting. 'The better part will be yours. The worse is projected on Alva. He will be the carrier of your irascibility, your neurotic outbursts, your flashes of unaccountable anger – anyway, you know yourself well enough, I don't have to spell it out for you. All that you want to get rid of will become Alva's. And you will be able to fully enjoy life. You will fall asleep as soon as your head touches the pillow, your sleep will be deep and untroubled. Your glance, the conductor and reflection of your integral will, will acquire hypnotic properties. People will be glad to obey you and do your bidding. But this bliss will have to be paid for. You will enjoy life, while Alva, your copy, deaf, blind, deprived of all senses, will dash about the city, searching for you, his antipode. Luckily, when Alva takes final shape and becomes externally a copy of you, his protective field will become more powerful – this is within my powers. So the radio signals sent off by you, will just barely penetrate through that magnetic armour. You'd be able to live in peace and fear nothing. But the moment you break your life's rhythm, become excited or develop a passion for something, the intensity of the signals radiated by your cells will grow and Alva will be able to catch them more easily. Then he will locate you sooner – you must see that for yourself.'

'It's late, I must go,' said Arben.

'One more thing,' Newmore said detaining his hand after their handshake. 'It is quite likely that when Alva is put at large and starts roaming the city, he will run into your acquaintances – for they, too, will be a bait for him, since each of them receives and reflects your biowaves, like the Moon reflects the sun's rays.'

'So they too . . .'

'No, no,' Newmore interrupted. 'A meeting with Alva entails no danger for them – he will be attuned to you alone. Remember it.'

VLADIMIR MIKHANOVSKY

---

from Frankenstein

I remained motionless. The thunder ceased, but the rain still continued, and the scene was enveloped in an impenetrable darkness. I revolved in my mind the events which I had until now sought to forget: the whole train of my progress towards the creation, the appearance of the work of my own hands alive at my bedside, its departure. Two years had now nearly elapsed since the night on which he first received life, and was this his first crime? Alas! I had turned loose into the world a depraved wretch whose delight was in carnage and misery; had he not murdered my brother?

No one can conceive the anguish I suffered during the remainder of the night, which I spent, cold and wet, in the open air. But I did not feel the inconvenience of the weather; my imagination was busy in scenes of evil and despair. I considered the being whom I had cast among mankind and endowed with the will and power to effect purposes of horror, such as the deed which he had now done, nearly in the light of my own vampire, my own spirit let loose from the grave and forced to destroy all that was dear to me.

MARY SHELLEY

The Double

WHEN Mrs Bloomgarden awoke at seven o'clock on Saturday morning the third of September, she discovered that her feet had come off sometime during the night. Small and sympathetic, her feet had tumbled to the floor and lay quietly on the rug – their fresh pink nail polish shining prettily in the sun.

'Well, I'll be damned!' she exclaimed. And turning to Leo Bloomgarden she whispered, perhaps more harshly than she intended, 'Leo! Wake up for God's sake; wake up, Leo!'

'I'm leaving,' said Leo simply after breakfast. 'Forgive me, Gloria, but I can't take it.' 'Poor Leo,' she said, stroking the back of his neck. 'Don't throw them out,' he indicated the bedroom as he left. 'Who knows? They might come in handy,' and he chuckled.

'That Leo,' she smiled to herself after he had gone. 'Always ready for a laugh.'

*   *   *

The next day she noticed that her feet were growing back. With a pang of secret understanding she went to find the shoe box hidden in the closet. In a moment her feet lay bare and vulnerable in her lap. She smiled. It was as she had thought. No, she was not surprised – hadn't she known all along? The feet were growing legs.

'Will they join?' she pondered. 'I suppose I'd better leave them out of the box now.' She lay them on the bed, being careful to place them in proper juxtaposition. If they were going to join, as undoubtedly they were (were not her own feet now half grown back?) there would be no malformation. And that is why, within a very short time, a new Gloria Bloomgarden grew perfectly and to full height. (I shudder to think what might have happened had she left her feet in the shoe box . . .)

That night she lay in bed beside the new Gloria (who had not yet attained consciousness) and watched her sleep. 'How beautiful I am,' she thought. She bent over the sleeping double and kissed her on the lips. 'When she awakens tomorrow' (and it was certain she would awaken – were not her own two feet fully regrown but for the nails?), 'when she awakens I will not tell Leo,' she decided. 'I will keep her to myself. She will be my secret as I will be hers. How lovely it is going to be!' Gently she caressed the double's perfect breasts (beneath which she distinctly heard the beating of a heart).

RIKKI DUCORNET

The Other

THE forest ended. Glad I was
To feel the light, and hear the hum
Of bees, and smell the drying grass
And the sweet mint, because I had come
To an end of forest, and because
Here was both road and inn, the sum
Of what's not forest. But 'twas here
They asked me if I did not pass
Yesterday this way. 'Not you? Queer.'
'Who then? and slept here?' I felt fear.

I learnt his road and, ere they were
Sure I was I, left the dark wood

Behind, kestrel and woodpecker,
The inn in the sun, the happy mood
When first I tasted sunlight there.
I travelled fast, in hopes I should
Outrun that other. What to do
When caught, I planned not. I pursued
To prove the likeness, and, if true,
To watch until myself I knew.

I tried the inns that evening
Of a long gabled high-street grey,
Of courts and outskirts, travelling
An eager but a weary way, In vain.
He was not there. Nothing
Told me that ever till that day
Had one like me entered those doors,
Save once. That time I dared: 'You may
Recall' – but never-foamless shores
Make better friends than those dull boors.

Many and many a day like this
Aimed at the unseen moving goal
And nothing found but remedies
For all desire. These made not whole;
They sowed a new desire, to kiss
Desire's self beyond control,
Desire of desire. And yet
Life stayed on within my soul.
One night in sheltering from the wet
I quite forgot I could forget.

A customer, then the landlady
Stared at me. With a kind of smile
They hesitated awkwardly:
Their silence gave me time for guile.
Had anyone called there like me,
I asked. It was quite plain the wile
Succeeded. For they poured out all.
And that was naught. Less than a mile
Beyond the inn, I could recall
He was like me in general.

He had pleased them, but I less.
I was more eager than before
To find him out and to confess,
To bore him and to let him bore.
I could not wait: children might guess
I had a purpose, something more
That made an answer indiscreet.
One girl's caution made me sore,
Too indignant even to greet
That other had we chanced to meet.

I sought then in solitude.
The wind had fallen with the night; as still
The roads lay as the ploughland rude,
Dark and naked, on the hill.
Had there been ever any feud
'Twixt earth and sky, a mighty will
Closed it: the crocketed dark trees,
A dark house, dark impossible
Cloud-towers, one star, one lamp, one peace
Held on an everlasting lease:

And all was earth's, or all was sky's;
No difference endured between
The two. A dog barked on a hidden rise;
A marshbird whistled high unseen;
The latest waking blackbird's cries
Perished upon the silence keen.
The last light filled a narrow firth
Among the clouds. I stood serene,
And with a solemn quiet mirth,
An old inhabitant of earth.

Once the name I gave to hours
Like this was melancholy, when
It was not happiness and powers
Coming like exiles home again,
And weaknesses quitting their bowers,
Smiled and enjoyed, far off from men,
Moments of everlastingness.
And fortunate my search was then

While what I sought, nevertheless,
That I was seeking, I did not guess.

That time was brief: once more at inn
And upon road I sought my man
Till once amid a tap-room's din
Loudly he asked for me, began
To speak, as if it had been a sin,
Of how I thought and dreamed and ran
After him thus, day after day:
He lived as one under a ban
For this: what had I got to say?
I said nothing. I slipped away.

And now I dare not follow after
Too close. I try to keep in sight,
Dreading his frown and worse his laughter.
I steal out of the wood to light;
I see the swift shoot from the rafter
By the inn door: ere I alight
I wait and hear the starlings wheeze
And nibble like ducks: I wait his flight.
He goes: I follow: no release
Until he ceases.
Then I also shall cease.

EDWARD THOMAS

The Spectral Self *or* My Phantom Double

'How still the night. The streets are deserted.
In that house yonder, one I loved did dwell.
She is far away. The place is forsaken,
And there stands the house dark and lone and chill.

And there is a man stands staring at her window,
He shakes and shudders in agony.
Saints in heaven! He turns his face towards me.
The moon comes out: tis myself I see!

Thou ghostly double, no man but a shadow,
What dost thou, aping my old cry
And all the pangs that I here suffered
So many a night in times gone by?'

HEINE

---

from 'La Nuit de Décembre'

Du temps que j'étais écolier
Je restais un soir à veiller
Dans notre salle solitaire.
Devant mon table vint s'asseoir,
Un pauvre enfant, vêtu de noir,
Que me ressemblait comme un frère . . .

. . . Partout où, le long des chemins,
J'ai posé mon front dans mes mains,
Et sanglotte comme un mouton,
Qui laisse sa laine au buisson,
Senti se dénuer mon âme;

Partout où j'ai voulu, dormir,
Partout où j'ai touché la terre,
Sur ma route est venu s'asseoir,
Un malheureux vêtu de noir,
Qui me ressemblait comme un frère.

Qui donc es tu, toi que dans cette vue
  Je vois toujours sur mon chemin,
Je ne puis croire, à ta mélancholie
  Que tu sois mon mauvais Destin.
Ton doux sourire à trop de patience,
  Tes larmes ont trop de pitié.
En te voyant, j'aime la Providence.
Ta douleur même est soeur de ma souffrance:
  Elle ressemble à l'amitié.

[When still a schoolboy, I was lying awake one night in our lonely
room, when there came in and sat down at my table a poor child
dressed all in black and as like me as a brother . . .

Wherever on my journey's way I set my head in my hands and wept like a woman, wherever I felt my heart stripped as bare as a sheep shorn by the shearer; Whenever I longed for sleep, wherever I touched land, there has come and sat on my path a wretch dressed all in black, and as like me as a brother.

Whoever you are that I keep seeing on my way, I cannot believe, observing your melancholy, that you are my ill fortune. Your sweet smile has too much patience, your tears are too full of pity. The sight of you makes me love providence. Your grief is even sister to my suffering. It seems like affection.]

ALFRED DE MUSSET, prose translation by Penelope Farmer

The solution that resolves the problems of the individual yearning for companionship is a parody of the desired synthesis of crowd and hermit: one creates society as God created Eve out of Adam – by splitting the self.

PAUL COATES

---

from Hapgood

WE´RE all doubles. Even you. Your cover is Bachelor of Arts first class, with an amusing incomprehension of the sciences, but you insist on laboratory standards for reality, while I insist on its artfulness. So it is with us all, we're not so one-or-the-other. The one who puts on the clothes in the morning is the working majority, but at night – perhaps in the moment before unconsciousness – we meet our sleeper – the priest is visited by the doubter, the Marxist sees the civilizing force of the bourgeoisie, the captain of industry admits the justice of common ownership.

TOM STOPPARD

---

from The Divided Self

A 'borderline' case – David

I shall give a straightforward account of David with the minimum of comment because I want the reader to be quite clear that such people and such problems exist in reality and are not matters of my invention. This case can also serve as a basis for much of the general discussion in the subsequent section.

David was eighteen when I saw him. He was an only child whose mother had died when he was ten. Since then he had lived with his father. From grammar school he had gone to university to study philosophy. His father could not see the point of his son consulting a psychiatrist as there was nothing, in his view, for him to see a psychiatrist about. His tutor, however, was worried about the boy because he seemed to be hallucinated and acted in various somewhat odd ways. For instance, he attended lectures in a cloak, which he wore over his shoulders and arms; he carried a cane; his whole manner was entirely artificial; his speech was made up largely of quotations.

His father's account of him was very meagre. He had always been perfectly normal, and he thought his present eccentricities were simply an adolescent phase. He had always been a very good child, who did everything he was told and never caused any trouble. His mother had been devoted to him. He was inseparable from her. He had been 'very brave' when she died and had done everything to help his father. He did the housework, cooked the meals, bought most of the food. He 'took over' from his mother or 'took after' her, even to the extent of showing her flair for embroidery, tapestry, and interior decoration. All this his father commended and spoke highly of.

The boy was a most fantastic-looking character – an adolescent Kierkegaard played by Danny Kaye. The hair was too long, the collar too large, the trousers too short, the shoes too big, and withal, his second-hand theatre cloak and cane! He was not simply eccentric: I could not escape the impression that this young man was *playing* at being eccentric. The whole effect was mannered and contrived. But why should anyone wish to contrive such an effect?

He was indeed quite a practised actor, for he had been playing one part or other at least since his mother's death. Before that, he said, 'I had simply been what she wanted.' Of her death he said, 'As far as I can remember I was rather pleased. Perhaps I felt some sorrow; I would like to think so anyway.' Until his mother's death he had simply been what she wanted him to be. After her death it was no easier for him to be himself. He had grown up taking entirely for granted that what he called his 'self' and his 'personality' were two quite separate things. He had never seriously imagined any other possibility and he took it equally for granted that everyone else was constructed along similar lines. His view of human nature in general, based on his own experience of himself, was that everyone was an actor. It is important to realize that this was a settled conviction or assumption about human beings which governed his life. This made it very easy for him to be anything his mother wanted, because all his actions simply belonged to some part or other he was playing. If they could be said to belong to his self at all, they belonged only to a 'false self', a self that acted according to *her* will, not his.

His self was never directly revealed in and through his actions. It seemed to be the case that he had emerged from his infancy with his *'own self'* on the one hand, and 'what his mother wanted him to be', his 'personality', on the other; he had started from there and made it his aim and ideal to make the split between his own self (which only he knew) and what other people could see of him, as complete as possible. He was further impelled to this course by the fact that despite himself he had always felt shy, self-conscious, and vulnerable. By always playing a part he found he could in some measure overcome his shyness, self-consciousness, and vulnerability. He found reassurance in the consideration that whatever he was doing he was not being himself. Thus, he used that same form of defence which has been already mentioned: in an effort to mitigate anxiety he aggravated the conditions that were occasioning it.

The important point he always kept in mind was that he was playing a part. Usually, in his mind, he was playing the part of someone else, but sometimes he played the part of himself (his own self): that is, he was not simply and spontaneously himself, but he *played* at being himself. His ideal was, *never to give himself away to others*. Consequently he practised the most tortuous equivocation towards others in the parts he played. Towards himself, however, his ideal was to be as utterly frank and honest as possible.

The whole organization of his being rested on the disjunction of his inner 'self' and his outer 'personality'. It is remarkable that this state of affairs had existed for years without his 'personality', i.e. his way of behaving with others, appearing unusual.

The outward appearance could not reveal the fact that his 'personality' was no true self-expression but was largely a series of *impersonations*. The part he regarded himself as having been playing most of his schooldays was that of a rather precocious schoolboy with a sharp wit, but somewhat cold. He said, however, that when he was fifteen he had realized that this part was becoming unpopular because '*It* had a nasty tongue'. Accordingly he decided to modify this part into a more likeable character, 'with good results'.

However, his efforts to sustain this organization of his being were threatened in two ways. The first did not trouble him too seriously. It was the risk of being spontaneous. As an actor, he wished always to be detached from the part he was playing. Thereby he felt himself to be master of the situation, in entire conscious control of his expressions and actions, calculating with precision their effects on others. To be spontaneous was merely stupid. It was simply putting oneself at other people's mercy.

The second threat was the more actual, and one upon which he had not calculated. If he had a personal source of complaint to bring to me, it was based on this threat, which indeed was beginning to disrupt his whole technique of living.

All through his childhood he had been very fond of playing parts in front of the mirror. Now in front of the mirror he continued to play parts, but in this one special instance he allowed himself to become absorbed into the part he played (to be spontaneous). This he felt was his undoing. The parts he played in front of the mirror were always women's parts. He dressed himself up in his mother's clothes, which had been kept. He rehearsed female parts from the great tragedies. But then he found he could not stop playing the part of a woman. He caught himself compulsively walking like a woman, talking like a woman, even seeing and thinking as a woman might see and think. This was his present position, and this was his explanation for his fantastic get-up. For, he said, he found that he was driven to dress up and act in his present manner as the only way to arrest the womanish part that threatened to engulf not only his actions but even his 'own' self as well, and to rob him of his much cherished control and mastery of his being. Why he was driven into playing this role, which he hated and which he knew everyone laughed at, he could not understand. But this 'schizophrenic' role was the only refuge he knew from being entirely engulfed by the woman who was inside him, and always seemed to be coming out of him.

R.D. LAING

> . . . Two souls, alas! reside within my breast,
> and each is eager for a separation:
> in throes of coarse desire, one grips
> the earth with all its senses;
> the other struggles from the dust
> to rise to high ancestral spheres . . .
>
> GOETHE, *Faust*, edited and translated by Stuart Atkins

---

from Confessions of St Augustine

FOR if there be so many contrary natures, as there be conflicting wills; there shall now be not two only, but many. If a man deliberate, whether he should go to their conventicle, or to the theatre: these Manichees cry out, Behold, here are two natures: one good, draws this way; another bad, draws back that way. For whence else is this hesitation between conflicting wills? But I say, that both be bad: that which draws to them, as that which draws back to the theatre. But they believe not that will to be other than good, which draws to them. What then if one of us should deliberate, and amid the strife of his two wills be in a strait, whether he should go to the theatre, or to our church? would not these Manichees also be in a strait what to answer? For either they must confess, (which they fain would not), that the will which leads to our church is good, as well as theirs, who have received and are held by the mysteries of theirs: or they must suppose two evil natures, and two evil souls conflicting in one man, and it will not be true, which they say, that there is one good and another bad; or they must be converted to the truth, and no more deny, that where one deliberates, one soul fluctuates between contrary wills.

Let them no more say then, when they perceive two conflicting wills in one man, that the conflict is between two contrary souls, of two contrary substances, from two contrary principles, one good, and the other bad. For Thou, O true God, dost disprove, check, and convict them: as when, both wills being bad, one deliberates, whether he should kill a man by poison, or by the sword; whether he should seize this or that estate of another's, when he cannot both: whether he should purchase pleasure by luxury, or keep his money by covetousness; whether he go to the circus, or the theatre, if both be open on one day: or, thirdly, to rob another's house, if he have

433

the opportunity; or, fourthly, to commit adultery, if at the same time he have the means thereof also; all these meeting together in the same juncture of time, and all being equally desired, which cannot at one time be acted: for they rend the mind amid four, or even (amid the vast variety of things desired) more, conflicting wills, nor do they yet allege that there are so many divers substances. So also in wills which are good. For I ask them, is it good to take pleasure in reading the Apostle? or good to take pleasure in a sober Psalm? or good to discourse on the Gospel? They will answer to each, 'It is good.' What then if all give equal pleasure, and all at once? Do not divers wills distract the mind, while he deliberates, which he should rather choose? yet are they all good, and are at variance till one be chosen, whither the one entire will may be borne, which before was divided into many. Thus also, when, above, eternity delights us, and the pleasure of temporal good holds us down below, it is the same soul which willeth not this or that with an entire will; and therefore is rent asunder with grievous perplexities, while out of truth it sets this first, but out of habit sets not that aside.

from Confessions of a Justified Sinner

IMMEDIATELY after this I was seized with a strange distemper, which neither my friends nor physicians could comprehend, and it confined me to my chamber for many days; but I knew, myself, that I was bewitched, and suspected my father's reputed concubine of the deed. I told my fears to my reverend protector, who hesitated concerning them, but I knew by his words and looks that he was conscious I was right. I generally conceived myself to be two people. When I lay in bed, I deemed there were two of us in it; when I sat up, I always beheld another person, and always in the same position from the place where I sat or stood, which was about three paces off me towards my left side. It mattered not how many or how few were present: this my second self was sure to be present in his place; and this occasioned a confusion in all my words and ideas that utterly astounded my friends, who all declared, that instead of being deranged in my intellect, they had never heard my conversation manifest so much energy or sublimity of conception; but for all that, over the singular delusion that I was two persons, my reasoning faculties had no power. The most perverse part of it was, that I rarely conceived *myself* to be any of the two persons. I thought for the most part that my companion was one of them, and my brother the other; and I found, that to be obliged to speak and answer in the character of another man, was a most awkward business at the long run.

JAMES HOGG

---

from The Case of the Dow Twins

'MISS Giles affirms that it was at the third apple tree next the stone wall of Hosea Getchell's orchard, just opposite the bars leading to Mr Lord's private road, that a sudden and most extraordinary change came over Jehiel. He jumped, she says, high into the air and landed sprawling in the sandy road alongside the hearse, yelling so hideously that it was with difficulty that she held the frightened horses. Picking himself up and uttering a round oath (something that had never before passed the virtuous lips of Jehiel), he turned his attention to the horses, kicking and beating them until they stood quiet. He next proceeded to cut and trim a willow switch at the roadside, and putting his decent silk hat down over one eye, and darting from the other a surly glance at the astonished Miss Giles, he climbed to his seat on the hearse.

'"Jehiel Dow!" said she, "what does this mean?"

'"It means," he replied, giving the horses a vicious cut with his switch, "that I have been goin' slow these thirty year, and now I'm goin' to put a little ginger in my gait. Gelang!"

'The hearse horses jumped under the unaccustomed lash and broke into a gallop. Jehiel applied the switch again and again, and the dismal vehicle was soon bumping over the road at a tremendous pace, Jehiel shouting all the time like a circus rider, and Miss Giles clinging to his side in an agony of terror. The people in the farmhouses along the way rushed to doors and windows and gazed in amazement at the unprecedented spectacle. Jehiel had a word for each – a shout of derision for one, a blast of blasphemy for another, and an invitation to ride for a third – but he reined in for nobody, and in a twinkling the five miles between Hosea Getchell's farm at Duck Trap at the village at Saturday Cove had been accomplished. I think I am safe in saying that never before did hearse rattle over five miles of hard road so rapidly.

'"Oh, Jehiel, Jehiel!" said Miss Giles, as the hearse entered the village, "are you took crazy of a sudden?"

435

'"No," said Jehiel curtly, "but my eyes are open now. Gelang, you beasts! You get out here; I'm going to Belfast."

'"But, Jehiel, dear," she protested, with many sobs, "remember Dr Gookin."

'"Dang Gookin!" said Jehiel.

'"And for my sake," she continued. "Dear Jehiel, for my sake."

'"Dang you, too!" said Jehiel.

'Drawing up his team in magnificent style before the village hotel, he compelled the weeping Miss Giles to alight, and then, with an admirable imitation of the war whoop of a Sioux brave, started his melancholy vehicle for Belfast, and was gone in a flash, leaving the entire population of Saturday Cove in a state of bewilderment that approached coma.

'The remains of the worthy Dr Gookin were borne to the graveyard that afternoon upon the shoulders of half a dozen of the stoutest farmers in the neighborhood. Jehiel came home long after midnight, uproariously intoxicated. The revolution in his character had been as complete as it was sudden. From the moment of Jacob's death, he was a dissipated, dishonest scoundrel, the scandal of Saturday Cove, and the terror of quiet respectable folks for miles around. After that day he never could be persuaded to speak to or even to recognize the young woman named Giles. She, to her credit, remained faithful to the memory of the lost Jehiel. His downward course was rapid. He gambled, drank, quarreled, and stole; and he is now in state prison at Thomaston, serving out a sentence for an attempt to rob the Northport Bank. Miss Giles goes down every year in the hopes that he will see her, but he always refuses. He is in for ten years.'

'And he, does he feel no remorse for what he did?' I asked.

'See here,' said Dr Richards, turning suddenly and looking me square in the face. 'Do you think of what you are saying? Now I hold that he is as innocent as you or I. I believe that the souls of the twins were bound by a bond which Dr Gookin's knife could not dissect. When Jacob died, his soul, with all its depravity, returned to its twin soul in Jehiel's body. Being stronger than the Jehiel soul it mastered and overwhelmed it. Poor Jehiel is not responsible; he is suffering the penalty of a crime that was clearly Jake's.'

My friend spoke with a good deal of earnestness and some heat, and concluding that Jehiel's personality was submerged. I did not press the discussion. That evening, in conversation with the village clergyman, I remarked:

'Strange case that of the Dow twins.'

'Ah,' said the parson, 'you have heard the story. Which way did the doctor end it?'

'Why, with Jehiel in jail, of course. What do you mean?'

'Nothing,' replied the parson with a faint smile. 'Sometimes when he feels well disposed toward humanity, the doctor lets Jehiel's soul take possession of Jacob and reform him into a pious, respectable Christian. In his pessimistic moods, the story is just as you heard it. So this is one of his Jacob days. He should take a little vacation.'

E. P. MITCHELL

---

from The Picture of Dorian Gray

HE winced, and, taking up from the table an oval glass framed in ivory Cupids, one of Lord Henry's many presents to him, glanced hurriedly into its polished depths. No line like that warped his red lips. What did it mean?

He rubbed his eyes, and came close to the picture, and examined it again. There were no signs of any change when he looked into the actual painting, and yet there was no doubt that the whole expression had altered. It was not a mere fancy of his own. The thing was horribly apparent.

He threw himself into a chair, and began to think. Suddenly there flashed across his mind what he had said in Basil Hallward's studio the day the picture had been finished. Yes, he remembered it perfectly. He had uttered a mad wish that he himself might remain young, and the portrait grow old; that his own beauty might be untarnished, and the face on the canvas bear the burden of his passions and his sins; that the painted image might be seared with the lines of suffering and thought, and that he might keep all the delicate bloom and loveliness of his then just conscious boyhood. Surely his wish had not been fulfilled? Such things were impossible. It seemed monstrous even to think of them. And, yet, there was the picture before him, with the touch of cruelty in the mouth.

OSCAR WILDE

from Dr Jekyll and Mr Hyde

THERE was no mirror, at that date, in my room; that which stands beside me as I write was brought there later on, and for the very purpose of those transformations. The night, however, was far gone into the morning – the morning, black as it was, was nearly ripe for the conception of the day – the inmates of my house were locked in the most rigorous hours of slumber; and I determined, flushed as I was with hope and triumph, to venture in my new shape as far as to my bedroom. I crossed the yard, wherein the constellations looked down upon me, I could have thought, with wonder, the first creature of that sort that their unsleeping vigilance had yet disclosed to them; I stole through the corridors, a stranger in my own house; and coming to my room, I saw for the first time the appearance of Edward Hyde.

I must here speak by theory alone, saying not that which I know, but that which I suppose to be most probable. The evil side of my nature, to which I had now transferred the stamping efficacy, was less robust and less developed than the good which I had just deposed. Again, in the course of my life, which had been, after all, nine-tenths a life of effort, virtue and control, it had been much less exercised and much less exhausted. And hence, as I think, it came about that Edward Hyde was so much smaller, slighter, and younger than Henry Jekyll. Even as good shone upon the countenance of the one, evil was written broadly and plainly on the face of the other. Evil besides (which I must still believe to be the lethal side of man) had left on that body an imprint of deformity and decay. And yet when I looked upon that ugly idol in the glass, I was conscious of no repugnance, rather of a leap of welcome. This, too, was myself. It seemed natural and human. In my eyes it bore a livelier image of the spirit, it seemed more express and single, than the imperfect and divided countenance I had been hitherto accustomed to call mine. And in so far I was doubtless right. I have observed that when I wore the semblance of Edward Hyde, none could come near to me at first without a visible misgiving of the flesh. This, as I take it, was because all human beings, as we meet them, are commingled out of good and evil; and Edward Hyde, alone, in the ranks of mankind, was pure evil.

ROBERT LOUIS STEVENSON

It was odd how the term 'Jekyll and Hyde' had passed into the language, so that even people who had never read Stevenson's story used the names as shorthand for internal divisions. Prior spoke of looking at his hands to make sure they had not been transformed into the hairy hands of Hyde, and he was not alone in that. Every patient Rivers had ever had who suffered from a fugue state sooner or later referred to that state as 'Hyde'.

PAT BARKER, *The Eye in the Door*

from The Nazi Doctors

THE key to understanding how Nazi doctors came to do the work of Auschwitz is the psychological principle I call 'doubling': the division of the self into two functioning wholes, so that a part-self acts as an entire self. An Auschwitz doctor could, through doubling, not only kill and contribute to killing but organize silently, on behalf of that evil project, an entire self-structure (or self-process) encompassing virtually all aspects of his behavior.

Doubling, then, was the psychological vehicle for the Nazi doctor's Faustian bargain with the diabolical environment; in exchange for his contribution to the killing, he was offered various psychological and material benefits on behalf of privileged adaptation. Beyond Auschwitz was the larger Faustian temptation offered to German doctors in general: that of becoming the theorists and implementers of a cosmic scheme of racial cure by means of victimization and mass murder.

One is always ethically responsible for Faustian bargains – a responsibility in no way abrogated by the fact that much doubling takes place outside of awareness. In exploring doubling, I engage in psychological probing on behalf of illuminating evil. For the individual Nazi doctor in Auschwitz, doubling was likely to mean a choice for evil.

Generally speaking, doubling involves five characteristics. There is, first, a dialectic between two selves in terms of autonomy and connection. The individual Nazi doctor needed his Auschwitz self to function psychologically in an environment so antithetical to his previous ethical standards. At the same time, he needed his prior self in order to continue to see himself as humane physician, husband, father. The Auschwitz self had to be both autonomous and connected to the prior self that gave rise to it. Second, doubling follows a holistic principle. The Auschwitz self 'succeeded' because it was inclusive and could connect with the entire Auschwitz environment; it rendered coherent, and gave form to, various themes and mechanisms, which I shall discuss shortly. Third, doubling has a life–death dimension: the Auschwitz self was perceived by the perpetrator as a form of psychological survival in a death-dominated environment: in other words, we have the paradox of a 'killing self' being created on behalf of what one perceives as one's own healing or survival. Fourth, a major function of doubling, as in Auschwitz, is likely to be the avoidance of guilt: the second self tends to be the one performing the 'dirty work.' And, finally, doubling involves both an unconscious dimension – taking place, as stated, largely outside of awareness – and a significant change in moral consciousness. These five characteristics frame and pervade all else that goes on psychologically in doubling.

[. . .] Mengele's own attitude toward the twins research was fiercely enthusiastic. Dr Lottie M. stressed how passionately involved Mengele was with 'his genetic idea,' and a Polish woman survivor told how he 'rushed through [his duties on the medical block] in order to have more time for his twins.' That passion made him 'totally blind to' the general misery of the camp. When he found identical twins in any transport, this woman went on to say, 'Mengele beamed – he was happy, . . . in a kind of a trance.' When deprived of possible twins – as on one occasion when he was not notified about the arrival of a transport – he was observed to become enraged and threatening.

As he also did when children, out of fear or fatigue, interrupted the examinations, or, as another survivor put it, 'if something didn't go right in experiments' or even if a temperature reading was not recorded on a twin's chart. Once when a child screamed that he felt like passing out, Mengele 'became enraged . . . [and] knocked the whole table down.' His attitude, according to this observer, seemed to be that if he could not complete the work immediately, he 'might not be able to achieve it.' He also became 'furious,' according to another survivor when a girl twin died at the wrong time – as in the case of one who succumbed to diphtheria while he was following her syphilis. He was attentive to and provided special care and medications for the surviving twin, who also developed diphtheria and whom he was said to like very much – until she recovered, at which time he had her killed so that her syphilis could be confirmed at post-mortem examination.

This duality – a confusing combination of affection and violence – was constantly described to me. The Polish woman survivor, for instance, described him as 'impulsive . . . [with] a choleric temper,' but 'in his attitude to children [twins] . . . as gentle as a father . . . [who] talked to them . . . [and] patted them on the head in a loving way.' He could be playful with them as well and 'jumped around' to please them. Twin children frequently called him 'Uncle Pepi'; and other twins told how Mengele would bring them sweets and invite them for a ride in his car, which turned out to be 'a little drive with Uncle Pepi, to the gas chamber.' Simon J. put it most succinctly: 'He could be friendly but kill.' And two other twins described him as 'like a dual personality, like Dr Jekyll and Mr Hyde, I think.'

Twins felt Mengele's appeal. One believed that Mengele liked him: '[He] immediately referred to me as his friend' and said that he was 'very fascinated with something in the Jew' and was generally pleasant and 'very human.' This man believed that Mengele protected the twins from Heinz Thilo, an SS doctor who wanted them killed, so that the latter was the 'devil of death' (an evil murderer) while Mengele was the 'angel of death' (who still had a little bit of feeling). But this survivor admitted that Mengele, in the laboratory, 'became a different person entirely, . . . a fanatic, . . . [and] if he didn't see blood on his white uniform, he wasn't content.' Tomas A. remained still more troublingly bound to Mengele: 'For twins Mengele was everything, . . . just marvelous, . . . a good doctor, . . . our backing [support]. If [it hadn't been for] him, we wouldn't be alive.' For a long time after liberation, A. found it impossible to believe the evil things he heard about Mengele, and he still struggles with the contradiction. He can now sum up the situation: 'For us, for the twins, [he was] like a papa, like a mama. For us. On the other hand, he was a murderer.'

ROBERT JAY LIFTON

For what better symbol after all of Mengele's dual nature – the angel and the monster, the gentle young doctor and the sadistic killer – than a twin.

L. M. LAGNADO AND S. C. DEKEL, *Children of the Flames*

Whereas twins are staple figures of comic literature which feeds on the confusion their similarity generates, the Double recaptures the image of the twin for non-comic literature: the Double is the emissary of death . . . One sees oneself at that moment at which one departs one's mortal frame.

PAUL COATES, The Double and the Other

———————

from The Doubles

'NEWMAN'S CLAIM was that as this sponge absorbs a man's ailments, it becomes more and more like him. And in the end they are alike as two peas in a pod . . .'

'Yes,' Arben drawled, 'And what happens to the sponge?'

'It begins to live a life of its own, a reflection as it were of a life of its own. It's a kind of spectre, which comes to find its other half and merge into one. But the man must avoid such a meeting . . . it bodes no good for him. I don't quite know how, because Newman could hardly get his words out by then . . . what was it he said would happen?'

'Annihilation?' Arben prompted.

'That's right,' Linda exclaimed.

VLADIMIR MIKHANOVSKY

———————

from Heautoscopy, Epilepsy and Suicide

HEAUTOSCOPY is the multimodal reduplicative hallucination of one's own person. As the classic *doppelgänger* experience it combines the features of autoscopy, which is a mere visual hallucination of one's body or body parts, such as seen in a mirror reflection, and those of the out of body experience or the primarily somaesthetic illusion of being physically separated from one's own body. It has been described in the frame of various neurological and psychiatric disorders and may also be experienced by healthy subjects, although in traditional folklore one's double is always considered a harbinger of death. [. . .]

Case history

A 21 year old right handed man had an uneventful medical history until

442

age 15, when he developed complex partial seizures. He reported that up to three times a day he experienced a series of biographical events passing by very quickly, during which he would drop objects from his right hand; on rare occasions, generalisation occurred.

[. . .] The heautoscopic episode, which is of special interest to the topic of this report, occurred shortly before admission. The patient stopped his phenytoin medication, drank several glasses of beer, stayed in bed the whole of the next day, and in the evening he was found mumbling and confused below an almost completely destroyed large bush just under the window of his room on the third floor. At the local hospital, thoracic and pelvic contusions as well as multiple bruises were noted. The patient was in a postictal confusion state and reacted with pain to manipulation of the spine and the right foot, but radiologically there were no fractures.

The patient gave the following account of the episode: on the respective morning he got up with a dizzy feeling. Turning around, he saw himself still lying in bed. He became angry about 'this guy who I knew was myself and who would not get up and thus risked being late at work'. He tried to wake the body in the bed first by shouting at it; then by trying to shake it and then repeatedly jumping on his alter ego in the bed. The lying body showed no reaction. Only then did the patient begin to be puzzled about his double existence and become more and more scared by the fact that he could no longer tell which of the two he really was. Several times his bodily awareness switched from the one standing upright to the one still lying in bed; when in the lying in bed mode he felt quite awake but completely paralysed and scared by the figure of himself bending over and beating him. His only intention was to become one person again and, looking out of the window (from where he could still see his body lying in bed), he suddenly decided to jump out 'in order to stop the intolerable feeling of being divided in two'. At the same time, he hoped that 'this really desperate action would frighten the one in bed and thus urge him to merge with me again'. The next thing he remembers is waking up in pain in the hospital.

PETER BRUGGER, *Journal of Neurology*

from William Wilson

IT was at Rome, during the Carnival of 18—, that I attended a masquerade in the palazzo of the Neapolitan Duke Di Broglio. I had indulged more freely than usual in the excesses of the wine-table; and now the suffocating atmosphere of the crowded rooms irritated me beyond endurance. The difficulty, too, of forcing my way through the mazes of the company contributed not a little to the ruffling of my temper; for I was anxiously seeking (let me not say with what unworthy motive) the young, the gay, the beautiful wife of the aged and doting Di Broglio. With a too unscrupulous confidence she had previously communicated to me the secret of the costume in which she would be habited, and now, having caught a glimpse of her person, I was hurrying to make my way into her presence. – At this moment I felt a light hand placed upon my shoulder, and that ever-remembered, low, damnable *whisper* within my ear.

In an absolute frenzy of wrath, I turned at once upon him who had thus interrupted me, and seized him violently by the collar. He was attired, as I had expected, in a costume altogether similar to my own; wearing a Spanish cloak of blue velvet, begirt about the waist with a crimson belt sustaining a rapier. A mask of black silk entirely covered his face.

'Scoundrel!' I said, in a voice husky with rage, while every syllable I uttered seemed as new fuel to my fury, 'scoundrel! impostor! accursed villain! you shall not – you *shall not* dog me unto death! Follow me, or I stab you where you stand!' – and I broke my way from the ballroom into a small antechamber adjoining – dragging him unresistingly with me as I went.

Upon entering, I thrust him furiously from me. He staggered against the wall, while I closed the door with an oath, and commanded him to draw. He hesitated but for an instant; then, with a slight sigh, drew in silence, and put himself upon his defence.

The contest was brief indeed. I was frantic with every species of wild excitement, and felt within my single arm the energy and power of a multitude. In a few seconds I forced him by sheer strength against the wainscoting, and thus, getting him at mercy, plunged my sword, with brute ferocity, repeatedly through and through his bosom.

At that instant some person tried the latch of the door. I hastened to prevent an intrusion, and then immediately returned to my dying antagonist. But what human language can adequately portray *that* astonishment, *that* horror which possessed me at the spectacle then presented to view? The brief moment in which I averted my eyes had been sufficient to produce, apparently, a material change in the arrangements at the upper or farther end of the room. A large mirror, – so at first it seemed to me in my confusion – now stood where none had been perceptible before; and, as I stepped up to it in extremity of terror, mine own image, but with features all pale and dabbled in blood, advanced to meet me with a feeble and tottering gait.

Thus it appeared, I say, but was not. It was my antagonist – it was Wilson, who then stood before me in the agonies of his dissolution. His mask and cloak lay, where he had thrown them, upon the floor. Not a thread in all his raiment – not a line in all the marked and singular lineaments of his face which was not, even in the most absolute identity, *mine own*!

It was Wilson; but he spoke no longer in a whisper, and I could have fancied that I myself was speaking while he said:

'*You have conquered, and I yield. Yet, henceforward art thou also dead – dead to the World, to Heaven, and to hope! In me didst thou exist – and, in my death, see by this image, which is thine own, how utterly thou hast murdered thyself.*'

EDGAR ALLAN POE

8

AUTHORS AS DOUBLES

ɞ&

Here is where we come full circle. To the point where this anthology turns still more unashamedly – doubly – autobiographical, my twoness not only twinly, but also professional. Of course it was not professional to start with; as with Daudet it was wholly inadvertent, natural, a matter of surprise, even shame. If it did presage my professional future, I hardly understood it as such. By the time I became fully conscious of the processes involved, though, I was a writer, which did not make me any less worried that such ways of thinking, feeling were in some way aberrant. For the occasion was the dying and death of my mother; it seemed wholly indecent to sit, as I did, by her deathbed, through her funeral, alongside my father's grief, grieving on the one hand, on the other, in some quite separate part of my head, working out how to describe her, him, the rest of the family, the congregation at the funeral; my own feelings, in the face of this grief and loss, not least. So indecent in fact, I did not put it into any book for twenty years.

Now, that this kind of splitting is not unique to authors, I know. All of us feel somewhat dissociated in the face of such agonies; feel ourselves looking at events as through a wall of glass. But I don't believe it's always as cold-blooded a process as it appears to be with writers – for so it seems to me at such times. As a means of survival,

447

even of creating something out of pain, it has its uses – but it can also cut us off from what is happening in some quite profound and uncomfortable way: as if no trauma – or joy for that matter – can be truly experienced until it can be expressed in words and on paper – and usually in a form which inevitably transmutes it into something other than it actually was. This may be, if one is charitable, a means of approaching the truth of the experience more nearly; or it may be pure lie and what finally distances one from it for good.

Until I started researching this book, though, I had never realised how unoriginal I was; how commonly writers do split themselves, see themselves as two. Some do it pathologically – de Maupassant, for instance, who observed himself sitting writing, teetered on the edge of madness for some time, and finally fell right in. Others are whimsical about it; Robert Louis Stevenson's Brownie writing self, for instance. Others may or may not call themselves double, yet themes of twoness, doubleness, shadowedness, recur in almost everything they write – as with that doubly-named writer, Samuel Clemens, otherwise known as Mark Twain, (or Mark *Two*; appropriately, his lecture partnership with another journalist quite unlike himself to look at was billed under the title 'The Twins of Genius'). Or as in the work of Michel Tournier, who not only wrote a whole novel on twins, *Gemini*, but who twins his Robinson Crusoe with Friday, and has his 'ogre' – in the *Erl King* – first attend the guillotining of his double and subsequently pursue twins of all kinds – even cloned twin pigeons – on behalf of his Nazi masters. Some other writers split themselves literally. Joyce Carroll Oates, for instance, has another writing self, Rosamund Smith, whose work, though unmistakably echoing that of her alter ego, is much more sensationalist and crude in subject and treatment – and infested with twins besides. Others, like Anita Brookner, 'keep separate addresses' as writer and social self. While Henry James approached the matter quite directly in his short story 'A private life' about a writer who appears so different from his work that it comes as no great surprise to anyone to discover it is written, literally, by a second self.

But Henry James was another author who addressed the theme of doubleness many times. His story 'The Jolly Corner' tells of a New Yorker like himself who has spent most of his adult life in Europe, and now sees his double in a house he had inherited in his home town. The double in this case is his neglected, undeveloped American self which raises the question – is the experience of doubleness part of what creates or at least drives the author, rather than vice versa? Exile is so very frequently a source both of metaphorical schizophrenia and of literature. In England, the colonial experience may have added to literature for just such reasons, through the experience of writers like Penelope Lively – or still more tellingly Jean Rhys – who spent their early childhood in countries like India and who never fitted into the 'native' country to which they returned. And also, in reverse, through the experience of colonised writers – Salman Rushdie, for instance, or Ben Okri – turned restless inhabitants of the country which colonised them. Self-chosen exile, like that of Henry James, and of his friend, Edith Wharton, of Joseph Conrad, is maybe a different matter; but in those cases, too, the sense of distance experienced in exile appears to be one major factor in the capacity of such writers to dissect the societies from which they came or in which they find themselves.

Henry James's Jolly Corner ghost haunts me in particular – because of its fictional depiction of the unlived, American aspects of his writing self. Last year I heard a philosophical paper on Herman Melville's story '*Bartleby the scrivener*', in which Bartleby, the legal writer, was seen as paradigm of some archetypal writer figure. The point about Bartleby is of course not just what he wrote – but what he could not, would not write. The statement 'I am not willing' reverberates throughout. This, it was suggested, indicates that the very nature of creation involves a potentiality which may or may not be realised, but is equally significant in either case (just as the yin potential of the yang twin, mentioned earlier, remains significant whether switched into or not). In some philosophies, apparently, a writer is indeed the original creator; that is, creation is, metaphorically speaking, an act of writing or sometimes, as writers know only too well, *not* writing. 'In the beginning is the word' precisely. Or, as Colin Tudge would have it in his *Engineer in the Garden* – on the basis of the theory that the subtlety of animal behaviour clearly indicates that though wordless they must think, and that, in the case of human animals, the constantly recurring themes of folklore and literature suggest that they, too, precede the words used to express them – 'In the beginning is the anecdote.' This makes the writer the original creator – who chooses to relate, or with equal validity *not* to relate the story inside her or him – twice over.

I've already pointed out in the introduction to the myth of the twin, that two is seen traditionally as the number of creation; that creation itself involves a split in the unity of God – whatever God is. In which case, the dual nature of writers seems appropriate, not to say essential. Without the capacity to split themselves or the world, and to put themselves together again, creators would create nothing. In creation, potential may remain unrealised; but by definition not all can. (And if, equally by definition, this names writers as devils, most of us, I daresay, would be flattered by that, not offended.)

Which brings me at last to the image of the doubly-split writer; the writer twin. If she or he is not only split by twinness but by writing, maybe the second split is engendered by the first. Maybe the will to reconnect, to put split parts together again by making stories, can be a grieving twin's way of healing the split and at the same time recreating the lost companion. The book as twin, in other words. Which would wholly explain the sense of loss when a book is delivered; a writer's instant need to start a new one – write another twin. (Did I begin writing seriously in Munich, because, having understood at last that such separation was inevitable, I too saw that such a twin could compensate for the real one?) Still more poignant and interesting is the case of those writers, such as Philip L. Dick, or Thornton Wilder, who lose their twin either at or before birth, or so very early that they never know them. Much of their work appears full of that loss and pain; the story of Estaban and Manuel in Wilder's *The Bridge of San Luis Rey* is a case in point. Elsewhere, too, lone twin survivors from such births are reported as feeling in some way incomplete, even where they have never been told of their dead sibling. I know of a woman sculptor, for instance, whose figurines always came in pairs, for reasons she did not understand until as an adult she learned at last about her stillborn twin. And if it's true that far more people than know it had a twin lost in the womb – including, in one recent hypothesis, all left-handers – could it be that many writers feel split, and so come to split themselves on paper, as writers, because they were at gestation two? Writers quite often are left-handed, after all.

The question I am left with finally, though, concerns writer twins who do grow to adulthood alongside their siblings. What of the twin who doesn't write? There are cases where both twins are writers – the Shaffers, for instance, Peter and Anthony. But more often than not, especially in the case of fraternal twins, only one takes up that profession. What of John Barth's female twin, for instance? What of Michèle Robert's twin, or Thomas Shapcott's? What of mine (who found it hard to cope with my writing – or rather the recognition it brought – but who, because she was always honest, admitted more than once that my life as writer was not one she'd ever have chosen). For it is true, it must be for all of us, that to some extent, consciously or unconsciously, our writing feeds on our twinship. And if there are betrayals, rejections by our other halves that we writer twins may find hard to forgive, how much greater a betrayal is ours of them, by putting them on paper, openly or covertly, in one way or another, whether they like it or not?

Homo Duplex! Homo Duplex! The first time that I perceived that I was two was at the death of my brother Henri, when my father cried out so dramatically, 'He is dead, he is dead!' While my first self wept, my second self thought, 'How truly given was that cry, how fine it would be in the theatre.' I was then fourteen years old.

This horrible duality has often given me matter for reflection. Oh this terrible second me, always seated whilst the other is on foot, acting, living, suffering, bestirring itself. This second me that I have never been able to intoxicate, to make shed tears, or put to sleep. And how it sees into things, and how it mocks!

ALPHONSE DAUDET, *Notes sur la Vie*, quoted in William James, *Varieties of Religious Experience*

---

from Gemini as a Creative Figure

THE Gemini path is one of paradox, contradiction, ambiguity, and the conjunction of opposites. Gemini rules the paired parts of our body, especially our hands, arms, shoulders, nervous systems, and brains. Its real genius lies in its ability to use both sides of the brain, to think literally and figuratively, logically and intuitively, intellectually and imaginatively. In fact, the Latin origins for the word *genius* contain the image of paired opposites, a reference to the genii, which come in pairs – one light and one dark – and are thought to preside over a person's birth and destiny. This intuitive image of genius has been confirmed by researchers investigating the ways creative people in all disciplines think. Polarities, ambivalence, and oppositional elements are pervasive in creative thinking, so much so that it is sometimes dubbed 'Janusian thinking' or 'divergent thinking.'

KAT DUFF, *Parabola*, June 1994

'A shadow always follows Graham Greene; that of another Graham Greene who is and who is not he . . .

MARIE CLAIRE ALLAIN, *The Other Man*

The writer god's tracing . . . of the theme of the double is an attempt to see himself, to confirm his own existence.

PAUL COATES

———————

I bear with me that double life which is the strength and simultaneously the misery of the writer. I write because I feel; and I suffer from everything which exists because I see it myself in the mirror of my thoughts, without being able to experience it.

MAUPASSANT

———————

Very many other things . . . can be said with reference to duality . . . that it directs, at a form of theft, a simultaneous praise and blame, that in playing with his dolls an author is playing with his doubles, and that a favourite doll has been the orphan and his opposite. The orphan author hides and seeks and soars. Duality is departure and return. It is theft and restitution. It is megalomania and magnanimity. It is weakness, illness and illusion, and it is the advantages they confer. It is divided and diffusive, hostile and hospitable. Duality is suicide and masturbation. It is bisexuality, and dual nationality. It courts and contemplates uncertainty, vacancy, doubt, dizziness and arrest. It is the behaviour and capacity of an author and it is the theory which explains him. It is the Eliot who encountered dissociation, and it is the Empson who encountered ambiguity.

KARL MILLER

———————

But you are trying to reconcile the book and the author. A book is the writer's secret life, the dark twin of a man: you can't reconcile them. And with you, when the inevitable clash comes, the author's actual self is the one that goes down, for you are of those for whom fact and fallacy gain verisimilitude by being in cold print.

WILLIAM FAULKNER, *Mosquitoes*

———————

In all my books perhaps I return to the duality which has marked my life from the time that I was a pupil in the school at Berkhamstead, whose head was my father. Hence my 'divided loyalties': I had friends, a few, but I was also my father's son – and they disliked my father. I belonged to neither side.

GRAHAM GREENE

For Sillitoe is, at least, a double man, a nature in disguise, aware continually of the splits in himself – in his own word, 'a foreigner.'

CANDIA MCWILLIAM on Alan Sillitoe,
Independent on Sunday, 16 July 1995

The repetitious sweat of producing over a thousand brass nuts a day did not worry me, because for one thing I was making it pay, and once accustomed to the process, could dream my way from morning till evening as if I was two people.

ALAN SILLITOE on himself, Ibid.

I was riding on the footpath towards Drusenheim, and there one of the strangest presentiments occurred to me. I saw myself coming to meet myself on the same road on horseback, but in clothes such as I had never worn. They were of light grey mixed with gold. As soon as I had roused myself from this daydream, the vision disappeared. Strange, however, it is, that eight years later I found myself on the identical spot, intending to visit Frederike once more, and in the same clothes which I had seen in my vision, and which I now wore, not from choice but by accident . . .

GOETHE, *Aus Meinen Leben*

from Scandal

THE cog-wheels rotating at the very core of his heart suddenly went berserk. The reason for the malfunction was clear. Something had intruded itself into Suguro's life on the night of the prizegiving and the internal machinery that had run in smooth synchronization up until then abruptly ran amok.

In his only refuge – his tiny study – Suguro lay his head down on his desk and lectured himself over and over again: It's nothing. You're exaggerating the whole thing.

That was surely the case. Other writers had had impostors annoy them, and they would regard his problem in the same light. All he had to do was ignore it like the others and the problem would vanish.

The thought should have been reassuring, but his mood did not improve.

Images floated before his eyes. The face identical to his own that he had seen at the prizegiving. Superimposed on that was the portrait hanging in the gallery. The base, loathsome, sneering smile was the same in both images.

Sometimes when his wife was not there he would go into the bathroom at his office and stare at his face in the mirror. A fatigue-worn face. Yellow-splotched eyes. A spray of white hair in his sideburns. The face of a sixty-five-year-old man. He was sixty-five and still full of doubts. He was restless and as jumpy as a mouse.

He stuck his tongue out at the mirror and remembered a scene from a German film he had gone to in his middle-school days. It was about an ageing – sixty-five, in fact – stage actor who fell in love with a young woman and ended up jilted and scarred by the experience. In the film the old man had scornfully stuck his tongue out at himself in the dressing-room mirror.

This is who you are. This is your face. Just how different is it from the face in the portrait? A voice deep inside him posed the question. It was directed at a man concerned solely with his public image, constantly aware of the eyes of his readers. The question was intended, it seemed, to nudge him in some direction or other.

Late in the middle of that night he woke up to the ringing of the telephone.

Who could that be? At this time of night?

His wife too had been awakened. 'Would you like me to answer it?'

'No, I'll get it.' He left the bedroom and turned on the hallway light. He brought the receiver to his ear, and in a voice that even he recognized as angry said, 'Hello. Hello?'

The caller did not respond.

Whoever it was seemed to be listening to his reaction. Eventually the line went dead. Suguro had the feeling it was not a mere hoax, and for a while he stood motionless in the darkness, scarcely even breathing.

SHUSAKU ENDO

———————

from Women and Ghosts

March

CHILL drenching rains, low and confused in spirit. I've had a viscid cold for weeks. Still intermittently feverish, barely meeting my classes. Not-Karo hasn't manifested herself again in any way I can tell anyone of, yet what happened last week in Buffalo has left a fog of fear over my life, especially whenever I appear in public.

It was in the Buffalo airport. As I entered the terminal I saw, fifty feet away behind the barrier, two obvious young-academic types, one carrying a white placard – evidently my welcoming committee. Then I saw them approach and greet someone else, a dark-haired woman only visible to me from behind, who after a moment walked on, leaving them to stare about and then wave tentatively at me. A minor case of mistaken identity, they explained as I stood there, nearly unable to speak.

Because a shudder of dread had gone through me: Not-Karo. I was only safe, I thought, because I hadn't seen her face; if I'd seen her face I would have died.

Don't be silly, it couldn't have been Not-Karo, I told myself on the way to town. She might have known I was giving a reading in Buffalo; she couldn't have known what plane I was arriving on. But whoever that woman was, if she had claimed to be Karo McKay they would have accepted her and left me standing in the terminal as if I didn't exist.

At the motel I still felt strained, strange. Took a little V, lay down on the bed but couldn't relax, got up, put on my cream lace dress and French chandelier earrings, brushed out my hair, redid my makeup, sprayed myself with Ma Griffe. In the glass I looked like Karo McKay.

But all through what followed I didn't feel like her. The food at the official dinner tasted strange, and whenever I spoke to anyone I felt as if I was reading from a script, a script I'd read from too often before.

Then when I came on stage it was wrong from the start. I could see the hands clapping in the half-dark, but they sounded like canned TV applause. There was no transforming rush and glow of energy, nothing. I smiled, spoke, started the tape. But as I gestured, as I modulated and projected my voice, every word sounded false, every movement was like time-lapse photography, artificially slowed down or speeded up.

And then, towards the end of the reading, I had this sensation that it wasn't me the audience was staring at, it was someone else, someone standing just behind me and a little to the left. I felt frightened, dizzy, literally dragged myself through the final two poems. As I left the stage I glanced over my shoulder; no one was there. But everything was still wrong; all the praises and thanks afterwards, and my replies, seemed coerced and artificial. I can't do this any more, I thought; I can't go on.

But I must go on. The world demands that I exhibit myself regularly on stage, and at the obligatory accompanying parties, lunches, dinners, receptions. It threatens me with poverty and obscurity if I don't perform, and bribes me with fame and fees – sometimes more for one reading than most of my books earn in years.

And it's not only me. Haven't I seen how many good writers – great writers – have gone on appearing in public far more often and longer than they should, because of these bribes and threats? Haven't I seen them on stage, worn down, slowed down physically and emotionally, stumbling and repeating themselves? Exhausting themselves, so that they haven't the energy or tranquillity to write? It could happen to me. Maybe it's already begun to happen, and that's why I can't – don't think about it.

Everything I felt in Buffalo can be explained rationally, no doubt: that I was tired, airsick, getting over a cold, had too much to drink etc. But what I can't explain is the absolute terror of that moment at the airport when I thought I saw the back of Not-Karo, whoever she was. Or what. She resembled a normal woman, but suppose she wasn't.

Suppose she never was real, but was, is, a kind of vampire or spectre, moving towards me. Oakland-Denver-Minneapolis-Chicago-Detroit . . . Buffalo. And in an almost straight line. Not a human being at all, but an evil spirit, like those demons in oriental folklore who can't turn corners.

That would explain how she always knows where I am, how she can slide from city to city. Spreading slime wherever she goes like a crawling snail, souring and destroying my life. So that once she's done the public things, I become unable to do them; it's as if they've been slimed and fouled. Already I can't smile at attractive strangers, sign books, or speak to fans in the easy, graceful way I once did. And now even being on stage feels false.

No, no, I mustn't think that way, that's mad. I've been ill, I must give myself time to recover. Call Bryan, cancel those last two readings. Yes, and tell him to hold off for a while on scheduling anything for the summer or fall. Panic: if I can't perform, can't teach, how will I survive?

And I daren't take too much time off. If I don't appear anywhere, gradually I'll cease to exist as far as the literary world is concerned. Lovers of poetry are as restless and fickle as most lovers; if you don't continually remind them of your existence they soon forget you. Especially if you haven't written any new – (Don't think about that.) Sooner than you can imagine you're unknown.

ALISON LURIE

---

from Notebook

LONDON, Jan. 7, '97. Last Sunday I struck upon a new 'solution' of a haunting mystery. A great many years ago I published in the Atlantic 'The Recent Carnival of Crime in Connecticut.'

That was an attempt to account for our seeming *duality* – the presence in us of another *person*; not a slave of ours, but free and independent, and with a character distinctly its own. I made my conscience that other person and it came before me in the form of a malignant dwarf and told me plain things about myself and shamed me and scoffed at me and derided me. This creature was so much its own master that it would leave the premises – leave its post – forsake its duties – and go off on a spree with other irresponsible consciences – and discuss their masters (no – their slaves).

Presently Stevenson published Dr Jekyll and Mr Hyde. That was nearer this thing. J. and H. were the dual persons in one body, quite distinct in nature and character and presumably each with a *conscience of its own*. Nearer, yes, but not near enough. Or, to put it differently, a truth and a falsity harnessed together; the falsity being the ability of the one person to step into the other person's place, *at will*.

I have underscored 'conscience of its own.' When I made my conscience my other person, and independent, with its own (original) character, it was a mistake. My conscience is a part of *me*. It is a mere machine, like my heart – but moral, not physical; and being moral is *teachable*, its action modifiable. It is merely a *thing*; the creature of *training*; it is whatever one's mother and Bible and comrades and laws and system of government and habitat and heredities have made it. It is not a separate person, it has no originality, no independence.

Inborn nature is Character, by itself in the brutes – the tiger, the dove, the fox, etc. Inborn nature *and* the modifying Conscience, working together make Character in man.

Jekyll and Hyde are correct in so far as each has its separate and distinct nature – *and* – conscience character.

But other cases show that the two persons in a man have no command over each other (as falsely pretended in Jekyll and Hyde). The two persons in a man do not even *know* each other and are not aware of each other's existence, never heard of each other – have never even suspected each other's existence.

And so, I was wrong in the beginning; that other person is not one's conscience; and Stevenson was wrong, for the two persons in a man are wholly unknown to each other, and can never in this world communicate with each other in any way.

Now I come to my *new* notion.

The French have lately shown (apparently) that that other person is in command during the somnambulic sleep; that it has a memory of its own and can recall its acts when hypnotized and thrown again into that sleep, but that *you* have no memory of its acts. You are not present at all.

Very good. That *is* distinct duality. To this arrangement I wish to add this detail – that we have a spiritualized self which can detach itself and go wandering off upon affairs of its own – for recreation, perhaps. I am not acquainted with my double, my partner in duality, the other and wholly independent personage who resides in me – and whom I will call Watson, for I don't know his name, although he most certainly has one, and signs it in a hand which has no resemblance to mine when he takes possession of our partnership body and goes off on mysterious trips – but I *am* acquainted (dimly) with my spiritualized self and I know that it and I are one, because we have common memory; when I wake mornings, I remember that it (that is, *I*) have been doing, and whither it (that is *I*) have been wandering in the course of what I took to be unreality and called Dreams, for want of a truthfuler name.

MARK TWAIN

---

from Borges and I

THE other one, the one called Borges, is the one things happen to. I walk through the streets of Buenos Aires and stop for a moment, perhaps mechanically now, to look at the arch of an entrance hall and the grillwork on the gate; I know of Borges from the mail and see his name on a list of professors or in a biographical dictionary. I like hourglasses, maps, eighteenth-century typography, the taste of coffee and the prose of Stevenson; he shares these preferences, but in a vain way that turns them into the attributes of an actor. It would be an exaggeration to say that ours is a hostile relationship; I live, let myself go on living, so that Borges may contrive his literature, and this literature justifies me. It is no effort for me to confess that he has achieved some valid pages, but those pages cannot save me, perhaps because what is good belongs to no one, not even to him, but rather to the language and to tradition. Besides, I am destined to perish, definitively, and only some instant of myself can survive in him. Little by little, I am giving over everything to him, though I am quite aware of his perverse custom of falsifying and magnifying things. Spinoza knew that all things long to persist in their being; the stone eternally wants to be a stone and the tiger a tiger. I shall remain in Borges, not in myself (if it is true that I am someone), but I recognize myself less in his books than in many others or in the laborious strumming of a guitar. Years ago I tried to free myself from him and went from the mythologies of the suburbs to the games with time and infinity, but those games belong to Borges now and I shall have to imagine other things. Thus my life is a flight and I lose everything and everything belongs to oblivion, or to him.

I do not know which of us has written this page.

JORGE LUIS BORGES, trs. J.E.I.

Some years ago, as retirement from the Courtauld Institute loomed and she needed to move her books and belongings, Anita Brookner bought *another* flat, in the same block, on the same floor, in fact literally next door. It seems odd, to have a second home on the doorstep of your first home: it's as if she were sending up the idea of a country cottage or the workplace within walking distance, or as if she were parodying herself as someone of almost agoraphobic unadventurousness. But the flat makes perfect sense: 'I simply work there. It's got a desk, and a bed, and a telephone number which nobody knows, so I can ring out but nobody can ring me.' It's hard to imagine a more respectable double life. But a double life, of sorts, is what it is: the woman and the novelist keep separate addresses.

BLAKE MORRISON, *Independent*, June 1994

---

from Reflection

I write with my left hand, but
the one in the mirror
holds a pen between the fingers
of the hand on her right. Her smile
slants lop-sided, her hair is combed
the wrong way, she stands so badly –
all contrary, changed, reversed.

I want to see photographs
(my own face and its reflection –
unlike each other
as matter is from anti-matter)
close together, and contemplate
resemblances, opposites,
the person they mistake me for:
reversed and changed and all contrary.

RUTH FAINLIGHT

HE was sitting at the desk in his study. His servant had strict orders not to enter while his master was working. Suddenly it seemed to Maupassant as if someone had opened the door. Turning round, he sees to his extreme astonishment his own self entering, who sits down opposite and rests his head on his hand. Everything Maupassant writes is dictated to him. When the author finished his work and arose the hallucination disappeared.

Quoted OTTO RANK, The Double, trs. Harry Tucker

---

from A Chapter on Dreams

FOR myself – what I call I, my conscious ego, the denizen of the pineal gland unless he has changed his residence since Descartes, the man with the conscience and the variable bank-account, the man with the hat and the boots, and the privilege of voting and not carrying his candidate at the general elections – I am sometimes tempted to suppose he is no story-teller at all, but a creature as matter of fact as any cheesemonger or any cheese, and a realist bemired up to the ears in actuality; so that, by that account, the whole of my published fiction should be the single-handed product of some Brownie, some Familiar, some unseen collaborator, whom I keep locked in a back garret, while I get all the praise and he but a share (which I cannot prevent him getting) of the pudding. I am an excellent adviser, something like Molière's servant; I pull back and I cut down; and I dress the whole in the best words and sentences that I can find and make; I hold the pen, too; and I do the sitting at the table, which is about the worst of it; and when all is done, I make up the manuscript and pay for the registration; so that, on the whole, I have some claim to share, though not so largely as I do, in the profits of our common enterprise.

I can but give an instance or so of what part is done sleeping and what part awake, and leave the reader to share what laurels there are, at his own nod, between myself and my collaborators; and to do this I will first take a book that a number of persons have been polite enough to read, the *Strange Case of Dr Jekyll and Mr Hyde*. I had long been trying to write a story on this subject, to find a body, a vehicle, for that strong sense of man's double being which must at times come in upon and overwhelm the mind of every thinking creature. I had even written one, *The Travelling Companion*, which was returned by an editor on the plea that it was a work of genius and indecent, and which I burned the other day on the ground that it was not a work of genius, and that *Jekyll* had supplanted it. Then came one of those financial fluctuations to which (with an elegant modesty) I have hitherto referred in the third person. For two days I went about racking my brains for a plot of any sort; and on the second night I dreamed the scene at the window, and a scene afterward split in two, in which Hyde, pursued for some crime, took the powder and underwent the change in the presence of his pursuers. All the rest was made awake, and consciously, although I think I can trace in much of it the manner of my Brownies. The meaning of the tale is therefore mine, and had long pre-existed in my garden of Adonis, and tried one body after another in vain; indeed, I do most of the morality, worse luck! and my Brownies have not a rudiment of what we call a conscience. Mine, too, is the setting, mine the characters. All that was given me was the matter of three scenes, and the central idea of a voluntary change becoming involuntary. Will it be thought ungenerous, after I have been so liberally ladling out praise to my unseen collaborators, if I here toss them over, bound hand and foot, into the arena of the critics? For the business of the powders, which so many have censured, is, I am relieved to say, not mine at all but the Brownies'.

ROBERT LOUIS STEVENSON

---

from The Private Life

I drew her out to the terrace and, before we had gone three steps, said to her: 'Who was with you here last night?'

'Last night?' – she was as wide of the mark as I had been.

'At ten o'clock – just after our company broke up. You came out here with a gentleman. You talked about the stars.'

She stared a moment, then gave her laugh. 'Are you jealous of dear Vawdrey?'

'Then it was he?'

'Certainly it was he.'

'And how long did he stay?'

She laughed again. 'You have it badly! He stayed about a quarter of an hour – perhaps rather more. We walked some distance. He talked about his play. There you have it all. That is the only witchcraft I have used.'

Well, it wasn't enough for me; so 'What did Vawdrey do afterwards?'
I continued.

'I haven't the least idea. I left him and went to bed.'

'At what time did you go to bed?'

'At what time did *you*? I happen to remember that I parted from
Mr Vawdrey at ten twenty-five,' said Mrs Adney. 'I came back into
the salon to pick up a book, and I noticed the clock.'

'In other words you and Vawdrey distinctly lingered here from about
five minutes past ten till the hour you mention?'

'I don't know how distinct we were, but we were very jolly. Où
voulez-vous en venir?' Blanche Adney asked.

'Simply to this, dear lady: that at the time your companion was
occupied in the manner you describe he was also engaged in literary
composition in his own room.'

She stopped short for it, and her eyes had a sheen in the darkness.
She wanted to know if I challenged her veracity; and I replied that
on the contrary I backed it up – it made the case so interesting. She
returned that this would only be if she should back up mine; which
however I had no difficulty in persuading her to do after I had related
to her circumstantially the incident of my quest of the manuscript –
the manuscript which at the time, for a reason I could now understand,
appeared to have passed so completely out of her own head.

'His talk made me forget it – I forgot I sent you for it. He made up
for his fiasco in the salon: he declaimed me the scene,' said Blanche.
She had dropped on a bench to listen to me and, as we sat there, had
briefly cross-examined me. Then she broke out into fresh laughter.
'Oh the eccentricities of genius!'

'Yes indeed! They seem greater even than I supposed.'

'Oh the mysteries of greatness!'

'You ought to know all about them, but they take me by surprise,'
I declared.

'Are you absolutely certain it was Vawdrey?' my companion
asked.

'If it wasn't he who in the world was it? That a strange gentleman,
looking exactly like him and of like literary pursuits, should be sitting
in his room at that hour of the night and writing at his table *in the dark*,' I
insisted, 'would be practically as wonderful as my own contention.'

'Yes, why in the dark?' my friend mused.

'Cats can see in the dark,' I said.

She smiled at me dimly. 'Did it look like a cat?'

'No, dear lady, but I'll tell you what it did look like – it looked like the author of Vawdrey's admirable works. It looked infinitely more like him than our friend does himself,' I pronounced.

'Do you mean it was somebody he gets to do them?'

'Yes, while he dines out and disappoints you.'

'Disappoints me?' she murmured artlessly.

'Disappoints *me* – disappoints every one who looks in him for the genius that created the pages they adore. Where is it in his talk?'

'Ah last night he was splendid,' said the actress.

'He's always splendid, as your morning bath is splendid, or a sirloin of beef, or the railway-service to Brighton. But he's never rare.'

'I see what you mean.'

I could have hugged her – and perhaps I did. 'That's what makes you such a comfort to talk to. I've often wondered – now I know. There are two of them.'

'What a delightful idea!'

'One goes out, the other stays at home. One's the genius, the other's the bourgeois, and it's only the bourgeois whom we personally know. He talks, he circulates, he's awfully popular, he flirts with you – '

'Whereas it's the genius *you* are privileged to flirt with!' Mrs Adney broke in. 'I'm much obliged to you for the distinction.'

I laid my hand on her arm. 'See him yourself. Try it, test it, go to his room.'

'Go to his room? It wouldn't be proper!' she cried in the manner of her best comedy.

'Anything's proper in such an enquiry. If you see him it settles it.'

'How charming – to settle it!' She thought a moment, then sprang up. 'Do you mean *now*?'

'Whenever you like.'

'But suppose I should find the wrong one?' she said with an exquisite effect.

'The wrong one? Which one do you call the right?'

'The wrong one for a lady to go and see. Suppose I shouldn't find – the genius?'

'Oh I'll look after the other,' I returned.

HENRY JAMES

466

from An Immaculate Mistake

OF all the games I played as a boy, this was the one I enjoyed most. It was fun being someone else, escaping from the Peter that I was into the Paul of my imagination, giving him different characteristics, different interests. Paul was a livelier creature than his dull impersonator, it seemed to me. He had to be created afresh, newly imagined, each time I decided to become him . . .

We rushed to meet Matthias, my cousins and Im whenever we saw him coming along the road. Unlike most of the grown-ups we knew, he found delight in the company of children. He enjoyed hearing as well as seeing us, and listened with unfeigned curiosity to our breathless accounts of the day's adventures.

'Which twin are you today?' he would ask me, with mock-seriousness.

When I said I was Peter I spoke in my own voice; when I was pretending to be my twin, I adopted his gentler tones.

'But where is your brother?' The question always tested my powers of invention.

My brother, I told him, was in the castle gardens, was down in the village, was in the churchyard, was where noone could find him.

'Some twins are inseparable, but not you two. When will I see you both together?'

'Tomorrow,' I promised, and added, 'Perhaps.'

Matthias was the only adult with whom I dared to play my game of being twins, for his eyes indicated that he appreciated mischief. He affected to be as gullible as the village children who did not know which twin was which, he allowed me to believe that I had fooled him.

PAUL BAILEY

---

from Gemini

JOHN Collier. [*Apology introducing collection of poems.*]

Siamese twins are generally two, but if by chance there were Siamese twins that were one, like semi-detached villas inhabited by the same person, it might be admitted that he might look at himself with some misgiving and vainly ask 'Which am I?'

These uneasy verses are some of the spasmodic gestures which each of me has made, during the last few years, in an attempt to usurp unity at the cost of the other. Something archaic, uncouth, and even barbarous is very obvious in one, and the other is an hysterically self-conscious dandy. What a pity that Orson with his labouring bosom insists on sucking all the blood away from Valentine, and what a pity Valentine will never condescend to trim that antique beard, and clip to cleaner points those clawing nails of Orson! Then they would grow so alike that it might be said that both were myself; but the fact is, that they are so at odds that I have long known I must choose between them, unless I could find some manner for them to lie in, in which their differences would be less aggressively marked.

JOHN COLLIER

---

from The Making of a Writer

IT is my fate, and equally my sister's, to have been born opposite sex twins, with an older brother and no younger siblings . . .

Much is known about 'identical' (monozygotic) twins, less about fraternal (dizygotic) twins, less yet about opposite-sexers (who, it goes without saying), are always dizygotic). But twins of any sort share the curious experiences of accommodating to a peer companion even from the beginning; even in the womb; of entering the world with an established side-kick, rather than alone, of acquiring speech and the other basic skills à deux, in the meanwhile sharing a language beyond speech and before speech. Speech, baby twins may feel, is for the Others. As native speakers of a dialect regard the official language, we may regard language itself: it is for dealing with the outsiders; between ourselves we have very little need of it. One might reasonably therefore expect a twin who becomes a storyteller never to take language for granted; to be ever at it, tinkering, foregrounding it, perhaps unnaturally conscious of it. Language is for relating to the Others.

Now, most opposite-sex twins come soon to shrug the shoulders of their imaginations at that congenital circumstance; to regard it as a more or less amusing detail. They can do so because it was not their additional fate to have a three year older brother who, upon hearing the unlucky news that he had not one but a team of rivals for his parents' hitherto undivided attention, gamely but fatefully remarked: 'Now we have a Jack and Jill.'

Poor firstborn. Thy day in the family sun wast shadowed from that hour, but thou hadst in advance thy more-than-justified revenge. Jack and Jill we became, and up childhood's hill we went – in scrappy East Cambridge, a crab-and-oyster town on the Eastern shore of Maryland – lugging between us that heavy pail. Our grade-school teachers oohed and aahed (doubtless privately laughed) at the awful cuteness of our names, while alley-wise classmates reddened our innocent ears with every bawdy version of the nursery rhyme. I can recite them still, those scurrilous varioria; my ears still redden.

Language, ohoboyohboy, c'est pour les autres: my sister and I were by it not let to forget our twinness. Until circumstance and physical maturation differentiated and tumbled us towards our separate fates [. . .] until the Commercial course and biological womanhood befell Jill, the Academic course and (a bit later) biological manhood Jack, we were a Jack and Jill indeed, between whom nearly everything went without saying.

With those closest since, I have had sustained and intimate conversation, but seldom in words except at the beginning and end of our connection. Language is for getting to know you and getting to unknow you. We converse to convert, each the other, from the Other into the extension of ourself; and we converse conversely.

[. . .] Once upon a time, in Myth, twins signified whatever dualisms a culture entertained: mortal/immortal, good/evil, creation/destruction, what had they. In Western literature since the Romantic period, twins (and doubles, shadows, mirrors) usual signify the 'divided self', our secret sharer or inner adversary – even schizophrenia some neo-Freudians maintain lies near the dark heart of writing. Aristophanes, in Plato's Symposium declares we are all of us twins, indeed a kind of Siamese twins who have lost and who eternally seek our missing half: the loss accounts for alienation, our felt distance from man and god; the search accounts for both erotic love and the mystics goal of divine atonement.

I have sometimes felt that a twin who happens to be a writer, or a writer who happens to be a twin, might take this stick by the other end and use schizophrenia, say, as an image for what he knows to be his literal case: that he once was more than one person and somehow now is less. I am the least psychological of all storytellers: yet even to me it is apparent that I write these words and all the others in part because I have no twin to be wordless with, even when I'm with her.

Less and less, as twins go along, goes without saying. One is in the world, talking to the Others, talking to oneself.

My books tend to come in pairs; my sentences in twin members.

JOHN BARTH

———————

ACKNOWLEDGEMENTS

Permission to quote copyright material is gratefully acknowledged: A. P. Watt Ltd and Random House UK on behalf of The Trustees of the Wodehouse Estate for the extract from 'George and Alfred' take from *Plum Pie* by P. G. Wodehouse; Reed Consumer Books for extracts from *East of Eden* by John Steinbeck, published by William Heinemann Ltd; Reed Consumer Books for 'The Blood of the Walsungs' from *Stories of a Lifetime* Volume 1 by Thomas Mann published by Martin Secker & Warburg Ltd; 'The Double Poet' from *Women and Ghosts* by Alison Lurie, published by William Heinemann Ltd; 'Reflection' from *This Time of Year* by Ruth Fainlight, published by Sinclair-Stevenson; *Fabrications* by Michael Ayrton, published by Martin Secker & Warburg Ltd; New Directions Publishing Corp. for extracts from 'The Flemish Double Portrait' – James Laughlin: *The Man in the Wall*, copyright © 1993 by James Laughlin, reprinted by permission of New Directions Publishing Corp.; Kat Duff and *Parabola* magazine for the extract from 'Gemini and the Path of Paradox' by Kat Duff; James Elniski and *Parabola* magazine for the extract from 'Finding One's Twin', both reprinted from *Parabola, The Magazine of Myth and Tradition*, vol. XIX, no. 2 (Summer 1994); 'The Heavy Bear Who Goes With Me' from Delmore Schwartz: *Selected Poems: Summer Knowledge*, copyright © 1959 by Delmore Schwartz, reprinted by permission of New Directions Publishing Corp.; Murray Pollinger, Victor Gollancz and Black Swan for the extract from *Absolute Hush* by Sara Banerji, published by Victor Gollancz and Black Swan; Oxford University Press for the extracts from *Conversaton with Ogotemeli* by Marcel Griaule, 1965, reprinted by permission of Oxford University Press; *A Zoroastrian Dilemma* by Zurvan, trans. R.C. Zaehner, 1955, reprinted by permission of Oxford University Press; Tavistock Publications for the extract from *The Divided Self* by R.G. Laing, reprinted by permission of Tavistock

Publications; University of Queensland Press for the extract from 'Portrait of a Younger Twin' from *Selected Poems* 1956–1988 by Thomas Shapcott, published by University of Queensland Press, St Lucia Queensland, 1989; Aitken, Stone & Wylie, USA for the extract from 'The Making of a Writer' by John Barth taken from Endfield, *New York Times* Book Review, May 9, 1982, copyright © 1982 by John Barth, reprinted with the permission of Aitken, Stone and Wylie Inc.; The Estate of Sinclair Lewis for the extract from 'The Willow Walk' in *Selected Short Stories* by Sinclair Lewis, copyright © 1946 by Sinclair Lewis; Faber & Faber for the extracts from *Hapgood* by Tom Stoppard, published by Faber & Faber; Rikki Ducornet for the extract from 'The Double' from *The Complete Butcher's Tales* by Rikki Ducornet, published by Dalkey Archive Press, copyright © Rikki Ducornet 1994, reprinted with the permission of the publisher; Lucinda Vardey Agency for the extract from 'Sylvie' by Barbara Gowdy, copyright © 1992 Barbara Gowdy, reprinted by permission of the author; Crown Publishers, Inc. for the extract from *From the Old Country* by Scholem Aleichem, translated by Frances & Julius Butwin, copyright © 1946, 1947 by Crown Publishers Inc., reprinted by permission of Crown Publishers Inc.; Marion Halligan for the extract from *Lover's Knot* by Marion Halligan, published by Reed Books UK, 1995; Peter Owen Publishers, London, for the extract from *Scandal* by Shusako Endo, published by Peter Owen Publishers; Aitken, Stone & Wylie, UK for the extract from 'I Like to Look: As in Music' by Kathy Page; Laurence Pollinger Ltd for the extract from *The God Hunters* by William Kelley, published by Simon & Schuster, Inc; Dow Jones & Company, Inc. for the extract 'Don't Worry if You See Double', from *The Wall Street Journal*, reprinted by permission of *The Wall Street Journal*, copyright © 1994, Dow Jones and company, Inc. All rights reserved worldwide; The University of Chicago Press for the extract from *Twins: A Study of Heredity and Environment* by H.H. Newman; Bloomsbury Publishing Plc for the extract from *The Robber Bride* by Margaret Atwood, first published by Bloomsbury in 1994; HarperCollins Publishers Ltd for the extract from *The Language of the Genes* by Steve Jones, published by HarperCollins Ltd and extracts from *Gemini* by Michael Tournier; *Crime as Destiny* by Johannes Lange, published by Allen & Unwin Ltd, an imprint of HarperCollins Publishers Ltd; Serpent's Tail for the extract from *Pillow Boy of the Lady Onogoro* by Alison Fell; *Twins Triplets & More* by E. Bryan, copyright © 1992 E. Bryan reproduced by permission of Greene & Heaton Ltd.; Barbara Schave and Janet

Ciriello *Identity and Intimacy in Twins*, (Praeger Publishers, 1983), pp. 12–13, copyright © 1983 by Praeger Publishers, reprinted with permission of Greenwood Publishing Group, Inc., Westport, CT. All rights reserved; Aitken, Stone & Wylie for 'All the Selves I Was' by Michèle Roberts; *The Sadeian Woman* by Angela Carter, copyright © Angela Carter 1979, reproduced by permission of the estate of Angela Carter c/o Rogers, Coleridge & White Ltd., 20 Powis Mews, London W11 1JN; *Wise Children* by Angela Carter, copyright © Angela Carter 1991, reproduced by permission of the estate of Angela Carter c/o Rogers, Coleridge & White Ltd., 20 Powis Mews, London W11 1JN; *Heat* by Joyce Carol Oates copyright © 1991 by The Ontario Review, Inc., reprinted by permission of John Hawkins & Associates, Inc.; 'Salient Facts' from *The Off Season* by Michael Covino, copyright © 1985 by Michael Covino, reprinted by permission of Persea Books; Dell Books for the extract from *Slapstick* by Kurt Vonnegut copyright © 1976 by Kurt Vonnegut, used by permission of Delacorte Press/Seymour Lawrence, a division of Bantam Doubleday Dell Publishing Group, Inc.; W.W. Norton & Company for extract from *Ecrits*: A Selection by Jacques Lacan, translated by Alan Sheridan – translation copyright – reprinted by permission of W.W. Norton & Company, Inc.; extract from *The Solid Mandala* by Patrick White, first published by Eyre & Spottiswoode 1966, copyright © Patrick White; 'The Other Side of Death' from *Innocent Erendira*; 'The Twins' reprinted from Gwen Harwood's *Collected Poems* (1991) by permission of Oxford University Press; extract from *The Nazi Doctors* by Robert Jay Lifton, copyright © 1986 by Robert Jay Lifton, reprinted by permission of BasicBooks, a division of HarperCollins Publishers, Inc.; Michael Donaghy for kind permission to use his poem 'The Break' from *Guardian New Poetry*, copyright © 1994 Michael Donaghy; extract from *The Dionne Years* by Pierre Berton published by Penguin reprinted by permission of Pierre Berton Enterprises; extract from *Brave New World* by Aldous Huxley reprinted by kind permission of Mrs Laura Huxley and Chatto & Windus publishers; 'The Twins' by Edogawa Rampo from *Japanese Tales of Mystery and Imagination* translated by James B. Harris reprinted by permission of Charles E. Tuttle Co., Inc.; 'About Men, About Women' by Mary Flanagan first published in the *Observer*, 30 July 1994, copyright © *Observer*; HarperCollins Publishers for extract from *The Profession of Violence* by John Pearson; Leslie Fiedler for extract from *Freaks* by Leslie Fiedler, published by Simon & Schuster, copyright © Leslie Fieldler.

Index

Donne, J. 367
Dryden, J. 389
Farquhar, G. 199
Locke, J. 390
Montaigne, 317
Molière 396
Rider, W. 54, 82, 162
Shakespeare, W. 49, 70, 229, 352, 378
Spenser, E. 22, 134
Webster, J. 268, 373

18th Century

Anon. 67, 349
Goethe 433, 455
Roget 1
Kleist, Von 101, 412
Potocki, J. 343

19th Century

Andersen, H. C. 374
Anon. 86, 104, 157, 213, 362
Bingham, J. F. 147
Bolton, G. B. 302
Bruce, M. G. 83
Carroll, L. 192
Daudet, A. 453
Dickens, C. 390
Dixon, J. 355
Dostoevsky 288, 410
Dumas, A. 246
Fouqué, Baron 190
Galton, F. 49, 77, 320
Gautier, T. 149
Gogol, N. 405
Grand, S. 72

1945–

Norris, H. 114
Oates, J. C. 54, 417
Obo, C. E. 339
Observer 318
O'Flaherty, W. D. 347
Page, K. 91
Pamuk, O. 373
Peake, M. 54, 76
Pearson, J. 19, 123
Piontelli, A. 136, 182
Poling-Kempes, L. 279
Pristavkin, A. 53, 54, 265
Radin, P. 405
Rampo, E. S. 214
Roberts, M. 221
Roper, R. 96
Sacks, O. 311
Schave, B. 99
Schimmel, A. M. 337
Seabrook, J. 186
Shapcott, T. 92, 107, 374
Sillitoe, A. 455
Smiley, J. 77
Sorensen, V. 173
Steinbeck, J. 27
Stewart, I. 394
Stoppard, T. 429
Strong, L. A. G. 218
Thompson, R. 274
Thompson, R. Faris 1
Tiempo, E. K. 403
The Sunday Times 275
The Times 57
Tournier, M. 55, 78, 112, 133, 291, 355, 384
Tymms, R. 409
Updike, J. 196
Vanderbilt, G. 63
Vogel, I. M. 261
Vonnegut, K. 315
Wallace, M. 113, 183, 195, 231, 275, 362
Wall Street Journal 287